The Battle to Control Femal in Modern Ireland

CW00546185

The Irish battle for legal contraception was a contest over Irish exceptionalism: the belief that Ireland could resist global trends despite the impact of second-wave feminism, falling fertility and a growing number of women travelling for abortion. It became so lengthy and so divisive because it challenged key tenets of Irish identity: Catholicism, large families, traditional gender roles and sexual puritanism. The Catholic Church argued that legalising contraception would destroy this way of life, and many citizens agreed. *The Battle to Control Female Fertility in Modern Ireland* provides new insights on Irish masculinity and fertility control. It highlights women's activism in both liberal and conservative camps, and the consensus between the Catholic and Protestant churches views on contraception for single people. It also shows how contraception and the Pro-Life Amendment campaign affected policy towards Northern Ireland, and it examines the role of health professionals, showing how hospital governance prevented female sterilisation. It is a story of gender, religion, social change and failing efforts to reaffirm Irish moral exceptionalism.

MARY E. DALY is Professor Emerita in Modern Irish History, University College Dublin. She is the author of ten books and co-author/editor of eight edited volumes, including *Sixties Ireland: Reshaping the Economy, State and Society, 1957–1973* (Cambridge, 2016) and, with Eugenio F. Biagini, *The Cambridge Social History of Modern Ireland* (2017). She was the first woman to serve as President of the Royal Irish Academy (2014–17) and was awarded a Royal Irish Academy Gold Medal in the Humanities in 2020.

The Battle to Control Female Fertility in Modern Ireland

Mary E. Daly

University College Dublin

To Shaaren + Gary

Best wishe[s]
Long a' Daly
Seplen 2023

CAMBRIDGE
UNIVERSITY PRESS

Shaftesbury Road, Cambridge CB2 8EA, United Kingdom

One Liberty Plaza, 20th Floor, New York, NY 10006, USA

477 Williamstown Road, Port Melbourne, VIC 3207, Australia

314–321, 3rd Floor, Plot 3, Splendor Forum, Jasola District Centre, New Delhi – 110025, India

103 Penang Road, #05–06/07, Visioncrest Commercial, Singapore 238467

Cambridge University Press is part of Cambridge University Press & Assessment, a department of the University of Cambridge.

We share the University's mission to contribute to society through the pursuit of education, learning and research at the highest international levels of excellence.

www.cambridge.org
Information on this title: www.cambridge.org/9781009314893

DOI: 10.1017/9781009314886

First published 2023

A catalogue record for this publication is available from the British Library.

A Cataloging-in-Publication data record for this book is available from the Library of Congress.

ISBN 978-1-009-31489-3 Hardback
ISBN 978-1-009-31487-9 Paperback

To my granddaughters, Isabel, Abigail and Emma

Contents

Acknowledgements

For a historian, the concept of a sole-authored book is something of a misnomer – we are very dependent on having access to source material. While researching and writing this book, I have accumulated a long list of debts, some sadly to people who are no longer alive. In addition to libraries and archives, this book draws on interviews and informal conversations, in coffee shops, private homes, across dining tables and walks beside Dublin Bay. My sister Patricia Crowley and Andrew Curtain, both gynaecologists, were valuable guides in this research, though they haven't read the manuscript and bear no responsibility for the contents. They introduced me to many of their colleagues: John Bonnar, James Clinch, Conor Carr, Anto Dempsey, the late Jim Dornan, the late Declan Meagher, the late Dermot MacDonald, Michael Mylotte, Colm O'Herlihy and Edgar Ritchie. If this book has a hero(ine), it is Edgar Ritchie. Anne Connolly, Tim Gleeson, Marie-Therese Joye, Joe Little, Jim Loughran, Tom O'Dowd, Maeve O'Dwyer, Áine Sullivan, the late Peter Sutherland, Niall Tubridy and the late Robert Towers were vital sources on various aspects of this story.

David McConnell, a founding member of Family Planning Services (FPS), tried unsuccessfully to locate their early records. A chance meeting with Dr Derek Freedman led to the later FPS records being transferred to University College Dublin (UCD) Archives. The late Brendan Walsh fended off my efforts to discuss his involvement with the Irish Family Planning Rights Association with a smile, so I am extremely grateful to Patricia Walsh, and her daughter Nessa, for locating his files, which enabled me to fill in an important but largely forgotten story. Former Minister for Health Barry Desmond gave me permission to access his uncatalogued papers held in UCD Archives, and even identified the correct boxes, and the late Gemma Hussey also granted me permission to consult her papers held in UCD Archives. My thanks yet again to UCD archivists, Seamus Helferty, Kate Manning and Orna Somerville. Harriet Wheelock, Keeper of Collections at the Royal College of Physicians of Ireland, located the files of the Institute of Obstetricians and Gynaecologists and gave me access, prior to their listing, to the files of the Irish Family Planning Association. I also wish to thank the staff of the National Archives, the National Library, the Newberry Library in Chicago and UCD Library.

My thanks also to Eugenio Biagini, Brian Casey, Catherine Cox, Anne Dolan, Michael Dwyer, John and Eithne FitzGerald, Carole Holohan, Greta Jones, John Logan, Ita Mangan, Patrick Maume, the late Peter Neary and Margaret O'Callaghan. Lindsey Earner-Byrne read an earlier draft of this book and provided perceptive and supportive comments. Paul Rouse, my second reader, was especially helpful advising on the introduction and conclusions. David Dickson and Mark Duncan helped me to identify the cover image.

A special thanks to John Bergin who compiled the index and acted as an informal copy editor. At Cambridge University Press, I wish to thank Liz Friend-Smith the commissioning editor for her consistent supporters and Laura Simmons for overseeing the production.

As ever, my family has been my constant supporter. I forgive my brother Kieran Crowley and his wife Caroline for repeatedly asking when the book would appear. Niall and Catherine, Denis and Anne Crowley, and the Daly family were more patient. Thanks yet again to Paul, Dee, Conor, John and Peter Daly; Elizabeth Daly and Dominik, Aidan, Kilian and Isabel Dahlem; Nicholas Daly and Stephanie Hutson and Alice, John, Abigail and Emma Keating. My greatest support throughout my career has come from my husband, P.J.

Abbreviations

AAC	Anti-Amendment Campaign
CAP	Contraception Action Programme
CMAC	Catholic Marriage Advisory Council
CMO	Chief Medical Officer
COSC	Council of Social Concern
CSO	Central Statistics Office
CSW	Council for the Status of Women
CSWB	Catholic Social Welfare Bureau
CTSI	Catholic Truth Society of Ireland
CYMS	Catholic Young Men's Society
DD	Dáil Debates
DDA	Dublin Diocesan Archives
DUWGA	Dublin University Women Graduates Association
EH	*Evening Herald*
EHB	Eastern Health Board
FF	Fianna Fáil
FGC	Fertility Guidance Clinic
FPS	Family Planning Services
FRCS	Fellow of the Royal College of Surgeons
GMS	General Medical Scheme
ICA	Irish Countrywomen's Association
ICC	Irish Council of Churches
ICDG	Irish Catholic Doctors Guild
ICTU	Irish Congress of Trade Unions
IER	*Irish Ecclesiastical Record,*
IFL	Irish Family League
IFPA	Irish Family Planning Association
IFPRA	Irish Family Planning Rights Association
II	*Irish Independent*
IMA	Irish Medical Association
IMT	*Irish Medical Times*
INO	Irish Nurses Organisation

IP	*Irish Press*
IPPF	International Planned Parenthood Federation
IPU	Irish Pharmaceutical Union
IT	*Irish Times*
ITQ	*Irish Theological Quarterly*
IUD	Intra-Uterine Device
IWLM	Irish Women's Liberation Movement
IWU	Irish Women United
JAMA	*Journal of the American Medical Association*
JIMA	*Journal of the Irish Medical Association*
MHB	Midland Health Board
MWHB	Mid-Western Health Board
NAI	National Archives of Ireland
NAOMI	National Association for the Ovulation Method in Ireland
NEHB	North-Eastern Health Board
NHC	National Health Council
NWHB	North-Western Health Board
OMAS	Ovulation Method Advisory Service
PLAC	Pro-Life Amendment Campaign
PSI	Pharmaceutical Society of Ireland
RCGPI	Royal College of General Practitioners of Ireland
RCPI	Royal College of Physicians of Ireland
RTÉ	Raidio Teilifís Éireann
SD	Seanad Debates
SEHB	South-Eastern Health Board
SHB	Southern Health Board
SOS	Save Our Society
SPUC	Society for the Protection of the Unborn Child
TCD	Trinity College Dublin
UCC	University College Cork
UCD	University College Dublin
UCDA	University College Dublin Archives
UCG	University College Galway
WHB	Western Health Board
WHO	World Health Organisation
WW	*Woman's Way*

Introduction

What Ireland has to offer to Europe and the World is its values.

> [F H, OSB, Glenstal Abbey to Taoiseach W.T. Cosgrave 5 Nov. 1973]

Down the centuries we have withstood all and everything an unscrupulous enemy has thrown at us in famine, war, persecution, emigration, and we have survived somehow. Now the ultimate evil is about to be perpetrated against us, especially against our young people.

> Mrs E.M, Ballina to Taoiseach Liam Cosgrave, 20 Nov. 1973[1]

if we enact legislation of this sort, however sincere and well intentioned our motives, this generation of Irish politicians will be called to account at the bar of history to answer the charge of our children and their children that we were the ones who publicly discarded the standards and values which, with conviction, I believe were the true standards and values which were treasured by Irish generations of the past.[2]

> Senator Michael O'Higgins, Fine Gael leader in the Seanad, 14 Nov. 1973

No western country experienced as protracted and passionate a debate on reforming the law on contraception as Ireland in the second half of twentieth century[3]. This book explores the social and cultural issues surrounding that debate. The longstanding Irish ban on contraception has commonly been seen as the consequence of Catholic church teaching and the near-universal religious observance by many Irish Catholics. Accordingly, Catholicism, or more precisely *Irish* Catholicism, plays an important part in this story. But the Irish debate on the availability and use of contraception went far beyond Catholic teaching. Indeed, the idea of large families and the laws banning contraception (as well as prohibition of divorce and abortion) was actually elevated to stand as a symbol of Ireland's national identity; the peculiar Irish approach to contraception was intimately bound up with ideas of Irishness.

---

[1] Quotations 1 and 2 are on National Archives Ireland (NAI) DT 2004/21/461.

[2] Seanad Debates (SD), 14 November 1973, cols 6–9. Debate on a private members family planning bill.

[3] This book examines contraception in independent Ireland. Under the 1937 Constitution, the name of the state (in English) is Ireland.

1

This merger of religious observance and expressions of Irishness in respect of contraception produced an extraordinary series of debates and actions. The logic of opposition to the use of contraception shifted over the decades. Initially, the belief that 'artificial' contraception was contrary to the teaching of the Catholic church was the engine that drove state policy and broader opposition to the use of contraception. By the 1970s, this argument was being abandoned, in favour of claims that permitting contraception would destroy the fabric of Irish society. Fear of committing sin was no longer seen as sufficient to prevent change. The battle to protect Irish society from the 'menace' of contraception, abortion and divorce continued into the present century, despite the fact that the rhetoric of Ireland's distinctive way of life was increasingly out of line with the reality of the lived experience of its people.

The context in which these debates took place includes both long-term demographic terms and global trends of modernisation. Ireland is the only country in the developed world whose population is not greater than that it was in the mid-nineteenth century.[4] This is a story of considerable complexity. The famine of the 1840s reduced the population by approximately two million through death and emigration. In its aftermath, Irish society adopted a survival strategy that entailed restrictions on marriage, plus the emigration of non-inheriting children. The key features of Ireland's population history since the famine include a chronically high rate of emigration, which since the 1990s has been complemented by a high rate of immigration. From the mid-nineteenth to the mid-twentieth century, the proportion of the population who married was the lowest in Europe and Irish men and women married at a later age. Yet in 1961, the number of children born to married women (marital fertility) was the highest in the developed world. The combination of a low marriage rate with sustained emigration made it possible to sustain high marital fertility.[5]

The global context of these demographic facts involves the emergence of reliable methods of fertility control. This book can be seen as the Irish chapter of this worldwide story. Contraception became a topic of public debate internationally in the 1920s and the 1930s. By 1930, the Catholic church was the only major religion to oppose the use of 'artificial' means of contraception, and Catholic church teaching, about marriage, the family and contraception, looms large in the Irish story. The newly independent Irish Free State, whose population was more than 90 per cent Catholic, sought to define its identity, and projecting an image of sexual purity and strong family life formed part

---

[4] The preliminary results of the 2021 Northern Ireland Census and the 2022 Census of Ireland show that the population of the island of Ireland has exceeded 7 million. This is higher than the 6.8 million recorded in 1851, but below the 1841 figure of 8.1 million.

[5] Tim Guinnane, *The vanishing Irish. Households, migration and the rural economy in Ireland, 1850–1914* (Princeton University Press, Princeton, 1997).

of that identity, with church and state combining forces to highlight this message. Ireland registered a uniformly high rate of church attendance among both men and women up to the last decades of the twentieth century; large numbers of women and men entered religious life, and the Catholic church exercised significant authority over Irish society. In most European countries, Catholicism was identified with the old order – the landed families and established elites. But in Ireland, Catholicism was associated with popular movements, such as campaigns for land reform and independence. While Catholic clergy tended to come from less-impoverished households, they were not members of the elite but the children of middling farmers or small businessmen, and the values that they upheld were those of respectable but modestly comfortable families.

By the early 1960s, many Catholics in other western countries were using methods of family planning that were incompatible with Catholic teaching. In the early years of the twentieth century, many countries in Europe, and US states, enacted laws restricting contraception that were not dissimilar to Ireland's, but there is no indication that they were enforced or observed elsewhere to the same degree as they were in Ireland. These laws had been repealed across the world by the early 1970s. However, a significant number of Irish people were convinced that making contraception available, (and, as repeatedly added) permitting divorce, would undermine Ireland's distinct identity. They believed that Ireland could withstand the moral decline associated with the modern world, despite the fact that Irish society was becoming more urban, better educated, and more open to external influences, and a growing number of Irish women were remaining in the workforce after marriage. The 1983 Pro-Life Amendment Campaign (PLAC), which affirmed the right to life of the 'unborn', and efforts to promote the Billings method of 'natural' family planning, can be seen as last-gasp attempts to signal Ireland's 'distinct way of life', despite the fact that by the 1980s, most Irish households had ready access to TV, films and publications from all parts of the English-speaking world, and a significant number of women travelled overseas to secure an abortion.

The emphasis in this book is primarily on family planning for married couples; this is essential to presenting the reality of the debate and the policies pursued in Ireland. But the book inevitably extends beyond married couples and the steadily rising incidence of pre-marital and extra-marital sex, cohabitation, and the growing number of births to single mothers form an important part of this story. Churchmen and lay activists repeatedly argued that prohibiting or restricting access to contraception would stem the sort of 'moral decline' which they considered to be represented in such developments; the statistics suggest otherwise. During the 1980s, despite the laws restricting access to contraception 'for bona fide family planning purposes' – which was commonly read as limiting access to married couples, the number of single women and men using contraception increased significantly, though the restricted Irish legislation precluded campaigns to promote contraception among sexually active single people.

Although the focus is on the laws and practice of contraception in Ireland, this book casts a sideways glance towards Northern Ireland. Recent works by Luddy and O'Dowd on marriage, Urquhart on divorce, and Earner Byrne and Urquhart on the abortion trail to Britain reveal that Ireland north and south and Catholics and Protestants had more in common than is commonly suggested.[6] There has been a tendency in many accounts of Irish family planning to suggest that the Irish Protestant communities were more liberal in their attitudes towards contraception; however the testimonies given by the Protestant churches to Minister for Health Charles Haughey in 1978/9, discussed in Chapter 5, suggests that their views were broadly in line with the majority of the Irish population, though, the Protestant churches had a different attitude towards the role of the state in enforcing sexual morality.

Other aspects to this history are also important. It is a history that must be read from a gendered angle: how Irish women belatedly secured access to reliable fertility control is obviously part of a wider story around the changing place of women in Irish society. The well-known images of the 1971 'contraceptive train', when a group of women travelled to Northern Ireland and returned brandishing contraceptives, has given rise to a popular impression that Irish feminists played a key role in making contraception available.[7] But the story is much more complex, and women activists were found in both the conservative and liberal camps. Added to this – as this book highlights – is the role, or non-role, of Irish men in controlling fertility. Until the 1960s, when the contraceptive pill became available, fertility control was determined by men, not by women.[8] So the primary responsibility for limiting pregnancies rested with men. In Ireland until the 1980s, it appears that most of the initiatives regarding family planning were taken by women, often with little support from male partners, and a number of surveys quoted in this book suggest that men were more conservative in their views on contraception and family size than their partners.

The Irish debate over contraception and 'pro-life' coincided with a time of social and economic change, a shift towards a more urban society and a

---

[6] Maria Luddy and Mary O'Dowd, *Marriage in Ireland, 1660–1925* (Cambridge University Press, Cambridge 2020); Diane Urquhart, *Irish divorce. A history* (Cambridge University Press, Cambridge 2020); Lindsey Earner-Byrne, Diane Urquhart, *The Irish abortion journey, 1920–2018* (Palgrave Macmillan, 2019).

[7] Mary Minihan, 'Laying the tracks to liberation: the original contraceptive train', *IT*, 28 October 2014; Linda Connolly, *The Irish women's movement. From revolution to devolution* (Palgrave Macmillan, Basingstoke, 2002), gives a much more nuanced account.

[8] The diaphragm was the only method of contraception before the pill that was initiated by women, and it was expensive, and not available to the majority of women.

significant rise in the proportion of younger adults who remained in Ireland rather than emigrate and the numbers of young adults with higher education. These were also the decades when the proportion of Irish women in the paid workforce began to rise, with more married women pursuing careers in the professions and senior positions in the public and private sectors. It was therefore to a considerable extent a debate about modernity and social change. The debate about contraception also coincided with the three decades of violence in Northern Ireland, which prompted a debate over the close identification between Irishness and Catholicism and the need to make an independent Ireland less of a 'cold place for Protestants'. Viewed from the perspective of 2021, this emphasis on access to contraception, and not enacting a Pro-Life Amendment, as gestures of inclusiveness towards Ulster Unionism is somewhat puzzling, given the strong hostility of many Ulster unionists towards marriage equality and access to abortion. The 1967 British Abortion Act was not extended to Northern Ireland; it would have been strongly opposed by the Catholic church but it was not extended because of Unionist opposition.[9] Many of the most vocal anti-contraception campaigners expressed deep hostility to any concessions towards Ulster unionism or the Protestant community in independent Ireland. The fact that Ireland was a partitioned island is an essential element of the story.

This book adopts a primarily chronological approach. Chapter 1 outlines some features that make Ireland's fertility pattern distinctive. Most of the decline in Irish fertility in the late nineteenth century was achieved by reducing the proportion of the population who married and postponing the age of marriage. Nevertheless by 1911, some Irish couples were limiting fertility and marital fertility continued to fall, though at a slow pace after independence. The gap between family size in Northern Ireland and Ireland widened in later decades as did the gap between Catholic and Protestant family sizes. The Irish Free State introduced legislation restricting access to information about contraception and prohibiting the sale and importation of contraceptives, legislation that reinforced Catholic teaching. Although similar legislation existed in other countries, it had much less impact than in Ireland. The near-universal practice of religion by men and women meant that Catholic teaching could be enforced in the confession box, and this teaching, combined with the valorisation of large families by Irish society, provided uncaring and other brutish husbands with a licence to continue to procreate, irrespective of the health or the wishes of their wife. Before the 1960s, there was little information available about the 'safe period', a church-permitted method of regulating fertility, which was increasingly being promoted by Catholic organisations in other countries,

---

[9] Earner-Byrne and Urquhart, *The Irish abortion journey*, pp. 70–1.

Whitty concluded that in Ireland 'Public ignorance was seen as the best basis for maintaining public morality'.[10]

As Chapter 2 shows that began to change in the 1960s, a decade marked by increased use of the contraceptive pill. The Pill had an especial significance for Ireland, given the absence of any other legally permitted forms of reliable contraception, and the fact that it gave women the initiative with respect to contraception. The timing was also apposite, because in the 1960s, Ireland embarked on a belated post-war marriage boom and couples married at an earlier age. The economy began to grow; access to secondary and university education was expanded, and pressure emerged to end the prohibition on women in paid employment after marriage.[11] This was also the decade of Vatican II. The Catholic church internationally was wrestling with the issue of contraception, in the face of growing non-conformity among Catholic couples. Although Irish Catholics remained more deferential to clerical authority than Catholics in other western countries, that was beginning to change. Chapter 2 also examines the cautious dissemination of information about the 'safe period' and clerical efforts to retain control over that process. Dublin maternity hospitals were contending with rising numbers of young mothers with uncontrolled fertility. In the initial years, 'fertility guidance clinics' only offered church-approved methods of family planning, but by the mid-1960s, they were prescribing the contraceptive pill. A number of Irish theologians were active in the emerging debate as to whether the contraceptive pill was compatible with Catholic teaching, and use of the Pill spread quietly in Ireland. Irish doctors were actively debating contraception, and the topic was being aired on Irish television and in print media, especially by women's magazines, but hopes of a more liberal future were dashed in 1968 when *Humanae Vitae* reaffirmed traditional teaching.

Chapter 3 concentrates on the years 1968–73, a key period in this story. The initial Irish response to the 1968 papal encyclical *Humanae Vitae* – reaffirming traditional Catholic teaching on contraception – was muted, compared with Europe or the United States, reflecting continuing Irish deference to clerical authority; clerical dissent was also limited. By 1972 however, two family planning clinics had opened in Dublin, and the ban on contraception was being challenged in the courts and the Oireachtas (parliament). This was happening against the backdrop of the Northern Ireland Troubles and a debate over minority rights. During the early 1970s, there was a possibility that Ireland would come into line with other European countries, liberalising its laws on contraception – but that didn't happen. Given the political challenges of enacting legislation to enable

---

[10] Noel Whitty, 'The law and the regulation of reproduction in Ireland', 1922–1992, *The University of Toronto Law Journal*, 43, no 4, autumn 1993, p. 854.

[11] A formal marriage ban only applied to the public service, but it was also a common practice in many private firms, especially those employing clerical and administrative workers.

even limited access to contraception, the government preferred to await the outcome of a Supreme Court judgment on the legality of the existing ban.

In December 1973, the Supreme Court affirmed the right of a married couple to plan their family. Chapters 4 and 5 cover the years 1973–79, and they can be read in alternative order. Chapter 4 examines the expansion of family planning clinics, and the emergence of grass-roots opposition to contraception, which happened in the legal vacuum following the Supreme Court Judgment. Chapter 5 discusses efforts to enact legislation to legalise contraception. Better access to contraception was driven by family planning clinics and by student's unions – reflecting the expansion in higher education during these years. Opinion polls during the 1970s show increasing support for legislative reform, but a majority of voters in rural areas and the west and north-west remained opposed, and most of those favouring reform wanted contraception to be restricted to married couples.

Irish women's organisations were divided on the issue. Women journalists played a key role in informing their readers about different types of contraceptive and contact details for family planning outlets, and second-wave feminists were active in the more radical wing of the family planning movement. But women were also prominent in the conservative pressure groups that emerged during the 1970s; these were modelled on anti-abortion movements in Britain and the United States. By the end of the decade, the Billings method of 'natural' family planning, which was mainly led by women, was being promoted as an opportunity for Ireland to demonstrate that fertility control was feasible without recourse to 'artificial' methods of contraception.

Government proposals for legislation permitting access to contraception reveal a consistent dilemma for politicians: how to make contraception available to married couples while restricting access by single people. Records of consultative meetings organised by the Department of Health (discussed in Chapter 5) suggest that by the late 1970s, there was consensus, sometimes grudging, among the main churches, medical groups, and the trade union congress that contraception should be available on a restricted basis, but it was also recognised that it would prove difficult to prevent access by single people. These consultations also reveal a determination on the part of doctors and pharmacists to protect their professional interests. The 1979 Family Planning Act legalised access to contraception, 'for bona fide family planning purposes' – terminology that was not defined, and it privileged 'natural methods' – in order to placate the Catholic hierarchy.

Chapter 6 examines the successful campaign to enact a constitutional amendment to protect the life of the 'unborn'. Readers who are primarily interested in contraception can skip this chapter if they wish. However, I see this campaign as an attempt to reinstate the image of Ireland as a morally conservative Catholic state, despite the enactment of the 1979 Act and the rising number of Irish women seeking abortions in Britain. The campaign was assisted by anti-abortion campaigners in the United States (where a pro-life amendment campaign had foundered) and Britain. Its success owes much to the political instability of the early 1980s. The PLAC made its case primarily on the urgent need to protect Ireland's distinctive cultural values. In contrast to other international anti-abortion movements, they failed to attract significant Protestant support, because the medical exemptions that they proposed reflected Catholic teaching. Despite claims that the 1983 referendum showed that Ireland was a moral beacon in the modern world, the number of women travelling to Britain for abortions continued to rise.

Despite the limitations of the 1979 Family Planning Act, Chapter 7 shows that the 1980s saw a marked increase in access to contraception, by single and married adults, and major advances in the training of medical personnel in family planning. However, surveys of mothers in maternity hospitals indicate that many pregnancies were unplanned, and access to both information and contraceptives remained limited in parts of provincial Ireland. The legal restrictions on contraceptives were gradually eased from the mid-1980s. Sterilisation was never banned in Ireland, and by the 1980s, male sterilisation was readily available, but access to tubal ligation, even in cases of acute medical need proved much more difficult. In some hospitals, including the Dublin maternity hospitals, the ethics committees, which were formed in the early 1980s at the behest of the Catholic hierarchy, and the hostility of nursing and other non-medical hospital staff made it almost impossible for doctors to carry out the procedure. This only eased in the 1990s.

This book concludes in the mid-1990s, when legal and practical restrictions on contraception disappeared, though many Irish women continued to travel to Britain for abortions. The decade was marked by a series of scandals that inflicted major damage on the standing of the Catholic church in Irish society, precipitating an acceleration in the decline in formal church attendance. It is also the decade when Ireland begins to experience significant immigration, and the 1998 Good Friday/Belfast Agreement, which was endorsed by over 94 per cent of the population of Ireland and 71 per cent of the population of Northern Ireland, accorded due recognition to Ulster Unionism and British identity.

Ultimately, what this history records is a peculiarly Irish aspect of a wider history of change in the second half of the twentieth century. It is a history which sets out to demonstrate how the Irish state legislated for the use of contraception within its boundaries. It is a history which examines the forces of religion and national identity, and how these were shaped by global forces. Returning to the wider question of Irish exceptionalism, the ending suggests that Ireland could not craft a *Sonderweg*, or an Irish variant of contemporary Chinese exceptionalism – combining an outward-facing economy and society, determined to enhance its place in the modern world, while upholding traditional sexual and demographic practices. Yet, the intensity of the debate over contraception is in other respects evidence of an Irish exceptionalism.

1   Late Marriages and Large Families
'The Enigma of the Modern World'?

In 1954, Rev John O'Brien, a professor at Notre Dame University in the USA, published an edited collection of essays, with the title, *The Vanishing Irish*[1]. He claimed that Ireland was 'teetering perilously on the verge of extinction' because of the large number of adults who never married. The one bright spot in a 'somber black' picture was the 'unusually high fecundity rate' of Irish women.[2] At this time, Ireland was a poor and predominantly rural society, with farming as the main occupation of the Irish people. Many adult women and men lived and worked (often unpaid) on the family farm or in a family business. Few married women were in paid employment, and the most common occupation for women was domestic or institutional service.

Irish couples had, by a considerable margin, the largest families in the developed world. In 1961, marital fertility[3] in Ireland was 195.5 per 1,000; the next highest figures were that of New Zealand, 154.6, and Canada, 152.9 per 1,000. By 1961, maternal mortality was 45 per 100,000, lower than Northern Ireland (53), but higher than England and Wales (34) and Scotland (37). This represented a dramatic improvement over the previous decade; in 1951, it stood at 164 per 100,000 births, almost double the English figure (84), and significantly higher than that in Scotland and Northern Ireland, both at 109. Infant mortality in 1961 at 31 per 1,000 births was also higher than that in Northern Ireland (27), England and Wales (22) and Scotland (26), but that gap had also narrowed significantly.[4]

On an international table of births per 1,000 of the population, Ireland ranked only eighth among nineteen countries.[5] From the late nineteenth century to the mid-twentieth century, approximately one-quarter of Irish adults remained permanently celibate, but those who married had large families. Although the

[1] John O'Brien (ed.), *The vanishing Irish: the enigma of the modern world* (McGraw-Hill, New York, 1953), Rev. O'Brien was the author of a best-selling guide to the church-approved rhythm method, discussed in Section 1.8.
[2] O'Brien, *The vanishing Irish*, pp. 36–9.
[3] The number of legitimate births per 1,000 married women aged 20–49.
[4] Central Statistics Office (CSO), *Annual report of the registrar general of marriages, births and deaths in Ireland, 1961, and 1951*.
[5] Robert Kennedy, *The Irish. Emigration, marriage and fertility* (University of California Press, Berkeley, London, 1973), p. 175.

marriage rate rose in the 1960s, in 1968, Brendan Walsh described Ireland's marriage rate as 'still perhaps the lowest in the world'. He believed that the large size of Irish families was a factor in the low marriage rate. He described it as 'remarkable to record .... that not only is Ireland's marriage fertility higher than that of other European countries similar in religion and level of economic development ... but also that it is at least as high as that of the Latin American countries for which data are available'.[6]

Beginning in France in the late eighteenth century, Europe and North America underwent a transition from high marital fertility, which was generally accompanied by high infant mortality, to smaller families. Tim Guinnane described Ireland's fertility transition as 'late and modest', when compared with other European countries.

The combination of large families but many unmarried adults gave Ireland a relatively low birth-rate at the turn of the twentieth century, but this low birth-rate was achieved in a way very different from the low birth-rates obtaining in England, France, or Germany at the same time. Elsewhere more people married but had ever-smaller families; in Ireland families themselves became rarer, and their size declined more slowly.[7]

Guinnane qualifies his argument by emphasising that there were parts of Germany and Austria where a high proportion of the population remained single and families were large: 'no one in Ireland was living a life that did not have a counterpart elsewhere in Europe, in prior centuries or in other peasant regions of Europe during the nineteenth century'.[8] But elsewhere this only occurred in specific regions – it did not apply to an entire country.

The marital fertility data in the 1911 Census forms have been mined by scholars seeking to discover whether Irish couples were controlling fertility, and which couples were doing so.[9] In 1911, family size varied by region, religion and class. Approximately half of the women who had been married for twenty years had given birth to between five and nine children; 30 per cent had given birth to ten or more. Mean fertility for these couples was 5.87 *live* children; for Belfast, the figure was 5.73; it was 5.6 in Dublin city and suburbs. Fertility in rural Ireland was much higher than that in Scotland or England, but urban fertility was similar to Scotland and 'though not as low as in some European cities elsewhere bore a closer resemblance to places outside Ireland than to rural Ireland'.[10]

---

[6] Brendan Walsh, *Some Irish population problems reconsidered ESRI paper 42*, (November 1968), pp. 4–5.

[7] Tim Guinnane, *The vanishing Irish. Households, migration, and the rural economy in Ireland, 1850* p. 7.

[8] Guinnane, *The vanishing Irish*, p. 223.

[9] Available online at National Archives Ireland. For a detailed description of the fertility date given in the 1911 Census, see Simon Szreter, *Fertility class and gender in Britain, 1860–1940* (Cambridge University Press, Cambridge, 1996); Guinnane, *The vanishing Irish*.

[10] Guinnane, *The vanishing Irish*, pp. 241–2, quote on p. 242.

Ó Gráda and Duffy estimated that in the middle-class suburb of Rathgar, home to many Protestant families, two-thirds of women who had been married for 5–9 years were controlling fertility; 20–25 per cent of rural couples were also limiting the number of children. He identified three zones: an area of 'light' fertility comprising Dublin, Louth and east Ulster; an area of high fertility in Connacht and North Munster; and an intermediate zone that included Leinster. Most of the intermediate zone was rural. The highest fertility was in areas with high emigration and a high proportion of Catholics. Areas with large farms and non-agricultural workers had smaller families. In Pembroke, a prosperous Dublin suburb, with a substantial Protestant population – which also contained working-class villages – Catholic couples had an average of 3.78 children compared with 2.78 for non-Catholic couples. This disparity applied in family size between Catholic and Protestant families regardless of length of marriage. Protestant couples who had been married for 20–29 years had an average of 5.15 children, whereas Catholics had 6.63. The differential fertility of Catholics and Protestants appears to have been a relatively recent development, and the analysis is complicated by the fact that a significant proportion of the Protestant population was middle class, whereas Catholics were more likely to be working class. Pembroke labouring families who were married for 20–29 years had an average of 7.64 children, semi-skilled workers had 9.47 and professional couples had 3.76 children.[11]

Guinnane emphasised that 'Irish people had available to them in this period, contraceptive methods that were sufficiently effective to account for the observed moderate declines in marital fertility .... fertility patterns reflected choice about contraception and family sizes and not strict adherence to canon law'.[12] The methods available in Ireland in 1911 were similar to those available throughout Britain and Europe. The fall in fertility during the nineteenth century took place with limited resort to barrier methods of contraception: these were most commonly used to prevent contracting venereal disease. Szreter's analysis of British fertility in the decades before 1914 suggests that abstinence and withdrawal were the key methods of contraception. He concluded that 'attempted abstinence within marriage was the single most widespread and frequently used method of birth control'.[13] Santow, using data from a number of studies of contraceptive methods, carried out in Europe, the United States and Australia, spanning from the 1930s to the 1980s concluded that withdrawal was almost as effective as using condoms and more effective

[11] Cormac Ó Gráda and Niall Duffy, 'The fertility transition in Ireland and Scotland c.1880–1930', in *Conflict identity and economic development, Ireland and Scotland 1600–1939* (Carnegie, Preston, 1995), pp. 90–3.

[12] Guinnane, *The vanishing Irish*, p. 243.

[13] Szreter, *Fertility class and gender in Britain*, p. 399.

than the rhythm method (discussed later); in other words, 'a far more effective method than generally believed'.[14] Postponing the age of marriage also played a significant role in reducing total fertility and marital fertility – and post-famine Ireland made full use of this. Szreter shows that it was part of the fertility limitation strategy deployed by the middle class in Victorian England.

The decision that a couple might make on the appropriate size of family is critical; it is even more critical that a couple makes such a decision as opposed to leaving conceptions to fate. In 1973, Ansley J. Coale of the Princeton fertility study project set out three preconditions for fertility decline, which remain relevant:

1. Controlling fertility must be 'an acceptable mode of thought and form of behaviour', within the 'calculus of choice'.
2. Reducing fertility must be seen as advantageous.
3. Contraceptive techniques must be known and available.

This became known as 'the "ready, willing and able" formula'.[15]

Guinnane suggests that Irish couples, Catholic and Protestant, may have wanted larger families than their English counterparts – four or five children – yet they were controlling their fertility.[16] Ó Gráda has shown that Catholic couples in Pembroke with Protestant neighbours tended to have smaller families, which suggests that example or the neighbourhood culture might have an impact. In the Netherlands, Catholic communities with a significant number of non-Catholic residents reduced their fertility at an earlier period than adjoining communities with few non-Catholics.[17] As to why Irish couples may have favoured larger families, Kennedy and Guinnane both suggest that we need to move beyond the automatic assumption that Irish couples had large families because of Catholic church teaching against contraception.[18] France, a predominantly Catholic country, which underwent a significant religious revival during the nineteenth century was the European leader in reducing family size. Abstinence was not incompatible with Catholic teaching.

David Kertzner argues that

If we are to better understand historical fertility behaviour and the historic decline in fertility this means doing real history and not some kind of highly stylized historical

[14] Gigi Santow, 'Coitus interruptus in the twentieth century', *Population and Development Review*, 19, no 4 (December 1993), p. 772.
[15] Dirk Van der Kaa, '"Ready, Willing, and Able"; Ansley J. Coale, 1917–2002', *Journal of Interdisciplinary History*, 34, no 3 (Winter 2004), p. 509.
[16] Guinnane, *The vanishing Irish*, p. 258.
[17] Ó Gráda and Duffy, 'The fertility transition in Ireland and Scotland c.1880–1930'; Marloes Schoonbeim, *Mixing ovaries and Rosaries. Catholic religion and reproduction in the Netherlands, 1870–1970* (Aksant Academic Publishers, Amsterdam, 2005), pp. 176–7.
[18] Guinnane, *The vanishing Irish*, pp. 260–1.

narrative. It means understanding what religious figures actually taught with regard to behaviour linked in some way to fertility, how this differed from time to time, from place to place, from group to group, how much influence and social control these religious specialists exerted, and all this in a larger changing context of social interaction, political control, and cultural meaning.[19]

Guinnane believes that in Ireland, before 1911, 'factors other than religion must be at work .... Religious affiliation had much less effect on fertility behaviors than did other factors such as social and economic status'.[20] In Montreal, in the late nineteenth century, Irish Catholics married at a much later age than French Catholics, and this was a means of limiting fertility.[21] The association between emigration and large families cannot be discounted. The strong tradition of emigrant remittances meant that an emigrant child could be an asset to a family rather than a liability. Emigration removed the need to subdivide holdings or make long-term provision for adult children. In the late nineteenth century, family size was generally smaller in areas where women had opportunities to engage in paid work; women outside Ulster had few opportunities. Guinnane also suggests that women who were unwilling to become mothers of large families might have emigrated; he cites some interesting pieces of evidence that show that 'Irish-born women in the United States in 1910 were more likely to control their fertility than other immigrant groups' or US-born white women.[22]

1.1   Fertility Post 1920

This examination of Irish fertility on the eve of World War I and independence sets the context for examining what happened after 1922. By 1911, many couples were limiting the size of their families, with significant effect, and the methods of contraception that most, if not all, were using – abstinence and coitus interruptus – continued to be available after independence.

The crude birth rate for Ireland (twenty-six counties) in the years 1911–26 was 305 per 1,000 married women aged 15–44; in 1961, it was 190 per 1,000. The decline in marital fertility was greatest among those women who married later in life and who were in marriage for longer duration. For women who married in their late thirties, whose marriages lasted for more than twenty-five years, fertility halved between 1911 and 1961, which was similar to the rate

---

[19] David I. Kertzer, 'Religion and the decline of fertility: conclusions', in Renzo Derosas and Frans van Poppel (eds), *Religion and the decline of fertility in the Western World* (Springer, Dordrecht, 2006), p. 261.

[20] Guinnane, *The vanishing Irish*, p. 262.

[21] Patricia Thornton and Sherry Olson, 'The religious claim on babies in nineteenth century Montreal', in De Rosas and Van Poppel, *Religion and the decline of fertility*, pp. 214–17.

[22] Guinnane, *The vanishing Irish*, p. 264.

of decline in England and Wales (though fertility in England and Wales was significantly lower in 1911). Fewer women were giving birth in their forties.[23] A falling age for the last birth is often one of the first indicators that couples are controlling fertility.[24] In 1961, 18 per cent of women who had married at the age of 25–29 had seven or more children; the comparable figure in 1911 was 50 per cent.[25] By 1946, all social groups had lower marital fertility than in 1911, though the average number of children born in the first four years of marriage had increased. Kennedy explains this by better nutrition; other factors would include the reduced incidences of tuberculosis and venereal disease. He concluded that 'apparently no greater effort was made to control fertility by newlyweds in 1961 than in 1911'.[26] Brendan Walsh noted that marital fertility fell between 1911 and 1946, but the decline then ceased. Fertility by social group was stable between 1946 and 1961.[27] The 1971 and 1981 population censuses show that marital fertility fell until the 1940s; for those marrying in the 1950s and early 1960s, it initially rose and then declined.[28]

1.2   Northern Ireland

In 1911, fertility rates in the six counties that became Northern Ireland[29] were not noticeably different from the rest of Ireland. Between 1911 and 1951, fertility in Northern Ireland fell much more sharply than in the rest of Ireland, though less than that in England and Wales. In 1951, fertility in Northern Ireland was similar to that in England and Wales in 1911. Northern Ireland did not collect information on birth by religion; however, Park calculated that in 1937, fertility in Catholics was 158 per cent of that of other denominations (ODs) – who were overwhelmingly Protestants; by 1951, this gap had widened to 186 per cent. The more rapid fertility decline in Northern Ireland and the widening religious divide appears to suggest that religion was a major factor. However, Park noted that in 1951, the fertility rate for Northern Ireland ODs was 148 per cent of that in England and Wales; so even if the entire population of Northern Ireland was Protestant, fertility would be significantly higher than that in England and Wales.[30]

---

[23] Kennedy, *The Irish*, pp. 179–80.

[24] John Knödel, 'From natural fertility to family limitation: the onset of fertility transition in a sample of Germany villages'. *Demography*, 16, no 4, 1979, pp. 501–7.

[25] Kennedy, *The Irish*, p. 181.   [26] Kennedy, *The Irish*, p. 177.

[27] Walsh, 'Some Irish population problems', p. 6; Kennedy, *The Irish*, pp. 177–8.

[28] Mary E. Daly, *The slow failure: population decline and independent Ireland, 1920–1973* (University of Wisconsin Press, Madison, 2006), p. 130.

[29] For the period after 1922, the term Ireland refers to the twenty-six county, independent Ireland. Article 4 of the 1937 Constitution states that 'the name of the state is Éire or in the English language Ireland'.

[30] A. Park, 'An analysis of human fertility in Northern Ireland', *Journal of the Statistical and Social Inquiry Society of Ireland*, 11, 1962, pp. 1–13.

The increasing gap between Catholic and Protestant fertility in Northern Ireland is not dissimilar to the gap between Catholic and Protestant fertility in the Netherlands, where Catholics constituted 40 per cent of the population. Van Heek suggested that Catholics in the Netherlands had a high level of fertility (though significantly lower than in Ireland or Northern Ireland), because the Dutch clergy strictly enforced Catholic teaching on birth control, and the Dutch Catholics' history of oppression had resulted in a fighting spirit, including a belief that Catholics could at some future date constitute a majority of the population – a belief that was shared and occasionally expressed by non-Catholics.[31] There are obvious similarities with Northern Ireland, where it was frequently alleged that Catholics were trying to outbreed the Protestants – however until the 1970s, higher fertility was offset by higher Catholic emigration.

Earner Byrne and Urquhart note that

Birth control was never explicitly banned in Northern Ireland, but nor did it become socially acceptable until the late 1960s and even then its reach was uneven …. For at least the first half of the twentieth century, the people on the island of Ireland shared a socially conservative outlook, bolstered by a traditional sense of faith and family life, and a belief that sexuality should be governed by a strict moral code.[32]

The first family planning clinic in Northern Ireland, a Marie Stopes Clinic, opened in 1936, later than England (1921) or Scotland and Wales (1925). It closed in 1947 because of lack of support and interpersonal difficulties between Stopes and the local committee. It had attracted a relatively small clientele.[33] A woman doctor who had been involved with the Marie Stopes clinic suggested that family planning in Northern Ireland was

religious and political, and they only see it as a means of reducing the birth rate. The Catholics are forbidden to have anything to do with it and the Protestants fear that if they reduce the size of their families they will eventually be outnumbered by the Catholics in the six counties and have to go in with Eire. They feel very strongly about it and the Ministry of Health would not be helpful.[34]

The Belfast Women's Welfare Clinic, a family planning clinic that opened in 1951 in a small Protestant maternity hospital, avoided publicity in order to reduce the prospect of opposition from the Catholic church.[35] When the BBC

[31] F. van Heek, 'Roman Catholicism and fertility in the Netherlands: demographic aspects of minority status', *Population Studies*, 10, no 2, November 1956, pp. 125–38.

[32] Lindsey Earner-Byrne and Diane Urquhart, *The Irish abortion journey, 1920–2018*, pp. 18–19; Leanne McCormick, *Regulating sexuality. Women in twentieth-century Northern Ireland* (Manchester University Press, Manchester, 2009), p. 180.

[33] Greta Jones, 'Marie Stopes in Ireland: the mothers' clinic in Belfast, 1936–1947', *Social History of Medicine*, 5, no 2, 1992, p. 265.

[34] Quoted in McCormick, *Regulating sexuality*, p. 183.

[35] McCormick, *Regulating sexuality*, pp. 184–5.

broadcast a documentary on the subject in 1966, a woman doctor explained that in addition to the Catholics, 'we have a strong Calvinist element to deal with, to whom we appear as the Scarlet Woman in person'.[36] In 1968, the Northern Ireland Family Planning Association received a grant from the Ministry of Health. By the end of the decade, there were seven family planning clinics, and family planning was available under the National Health Service.[37]

1.3   Fertility in Ireland (1920–1961)

The gap between Catholic and Protestant family sizes increased in Ireland from the 1920s. Guinnane describes the divergence as 'a twentieth-century development'.[38] By 1946, over half of non-Catholic couples had 1–3 children; by 1961, almost two-thirds of non-Catholic families consisted of 1–3 children. Social class does not account for the discrepancy, although professional and middle-class families of all religions had smaller families than working class and farming households. In 1946, Catholics salaried employees, higher professionals, employers and managers, who were married for 25–29 years had approximately twice as many children as their Protestant counterparts; the gap had narrowed somewhat by 1961 because of rising or stable family size for Protestants, whereas Catholic families were smaller.[39] Brendan Walsh using 1960s data for both parts of Ireland concluded that 'the general tendency is for completed family size to be about 50 per cent higher among the RC population'. Catholics and ODs in both Northern Ireland and the Republic show similar differential fertility by social class, with farming and manual workers having larger families than professional and non-manual workers'.[40] Kennedy claims that

The pattern of non-Catholic marital fertility shows that effective birth control techniques, including abstinence, were available to those who wished to use it. The higher marital fertility of Irish Catholicism can be traced to a greater reluctance to use, rather than an ignorance of effective birth control methods or an inability to obtain them.... couples who desired to limit their family size were able to do so. Knowledge about and access to artificial birth control methods explain part of the differences, of course, but traditional methods such as coitus interruptus and either periodic or permanent abstinence were widely known and available to all married couples, given sufficient motivation.[41]

Statistics suggest that religion was a critical factor in the rate of fertility decline after 1920, though Irish Protestants had larger families than their British

[36] Leanne McCormick, '"The scarlet woman in Person": the establishment of a family planning service in Northern Ireland, 1950–74', Social History of Medicine, 21, no 2, 2008, pp. 345–60.
[37] Earner-Byrne and Urquhart, Abortion, pp. 64–6.
[38] Guinnane, The vanishing Irish, p. 278.   [39] Kennedy, The Irish, pp. 184, 188.
[40] Brendan Walsh, Religion and demographic behaviour in Ireland, ESRI paper 55 (May 1970), pp. 8–9.
[41] Kennedy, The Irish, pp. 184, 189.

counterparts. Guinnane states that 'Ireland's marital fertility has received little systematic attention because the explanation seemed self-evident: the Church discouraged conception and the Irish accepted the Church's teaching'. But fertility patterns before 1920 complicate that argument. He suggests that 'We cannot simply invoke Catholicism as a set of beliefs and institutions; we must explain why, if Catholicism really is the answer, Irish couples accepted this facet of their Church's teaching'.[42] In the early 1960s, Spain, Portugal and Poland – countries that were generally recognised as Catholic had significantly lower marital fertility than Ireland. Does the explanation lie in *Irish* Catholicism, as opposed to Catholicism?

McQuillan and Goldscheider both suggest that religion influences demographic behaviour in a number of ways. Church teaching exercises an influence, not just on issues such as contraception but also on the merits of large families and gender relations. Social organizations, such as denominational schools and community groups that transmit church teaching and the importance of compliance are important as is the degree to which religion and religious values, form an important part of personal identity. In Muslim countries, fertility is higher among those who had attended Islamic schools.[43] Goldscheider concluded that 'the values that most influence fertility are those that relate to the centrality of the family, the roles of men and women, and the roles of parents and their children. These values are significantly more important than religious views on contraceptive usage or ideal family size'. The evidence suggests that the differential fertility between Catholics and Protestants in Ireland was a relatively recent occurrence, beginning probably in the closing decades of the nineteenth century, and it accentuated after 1920. One factor may be when the 1930 Lambeth Conference signalled a qualified approval for family planning, Catholicism became an outlier in its opposition to birth control and this opposition, and the continuing affirmation of the merits of large families becomes a statement of Catholic identity, and a statement of Irish Catholic identity.

The *Commission on Emigration and other Population Problems*, which sat from 1948 to 1954 reflected an Irish church-state consensus on the merits of large families. It stated that the decline in family size was 'unwelcome and every effort should be made to arrest it'. Without citing supporting evidence, it claimed that large families were only a burden for a relatively short time; they had no evidence that might suggest that large families 'makes for a general condition of poverty'; or that 'our family pattern imposes an undue strain

---

[42] Guinnane, *The vanishing Irish*, pp. 260–1.
[43] K. McQuillan, 'When does religion influence fertility?' *Population and Development Review*, 30, no 1, 2004, pp. 25–56; Calvin Goldscheider, 'Religion, family and fertility: what do we know historically and comparatively?', in Derosas and van Poppel, *Religion and the decline of fertility*, pp. 41–58, quote on p. 57.

on mothers in general', or that *'apart from the increased risk associated with more frequent child-bearing'* [my italics] they had an adverse effect on the health of mothers. Furthermore, the number of families with a large number of dependent children – defined as ten or more was 'relatively few'.[44] A published personal reservation written by Rev. A.A. Luce, a professor of philosophy at Trinity College Dublin and a member of the Commission, stated that he had considered it to be 'a public duty' to collect information on contraceptives, and he believed that the commission should examine this issue however that did not happen. In Chapter 9 'Population Policy', this government commission faithfully and unquestioningly repeated Catholic social teaching: 'The primary purpose of marriage, in the natural order of things, is the birth and bringing up of children. The principle which rightly guides the normal Christian married couple in this matter is to have as many children as they can reasonably hope to bring up properly'. Three Protestant members dissented, as did a number of Catholic members, though not all of the latter recorded their dissent in the published report. Some suggested that large families were the primary explanation for Ireland's low marriage rate. The Bishop of Cork, Dr Lucey, who was a member of the Commission, believed that the endorsement of large families in the majority report (a compromise) was not sufficiently strong, so he submitted a minority report that included the biblical injunction to '"Increase and Multiply" and fill the earth'.[45] While comparatively few Irish people – even politicians or public servants – waded through the majority and minority reports of the *Commission on Emigration*, the contents suggest that in the 1950s, large families were widely valorised by both church and state – though there were dissenters.

A number of studies of fertility control emphasise the importance of motivation: the wish to limit family size. Economic factors such as the cost of raising and educating children and opportunities for female employment are commonly cited as factors resulting in smaller families.[46] Birth rates fell throughout Europe during the depression of the 1930s. In Ireland, emigration reduced the cost of large families, especially for farming households, because it avoided pressures to subdivide holdings, and provided job options for non-inheriting children – including manual/labouring jobs that family pride might have regarded as unsuitable in Ireland. Middle-class and large farming families tried to give their children a secondary, and perhaps, university education, but until the 1970s, compulsory schooling ceased at the age of fourteen, so for many households, the cost of schooling – in terms of income foregone and child support was

---

[44] Daly, *The slow failure*, p. 123. The report appears to have predated the publication of Irish journal articles describing the significant rise in maternal mortality and morbidity in high parity births.

[45] Daly, *The slow failure*, pp. 122–8.

[46] Gary Becker, *A treatise on the family* (Harvard University Press, Cambridge, MA, 1991 edition), pp. 138–51.

relatively short. Irish society continued to expect older children to contribute to family income – handing over all or part of their pay; working unpaid in the family farm or business, or sending remittances home, which helped to reduce the burden associated with large families. Given these expectations, a large family was a good insurance policy. Family supports were important in a society that lacked a comprehensive welfare state and one where widows often had to depend on family or charity to survive at any level above basic subsistence.

1.4   Contraception and Censorship in Independent Ireland (1922–1935)

In our views on [contraception] we are perfectly clear and perfectly definite. We will not allow ... the free discussion of this question ... We have made up our minds that it is wrong. That conclusion is for us unalterable ... That question shall not be advocated in any book or in any periodical that circulates in this country.[47]

The aftermath of the Great War prompted an international backlash against the relaxed moral codes of the war years – as evidenced by greater freedom for women, shorter skirts, smoking and rising illegitimacy. The emergence of the cinema as a form of mass entertainment was another cause for concern; likewise, the motor car – which offered both a means of private transport and a private space for courting couples. While the impact of the Great War was less significant in Ireland, the war of independence created opportunities for some women to drive cars, and mix more freely with men, and the rate of recorded illegitimate births increased (as it did in Britain and elsewhere). The foundation of the Irish Free State was seen as an opportunity to reverse this moral decline; indeed, some believed that Irish independence made it imperative to enforce a new national moral order.

In 1923, Ireland signed the International Convention for the Suppression of the Circulation and Traffic of Obscene Publications, which required each signatory to examine whether they needed to introduce legislation relating to obscene publications, and to determine how obscene publications should be defined.[48] In 1926, the Minister for Justice established the Committee on Evil Literature to determine whether it was 'necessary or advisable in the interest of public morality to extend the existing powers of the state to prohibit or restrict the sale and circulation of printed matter'. The committee provided a platform for the Catholic Action movement to campaign for restrictions on obscene

[47] DD, 18 October 1928, col 608, Fitzgerald Kenney.
[48] Sandra McAvoy, '"A perpetual nightmare": women, fertility control, the Irish state, and the 1935 ban on contraceptives', in Margaret Preston and Margaret Ó hÓgartaigh (eds), *Gender and medicine in Ireland, 1700–1950* (Syracuse University Press, Syracuse, New York, 2012), p. 194.

literature and for the definition of 'obscene' to be extended to include literature relating to contraception. Peter Martin noted that 'the most contentious item on the reformer's agenda was birth control ... the government was afraid of alienating the Protestant community and interfering in people's lives' but Catholic Action believed that 'advertisements for contraceptives and articles supporting birth control were, as far as the pro-censorship lobby was concerned, among the most objectionable features of the foreign press'.[49]

Within a decade of independence, the Irish Free State enacted laws to regulate access to alcohol, impose licensing restrictions on dances and censor films and printed matter. These campaigns were driven by a Catholic Action movement, which saw a native government as a sympathetic instrument in their campaign to bring Irish laws into conformity with Catholic teaching.[50] The primary demand of the Catholic Truth Society of Ireland – a publisher of widely available leaflets on faith and morals, directed at a lay audience, was that 'neo-Malthusian birth control' be made illegal. They wanted a ban on all publications that advocated birth control or published advertisements for birth-control literature. Concerns about contraception were at the heart of this wider moral panic; dance halls, motor cars, cinemas and evil literature were all viewed as promoting a receptive attitude towards birth control, and birth control was linked with rising illegitimacy.[51]

In the mid-nineteenth century, advertisements for birth control devices were carried out in the Dublin popular press. Whether the advertised products were effective, does not concern us. The *Dublin Medical Press* – the journal of the medical profession – waged a long campaign to suppress these advertisements, 'naming and shaming local newspapers in Ireland that carried "indecent" advertisements'. Over time, the *Dublin Medical Press* shifted its position, arguing that information about birth control should be scientific – that is provided by the medical profession.[52] Although these advertisements were not new, one can argue that with the publication in 1918 of Marie Stopes' book *Married Love*, birth control had moved from small ads to a more respectable and more public position, resulting in a greater sense of 'moral panic' over the dangers of contraception. Some Irish people wrote to Marie Stopes seeking advice on family planning, indicating that her work was not unknown in Ireland. Ó Gráda noted that more letters came from Northern Ireland than from the

[49] Peter Martin, *Censorship in the two Irelands, 1922–1939* (Irish Academic Press, Dublin, 2006), p. 62.

[50] Maurice Curtis, *The splendid cause. The Catholic Action movement in Ireland in the twentieth century* (Original Writing, Dublin, 2008).

[51] David Fitzpatrick, *The two Irelands, 1912–1939* (Oxford University Press, Oxford, 1998), p. 228.

[52] Ann Daly '"Veiled obscenity"; contraception and the Dublin Medical Press, 1850–1900', in Elaine Farrell (ed.), *'She said she was in the family way'. Pregnancy and Infancy in modern Ireland* (Institute of Historical Research, London, 2012), pp. 15–34, quote on p. 30.

Irish Free State. In the years 1918–21, some correspondents may have been members of the British Army stationed in Ireland; thirty-six correspondents were of middle- or upper-class backgrounds, and only three were identifiably working class. The 1929 Censorship of Publications Act does not appear to have impacted on the flow.[53]

Periodicals explaining methods of contraception were available in the 1920s – at least in Dublin. McAvoy records the case of a Dublin chemist who was prosecuted in 1920 (before independence) for displaying posters advertising contraceptives and books containing contraceptive information; the authorities burned his stock of 240 books.[54] The large number of books suggests that he had a ready market. Marie Stopes' pamphlet *A Letter to Working* Mothers was available in a shop in Stephen Street; in 1928, the owner was prosecuted for selling *Family Limitation*, a pamphlet by American birth-control pioneer, Margaret Sanger, which was described as an 'obscene libel'.[55] Many witnesses who gave evidence to the Committee on Evil Literature called for, either a ban or the censorship of birth control literature, among them, a deputation from the CTSI whose members included the Master of the Coombe maternity hospital, and a future Minister for Justice; representatives of teaching organisations, and the Irish Retail Newsagents, Booksellers and Stationers Association.[56] Ferriter suggests that the main targets were imported publications from England – newspapers and periodicals giving racy details of divorce proceedings, answers to queries about sexual problems, and 'papers and books containing advertisements of certain drugs and instruments which urge people to the most monstrous crimes'.[57] It is unclear how widely they circulated, especially outside Dublin. The censorship files in the National Archives suggest that advertisements for contraceptives or information about birth control were widely carried in British magazines; the files contain copies of magazines that targeted poultry producers, racing tipsters and people with an interest in cage birds, and these advertisements were a common feature of best-selling Sunday newspapers such as the *News of the World*.[58] During the Senate debate on the 1929 Censorship of Publications Bill, Senator Oliver St John Gogarty, a medical doctor, reported that new mothers who placed birth notices in newspapers had received literature

---

[53] Ó Gráda and Duffy, 'Fertility transition in Ireland and Scotland', pp. 97–100.

[54] McAvoy, 'A perpetual nightmare?', p. 192.

[55] Sandra McAvoy, '"Its effect on public morality is vicious in the extreme": defining birth control as obscene and unethical, 1926–32', in Elaine Farrell (ed.), *'She said she was in the family way'*, p. 43.

[56] McAvoy, 'Its effect on public morality is vicious in the extreme', p. 42.

[57] Diarmaid Ferriter, *Occasions of sin: sex and society in modern Ireland* (Profile Books, London, 2012), p. 187.

[58] Daly, *Slow failure*, pp. 87–9. McAvoy, 'A perpetual nightmare', p. 42 gives an extensive list of Sunday newspapers and periodicals that carried such advertisements, including *Old Moore's Almanac*, which appears to have been a staple in many Irish homes.

from British mail order firms attempting to sell them information or contraceptive devices.[59] This was also happening in Britain at this time.[60]

In December 1926, the Committee on Evil Literature unanimously recommended that 'the sale and circulation, *except to authorised persons*, [my italics] of books, magazines and pamphlets that advocated the unnatural prevention of conception should be made illegal and be punishable by adequate penalties' – wording that would appear to leave open the possibility that doctors would have access to such literature.[61] The Committee was of the opinion that for young and single people birth control literature would 'open[ing] the way to sensual indulgence for those who desire to avoid the responsibilities of the married state'.[62] In other words, married couples were *not* the primary target. Ferriter notes that while there was widespread opposition to the censorship of literature, this opposition did not always extend to proposals to ban books advocating birth control. He cites a Senate speech by St. John Gogarty, who had a large circle of literary friends: 'No one who has any care for a nation's welfare can for one moment countenance contraceptive practices which are a contradiction of a nation's life'. Professor W.E. Thrift TD for Trinity College, while not condemning birth control described some of the literature on the topic as 'disgusting to all decently minded people'.[63] The 1929 Censorship of Publications Act gave the Censorship Board the power to recommend that the Minister should prohibit the sale and distribution within the state of any publication that 'advocates the unnatural prevention of conception or the procurement of abortion or miscarriage or the use of any method, treatment or appliance for the purpose of such prevention or such procurement' and advertisements for these products were defined as 'indecent and obscene'. Whitty concluded that 'Public ignorance was seen as the best basis for maintaining public morality'.[64]

Given that contraceptives were widely advertised in periodicals during the 1920s, it is probable that Irish couples were purchasing them by mail order. McAvoy discovered that in 1926 the Irish postal authorities were returning packages of contraceptives that they had identified in the mail to Britain, although they had no legal authority to do this, but there was no systematic scrutiny of postal packages.[65] Irish men who had lived or worked in Britain may have become familiar with condoms – especially those who had served in the British army; there is no evidence that the Irish army distributed condoms as

59 Seanad Debates, vol 12, 11 April 1929, col 87.
60 Kate Fisher, *Birth control, sex & marriage in Britain 1918–1960* (Oxford University Press, Oxford, 2006), p. 37.
61 Martin, *Censorship in the two Irelands*, pp. 67–8.
62 *Report of the Committee on Evil Literature* (Government Publications, Dublin, 1926), p. 14.
63 Ferriter, *Occasions of sin*, p. 188. McAvoy, 'A perpetual nightmare'.
64 Noel Whitty, 'The law and the regulation of reproduction in Ireland, 1922–1992', *The University of Toronto Law Journal*, 43, no 4, autumn 1993, p. 854.
65 McAvoy, 'A perpetual nightmare', p. 190.

part of their effort to contain venereal disease.[66] The Committee on the Criminal Law Amendment Acts (1880–85) and Juvenile Prostitution – the Carrigan Committee, which reported in 1931 claimed with respect to contraceptives that

so common in some places were such articles in use that there was no attempt to conceal the sale of them, and places were mentioned to which the supply of such articles come regularly by post to recognised vendors. At the same time, quantities of contraception advertisements are in circulation, and price lists are extensively distributed throughout the country by cross- channel agencies in order to facilitate the direct purchase by private persons of the articles offered by sale.[67]

These claims were made by groups who were determined to foment a sense of moral panic, and so far, they have not been supported by independent evidence. The only information that I have found to date about the sale and distribution of contraceptives in Ireland around this time comes from a much later date, though there is no reason to discount its accuracy.

In June 1972, when the question of amending the laws on contraception was attracting attention, a Dublin man wrote to the Taoiseach Jack Lynch offering to provide information about the supply of contraceptives before 1935. He received a polite reply thanking him for his letter, with the comment that nothing that he had to communicate would be of interest to the Attorney General. Despite this brush-off, he wrote a second letter to the Taoiseach. This man started work with the wholesale chemist May Roberts in 1926. In 1928/9, he became an assembler in sundries – he and a colleague had sole charge of a press with a Yale lock which was stocked with cigarettes and other items including two gross of rubber preventatives. These were supplied 'occasionally' to 4–5 chemists in Dublin: Blake's with branches in Fownes St and Liffey St; Rosenthal in Merrion Row, Hamilton Long in O' Connell Street, and Price's pharmacy of Clare St. where Leopold Bloom memorably bought lemon soap on 4 June 1904.[68] Michael Solomons, a gynaecologist recalled that when he was a child Rosenthal was fined for selling contraceptives, and his father, also a gynaecologist paid the fine.[69] May Roberts supplied a gross every fortnight to Blair's in Cork city (presumably John Blair and Son of Patrick Street), and they occasionally posted a gross to the British naval bases in Spike Island and Lough Swilly. Although one-third of the staff at May Roberts was Protestant, he claimed that only one man 'availed of contraceptives' – and this was usually covered up by putting in an order for a sponge.[70] The general tenor – especially the phoney order for a sponge – indicates a surreptitious attitude towards their

[66] My thanks to Susannah Riordan for discussing this matter with me.
[67] As quoted by Chrystel Hug, *The politics of sexual morality in Ireland* (Macmillan, Basingstoke, 1999), p. 80.
[68] NAI DT S2003 NAI, DT,/16/453.
[69] Michael Solomons, *Pro-life. The Irish question* (Lilliput Press, Dublin, 1992), p. 22.
[70] NAI, DT, S2003/16/453.

use, and a limited market. There may have been other outlets. In Britain, contraceptives were often sold at market stalls and the barber shops of popular memory, but so far, no information regarding such sales has come to light for Ireland. The majority of Dublin street traders were women, which makes it less likely that they would sell contraceptives. McAvoy failed to get any useful statistical data on imports of contraceptives.[71] The evidence available at present suggests very limited availability before 1935. This should not surprise us. In Britain, Boots the leading chain of pharmacies did not sell condoms until the 1960s; neither did many of the independent chemist shops; those that did, tended to keep them out of sight, and on occasion, they were only sold by a senior member of staff.[72] I have found no information about sales of condoms in Northern Ireland during these years.

1.5   The Lambeth Conference and *Casti Connubii* (1930)

Family planning featured prominently in religious and political debates in the 1930s, to a degree not again seen until the 1960s. Noonan, writing about the Catholic church and contraception describes the early 1930s as 'the high point not only of active teaching against contraception, but of an absolute stand against cooperation with instruments'.[73] At the 1930 Lambeth Conference, the Anglican church modified its opposition to birth control and endorsed the use of contraception in limited circumstances: – where an additional birth would present a risk to the life or health of the mother, or the mother would be so exhausted that an additional child would prevent her fulfilling her duties to her family. The emphasis placed on the mother's health and well-being is significant. This conference was attended by thirteen bishops of the Church of Ireland, and two were members of the team that drafted the resolution on family planning.[74] The resolution received limited coverage in Irish newspapers. The *Irish Times* (the newspaper read by many Irish Protestants), and the *Belfast Telegraph* limited their coverage to the brief official statements from the Conference. When the Church of Ireland Home Mission Society gave a series of sermons on the Conference decisions, the sermon on Christian Marriage emphasised the preservation of family life, that marriage was a lifelong union, and the sacredness of sex within marriage. The summary in the *Irish Times* did not mention family limitation.[75]

---

[71] McAvoy, 'A perpetual nightmare', pp. 189–90.
[72] Stuart Anderson and Virginia Berridge, 'The role of the community pharmacist in health and welfare, 1911–1986', in Joanna Bornat, Paul Thompson, Robert Perks, Jan Walmsley (eds), *Oral history health and welfare* (Routledge, London and New York, 2000), p. 66.
[73] John Noonan, *Contraception. A history of its treatment by the Catholic theologians and canonists*, (Belknap Press, Cambridge, MA, 1965), p. 506.
[74] McAvoy, 'A perpetual nightmare', pp. 196–7.
[75] *Irish Times*, 23 February 1931. I have also scanned the *Irish Times* and *Belfast Telegraph*, July 1930–May 1931. Irish Newspapers Archives, accessed 7 March 2022.

The Catholic church was now the only Christian church that was unequivocally opposed to contraception, and the church's reaction, indeed sense of panic is evident. The papal encyclical *Casti Connubii* [on Christian Marriage] was published on 31 December 1930. The timing was not accidental. Noonan claims that it was a response to the Lambeth Conference resolution, and this was also stated in the *Irish Times,* which carried a report by the Rome correspondent of the *Times*.[76] The other precipitating factors were a call by the German Catholic church for a change in church teaching on contraception, and the Vatican's belief that church teaching was not being enforced.[77] The encyclical dealt with all aspects of marriage; it rejected divorce and trial marriages (pre-marital sex), and sterilisation. It urged the faithful to 'bear offspring for the Church of Christ, to procreate saints and servants of God, that the people adhering to the worship of God our Saviour should daily increase'. It condemned any use of the marriage act, which was deprived of its power to procreate.[78] Confessors should inform penitents of their duty to procreate, and should disabuse those who practised contraception in good faith – that is not realising that it was wrong to use withdrawal. They were also instructed to tell a wife whose husband was using contraception that she should resist sexual relations – even if this resulted in assault; a husband whose wife was using contraception was instructed to take steps to remove her contraceptive instruments.[79] The 1931 Lenten pastorals issued by Irish bishops were inspired by the papal encyclical. Twelve bishops 'reaffirmed the sanctity of marriage and inadmissibility of divorce; eleven deplored the insidious effects of the press, wireless or evil literature; eight inveighed against the cinema or theatre; six warned of the dangers of dancing; four alluded delicately to contraception, abortion or infanticide; three condemned company-keeping; irregular unions and immodesty in female dress each provoked two admonitions'.[80] The extensive publicity by the Catholic Hierarchy of papal teaching on marriage and contraception contrasts with the lack of publicity given to the Lambeth Conference statement by the Church of Ireland.

Members of the Irish Catholic Hierarchy opposed the appointment of Protestant doctors to public appointments, such as dispensary doctor or medical officer of health, alleging that they might prescribe contraceptives, and contraception became a major issue in the debate over legislation to regulate the Pharmaceutical Society of Ireland [PSI]– the representative organisation for dispensing chemists. [This legislation was necessary to take account of the formation of the Irish Free State and of Northern Ireland]. The PSI was the first organisation to demand the introduction of legislation banning the sale,

[76] *IT*, 13 January 1931.   [77] Noonan, *Contraception*, p. 424.
[78] Noonan, *Contraception*, p. 426.   [79] Noonan, *Contraception*, p. 504.
[80] Daly, *Slow failure*, p. 90.

manufacture and distribution of contraceptives in 1931. A number of pharmacists pressed for the inclusion of a provision to remove pharmacists, who were guilty of professional misconduct from the register, and they urged that the manufacture, stocking, procuring or possessing of any drug or article used for the purpose of abortion or contraception should be deemed professional misconduct. May Roberts – the wholesaler described in that 1972 letter, told the PSI that they would cease to stock contraceptives, 'if it is considered desirable'; another wholesaler made it known that they did not stock contraceptives; a third appeared to indicate that he was not in favour of contraceptives – which would appear to confirm that they were not widely distributed. Pharmacies that stocked contraceptives came under pressure from Catholic Action groups. McAvoy quotes a Department of Justice memorandum in 1933 stating that 'reputable chemists have of late refrained from stocking them'; however, Fr Devane – a prominent figure in Catholic Action – reported that they continued to be stocked by four Dublin chemists (three in Fownes St).[81]

1.6   The Criminal Law Amendment Act 1935

The campaign by Catholic Action groups against contraception became embroiled in proposals to amend the 1885 Criminal Law Amendment Act, which set the age of consent for sexual relations. The Act was amended by Westminster in 1922 and in Northern Ireland in 1923. These amendments raised the age of consent and tightened the position with respect to mitigating arguments.

Susannah Riordan suggests that similar changes were under consideration by Minister for Home Affairs, Kevin O'Higgins, and if the amendment had been introduced in the mid-1920s, it might have been confined to raising the age of consent. But the delay coincided with growing activity by Catholic Action groups and an increased focus on contraception. In 1930, the Minister for Justice, James Fitzgerald-Kenney, set up a committee to examine possible amendments to the Act – this followed attempts by the opposition Fianna Fáil party to introduce a private members bill to this effect. Riordan noted that the report of the Committee appointed to review the Criminal Law Amendment Act, which is known as the Carrigan Committee, 'went well beyond this brief. It ranged widely and damningly over the state of Irish sexual morality'. She suggests that 'Far from assessing the desirability of law reform, it indiscriminately collected such evidence as suggested the state was experiencing moral decay and extrapolated from this the need for legislative intervention' in matters such as brothels, public dance halls and contraceptives.[82] Prostitution and

---

[81] This paragraph is based on McAvoy, 'A perpetual nightmare', pp. 46–51.
[82] Susannah Riordan, '"A reasonable cause": the age of consent and the debate on gender and justice in the Irish Free State, 1922–35', *Irish Historical Studies*, 34, no 147, 2011, pp. 429, 439–40.

birth control were discussed in the same section – reinforcing the association between contraception and sexual licence. The report was circulated to the Executive Council, with the recommendation that nothing further should be done until expert advice had been sought. When Fianna Fáil came into office in 1932, a decision was taken to suppress the report, and Justice Minister James Geoghegan determined to legislate without debate. A cross-party committee of the legislature began work on draft legislation. The Minister asked the Catholic Hierarchy to submit a memorandum setting out their wishes, which would be considered by the cross-party committee. Their memorandum sought legislative action on four matters: a prohibition on contraceptives; raising the age of consent; restrictions on public dance halls and 'the moral abuse of motorcars'.[83]

The clauses relating to contraceptives drafted by the cross-party committee followed the recommendations of the Carrigan Committee. They involved a ban on contraceptives, which would not apply in 'exceptional circumstances' based on religious conviction or medical need, but this was rejected by the Cabinet, who sought an absolute ban.[84] McAvoy suggests that Seán T. O'Kelly – Minster for Local Government and Public Health was responsible for the total ban implemented in the 1935 Criminal Law (Amendment) Act – an act whose primary purpose was to strengthen the law relating to sexual offences, particularly those involving under-age females. The inclusion of the ban on contraception in legislation relating to sexual offences with minors reinforced a sense that contraception was obscene, and offensive. The Dáil and the Seanad were loath to discuss the legislation in the full house – preferring to refer legislative scrutiny to committees, whose proceedings were not reported in the published Oireachtas Debates. The Minister for Justice discouraged debate, arguing that the bill was the work of 'an informal Committee of the Dáil', and therefore came with all-party support.[85] A member of the opposition front bench agreed, describing it as 'the work of a Committee formed from all parties in this House' – an 'entirely non-political Committee'.[86] The reluctance to discuss child prostitution extended to contraception. Even Senator Kathleen Clarke, widow of the 1916 leader Tom Clarke, who was in favour of deleting the clause on contraception, referred to contraceptives as 'these things', and this phrase was adopted by a fellow-Senator. The Dáil Committee recommended minimal changes, none relating to contraception however the Special Committee of the Seanad recommended the deletion of Article 17 relating to the sale manufacture and distribution of contraceptives. Kathleen Clarke expressed support for Church and State 'in trying to get rid of these things',

---

[83] James Smith, 'The politics of sexual knowledge: the origins of Ireland's containment culture and the 1931 Carrigan report', *Journal of the History of Sexuality*, 13, no 2, 2004, p. 217.
[84] Smith, p. 218.   [85] Seanad Debates second stage, 19 December 1934, vol 19, no 8.
[86] SD 28 June 1934, col 1248, vol 53, no 10.

but she argued that prohibition would encourage an illicit trade. She was supported by Senator Bagwell (Unionist) who claimed that there were differences of opinion on the topic, and the matter was best left to individuals. Labour Senators Thomas Foran and Tom Johnson argued that contraception should not be included in this bill – it was a matter for separate legislation. Oliver St. John Gogarty spoke of the medical benefits of contraception, such as controlling venereal disease (which was rife in Dublin), and he suggested that public opinion might change. Despite these views, the amendment was not carried. Senator Comyn was more in tune with majority opinion, describing the clause relating to contraception as the most important aspect of the legislation – he claimed that trade in contraception 'would mean the destruction of this race'.[87] The Senator's argument linking contraception with race destruction was common in 1930s Europe, but it did not feature prominently in Ireland, where the rhetoric concerning population decline focused on emigration and on the baleful effect of internal migration from the healthy countryside to disease-ridden cities, an argument that echoed Catholic social teaching.[88]

The 1935 legislation that prohibited access to contraceptives for almost fifty years was passed as an addendum to legislation on sexual offences. Public debate was confined to short statements in the Seanad. Contrary to Mrs Clarke's fears, there is no evidence of any significant black market in contraceptives until the early 1970s. I would argue, however, that the 1929 Censorship of Publications Act was probably more significant than the 1935 Act, because it denied Irish people's access to knowledge about contraception. Although Peter Martin suggests that the importance of birth control as a factor in the banning of books has been overstated,[89] the Censorship of Publications Act resulted in the banning of numerous guides to family planning, including those produced by the Mothers' Union, and family health manuals produced by *Good Housekeeping*, Pan Books, and *Pear's Encyclopaedia*, some editions of *Old Moore's Almanac*, and books by Margaret Sanger, Marie Stopes and Bertrand Russell. The ban extended to manuals written for new mothers, whose titles suggest that they were primarily about babies and child care.[90] Michael Solomons noted that many books relating to sex or marriage were banned if they contained a chapter or even a paragraph about contraception.[91] The 1929 Act also prevented and/or restricted the circulation of books and periodicals dealing with marriage, and reproductive biology.

The only known instance of a book being banned, that gave details of the 'safe period', which was not prohibited by the Catholic church, was the notorious ban imposed in 1941 on Halliday Sutherland, *Laws of Life* which carried the approval

---

[87] SD, 6 February 1935, vol 19, no 15, cols 1247–59.
[88] Daly, *The slow failure*, pp. 26–30.   [89] Martin, *Censorship in the two Irelands*, pp. 193–4.
[90] *Iris Oifigiúil. Register of Prohibited Publications*: successive editions.
[91] Solomons, *Pro-life*, p. 16.

of the Catholic Archdiocese of Westminster – though some titles on the list of banned publications, such as *Modern Rhythm*, or *The Natural Method* might also have fallen into this category. *Laws of Life* was not banned because it advocated the unnatural prevention of conception, but on the grounds of indecency. Sutherland was a Catholic gynaecologist, best known for challenging Marie Stopes, and his book was banned following a complaint by a 'Protestant father' that the information that it gave on the 'safe period' might be abused by young people. The Catholic Vigilance Society approved of the book.[92] The complaint may have been motivated by resentment at Sutherland's challenge to Marie Stopes; whatever the reason, it generated a major debate in the Seanad – but censorship was imposed – and the passages that Senators read from this, and other banned books were redacted in the official debates. The 1949 *Royal Commission on Population* was also banned – presumably because it discussed methods of fertility control being used in Britain,[93] though this ban was short-lived.

Ireland was by no means unique in introducing legislation to restrict access to contraception. Noonan noted that in Spain, Belgium and Ireland, the legislation reflected Catholic teaching on contraception.[94] In other countries, it was often prompted by efforts to counteract the falling birth rate. Legislation restricting access to contraception was introduced in many US states. In Australia, the customs department kept a watch on publications dealing with family planning and thousands of titles were suppressed.[95] In the Netherlands, legislation was passed in 1911 restricting the dissemination of advice on birth control and the sale of contraceptives. In France, whose population had been growing at a much slower rate than elsewhere in Europe for over a century and fears of population decline were aggravated by the appalling losses of young men during World War I, laws were passed in 1920 prohibiting the spread of birth control information and the sale of contraceptives, and measures were introduced against abortion, though condoms – defined as a protective against venereal disease were exempted. Belgium had laws countering the sale of contraceptives and dissemination of information.[96] In Portugal where the Salazar government had banned the sale and advertisement of contraceptives, condoms continued to be sold in pharmacies and distributed in the army.[97] Most of these

---

[92] Michael Adams, *Censorship. The Irish experience* (Scepter Books, Dublin, 1968), pp. 88–9 and p. 214.

[93] Paul Blanshard, *The Irish and Catholic power* (Derek Verschoyle, London, 1954), p. 105.

[94] Noonan, *Contraception*, p. 411.

[95] Frank Bongiorno, *The sex lives of Australians* (Collingwood, Victoria, 2015 edition), p. 180.

[96] D.V. Glass, 'Western Europe', in *Family planning and population programs. A review of world development* (Proceedings of the International Conference on Family Planning Programs, Geneva, Chicago, August 1965), pp. 183–92.

[97] Tiago Pires Marques, 'The politics of Catholic medicine: "The Pill" and Humanae Vitae in Portugal', in Alana Harris (ed), *The schism of '68. Catholicism, contraception and Humanae Vitae in Europe, 1945–1975* (Palgrave Macmillan, London, 2018).

laws remained in existence until the 1960s, though compliance may have been limited because statistics show that all these countries recorded significantly lower marital fertility than Ireland.

1.7   Enforcing Catholic Teaching in Confession

Priests did not generally preach about sexuality and associated topics at Sunday mass, because the attendance included single adults and children, and anything other than vague references to this topic, would have been avoided.[98] What priests said or failed to say in confession to couples who were limiting families appears to have varied widely. In the United States, according to Tentler, some priests avoided the topic entirely, leaving it to parish missions; some large US parishes held separate missions over four weeks for single men, single women, married men and married women.[99] Missions offered scope for addressing sensitive topics – attendance was limited to adults, and they were generally segregated by gender. Some priests may have been extremely intrusive about family size; others opted for a quiet life. None of the elderly Quebec priests and former priests who were interviewed by Gervais and Gavreau admitted denying absolution to women or men using contraceptive methods not approved by the Catholic church.[100] In Italy, where coitus interruptus was one of the main methods of contraception well into the 1980s, many priests in the diocese of Padua in the 1930s appear to have made a conscious decision not to press those in confession about this practice, and a similar silence has been reported in the Netherlands. All four Swiss women, interviewed by Rusterholz, who had confessed to using withdrawal received absolution.[101]

Irish priests may have shown less understanding. A doctor in county Clare, who was the father of two children, told the Harvard anthropologist Solon Kimball that 'the Catholic church is a bloody tough religion'. If a man confessed that he was taking steps to prevent conception, the priest would refuse absolution unless the man gave an undertaking to desist. He would also be asked whether he had made a similar confession in the past. Failure to confess all your sins would be a mortal sin. This doctor was 'on the abstention route', because he could not afford to educate a larger family. He claimed that

---

[98] This was noted in interviews with elderly Swiss Catholics, Caroline Rusterholz, 'Reproductive behaviour and contraceptive practices in comparative perspective', *The History of the Family*, Published online 1 December 2014, p. 11.

[99] Leslie Tentler, *Catholics and contraception. An American history* (Cornell University Press, Ithaca and London, 2004), pp. 23–38.

[100] D. Gervais and D. Gauvreau, 'Women priests and physicians: family limitation in Quebec, 1949–1970', *Journal of Interdisciplinary History*, 34, no 2, 2003, p. 306.

[101] Gianpiero dalla Zuanna, 'Tacit consent. The Church and birth control in Northern Italy', *Population and Development Review*, 17, no 2 (June 2011), pp. 361–74; Angelo Somers and Frans Van Poppel, '*Priest, parishioner and posterity. A Dutch urban legend or historical fact? History of the Family*, 15, (2010), pp. 174–90. Rusterholz, 'Reproductive behavior', p. 12.

a priest told him that this was 'all right' provided that the couple had agreed, but if one party wished to have sexual relations and was denied, it would be a mortal sin.[102] Another father of two children said that 'sometimes it is a problem because the priests are always after you to have more'.[103] One father of a large family was described as 'always in a row with priests'; he no longer went to confession or communion though he attended mass occasionally. This man had been denied absolution in confession by a missionary priest because he was no longer having sexual relations with his wife. When he complied with the priest's demand, his wife again became pregnant.[104] One of Kimball's closest acquaintances in Clare, who related this man's story, described it as 'a very delicate matter'. He did not regard his sexual relations with his wife as 'the priest's business' and never spoke of it in confession. This man's wife almost died following a miscarriage and she was extremely ill following the birth of their only child, so they had decided that they could not risk another pregnancy.[105]

The wife of the doctor quoted above, also spoke to Kimball when her husband was not present. 'She had been to a new priest, and he had said some things to her, and she thought to herself that she wouldn't go back to him again. She knew a nice little priest who was very nice.' She claimed that one local woman had given birth to a third child, 'because the confessing father made her do it and she blamed it entirely on him' and was determined not to have any more children. This doctor's wife said that priests had told her that 'God might be angry with her for not having more children and would punish her'.[106] A farmer's wife, recounted that when the priest who was conducting the parish mission, asked her 'did I give my husband his lawful rights. I nearly laughed at him but didn't answer. They never ask you about your married life and you don't need to tell them'[107]

The capacity of the Catholic church to enforce this tough regime was heavily dependent on the piety and obedience of the laity. Many men and women were members of religious associations – confraternities or sodalities – whose members were required to attend confession and communion together several times a year. Absences were recorded, and delinquent members were visited by the section prefect, who lived in their neighbourhood, and perhaps by a local priest.[108] These communal religious celebrations helped to ensure conformity on the part of women and men.

---

[102] Newberry Library Chicago, Kimball Papers, Box 1.3.69.
[103] Kimball Papers, Box, 1.3.161.   [104] Kimball Papers Box, 2.8.9.
[105] Kimball Papers, Box 2.8.10.   [106] Kimball Papers Box,1.3.161.
[107] Kimball Papers, Box 1.5. 58.
[108] On confraternities, see Síle de Cléir, *Popular Catholicism in twentieth-century Ireland. Locality, identity and culture* (Bloomsbury, London and New York, 2017), pp. 29–43; Colm Lennon (ed), *Confraternities and sodalities in Ireland* (Columba Press, Dublin, 2012).

1.8   The 'Safe Period': Catholic Church Teaching in Ireland and Beyond

These stories suggest that many men and women in 1930s Ireland wished to limit the number of children, and the Harvard researchers were quizzed on many occasions about birth control. If the Irish Catholic clergy had wished to assist married couples in this respect, they could have promoted the 'safe period'. *Casti Connubii* made only brief reference to the 'safe period' as a means of family limitation. It stated that this method was lawful 'provided always the intrinsic nature of that act was preserved, and accordingly, its proper relation to the primary end'[109] – conceiving children.

The belief that women were not fertile at all times was not new, but during the nineteenth century, the 'safe period' was believed to occur in mid-cycle, with peak fertility during or near menstruation.[110] This misunderstanding existed in Ireland. In 1933, a general practitioner in Ennis told Kimball that 'You would be surprised at some of the queer ideas they have regarding sex and pregnancy. I have had men tell me and seriously that the only time they were sure that they could make their wives pregnant was during the time they were unwell, I suppose it comes from their ideas in dealing with cattle in that this is the time that a woman is in heat and should be made pregnant, for the man and the women to have relations during this period, and it will ruin both of them, and they never taught us in the books that pregnancy could take place at this time, in fact I don't think it can'.[111] (The doctor's uncertainty about fertile and infertile periods is worth noting).

An accurate description of the female reproductive cycle emerged in the early 1930s. Kyusaku Ogino was first in the field with research published in Japan in 1924, but his findings were not translated into German until 1930, and English in 1932. In 1929, an Austrian doctor Herman Knaus reached similar results independently. Their findings were widely publicised in Europe and North America. Campbell suggests that 'The increasing number of Roman Catholic theologians who were becoming keenly aware of the conflict between what was described as "the irresistible pressure of society in favour of contraception" and the "immovable condemnation of the church" warmly welcomed the discoveries of Ogino and Knaus'.[112] A best-selling 1932 book by Leo Latz, a member of the medical faculty at the Loyola University in Chicago, titled *The Rhythm of sterility and fertility in women* – 60,000 copies were sold in 1932/33 – led to the term 'the rhythm method'. By 1946, this book was in its sixth edition and had sold nearly 300,000 copies. It was one of several books

---

[109] As quoted in Noonan, *Contraception*, p. 442.   [110] Noonan, *Contraception*, pp. 438–41.
[111] Kimball Papers, Newberry Library, Box 1.3.67.
[112] Flann Campbell, 'Birth control and the Christian churches', *Population Studies*, 14, no 2, November 1960, p. 140.

on the safe period, published in the early 1930s, which carried the approval of Catholic bishops.[113]

News of the rhythm method reached Ireland relatively quickly. In November 1933, Kimball described one of his Ennis companions quizzing the local doctor about the safe period. The doctor's response was 'I buy books on the subject and I have the word of authorities all over the world and I read these books but there isn't any safe period because they don't agree on it. ….The general idea is that from the 17th to the 24th day, but if you take my advice you will get caught even then. There is no safe period. I have known men who have been all right for several years and then all of a sudden they get caught.'[114] I suspect that there is an element of braggadocio about the doctor's response; the scientific information was relatively new, so it is unlikely that men could have been 'all right for several years' using this method; nevertheless, the exchange reflects a degree of knowledge. On another occasion, a bank clerk, who was single and claimed to have no interest in marriage, reported that a friend had informed him that the safe time to have sexual relations was shortly after menstruation.[115] In a 1937 paper, 'The Problem of Population', UCC economics professor John Busteed, claimed that information about the safe period had been spreading throughout the Irish middle class for the past two years.[116] Ferriter dismisses Busteed's suggestion that knowledge was confined to methods approved by the Catholic church as 'far-fetched', going on to suggest that 'there were some who went over the border to Belfast to source contraceptives – but he gives no source for this statement, and it is unclear whether contraceptives were widely available in Northern Ireland at that time. Given that Busteed was an active member of Catholic Action, it is probable that he would have highlighted such dangers if he was aware of them.[117]

By modern standards, the 'safe period' is not a reliable form of fertility control, but it is effective in reducing the number of births. John Marshall, a neurologist who worked closely with the Catholic Marriage Advisory Council [CMAC], in Britain described it as 'not without value'. He claimed that 80 per cent of women having regular unprotected sex would become pregnant within a year. If they followed the calendar method – the most basic version of the safe period – this would fall to 25 per cent,[118] admittedly a high failure rate by modern standards, but a significant reduction in births.

In 1934, the *Irish Ecclesiastical Record* [IER] answered a query from a priest: 'Is it permissible to teach publicly knowledge of the Ogino and Knaus

---

[113] Noonan, *Contraception*, p. 443.   [114] Kimball Papers, Box 1.3.69.
[115] Kimball Papers, Box 1.6.211.   [116] Daly, *Slow failure*, p. 92.
[117] Ferriter, *Occasions of sin*, p. 195.
[118] John Marshall, *Love one another. Psychological aspects of natural family planning* (Sheed and Ward, London, 1995), p. 13.

method... preaching, disseminating and broadcasting popular booklets with minute explanations of the recurrence of the so-called sterile period, and all public utterances by clerics or laymen *in any way* recommending the practice.... is it permissible to teach publicly the doctrine of the empty cradle?' He was told that if couples began to make widespread use of periodic continence, the practice 'might be as socially calamitous as the intrinsically immoral practice of birth control'. Widespread use of the safe period would be an abuse.

We hope and believe it is true that the married couples who have a sufficiently justifying cause for availing of the Ogino-Knaus system are comparatively few. That in itself should be ample reason why the knowledge of this system should not be spread indiscriminately. For it is unfortunately only too easy for people to persuade themselves that the medical or social or eugenic indications of which we have spoken are verified in their case. Accordingly, we find the moralists who have written on the subject practically unanimous in urging that instruction on these matters should be as far as possible individual. A distinguished medical practitioner, himself a firm believer from experience in the scientific accuracy of the system, laments the wide publicity it has been given in popular pamphlets, and regrets that such matters should not have been reserved for the columns of scientific periodicals.

The respondent, who was probably Professor Canon John McCarthy of Maynooth College was 'rather startled ....that these matters have been made the subject of discourse in the church. It would be difficult to conceive of circumstances that would justify public instruction to congregations of every age and condition on matters which are of their nature delicate and dangerous'.[119] The *IER* also answered several queries as to whether a married woman, whose husband had venereal disease, or was suspected of being a carrier, could use some form of contraception, such as a sterile cream that would prevent infection while also acting as a contraceptive. The advice in these cases was generally given in Latin – presumably to prevent the uninitiated (laity) reading it. It indicated that a woman could not take any steps that would with moral certainty prevent conception, but she could use treatments that would prevent infection and make conception less certain (the double effect).[120]

In 1946, Canon McCarthy published an article on 'The use of the safe period'. He was obviously well informed. He cites Latz, *The Rhythm*, which had sold almost 600,000 copies by 1946; articles by Ogino and Knaus, Halliday Sutherland – whose book had been banned in Ireland, and an article by Holt in the March 1944 issue of the *American Journal of Obstetrics and Gynaecology*. He states that 'it is clear that knowledge of the "safe period" has become widely

---

[119] *IER* vol 43, '1934 Notes and queries: diffusion of Knowledge regarding the safe period', pp. 414–18.
[120] John Canon McCarthy, *Problems in theology*, vol 2 (Browne and Nolan, Dublin, 1959), pp. 253–9.

diffused in some countries' and suggested that the authors that he cited 'will be familiar to our readers'. The Canon was sceptical about its effectiveness: 'even the most ardent supporters of the "safe period" theory generally admit that there are difficulties and uncertainties in its practical application....they insist for success on long observation of the menstrual cycle ...based upon a scientific calculation which needs careful and scientific application in the individual cases'.

So much for the technique, what about the theology? 'If then, a confessor or director is asked about the liceity of the exclusive use of the "safe period", he will have to elicit whether or not there is a justifying cause and give his verdict accordingly. There are many reasons relating to health, housing and poverty which may justify, for a time or even permanently, the restriction of marital intercourse to the sterile period.' That statement might be taken as expressing support for the 'safe period', but the Canon was determined to restrict knowledge. He dismissed the argument that it was better to educate couples about the 'safe period', because otherwise they might use contraceptives.

Indiscriminate diffusion of knowledge of the 'safe period' could easily enough lead to its indiscriminate use – a situation fraught with calamitous social consequences. Accordingly, we would deprecate the suggestion that this knowledge should be generally disseminated... We suggest that information....should only be given individually as far as is possible and only to those who are entitled to use it. And they in turn should be exhorted not to pass on the information to others.

This article sets the scene for the dissemination – or more realistically – the control of information about the 'safe period' in Ireland. The motives for limiting family size, as set out by Canon McCarthy are quite broad – the limitations related to information. The confessor is the gatekeeper; if he determines that a couple have valid motives for controlling fertility he can refer them to a Catholic doctor, though this doctor might not be knowledgeable about the 'safe period'. In such circumstances, a confessor may recommend a book that was approved by the Catholic church – but the couple would have to order the book, read it – and take care not to share it. Given the deference shown by Irish people towards their priests and the generally low level of education, few couples would have had the self-confidence to articulate a case for the 'safe period' to a confessor or ask him to recommend a suitable book. And this assumes that the priest was comfortable discussing the topic.[121]

Thousands of American couples learned about the safe period from Latz and other approved authors, though Latz, lost his job at Loyola (a Jesuit university), and the Archbishop of Chicago subsequently withdrew his imprimatur, indicating that the attitude of the US Catholic church was not one of universal approval. But American couples had multiple sources of information. John A. O'Brien,

---

[121] McCarthy, *Problems in theology*, vol 2, pp. 259–64.

who is quoted at the beginning of this chapter, was the author of a 1934 book *Legitimate Birth Control,* which was serialised in the *Sunday Visitor* – a family magazine 'though discreetly minus the "how-to" section'.[122] In 1936, Boston gynaecologist John Rock – who was to play a major role in developing the contraceptive pill – opened the first clinic in the United States, and 'possibly in the world' teaching couples how to calculate the safe period. Rock, a Catholic and a graduate of Harvard Medical School, had signed a petition in 1931 urging the removal of the ban on birth control imposed by the Commonwealth of Massachusetts.[123] Joannes Smulder, a Catholic doctor practising in the Netherlands, published a guide to the safe period, written in simple language which was in its seventh reprint by 1939.[124] A Dominican priest in Quebec published a pamphlet explaining the safe period at his own expense, and the method was taught in pre-marriage courses organised by the Catholic Action movement.[125] A 1971 study of older married couples in Quebec revealed that 64 per cent of those marrying in the early 1930s had used contraception; an estimated 80 per cent of Catholic couples who tried to limit their families had used the rhythm method, compared with 25 per cent of non-Catholic couples.[126] In Brittany, *Foyers Rayonnants,* a positive account of the safe period, written by a Catholic priest, sold 200,000 copies.[127] In Britain, Halliday Sutherland's book, *Laws of Life,* first published in 1935 by the leading Catholic publishing company, Sheed and Ward, with the *permissu superiorum* from the archdiocese of Westminster, provided a detailed account of the safe period, complete with diagrams of the female reproductive organs, a clear explanation of reproductive biology and several pages with calendars highlighting fertile and infertile periods, including charts that a woman could fill out to calculate her safe period. By 1943, the book was in its sixth edition; a 'cheap edition' costing 3/6 was published in 1946.[128] As noted earlier, *Laws of Life* was banned in Ireland.

According to John Marshall, the calendar method – a purely mathematical estimate of the fertile period – reduced the annual rate of conception to 25 per cent. A Dutch gynaecologist J.G.H. Holt discovered that it was possible to determine the timing of ovulation by tracking minor changes in a woman's basal

---

[122] Tentler, *Catholics and contraception,* pp. 106–7.
[123] Loretta Mc Laughlin, *The Pill, John Rock and the Church: the biography of a revolution* (Little Brown, Boston, 1982), p. 27.
[124] Schoonheim, *Mixing ovaries and rosaries,* pp. 195–6.
[125] Gervais and Gavreau, 'Women priests and physicians', pp. 301–3.
[126] Danielle Gavreau and Peter Gossage, 'Empechez la famille. Fecondité et Contraception au Quebec, 1920–1960', *Canadian Historical Review,* 78, no 3, September 1997, pp. 478–510.
[127] Martine Segalen, 'Exploring a case of late French fertility decline: two contrasted Breton examples', in John Gillis, Louise Tilly and David Levine (eds), *The European experience of declining fertility* (Oxford University Press, Oxford, 1992), pp. 240–4.
[128] Publication details taken from Halliday Sutherland, *Laws of Life* (Sheed and Ward, London, cheap edition 1946) frontispiece; diagrams, etc. on pp. 48–69.

body temperature.[129] The temperature readings were only reliable if a woman had been lying immobile for three hours; if she had to get up in the middle of the night to calm a fractious infant, the reading would not be accurate. This method required more training and access to the appropriate thermometer, although there are claims that it could be done using a standard thermometer purchased in any pharmacy, it would probably prove difficult to read the minute temperature changes on these devices. John Bonnar, TCD gynaecologist, claimed that 'the scale of the graph paper recording the temperature' was critical. In 1959, Marshall and Fr. Maurice O'Leary, the director of the CMAC, travelled to the Netherlands to learn about the basal body temperature method of determining female ovulation, and they subsequently adopted that method and taught it to clients.[130] In Quebec, Sérena (SErvice de RÉgulation des NAissances) was founded in 1955 by a young married couple to teach the thermal method. It spread widely throughout Quebec, reaching large numbers of working-class families; many parish priests supported Sérena, though not the cardinal.[131]

Marshall, who conducted the first scientific studies of the effectiveness of this method, claimed that the basal body temperature method resulted in a significant decline in the rate of conception. A field trial of 502 couples recruited by the UK CMAC in 1965 and 1967 showed that 381 couples who opted to confine sexual intercourse until after ovulation had occurred (as determined by changes in body temperature) had an accidental pregnancy rate of 1.2 per 100 women per year. There were 4.2 per 100 pregnancies caused by method failure – breaking the rules. The figures were higher for those who did not confine sex until after ovulation: 5 per 100 per year 'accidental' pregnancies and 13.3 per 100 per year pregnancies when couples failed to follow the guidelines.[132] The effective rates cited here (including method failure) are superior to those cited by Cook for cervical caps, spermicides, sponges and condoms during the inter-war years.[133] In 1959, just before oral contraception became widely available, 16 per cent of UK wives married in the years 1930–60 and 34 per cent of American wives married between 1935 and 1955 claimed to use natural methods of family planning. (The percentages for all methods totalled 157 per cent in the UK and 174 per cent in the USA indicating that some used more than one method.)[134]

---

[129] Marshall, *Love one another*, pp. 4, 13.

[130] John Marshall, *Fifty years of marriage care* (Catholic Marriage Care, London, 1996), p. 104.

[131] Diane Gervais, 'Morale catholique et détresse conjugale à Quebec. La réponse du service de régulation des naissances, Seréna 1955–1970', *Revue de l'histoire de l'amerique francaise'*, 55, no 2, 2001, pp. 188–95; Gervais and Gavreau, 'Women priests and physicians'.

[132] John G. Turner, Foreword, to Marshall, *Fifty years*, pp. 1–2; Marshall, *Love one another*, pp. 4, 20–1.

[133] Hera Cook, *The long sexual revolution, sex and contraception, 1800–1975* (Oxford University Press, Oxford, 2004), pp. 140–2.

[134] Lara Marks, *Sexual chemistry. A history of the contraceptive Pill* (Yale University Press, Newhaven and London, 2001), p. 187.

Separate questionnaires issued to husbands and wives who took part in the UK trial of the 'safe period' (410 couples filled in separate questionnaires) revealed that 42 per cent of wives and 41 per cent of couples who had been instructed in this method continued to worry about the possibility of an unplanned pregnancy. Forty per cent of husbands and 22 per cent of wives said that it was often difficult to abstain from sex during the fertile period, and 53 per cent of husbands and 56 per cent of wives said that it was sometimes difficult to abstain. One-quarter of men and women felt that abstinence had a bad effect on their relationship, though the majority disagreed. But despite these difficulties, 66 per cent of men and 75 per cent of women regarded the safe period as a satisfactory method of birth control.[135] Their comments reflected a 'wide spectrum of opinion', both positive and negative. Many couples undoubtedly found that it had major drawbacks. In recent years, David Geiringer, Marshall's grandson, has revisited letters that Marshall received, and he has interviewed older British Catholics about their experiences of 'natural family planning'. A number spoke about the 'de-eroticising routines' that it entailed – marking charts, taking a temperature; the emotional impact of the necessary abstinence, though some claimed that it enhanced the sensual pleasure.[136] Their diverse reactions – both positive and negative – are not dissimilar to those reported by Cook for couples who used condoms, diaphragms and other barrier methods in the early/mid-twentieth century. Cook concludes that 'By the 1930s, those women and men who had co-operative partners, self-discipline, an adequate income, and private washing facilities could, by using a spermicidal pessary *and* a douche *and* either a condom, rubber cap, or diaphragm, obtain a high level of protection from pregnancy'.[137] One favourable aspect of natural family planning noted by Marshall was the fact that couples did not need to insert a diaphragm or put on a condom. When Marshall contacted natural family planning groups in continental Europe, hoping to get statistical data that could be used for comparison with UK data, he discovered that in Europe, natural family planning was commonly used in conjunction with barrier methods, so that couples could dispense with a condom at certain times: 'no less than 40 per cent of couples were having intercourse during the fertile time, whilst trying to avoid conception either by withdrawing or by using a condom or diaphragm'.[138]

What information was available in Ireland about the safe period? Veritas, the Irish Catholic publishing house appears to have distributed Latz, though no copy exists in the National Library, Trinity or UCD libraries. The RCPI

---

[135] Marshall, *Love one another*, pp. 22–4.
[136] David Geiringer, *The Pope and the Pill* (Manchester University Press, Manchester, 2020), Chapter 4.
[137] Cook, *The long sexual revolution*, pp. 140–2.   [138] Marshall, *Love one another*, p. 98.

library copy came from the library of the late Dr John Fleetwood, a general practitioner based in the Dublin suburb of Blackrock, who had a strong interest in the history of medicine. It carries the stamp of a commercial business in Mountrath [Laois]; it may been in a circulating library. I failed to locate a copy of Halliday Sutherland's book in any Irish library. An American Jesuit sociologist who carried out research in Dublin in the late 1940s/early 1950s noted that one doctor and a number of priests informed him that the rhythm method was used 'in the managerial and clerical classes', and they believed that its use was increasing.[139]

The Vatican's attitude remained guarded until October 1951 when Pope Pius XII, speaking to the Congress of the Italian Catholic Union of Midwives, endorsed the use of the rhythm method by married couples. Pius XII said that whether its use was right or wrong depended on the motives; serious reasons, medical, eugenic, economic and social could justify the safe period, 'even for the entire duration of the marriage'. He spoke about 'the legitimacy and – at the same time the limits – in truth very wide – of a regulation of offspring' – distinguishing between 'a regulation of offspring' and 'so-called "birth-control"'.[140] Noonan suggests that the permitted economic motives went beyond a fear of living in acute poverty, and the social motives might even extend to concern about the rapid increase in world population. Pius XII repeated this message one month later, in an address to two Italian Catholic associations that promoted large families.[141] In the United States, papal approval encouraged a more open discussion of the rhythm method. According to Tentler, 'Periodicals aimed at the laity, which even in the 1940s had seldom or never referred to rhythm, now carried features on the subject that were typically frank and sometimes markedly sympathetic'. Although some priests maintained a conservative approach, they were outnumbered, and their advice was increasingly questioned by married couples.[142]

In Britain, CMAC was founded in 1946 by Catholic laymen and women, independent of the Catholic church but 'with the blessing of Cardinal Griffin the Archbishop of Westminster', who became the first president. Within a few years, it came under clerical control. Most CMAC members and counsellors were from professional or comfortable middle-class backgrounds, including significant

---

[139] Alexander Humphreys, *New Dubliners. Urbanization and the Irish family* (Routledge & Kegan Paul, London, 1966), p. 211. When a UCD colleague, a historian and son of a doctor, saw me carrying a copy of *Laws of Life*, he recalled finding this book, carefully hidden at the back of a bookshelf in his parental home.

[140] *Marriage and the moral law. What the Pope really said* (Pontifical Court Club, London, 1957) with a foreword by Dr Godfrey President of the Pontifical Court Club, p. 13.

[141] Noonan, *Contraception*, pp. 446–7. *The teachings of Pope Pius XII. Compiled and edited with the assistance of the Vatican Archives* by Michael Chinigo (Methuen, London, 1958), p. 49.

[142] Tentler, *Catholics and Contraception*, pp. 182–3.

numbers of doctors. Information and training in natural family planning was one of the Council's three main activities – the others were pre-marriage courses and marriage counselling.[143] From its earliest years, many people contacted the CMAC seeking advice and information about the 'safe period', and the CMAC had to skirt between the different views of Catholic clergy on this issue.[144] Dr John Marshall, a prominent member of the CMAC for almost fifty years, noted that 'in 1946 family planning or birth regulation were dirty words in Catholic circles.... Counsellors in the London centre were instructed that they should only refer a couple to a medical adviser for NFP (natural family planning) instruction if they were married, had at least two children and had written permission from their parish priest'.[145] The majority of referrals were women with serious health problems; many priests and lay Catholics were opposed to instructing newly-weds or engaged couples. That changed after 1951.[146]

There were no comparable developments in Ireland. The Irish Catholic professional laity probably lacked the confidence of their English counterparts, and unlike England, Irish Catholicism did not have to contend with the availability of divorce and contraceptives, a Marriage Guidance Council, and a religiously diverse society. UCD Medical School Library holds a copy of Pius XII's address to the Catholic Union of Midwives, dated 1952, but it was published in Britain; the CTSI did not publish this important address until 1957. While Noonan, the leading authority on the subject, described Pius XII's 1951 statement as evidence of 'a new spirit ... for the first time ... a method open to all Christian couples'[147] an article in the 1952 Irish Theological Quarterly by Rev. William Conway, Maynooth theologian and future primate of all Ireland, opened with the statement that 'the Holy Father's discourse.... introduced no new orientation into the Church's teaching'; he described it as 'a confirmation of what is already taught'.[148] A query to the IER, in 1952, which specifically mentioned the papal statement, asked whether a married couple 'say with one or two children' who determined to confine sexual intercourse in future to the sterile period acted unlawfully. The correspondent also asked whether it was permissible for a priest to give instruction, in private consultation on the safe period outside confession. He was told that such instruction would be both 'imprudent and unlawful'....'besides the confessor should not be a counsellor of infecundity'. Pius XII had mentioned social and economic factors as

---

[143] Marshall, *Love one another*, pp. 3–4. Marshall, *Fifty years of marriage care*.

[144] Alana Harris, 'Love divine and love sublime: the Catholic Marriage Advisory Council, the marriage guidance movement and the state', in Alana Harris and Timothy Willem Jones (eds), *Love and romance in Britain, 1918–1970* (Palgrave Macmillan, Basingstoke, 2015), pp. 211–12.

[145] Marshall, *Fifty years of marriage care*, p. 103.

[146] Marshall, *Love one another*, pp. 5–6.   [147] Noonan, *Contraception*, pp. 445–6.

[148] William Conway, 'The recent papal allocution: the ends of marriage', *Irish Theological Quarterly*, 19, no 1, 1952, p. 75.

justification for limiting family size, but this respondent emphasised that these should be 'serious personal reasons .... only grave or serious reasons'.[149] If the respondent was Canon John McCarthy, his attitude had become more stringent. The *IER* message was clear – limiting the number of children by using the safe period should be an exceptional measure, not the norm. A 1954 article titled 'Catholic Approach to Marriage' by Rev. A. Regan CSSR stated that the Pope's address to the Catholic midwives had 'emphasized, once again the importance of never forgetting that the generation and education of children is the primary purpose of marriage'. In cases where people had a good reason not to have children, he quoted the Pope 'But God obliges married people to abstain, if their union cannot be fulfilled according to the laws of nature. Therefore, in this case abstinence is possible'.[150]

The Belfast Welfare Women's Clinic, established in 1951, which was for many years the only family planning clinic in Northern Ireland, reported that they received queries from the Republic, and Britain's Family Planning Association in London appears to have referred Irish queries to the Belfast clinic. They posted supplies to the Republic, addressed by hand, and in plain packaging to avoid customs. It is impossible to estimate how many clients the clinic had in the Irish Republic.[151] Importing packages of contraceptives on a regular basis would have been risky, especially for Protestant couples living in rural and provincial Ireland (see Chapter 4 about the fate of packages of condoms posted in the 1970s). Postal and customs staff acted as moral policemen – intercepting packages to check the contents. In the 1960s, they confiscated leaflets on the safe period published by the CMAC that were posted to Holles St consultant obstetrician Dr Declan Meagher, although he successfully retrieved them. Travellers through Irish ports or airports routinely had their luggage searched; publications were inspected to see if they offended Irish censorship regulations – any substantial quantity of contraceptives would have been seized.

In 1977, UCD law lecturer James O'Reilly claimed that the scope of an indecent advertisement 'was so wide as to prohibit the advertisement or promotion in print of methods of family planning the Catholic Church now approves of'.[152] While in theory, the border with Northern Ireland was much more open – given that it was impossible to police a border that ran through fields and 'unapproved roads' (roads without customs posts that were accessible for local traffic), cars using the major highways were routinely searched and goods impounded to protect Ireland's high-tariff regime. Travellers from the Republic would have needed to know which pharmacies in Northern Ireland

---

[149] *IER*, Notes and queries, vol 77, 1952, p. 441.
[150] A member of the Redemptorist Order; *ITQ* 21, 1954, pp. 259, 261–2.
[151] McCormick, 'The scarlet woman in person', pp. 356–7.
[152] James O'Reilly, 'Marital privacy and family law', *Studies*, 66 (spring 1977), p. 10.

stocked condoms, and it would have been advisable to seek them in Belfast rather than smaller towns. If condoms were imported – it was in limited quantities and probably only for personal use. Paul Blanshard, writing in the early 1950s, claimed that a recent petition by a Protestant physician and a Protestant chemist to import a small quantity of contraceptives for a couple, who were both suffering from advanced tuberculosis, was rejected. Blanshard remarked that 'Nowhere in the Republic could any young person discover for himself that his nation stands alone among English-speaking countries in its position on birth control, and that the overwhelming majority of the people of the West accept contraception as a respectable practice.'[153]

For Irish couples wishing to limit their families, the options in the 1950s were not dramatically different to 1911 – abstinence and coitus interruptus. Some couples were aware of the safe period, but information was tightly controlled. In 1951, Pope Pius XII emphasised that it was the duty of midwives, not the duty of priests to give advice on fertility, and midwives should be aware of the moral issues associated with the use of the safe period. However, Canon McCarthy presented their responsibilities in a different manner: 'An attitude of willing acceptance of motherhood is a natural corollary of the use of the conjugal rights…The midwife should foster this attitude in the minds of parents… The midwife must refuse categorically to accede to any request from parents to help them to violate this unchangeable principle of the moral law….'[154]

Irish midwives were not given any training in the safe period, or access to relevant literature before the mid-1960s and perhaps later. Domiciliary midwives were hard-pressed, coping with home births and mothers with very large families; maternity hospitals and nursing homes were contending with rising numbers of births, as Irish women took advantage of the 1953 Mother and Child Scheme, entitling them to free maternity care in a hospital or approved nursing home. One of the objections voiced by the Catholic hierarchy to Noel Browne's Mother and Child Bill was the fear that doctors might advise women on fertility limitation. Although the maternity and post-partum aspects of that legislation were introduced in 1953 following negotiations with the Catholic hierarchy[155] (the most significant difference was the requirement that women in higher-income households, would have to make a modest payment to benefit from its provisions), there is no indication that they received any form of fertility advice. Nevertheless in 1960, Flann Campbell wrote that 'Even in the Republic of Ireland, where a strict literary censorship operates, and where the Roman Catholic hierarchy are almost Manichean in their hostility to discussion about sex, it is now possible to buy for a few shillings a booklet giving the

---

[153] Blanshard, *The Irish and Catholic power*, pp. 162–4.
[154] McCarthy, *Problems in theology*, p. 2, pp. 221–5 (check).
[155] Ronan Fanning, *IT*, 13 and 14 February 1985.

most precise details about how to avoid conception after coitus by means of the safe period'.[156] So far I have failed to identify that booklet.

By the late 1950s, and probably earlier, Irish Catholic couples were increasingly out of line with Catholic couples in Britain, North America and western Europe, where family planning appears to have been widely accepted as part of married life. Many couples elsewhere had managed to reconcile their Catholicism by using contraceptive methods that were not sanctioned by the Catholic Church. In 1949, the *Royal Commission on Population* reported that 46 per cent of British Catholics who married between 1930 and 1939 had used methods of birth control that were not sanctioned by the Catholic church.[157] The Canadian province of Quebec had an overwhelmingly Catholic population; couples married early and families were large, but many Quebec Catholic used contraceptive methods not approved by the Church, such as withdrawal, and while some clergy condemned this behaviour others viewed it 'with a fickle and capricious tolerance'.[158] Interviews with Swiss Catholics, who became parents between 1950 and 1970, revealed that many used methods of contraception that were not approved by the Catholic church.[159] In a study of British women carried out in the mid-1950s, 47 per cent of married Catholic women used some form of birth control and 39 per cent of single Catholic women thought that they should use it.[160] A detailed survey of British married couples, carried out in 1959 as part of the Rockefeller Institute's research into fertility control, showed that 36 per cent of Catholic couples approved of birth control, compared with 68 per cent of Protestant informants. The gap between Catholics and Protestants was narrowing: of those who married before 1929, 54 per cent of Protestants but only 17 per cent of Catholics were in favour of birth control; the figures were 74 per cent and 42 per cent, respectively, for couples who married between 1950 and 1959. If the numbers who approved of contraception was rising and the proportion who disapproved was declining, the proportion of disapprovers who cited religious reasons was rising: 55 per cent of disapprovers in the 1950–59 cohort (all religions), compared with 43 per cent among those who had married before 1929. Catholic users of birth control were more reticent than others surveyed.

The highest percentage of Catholic couples using contraception was found among those who were married between 1940 and 1949, 61 per cent

---

[156] Campbell, 'Birth control and the Christian churches', p. 132.

[157] Alana Harris, *Faith in the family. A lived religious history of English Catholicism, 1945–82* (Manchester University Press, Manchester, 2013), p. 153.

[158] Gervais and Gavreau, 'Women priests and physicians', p. 305.

[159] Rusterholz, 'Reproductive behaviour', pp. 11–12.

[160] Eustace Chesser, Joan Maizels, Leonard Jones and Brian Emmet, *The sexual, marital and family relationships of the English women* (Hutchinson's Medical Publications, London, 1956), as cited in Campbell, p. 147.

of Catholics against 74 per cent of Protestants. In Britain, the proportion of Catholics using the safe period had increased from 3.9 per cent of the 1930s cohort to 16 per cent of the 1940s cohort, but the proportion who remained faithful to Church teaching fell from 65 per cent of the 1930s cohort to 49 per cent of the 1940s cohort. Catholic couples tended to only consider limiting their fertility, after they had given birth to a number of children, whereas non-Catholics were more likely to use contraception early in their marriage. This pattern was also found in a contemporaneous US study. Catholic couples only turned to non-approved methods of contraception having first tried the 'safe period' and found it ineffective; almost half of US Catholics who married in the 1940s had used methods not approved by the Church. In the British study, '60% of the Catholic informants had complied with the Church's teachings', as had 70 per cent of Catholics in the US survey.[161] Conformity was closely associated with religious practice: 71 per cent of those who described themselves as 'devout' conformed to Church teaching, compared with 51 per cent of 'moderate' and 31 per cent of 'indifferent' Catholics. Those who attended church irregularly had an almost identical pattern of birth control to Protestants.[162]

The timing of both the USA and the British studies is significant, in that they were conducted shortly before the dissemination of the contraceptive pill. They suggest, as is evident from data on marital fertility that Ireland was an outlier. Many Catholics elsewhere were adopting some form of family limitation, including methods that were not approved by the Catholic church. Ireland's outlier status *may* reflect cultural values favouring large families; however, the fact that the overwhelming majority of the population was Catholics (and often devout Catholics) was also important, as was the failure of the Irish Catholic church to provide any support or education for couples to use the 'safe period'. Campbell determined that 'The extent to which this "heresy" [contraception] has spread naturally depends upon the strictness of the particular Church's rules, the powers – clerical and lay – which the Church may have to enforce its edicts, and the kind of society in which the Church operates'.[163] A study of fertility decline in Switzerland emphasises how religious norms and values impacted on individual behaviour through state policies and state institutions.[164] Campbell noted that the Catholic Church was concerned about contraceptive practice among Catholics who were living in countries where

---

[161] Griselda Rowntree and Rachel M. Pierce, 'Birth control in Britain' Part II, *Population Studies*, 5, no 2 (Nov 1961), p. 143. The US study is Ronald Freedman, Paschal Whelpton and Arthur Campbell, *Family planning, sterility and population growth* (McGraw-Hill, New York, 1959).

[162] Rowntree and Pierce, 'Birth control in Britain', p. 145.

[163] Campbell, *Population studies*, pp. 144–5 and footnote 51.

[164] Anne-Françoise Praz, 'State institutions as mediators between religion and fertility: a comparison of two Swiss regions, 1860–1930', in Derosas and Van Poppel (eds), *Religion and the decline of fertility*, pp. 147–76.

they constituted a minority of the population.[165] Judged by those yardsticks, Ireland was arguably the country where conformity to Catholic teaching, and a strict interpretation of that teaching was most likely to prevail. Church attendance was almost universal and religious practice by many men and women extended far beyond attending Sunday mass and their Easter duty; the Irish Catholic laity tended to defer to their clergy. Catholic teaching on contraception was reinforced by the state – with stringent censorship controlling access to literature on contraception and a ban on the manufacture, sale or distribution of contraceptives, not to mention stringent custom controls over all imported goods. Access to information about the safe period was controlled by the Catholic clergy and Catholic doctors, though individual couples may have gained access to books, or leaflets via family or friends in Britain, or through a sympathetic doctor or priest. If a couple contacted their family doctor seeking advice on the safe period, it is not certain that he/she would have had sufficient knowledge of the method. The best prospects would have been to approach a doctor who had worked in Britain at an earlier stage in his/her career, where they might have come into contact with the CMAC. Nevertheless, by the late 1950s, a number of commercial firms were trying to sell devices in Ireland that claimed to make it possible for a woman to calculate her safe period – and this development, together with the contraceptive pill challenged the Catholic church and Catholic doctors, though not yet the state.

[165] Campbell, *Population studies*, pp. 144–5.

2   The Pill, the Pope and a Changing Ireland

'Although there was no law preventing people from talking about family planning or the use of contraception for the majority of men and women there was no one to discuss it with'.[1]

2.1   International Developments

The 1960s revolutionised contraception and fertility throughout the developed world, and the later years of that decade were marked by a sexual revolution, with increasing numbers of young single adults openly enjoying sexual relations. This contrasted with the conservatism of the immediate post-war years, when couples married at an early age, marriage was almost universal, and a 'baby-boom' resulted in a higher birth rate than during the 1930s. The 1950s was the golden age of the housewife, when stay-at-home mothers, increasingly relieved of having to work within the family economy, and heavy household chores, such as washing clothes by hand, could focus on homemaking and child-rearing, and motherhood and domesticity were valorised. But Caitriona Clear is correct that this domestic idyll did not apply to Ireland.[2]

In Britain, marital fertility rose in the 1940s and 1950s, and while some couples chose to have larger families, in many instances this was due to inadequate control of fertility.[3] Information and access to contraception was much more widely available than in Ireland, but it remained limited until the 1960s: there were only 340 Family Planning Association clinics, operated by volunteers. The 188 local authority clinics only advised women who needed contraception for medical reasons; many GPs did not regard contraception as part of their function. Clinics were poorly advertised, and access to birth control information was concentrated in particular areas.[4] Contraception was seen as a matter

---

[1] Solomons, *Pro-life*, p. 15.
[2] Caitriona Clear, *Women of the house: Women's household work in Ireland 1922–1961* (Irish Academic Press, Dublin, 2000), p. 214.
[3] Cook, *The long sexual revolution*, pp. 264–5; Fisher, *Birth control, sex, & marriage*, pp. 29–30; 44–46.
[4] Fisher, *Birth control, sex, & marriage*, pp. 29–30; 44–46.

for married couples. In the United States where the Comstock laws still prevailed, thirty-one states banned sales of books about contraception on grounds of obscenity, and twenty-four banned sales of contraceptive devices, though some exempted pharmacists or physicians from these regulations. Condoms were sold with a medical prescription 'for the prevention of disease'.[5] Women who could afford a private gynaecologist could be fitted with a diaphragm.

The Brook Clinic, the first birth control clinic to state that it catered to single women opened in London in 1964.[6] In the United States, the Comstock laws were gradually repealed, state by state. In Griswold v. Connecticut (1965), the US Supreme Court declared the prohibition on the use of contraceptives to be illegal – Connecticut was the last US state to enforce such a ban. This decision removed all residual prohibitions on the sale of contraceptives or books about contraception throughout the USA. By 1968, it could be said that 'local state and federal government support of family planning is evident throughout the land'.[7] The right to bring contraceptive devices into the USA for personal use was not established until 1971.[8]

In Belgium, a family planning association, established in 1949 to take advantage of a legal loophole formed a national federation in 1963, opening clinics in the major cities, but it continued to operate in 'a legal grey zone' until 1972 when the ban on '"propaganda" for contraceptive purposes was removed'.[9] France failed to secure the repeal of laws restricting access to contraception in 1956, but advice centres that informed clients about ways of obtaining access to contraceptives opened. Restrictions on contraceptives were repealed in 1967, much to the chagrin of Madame de Gaulle. In Italy, the ban on contraception introduced under Mussolini ended in 1971.[10] In West Germany, laws prohibiting contraception during the Nazi era were repealed in 1961.[11] In Quebec, an overwhelmingly Catholic province, where fertility

---

[5] James W. Reed, 'The birth control movement before Roe v. Wade', in Donald T. Critchlow (ed), *The politics of abortion and birth control in historical perspective* (The Pennsylvania State University, University Park, 1996), p. 35.

[6] Cook, *The long sexual revolution*, pp. 288–9.

[7] Martha T. Bailey, '"Momma's got the Pill": How Anthony Comstock and Griswold v. Connecticut shaped US child-bearing', *American Economic Review*, 100, no 1, March 2010, p. 101. Leslie Corsa, 'The United States: public policy and programs in family planning', *Studies in Family Planning*, 3, 1968, pp. 259–76.

[8] James Reed, *From public vice to private virtue. The birth control movement and American society since 1830* (Basic Books, New York, 1978), p. 121.

[9] Wannes Dupont, 'Of human love: Catholics campaigning for sexual aggiornamento in post-war Belgium', in Harris (ed), *The schism of '68*.

[10] Francesca Vassalle and Massimo Faggioli, 'A kind of reformation in miniature: the paradoxical impact of *Humanae Vitae* in Italy, in Harris (ed), *The schism of '68*.

[11] D. V. Glass, 'National programs', in *Family planning and population programs: A Review of World Developments* (University of Chicago Press, Chicago, 1966), pp. 188–92. Julian Jackson, *A certain idea of France: The Life of Charles de Gaulle* (Penguin, London, 2018).

was among the highest in the world, the typical family size plummeted from 4 children in 1957 to 2.27 in 1968. By 1970, fertility had fallen below the natural replacement level.[12] While the sharp fall in fertility throughout the western world, and the revolution in sexual behaviour are often seen as a consequence of the Pill, the relationship is unclear. Was this 'a "contraceptive revolution" or a revolution of the times'? Most early adopters of the Pill were married women.[13] Marks has suggested that a sexual revolution was underway before the Pill became widely available; in Britain, the numbers of extramarital births were rising sharply.[14]

The rapid expansion in world population after World War II was widely discussed in the international media – sometimes with sensational headlines such as the Population Bomb. Tyler May notes use of Cold War rhetoric in the population debate, and the foundation in 1952 of the International Planned Parenthood Federation and the Population Council.[15] During the 1960s, reducing mortality and fertility in the developing world became goals of US foreign policy.[16] Concerns about global population prompted research into fertility control, and it filtered into discussions of Catholic teaching on contraception. The Vatican was showing a greater interest in developing countries, and this brought an awareness of the consequences of a rapidly expanding population, though the Catholic solution was to promote an expansion in food production.[17] Pope John XXIII referred to population problems in two encyclicals, *Mater et Magistra*, and *Pacem in Terris*. When a senior Vatican official met the president of the International Planned Parenthood Federation in Rome in 1963, he assured him that the Catholic church was concerned about the population explosion.[18]

2.2   Ireland: Family Planning and Clerical Authority

The relaxation of the laws on contraception and the expansion of family planning services internationally meant that Ireland was even more out of step with western Europe and the United States by the end of the 1960s, than at the beginning of that decade. By the early 1960s, Ireland had belatedly embraced the post-war marriage boom, with a fall in the age of marriage and a

---

[12] Kevin J. Christiano, 'The trajectory of Catholicism in twentieth century Quebec', in Leslie Woodcock Tentler (ed), *The Church Confronts Modernity. Catholicism since 1950 in the United States, Ireland & Quebec* (Catholic University of America, Washington, DC, 2007), p. 34.

[13] Bailey, '"Momma's got the Pill"', p. 100. Elaine Tyler May, *America and the Pill. A history of promise, peril and liberation* (Basic Books, New York, 2010), pp. 72–4.

[14] Marks, *Sexual chemistry*, p. 203.   [15] May, *America and the Pill*, pp. 35–46.

[16] John Sharpless, 'World population growth, family planning, and American foreign policy', in Critchlow (ed), *The politics of abortion and birth control*, pp. 72–102.

[17] Philbin, *Catholic Standard*, 25 October 1963.

[18] Robert Blair Kaiser, *The encyclical that never was. The story of the Pontifical Commission on Population, Family and Birth 1964–66* (Sheed and Ward, London, 1985 and 1987), pp. 42 and 47.

rising marriage rate, which created increasing pressure for some 'solution' to Ireland's large families. The medical consequences of giving birth to 8–10 children or more, and giving birth after the age of forty, as many Irish women did, were not discussed in the media, but they begin to feature more prominently in medical publications, especially the annual clinical reports of the Dublin maternity hospitals. In 1967, an amendment to the Censorship of Publications Act provided that a ban on published works would automatically lapse after twelve years, though significantly that relaxation did not apply to publications advocating birth control. There was a growing interest in the rhythm method, but the information was controlled by a confident Catholic hierarchy. In the early 1960s, the authority exercised by Catholic clergy did not face a serious challenge. This was the peak of post-Tridentine Catholicism in Ireland – with record numbers of men and women entering religious life; near-universal mass attendance, and large numbers of adults participating in parish missions, pilgrimages and confraternities.

In the early 1960s, an American psychologist and Jesuit priest Bruce Biever interviewed a large sample of Catholics in the greater Dublin area on a range of topics, including marriage and family. He presented interviewees with a series of statements and recorded their responses. Dublin Catholics dismissed his assertion that many parents believed that the Church was advocating a type of family which they could not support; or that parents had an obligation to have as many children as possible, as over-simplification, a distortion of church teaching; 80 per cent rejected a statement that 'the more children; the better Catholics the parents are', but 'fewer than one in five gave an unqualified denial'.[19] A remarkable 88 per cent disagreed with the statement that a celibate clergy could not give worthwhile advice on the problems of marriage;[20] 58 per cent agreed that 'the use of sex is allowed for only one reason: to beget children. All other considerations are secondary'. Biever was intrigued that one-quarter of respondents disagreed with that statement (the remainder expressed no opinion) 'since the opinion as stated reflects accurately the only doctrine on the use of sex which is being presented to them currently by their clergy'. The dissenters tended to be younger, and a majority were women.[21]

On birth control Biever concluded that

Basically for the Irish there is no problem… Interviews confirmed that the Irish by and large consider abstinence the only legitimate manner of curtailing procreation, but more important than this is the equally strong conviction expressed throughout the interviews that even this was somehow 'frustrating' God's will. There is a great positive value

---

[19] Bruce Biever, *Religion, culture and values: A cross-cultural analysis of motivational factors in native Irish and American Irish Catholicism* (Arno Press, New York, 1976), p. 481.

[20] Biever, *Religion, culture and values*, pp. 404, 412.

[21] Biever, *Religion, culture and values*, p. 479.

placed upon procreation, and many of the Irish expressed total lack of comprehension on how the matter of birth control could be seriously treated in the Catholic context at all. Children are the gift of God, and men have nothing to say as to whether they come or not; parents are only the conditions for the implementation of the divine will in this respect, and the Irish regard this as a sacred function which is not to be tampered with. Likewise, they are completely satisfied with accepting the guidance of their clergy in this matter.

Almost 80 per cent of those surveyed rejected the statement that a celibate priest never had to face the problem of birth-control, 'so what can he tell me about it?'

The simple fact is that the majority of the Irish population seemingly are quite convinced that the current sexual mores of Ireland are quite proper and healthy, both individually and socially. They are convinced they are doing God's will in this regard, and exhibit both hostility and lack of comprehension when the suggestion is made, by their own people, or by foreigners, that such is not the case.[22]

When Biever compared the views of Irish and Irish-American Catholics significant differences emerged: 68 per cent of Irish Americans agreed with the statement that the Church's only answer to birth control was to abstain and his interviews with Irish-Americans

revealed a deeply concerned and troubled laity who were dissatisfied with what in some instances was termed a "clerically smug" complacency in viewing the problem, and many went so far as to say that they considered birth control to be a moral imperative in many cases.

Just under 60 per cent of Irish-Americans agreed with the statement (to which the Irish were unalterably opposed): 'It's easy for a celibate priest to talk about birth control – what can he tell me about it'.

Significantly, the American sample revealed upon questioning that they did not think the church could not come up with an answer, but rather the failure to provide a suitable remedy for uncontrolled procreation was the result of clerical complacency and theological lack of awareness and/or sympathy for the plight of the laity.[23]

He detected no consciousness in Ireland that the laity should be more vocal. The strong religious commitment of the Irish people 'reinforces and makes invulnerable the participation in and dictation of social policy by the church, and the social leadership function which the church has and does exercise cannot be understood without the fact of religious commitment....'[24]

By the early 1960s, Irish Catholics were out of line with Catholics in the USA and elsewhere in their unquestioning deference to the clergy. In Britain,

---

[22] Biever, *Religion, culture and values*, pp. 481–2.
[23] Biever, *Religion, culture and values*, pp. 768–9.
[24] Biever, *Religion, culture and values*, pp. 489–90.

according to Harris, 'an increasingly educated Catholic audience', interrogated Church teaching on issues such as contraception and mixed marriages, in 'loyal dissent'.[25] Likewise 'an urban and increasingly well-educated Quebec posed unprecedented challenges for what had only recently been a mostly agrarian Church. The critics were also a force for change not just in the Church but in the society the Church had done so much to define'.[26]

Biever captured opinions among Dublin Catholics at a time when new challenges were emerging with respect to sexuality and contraception – though we should not overstate their impact. The coming of an Irish television service (some parts of the country had been watching British television for several years), a new wave of Irish women's magazines, the Second Vatican Council, and knowledge of the Pill all offered potential for social change and changing attitudes towards contraception and the clerical authority. Emigration had fallen sharply from the record levels of the 1950s; in 1966, the population, aged from 20 to 29 was 10 per cent higher than in 1961. The 1960s also saw a significant increase in the number of men and women (especially younger men and women) in waged and salaried jobs, as opposed to working in domestic service or the family economy, and rising participation in secondary and university education.

2.3   'The Safe Period'

The widespread use by Catholics elsewhere of the 'safe period', and the search for more reliable methods had created a market for devices that allegedly assisted women in detecting ovulation. By the early 1960s, manufacturers and distributors appear to have seen Ireland as a potential market for their products. This suggests that there *was* a market; John Marshall noted that 'a substantial minority' of letters to the CMAC in London came from Ireland, north and south.[27] In 1959, the Archbishop of Dublin, Dr McQuaid was contacted by the Gynometers Limited, a London company who claimed to be the patentees of the Safe Period Indicator. They explained that Irish newspapers and periodicals had been reluctant to publish advertisements for their product. In their letter, they quoted Pope Pius XII and the 1958 Lambeth Conference, which had liberalised Anglican teaching on family planning – including a statement that Family Planning is a right and important factor in Christian life. They hoped that the Archbishop would have 'no qualms' in approving their device – a note

[25] Harris, *Faith in the family*, p. 164; Harris *The schism of '68*. Introduction.

[26] Tentler, Introduction, to Leslie Tentler (ed), *The Church confronts modernity. Catholicism since 1950 in the United States, Ireland and Quebec* p. 6; Kevin Christiano, 'The trajectory of Catholicism in twentieth century Quebec' in Tentler (ed), *The Church confronts modernity*, p. 24.

[27] Marshall, *Love one another*, p. 9.

in his instantly recognisable hand – indicates otherwise.[28] He received similar solicitations from the makers of the CD indicator – sent yet again from a London address, complete with a pamphlet outlining its merits, and order forms! On this occasion, Monsignor Horgan, (Professor of Metaphysics at UCD, 1942–71) and a confidant of the Archbishop, sent the material to Professor John Cunningham, Professor of Obstetrics and Gynaecology at UCD and a consultant at the National Maternity Hospital. He dismissed the device as 'simply a small calculating machine, there are a number of them on the market....It does nothing to help the woman concerned except to make it easier to count days. This she can do herself without much trouble.' Professor Cunningham claimed that it could be misleading and had 'no scientific value'. Monsignor Horgan forwarded this report to McQuaid, who concurred: 'I thought the machine of no special value. Tables are found in standard books.'[29]

In 1965, the sales manager of the *Irish Times* contacted the director of the Dublin archdiocese's press office, asking for his comments on a letter from the CD Indicator Company, which he enclosed, stating that the device had the Archbishop's approval. The company wished to advertise in the *Irish Times* and apparently in other newspapers. The accompanying letter explained that they were 'a world-wide organisation'; the device was 'fully approved by the Roman Catholic Church and our advertisements in women's magazines are with the knowledge and approval of Archbishop McQuaid'. It also claimed that they had the 'full approval and assistance of the Irish Medical Association, who also advertise in their journal for us', as does the *Lancet* for the past seven years. The diocesan press officer contacted the Dublin offices of CD Indicator and asked that they withdraw the statement that they had the Archbishop's approval; he received their assurance that it would not happen again. He informed the Archbishop that the *Irish Times* would 'not now' be carrying their advertisement and he sent messages explaining that the advertisements did not have the Archbishop's approval to other newspapers and to the state broadcasting companies, Raidio and Teilifís Éireann. He also suggested that the Archbishop should consult a doctor (he suggested Dr Jennings, a local GP), as to whether such advertisements should be carried in journals, 'other than medical or medico-moral journals'. The sales director was described as 'a Jew formerly of Prague', who had, he believed arrived in Dublin from Australia.[30]

The informal restrictions on newspaper advertisements continued, but in July 1965, *Woman's Way*, which was published by the Dublin-based Creation Group, began to publish advertisements for the CD indicator, under the heading, 'Science & Nature go hand in hand' – the advertisement stated that it was 'the

[28] Dublin Diocesan Archives (DDA), McQuaid Papers, XXV/339.
[29] DDA XXX/360/6, 6 January 1960; XXV/340/7.   [30] DDA XXVI/26/30-53.

only method approved by the Catholic church'.[31] In 1966, *Woman's Way* carried an advertisement for 'The Ovula' – a thermometer designed and calibrated to assist in identifying ovulation, which was available by post from a Dublin address.[32] In August 1968, shortly after the papal encyclical *Humanae Vitae* was published, the advertising manager of the *Irish Press* contacted Archbishop's House requesting sanction to publish an advertisement for a 'conception days' indicator' – the precise brand was not mentioned. He explained that they had been offered a similar advertisement some years earlier but had rejected it as suitable only for a woman's magazine, but given that the publication of *Humanae Vitae* has resulted in 'very frank discussion of the fertile period', they viewed the topic as 'a matter of general discussion' and would like to reconsider their position. The Archbishop's view had not changed. The *Irish Press* was told that he never gave sanction to any commercial enterprise; he never passed judgement on 'any particular medical arrangement for the rhythm controls'. 'If this advertisement should be printed at all', it should be confined to medical journals and under medical auspices. It was 'quite out of place in the daily press – no matter what publicity has been already given to sexual matters'.[33]

Information on a more exotic device made its way to Archbishop's House in 1961, when Dr McQuaid's secretary reported that a (named) Catholic salesman, employed by a 'chemical firm' wanted to draw the Archbishop's attention to 'an instrument for the purpose of calculating ovulation time', for which his firm had distribution rights. He enclosed a copy of the brochure describing how 'the instrument' worked, together with a copy of an article from the *Journal of the American Medical Association*, allegedly endorsing the product. The device would be distributed to obstetricians and general practitioners – it would not be available to the public in retail chemists. They were anxious to have Dr McQuaid's views on the product; although the manager of the firm was not a Catholic, 'he was an honourable man who was anxious to do what was ethically right'. The accompanying brochure explained that the Fertility Testor (sic), 'operates on the principle that a woman secretes glucose in the cervical mucous cascade approximately three days prior to ovulation'. It consisted of a plunger to be inserted into the vagina and cervix to collect mucous, which would then be analysed, apparently by spreading it on a tape. The brochure emphasised that it had been developed after eighteen years research in St. Elizabeth's Hospital in Boston – a Catholic hospital. Dr McQuaid referred this literature to Mgr Horgan and Rev Conor Martin (Professor of Ethics and Politics at UCD) for their opinion. Monsignor Horgan enlisted two further clergymen and Professor John Cunningham to determine the merits of this device.

[31] *Woman's Way*, July 1965.   [32] *Woman's Way*, 1 June 1966.
[33] DDA XX/14 *Humanae Vitae*, 12 August 1968.

Monsignor Horgan (writing on UCD headed stationary) reported that Professor Cunningham and the two priests that he had contacted were 'in complete agreement'. It was reassuring that St. Elizabeth's was a Catholic hospital. Rev Clarke could see 'no moral objection to the use of this method in married life, whenever the use of periodic abstinence is permissible. It is medically sure. It is in keeping with the hope of Pius XII expressed in his address to the Family Front Congress, 1951, "that medical science would success in giving the legitimate method of regulating births a sufficiently sure basis"'. Rev Dr Curtin disclaimed any capacity to pronounce on the scientific accuracy but he also cited Pope Pius XII's 1951 address – adding that 'the Fertility Testor is a step in this direction'. He determined that using the device 'will be lawful if the avoiding, postponing or spacing of pregnancies is itself lawful. A married woman, then, who is justified in having recourse to the infertile period is justified in using it'. Doctors could lawfully prescribe it and comment on it. The least enthusiastic report came from Professor Cunningham, who described this fertility test as 'fairly simple' and having 'considerable accuracy'. However, he warned that 'it is not, however reliable in all cases. There is still the human variation and this may result for any one of several reasons'. He cautioned that it 'is not always accurate. I doubt if it would be of much help in the case of uneducated people'.[34] It is unclear whether these views were communicated to the salesman or the distributor.[35]

Monsignor Horgan was chaplain to the Guild of St. Luke, SS Cosmas and Damien – an international guild of Catholic doctors. In the 1930s, Stafford Johnson, Master of the Irish branch of the Guild had objected to the insertion of a passage in a League of Nations report on maternal and child welfare about giving advice on birth control to mothers who were suffering from serious diseases, such as nephritis, heart disease or tuberculosis.[36] However we should not overstate the Guild's influence. In 1965, the general secretary, Raymond Magill, who was based in Belfast, stated that in its thirty-four years' existence, 'the Guild has existed rather than flourished'. There were branches in Dublin (fifty-one paid up members), Belfast, seventy-one; Cork, twenty; Kilkenny, thirty-seven, Waterford, twenty-one, and Galway, sixteen – approximately 10 per cent of Catholic doctors practising in Ireland. Dr Magill claimed that 'its impact on medical life in Ireland has been too small.... Apathy is the main

---

[34] DDA Irish Guild St. Luke, SS Cosmas and Damien 66/4/1-.

[35] J.B. Doyle, Frank Ewers, 'The fertility testor', *Journal of the American Medical Association*, 170, no 1, 1959, pp. 45–6. Accessed 14 March 2022: A letter in the *JAMA* in May 1961 by A. R. Arbarbanel claimed that advertising The Fertility Testor Tape 'as a method of birth control – for either conception or contraception – is to put it mildly, premature'. J. B. Doyle, replying to this letter stated the primary purpose of the fertility testor was as a fertility aid. *JAMA* 176, 6, May 1961, pp. 174–5. Although patents for the Fertility Testor were sought in 1964 and 1965, I have failed to find any further reference to this device.

[36] Lindsey Earner-Byrne, *Mother and child: maternity and child welfare in Dublin, 1922–60* (Manchester University Press, Manchester, 2007), p. 43.

opponent, a general feeling that in Ireland such a Guild is unnecessary, that the matters with which it concerns itself are best left to the Church or to the State'.[37] [The fact that the largest membership was in Belfast would appear to confirm this point of view]. Magill's comments prompted some resentment from the Dublin branch, although the close relationship between the Guild and Archbishop's House confirms Magill's view that doctors tended to leave matters to the clergy. The evidence suggests that the Guild was effectively controlled by a select group of priests, who were close to McQuaid, most of them holding academic positions in UCD.

In February 1963, the Irish Guild held a seminar on natural family planning, which was attended by approximately ninety doctors and medical students and ten priests. Dr Jennings, Master of the Dublin branch, who was a GP in Drumcondra, close to Archbishop's House, informed the Archbishop that Dr Raymond Cross, consultant obstetrician at the Rotunda – where he specialised in infertility – gave a talk on methods used to determine ovulation, and 'He also spoke of the Porto Rican pill (sic)[38] and its use as a therapeutic drug.' [This is the earliest Irish reference to the Pill that I have found.] Maynooth theologian Dr Denis O'Callaghan spoke about 'the present Catholic teaching on planned parenthood'.[39] He emphasised that 'the primary purpose of marriage is not only to procreate children – it is to procreate and *educate* children'; 'it is reasonable to desire a family so constructed that its own well-being and success in fitting out children for life are assured'. He placed considerable emphasis on responsible parenthood; 'there is no special virtue in the mere uncertainty of births nor in the biological naturalness of pregnancy after pregnancy', though at a later point, he noted that 'All factors considered the larger family is normally the better and happier family'. He cited a claim by Pope Pius XII that large families combat materialism and are consequently 'the cradle of saints'. 'If then both parties consent to use the rhythm, and if they can preserve the continence which it demands, it may be employed to space births and finally, if the parties so wish, to limit the size of the family'. But the couple's attitude 'is all important'. He expressed fears that 'if it [rhythm] is adopted as a device of cheating life and love in the interests of pleasure it will pave the way to a contraceptive mentality... hostile to children'. He mentioned the success of the English CMAC, referencing Dr John Marshall, and suggested that doctors should have 'a new confidence in the safe period and make obsolete the notion that the safe-period is basically unreliable'. Catholic doctors had a duty to be well informed about the theory and practice of the rhythm method.

[37] DDA 66/5/14, Raymond Magill to Archbishop of Armagh, 2 September 1965.
[38] The early trials of the contraceptive pill took place in Puerto Rico.
[39] The terminology is interesting reflecting growing international interest in measures to control the world's population – but a terminology that was often regarded with hostility by the Catholic church.

When Rev Dr O'Callaghan spoke about the Pill, he emphasised that it 'must never be used as anti-fertility Pill no matter what the motive be it therapeutic or frankly contraceptive'. It was impossible to justify the Pill 'as a variant or extension of the safe period' – which was the argument made by John Rock (see below), though he was not cited. Dr O'Callaghan conceded that the Pill could be used to treat 'a pathological conditions … if a more conservative treatment were not available or equally effective', provided that the pathological condition was not the danger of a future pregnancy – in which case the Pill was not permissible.[40]

Dr Jennings noted that the discussion that followed 'showed how much misunderstanding there is of the principles of Catholic teaching even among Doctors, and how much need there is to let couples know that the practice of period continence when advisable is morally correct'. It was important 'to make Doctors and nurses understand this and aware of their responsibility'. He suggested holding a 'semi-public meeting' in UCD to inform the medical profession 'if Your Grace thought well of it'. His report concluded by noting that 'this question of Church teaching to medical students, doctors, and nurses and some instruction to young married couples is constantly coming up in group discussions nowadays'. Dr Jennings' deference is marked – he introduced the sentence quoted above, with the phrase 'I regret giving Your Grace more problems'.[41]

Having read Dr Jenning's report, Monsignor Horgan recommended establishing a small committee to 'keep the activities of the Dublin branch under review, and propose ways of expansion'. The committee consisted of Dr Jennings, the Monsignor and four clerical colleagues who lectured in UCD, including Des Connell, a future Archbishop of Dublin. This group sent Dr McQuaid proposals for future activities: publishing a pamphlet every year targeted at doctors and medical students, where a doctor and moralist would each write on a topic – they suggested 'the Porto Rican pill, or the Catholic concept of family planning'; a course of lectures in medical ethics, given by a priest for students in institutions where Catholic medical ethics was not taught – such as the Rotunda Hospital and the Royal College of Surgeons in Ireland– which was attracting a growing number of foreign students.[42] These proposals suggest that Horgan and his colleagues were conscious of a need to ensure that future doctors were grounded in Catholic teaching, and equally determined to retain clerical control. In a follow-up comment, Horgan told the Archbishop that 'Experience shows that by themselves the doctors co-operate only passively. But a few faithful members like Dr Jennings can provide a framework through which our Faculty may hope to educate the doctor'.[43]

---

[40] 'Family Regulation. The Catholic View, address to the Dublin branch of the Guild of St Luke, SS Cosmas and Damien', 20 February 1963, *Irish Theological Quarterly,* 30, 1963, pp. 163–68.
[41] DDA 66/4/10, Guild.   [42] DDA 66/4/17, 11 May 1963.   [43] DDA 66/4/18.

By December 1963, the Guild had produced a pamphlet titled *The Catholic Concept of Family Planning*. The section on ethics and Catholic teaching was written by UCD ethics lecturer, Rev Bertie Crowe. Dr Jennings provided a medical commentary. A copy was dispatched to McQuaid, who was in Rome attending the Second Vatican Council. He replied with his customary speed and courtesy, noting that 'The booklet is excellent. I have waited years for it. Very grateful'. The moral case set out by Rev Crowe reflected a moderately liberal Catholic attitude. Having noted potential medical reasons for family limitation, he continued,

more commonly, there will be social or economic factors; perhaps the family cannot afford another child either because of the cost of feeding and clothing it or, more likely because of the difficulty of providing properly for its education; or it may be that the housing accommodation does not allow for another child; or there may be already in the family a handicapped child who requires more than ordinary care and attention. Such factors – and more so, a combination of such factors – may make pregnancy an unreasonable burden.

Dr Jennings described the female cycle, and how to identify the fertile and infertile periods. He outlined the calendar method, the temperature method and offered some guidance to doctors on how to advise a couple. Where there were serious contraindications to a future pregnancy, he declared that the temperature method was essential; if a woman's condition was so serious as to constitute an absolute contraindication to a future pregnancy, she should be referred to an obstetrician 'who may carry out further tests chemical and cytological' – though how these would assist in preventing pregnancy remains a mystery to me. Women with irregular cycles should use the temperature method, combined with the calendar. He advised that couples 'should not be sent away to collect records, for this is going to take at least three months and abstinence for that time may be difficult' – though it is unclear how that could be avoided while observing Catholic teaching. He also recommended that husband and wife should be present for the doctor's advice session; if that was not possible, the husband should have a separate consultation. Dr Jennings noted that 'research aimed at accurate prediction is going on....but while awaiting perfection in the solution of the problem, they should be prepared to use the present methods, which are sufficiently reliable to be recommended with confidence'. The concluding section is worth quoting:

The practical application of the infertile period is too little known in this country. Yet Family Planning is for many Catholic families a constant source of anxiety. Practising doctors have an obligation to be able to help their patients by instruction in lawful methods. For too long they have been hesitant about the rhythm method, rejecting it – wrongly – on moral grounds, or doubting its reliability, or possibly not fully conversant with it. The purpose of this pamphlet is to state clearly the Catholic concept of

Family Planning, to show that it is an integral part of married chastity and that means are available that are morally licit and medically reliable.[44]

In January 1964, the *Journal of the Irish Medical Association* – the representative body for doctors – reported on the 'recent' meeting of the Catholic Doctor's Guild of St Luke, SS Cosmas and Damian on family planning, and the pamphlet – which was available free of charge from the Guild office in Dublin. It emphasised that the purpose was 'to state clearly the Catholic concept of family planning, to show that it is an integral part of married chastity and that means are available that are morally licit and medically reliable'.[45]

The June issue of the *Journal of the Irish Medical Association (JIMA)* included an article titled 'The medical aspects of the safe period' by John O' Sullivan a consultant obstetrician in Northern Ireland. He outlined the basic science of ovulation, the calendar method, how to calculate fertile and infertile periods, mentioning calculating aids such as the CD Indicator and Safecaster. He discussed the temperature method and the views of named medical experts as to how long a temperature needs to be taken in the morning, and whether this should be done orally or rectally. He advised that 'an ordinary clinical thermometer is sufficient', but recommended named special ovulation thermometers and 'special charts for recording the temperature' – available from the British CMAC. A woman should take her temperature every day for several months before relying on this method! Dr O'Sullivan claimed that the temperature method 'instils confidence in a patient especially if there has been a failure by the calendar method. In consequence the patient more readily accepts the burden of recording the temperature'. He suggested that district nurses could provide invaluable assistance to women who found it difficult to determine ovulation from reading their temperature charts – no such assistance would have been available in the Republic. He also quoted extraordinarily optimistic figures for successful avoidance of pregnancy – using either the Ogino [calendar] or temperature methods, citing Tietze and Potter, who claimed that the Ogino formula gave women a 90 per cent chance of avoiding pregnancy for 5–10 years, figures similar to using a diaphragm; the temperature method was 100 per cent successful if intercourse was restricted to after ovulation.[46]

This article and the Guild's pamphlet indicate a growing interest in fertility control among general practitioners and the public. In April 1964, it was suggested that the Guild's pamphlet should be made available for general

---

[44] DDA 66/4/29.   [45] *JIMA*, January 1964, p. 36.
[46] *JIMA*, June 1964, p. 175. Christopher Tietze and Robert G. Potter Jr., 'Statistical evaluation of the rhythm method', *American Journal of Obstetrics and Gynecology*, vol 84, no 5, September 1962, pp. 692–98. The Knaus method, which had a shorter period of abstinence, had a lower success rate. The statistical methods used by Tietze and Potter were criticised in later studies of contraceptive methods. Anrudh K. Jain, Irving Sivin, 'Life table analysis of IUDS: problems and recommendations', *Studies in Family Panning*, 8, no 2, February 1977, pp. 25–47.

circulation, perhaps through the Catholic Truth Society of Ireland. Monsignor Horgan favoured this, noting that doctors were requesting several copies for their patients; however, he suggested that 'medical details, concerning for example, the application of the Rhythm method which might be misinterpreted by the people' should be omitted. Detailed advice should be controlled by doctors.[47] When Dr Jennings told Archbishop McQuaid that a revised version of the pamphlet would soon be available, the archbishop cautioned that it would need 'much simplification for the ordinary reader'. He told another doctor that 'it needs serious revision to help such people to understand the highly technical language used. Further, the medical section could be used ignorantly as a substitute for consultation with a conscientious doctor, with of course, error in application and mischievous frustration.'[48] There is recurring evidence of clerical paternalism towards both the medical profession and married couples, and a refusal to give couples sufficient information to enable them to use this non-medical method of contraception, without recourse to a doctor. This insistence on an individual consultation restricted access – given the cost of a surgery visit – 15/- roughly 1 euro,[49] and it is highly improbable that the 30 per cent of the population, who attended a public dispensary doctor, would have been accorded a consultation, or that many dispensary patients would have had the self-confidence to request one. Dr McQuaid preferred that the booklet should be published by Michael Gill, rather than the CTSI, which would make it less accessible. Bookshops were confined to larger towns, and local newsagents were unlikely to stock it. CTSI pamphlets were widely available in church porches.

In 1963, Ireland's largest maternity hospital, the National Maternity Hospital in Holles Street – whose board was chaired by the Archbishop of Dublin Dr McQuaid (though he did not attend meetings), opened a fertility guidance clinic providing advice 'in conformity with Catholic moral teaching'. Family planning – presumably the safe period – became an integral part of the training programme for medical students, doctors and student midwives. The hospital's annual report indicated that the clinic was established 'with the full knowledge and at least tacit support of the Archbishop of Dublin'.[50] This reflected a wish to address the problem of large families, a problem which according to Dr Dermot MacDonald, then an assistant master, was becoming worse, with an increase in earlier marriages, and a declining incidence of tuberculosis – a disease that could result in infertility. In 1960, a Dublin street trader gave birth to her twentieth child in the Rotunda Hospital at the age of fifty-four, and although she is exceptional – the oldest mother to give birth in the history of

---

[47] DDA 66/4/33.   [48] DDA 66/4/41 and 44.

[49] Mary E. Daly, *Sixties Ireland: Reshaping the economy, state and society, 1957–1973* (Cambridge University Press, Cambridge, 2016), p. 234.

[50] Tony Farmar, *Holles St, 1894–1994: The National Maternity Hospital: a centenary history* (A&A Farmar, Dublin, 1994), p. 152.

the Rotunda, many women gave birth to more than ten children and continued to give birth over the age of forty.[51]

The new Master of Holles St, Kieran O'Driscoll in a lecture to the Dublin Institute of Catholic Sociology, emphasised that artificial birth control 'is of course morally wrong and has no place in our philosophy'; however theologians were now of the opinion that the ideal family 'is the one that couples can procreate and rear, having due regard to the physical and intellectual welfare of the children, health and reasonable comfort of the parents'.[52] When he addressed the Irish Medical Association Conference, Dr O'Driscoll noted that 'instructions on birth control had been available to private patients for some time, and while a large percentage availed of it, he felt the same knowledge should be available to public patients in every hospital in the country'.[53] It was important that trainee doctors and midwives should be given instruction in family planning (albeit only the method approved by the Catholic church), given that some would work in developing countries.[54] The growing acceptance of natural family planning is evident in the *Catholic Standard*, which was published in Dublin. In January 1964, one of the regular Family Doctor columns was titled 'The doctor and family planning'. It emphasised that 'parents are the arbiters. If they want a big family and feel they can cope with them then they should go ahead....', but the columnist went on to condemn contraception and outline approved methods.[55] John Marshall (CMAC) was a guest speaker at the Social Studies Congress in the summer of 1964; by this time, he was writing regular columns in an Irish Sunday newspaper.

But change was slow. Although the Catholic Workers College – which was run by the Society of Jesus, introduced optional pre-marriage courses in the mid-1950s, there is no indication that they included a discussion of sexuality, reproduction or fertility control, and this course formed the model for the pre-marriage course introduced by the Dublin archdiocese in some parishes. By 1966, 972 couples attended a pre-marriage course, roughly one in seven of the 6,559 who married that year.[56] The priest who was in charge believed that it should be updated. The doctor's talk should be revised, and it should be given by a young doctor.

In 1965, Rev Cornelius Lee, a curate at Westland Row, the church closest to Holles St informed McQuaid that 'As many of the nurses doing their midwifery training in the hospital have received their general training in England, I have conceived it my duty to give each group of nurses entering the hospital a series of conferences on the Address to Midwives of Pope Pius XII.'[57]

---

[51] Deirdre Foley, '"Too many children?" Family planning and *Humanae Vitae* in Dublin', 1960–72, *Irish Economic and Social History*, 46, no 1 2019, p. 143.
[52] *Catholic Standard*, 6 December 1963.   [53] *Women's Way*, 30 November 1963.
[54] *Catholic Standard*, 6 December 1963.   [55] *Catholic Standard*, 31 January 1964.
[56] DDA/CSWB (Catholic Social Welfare Bureau) Agencies AB8/B/XIX Pre-marriage courses.
[57] DDA CSWB Agencies, AB8/B/XIX, 14 February 1965.

In 1965, Msgr. Barrett, director of the archdiocese's Catholic Social Services Conference, asked McQuaid for permission to send Fr. Peter Cunningham, the recently appointed director of the Dublin archdiocese's pre-marriage courses, to a fertility conference run by the British CMAC. The conference included a paper on 'the present role and future prospects of progestegens', lectures on the infertile period by Dr John Marshall and a talk on psychological aspects of 'the infertile period' by consultant psychiatrist Dr Jacobus Dominian. Declan Meagher, assistant master in Holles St, spoke about the role of an advice centre in a maternity hospital. A French couple spoke about training couples in use of the safe period.[58] The inclusion of Mass as part of the programme testified to its religious orthodoxy. Barrett informed McQuaid that the conference would give Fr. Cunningham an opportunity to meet priests who were 'engaged in the work in London'.

In 1962, the Catholic Marriage Advisory Council opened its first branch in Ireland – in Belfast, and by 1964, centres had opened in Limerick, Kilkenny and Cork, with staff being trained by London. A CMAC branch in Dublin did not open until 1968.[59] Ireland was very much an outlier in the numbers of couples who attended pre-marriage courses. It seems probable, though I have found no evidence to confirm my views, that Dr McQuaid preferred that any pre-marriage courses and associated activities should be controlled by the archdiocese and he may not have welcomed the arrival of the CMAC. In Britain and in Quebec, pre-marriage courses offered by the Catholic church included significant material on the 'companionate marriage', and the modern theology of marriage, which saw marriage as 'a spiritual partnership [and] entailed an explicit divinization of the sexual act itself within the bonds of marriage, thus assigning almost exclusive weight to sex as the one element that provided an ongoing sanctification to marriage'.[60] Perhaps the Irish Catholic church was wise to avoid such teachings, because placing sex at the heart of a Catholic marriage might cause couples to question the high rate of abstinence involved in church-approved family planning.

2.3.1   The Pill

It is no coincidence that the Irish Catholic Church began to show an interest in educating doctors and couples about the 'safe period' in 1963, because this

---

[58] In 1966, Fr Cunningham asked permission to spend some weeks in London observing the pre-marriage course run by the archdioceses of Westminster. He told McQuaid that the courses on offer – now eleven years old – needed major overhaul. He was keen to involve specially trained married couples in giving many of the talks.

[59] Marshall, *Fifty years of marriage care,* p. 73.

[60] Michael Gauvreau, '"They are not of our generation". Youth, gender, Catholicism and Quebec's dechristianization 1950–1979', in Tentler (ed), *The Church confronts modernity*, p. 69. See also Harris, *Faith in the family*, pp. 154–62.

was the year when the contraceptive pill came to public attention. The Pill had a dramatic impact on women's lives. It enabled women for the first time, to control their fertility in an unobtrusive manner that was independent of men. It was the first contraceptive to separate birth control from sexual intercourse and it was almost 100 per cent effective.[61] Initially marketed as a reliable means for married women to limit family size, by the end of the decade, the Pill was playing a key role in a sexual revolution, and although originally designed to assist in reducing population growth among poorer families and poorer countries, middle-class women – married or single – in developed countries were the major beneficiaries.[62]

The first large-scale trials took place in Puerto Rico in 1956 with further trials in the USA, Australia, Hong Kong, Haiti, Mexico and Britain.[63] The first contraceptive pill Enovid/Enavid came on the market in Britain and the United States in 1957 as a treatment for infertility and menstrual disorders. By 1959, over 500,000 American women were taking the Pill, allegedly for menstrual disorder. Initially, the regulatory authorities only approved the Pill for this purpose, but it was known to prevent conception. Many women in the United States were demanding it, before it had been approved as a contraceptive.[64] In 1960, the pharmaceutical company Searle applied for a license to distribute it as a contraceptive, but the British authorities refused, because the issue was 'too politically and morally sensitive'.[65] The practice of describing the Pill as a fertility regulator, rather than a contraceptive, was not unique to Ireland. In June 1960, the US Food and Drugs Administration gave approval for its use as a contraceptive, though they insisted that a woman could only use it for a maximum of two consecutive years.[66] First marketed as a contraceptive in Britain in 1961, it was initially used by middle-class women, but soon spread to the working class. As usage increased, the proportion of couples relying on withdrawal fell. Marks claims that in Britain, the Pill 'marked a radical turning point in working class contraceptive culture, whereby women, rather than men, now took responsibility for contraception'.[67]

It has proved impossible to determine when the contraceptive pill was first used in Ireland. The earliest references appear to be in a theological context, whether in religious periodicals or in the general press. This suggests a reticence on the part of the medical profession about fertility limitation – a reticence, perhaps even a fear, that reflects stringent censorship laws, and the authority of the Catholic church; only the Catholic church would write about contraception! This began to change in 1963/64.

---

[61] May, *America and the Pill*, pp. 1–4. Marks, *Sexual chemistry*, p. 3.
[62] Marks, *Sexual chemistry*, pp. 184–5.   [63] Marks, *Sexual chemistry*, p. 103.
[64] Marks, *Sexual chemistry*, pp. 4–6.   [65] Marks, *Sexual chemistry*, p. 32.
[66] May, *America and the Pill*, p. 34.   [67] Marks, *Sexual chemistry*, pp. 191–2.

2.3.2   The Pill and Catholic Theology

Contraception and fertility were the main medical ethics concerns for Catholics during the 1960s. In a standard book, such as Gerald Kelly, S.J. *Medical-Moral Problems*,[68] the majority of the text relates to male and female reproduction and associated issues. Marks claims that the Pill presented 'an unprecedented challenge to Catholic teaching on contraception', because it 'was not mechanical, did not kill or hinder the passage of sperm'. It 'seemed to mimic the natural functions of the female human body'. This was the argument made by John Rock, in his 1963 book *The Time has Come: A Catholic doctor's proposals to end the battle over birth control*. Rock set out the case for 'a "pill-established safe period"... a morally permissible variant of the rhythm method'.[69]

When Pius XII endorsed the rhythm method in 1951, he indicated that he would welcome improvements to that technique.[70] In 1958, when the Pill was in the experimental stages Pius XII recognised its use for therapeutic purposes, though not as a contraceptive.[71] He deployed the established Catholic argument of the indirect effect: whether the Pill was permissible or not depended on the woman's intent. If she was advised by her doctor not to become pregnant for some medical reason – such as the condition of her uterus – the Pill could be taken to address that condition, knowing that it would have the indirect effect of preventing pregnancy. By the late 1950s, a number of theologians were debating the possible use of the Pill in cases where a woman had a heart condition, or to achieve a regular menstrual cycle.[72] Shortly before Pius XII's pronouncement, Canon Louis Janssens a Louvain theologian suggested that it could be used by lactating women to ensure that they would not become pregnant.[73] In December 1961, following reports that many nuns in the Congo (which was experiencing civil war), had been raped, three prominent theologians determined that they could take the contraceptive pill to prevent pregnancy.[74]

One of the first theologians to enter the fray was Denis O'Callaghan, a professor at the National Seminary in Maynooth. In a 1960 article, he determined that using these drugs to prevent pregnancy 'will be tantamount to contraception

---

[68] First published in pamphlet form in the United States and later published in Dublin by Browne and Nolan (1955) for the UK religious publisher Clonmore and Reynolds.

[69] John Rock, *The time has come: A Catholic doctor's battle to end the battle over birth control* (Knopf, New York; Longman, London, 1963).

[70] Marks, *Sexual chemistry*, p. 218.

[71] In an Address to the Seventh International Congress of Hematology, 12 September 1958, Noonan, *Contraception*, p. 461.

[72] Noonan, *Contraception*, pp. 462–3.

[73] Denis O' Callaghan, 'Fertility control by hormonal medication', *Irish Theological Quarterly* 27, 1960, p. 14.

[74] Kimba Allie Tichenor, *Religious crisis and civic transformation: how conflicts over gender and sexuality changed the West German Catholic Church* (Brandeis University Press, Waltham, Massachusetts, 2016), p. 117.

and will therefore be judged illicit'; using them for therapeutic purposes 'will be justified with certain qualifications', and 'in a number of borderline cases the judgement will depend on a close analysis of the facts and a sharp definition of moral concepts'.[75] He reiterated Pius XII's views, as stated in 1958, that sterilisation, temporary or permanent is wrong; using these drugs with 'a contraceptive intent' sinned against both the Fifth and Sixth Commandments.

> Therefore, when the hormonal or other sterilizing preparations are used precisely as anti-fertility, anti-pregnancy, or contraceptive pills, their employment is absolutely unlawful and no reason however serious can justify what is contrary to nature. If it is feared that a pregnancy will endanger a wife's health she may use the safe period or she may abstain completely from intercourse, but she may not use the progestational steroids to suppress ovulation and so exclude the possibility of pregnancy.[76]

Little comfort here for couples trying to limit their families, even where a future pregnancy posed a risk to the woman's health! Yet when Dr O'Callaghan examined indirect effects, he determined that it was morally permissible to use the Pill 'to correct a pathologically irregular cycle, even if this is done for the ultimate purpose of making the use of the safe period more secure'. Having discussed the unreliable nature of a woman's menstrual cycle 'due to mental or physical over-exertion, excessive emotional disturbances, sudden changes of climate or altitude', he determined that it would be permissible to use the Pill as a cycle regulator, 'there is no moral problem when one merely assists nature to maintain its uniformity'.[77]

The *Irish Theological Quarterly* kept readers informed about the ongoing debate. In 1962, Rev Enda McDonagh reviewed three books by leading European theologians.[78] His review focused mainly on Rev Stanislas de Lestapis – 'a well-known expert on family and population problems', who provided 'a gloomy picture of the implications of "Contraceptive Civilization"'. De Lestapis condemned 'the crusade' by the US Planned Parenthood Federation, Britain's Family Planning Association and the International Federation of Planned Parenthood to spread the message of birth limitation, and the recent endorsement of 'responsible parenthood' by the Lambeth Conference (1958) and the World Council of Churches (1959). He refuted the argument that family planning was the only solution to world hunger; and he rejected the argument that contraception prevented abortion – 'birth-control has already proved to be a result rather than a cause of social advancement', before going on to

---

[75] O'Callaghan, 'Fertility control by hormonal medication', p. 1.
[76] 'Fertility control by hormonal medication', p. 6.   [77] *ITQ*, pp. 11–12.
[78] S de Lestapis, SJ. *Family planning and modern problems* (Herder and Herder, London, 1961), translation of *La Limitation des Naissances* (Paris, second edition, 1959); Bernhard Haring, *Sociology of the family* (Cork, 1959, translation of *De Ehe in dieser Zeit*, first published 1954); and Leon Suenens, *Love and control* (London, 1961), translation of *Un Problème crucial: amour et matrice de soi* (Bruges, 1960).

denounce the suggestion that 'the burden of childbearing is a natural injustice to women, which must be righted'.[79]

Dr McDonagh drew on all three works to discuss the two purposes of marriage – an expression of love and the procreation of children. He suggested that there is 'no opposition between these two ends'. That did not meant that couples should have the maximum number of children physically possible; 'love and prudence', including the requirement to educate their children, may demand that births be spaced and the number of children limited, but only through lawful means – birth-regulation, not birth control.[80] He was conscious of the difficulties that the church was facing because of its teaching on marriage and fertility: 'In the comparative stability of Irish life, it is difficult to realize the extent of the threat to Christian living which marriage and family problems present'.[81]

The 'comparative stability of Irish life' was exceptional. Just as the Pill did not initiate a sexual revolution in western society, neither did it precipitate Catholic church difficulties with respect to marriage and fertility control. In Belgium, from the late 1940s, Catholic clergy centred around the Catholic University of Louvain 'moved by the plight of the pious, committed themselves to relaxing the restrictions imposed by *CC'*[*Casti connubii*].[82] In 1955, 30 per cent of American Catholic women aged 18–39 were using methods of contraception that were not approved by the Catholic church.[83] The Pill appeared to offer a solution that might be consistent with Catholic teaching.

1963 was the year when the Pill emerged as a major issue within the Catholic church. 'No Catholic writer before 1963 had asserted that the general prohibition of contraception was wrong'.[84] In March 1963, Willem Bekkers, Bishop of the Dutch diocese of s-Hertogenbosch, in an interview on a Dutch Catholic radio station, queried Catholic teaching on birth control. He said that 'birth regulation' was 'an integral part of the total task entrusted to married people' and suggested that 'there is no particular merit in having a large or a small family'. His comments may have been prompted by a recently completed two-year survey of marriage carried out by the Dutch hierarchy among doctors and clergy, which recorded widespread dissatisfaction with church teaching on marriage; eighteen of the twenty theologians surveyed approved or acquiesced in the Pill as a means of contraception.[85] By 1965, it was reported that 44 per

---

[79] Enda McDonagh, 'Moral theology to-day. Marriage and family planning', *Irish Theological Quarterly*, 29, no 1, 1962, pp. 70–75.

[80] McDonagh, 'Moral theology to-day', pp. 75–78.

[81] McDonagh, 'Moral theology to-day', p. 68.

[82] Wannes Dupont, 'Of human love: Catholics campaigning for sexual aggiornamento in postwar Belgium', in Harris (ed), *The schism of '68*.

[83] Charles Westoff and Norman Ryder, *The contraceptive revolution* (Princeton University Press, Princeton, 1977), p. 23.

[84] Noonan, *Contraception*, p. 512.

[85] Noonan, *Contraception*, p. 531; Kaiser, *The encyclical that never was*, pp. 41–45.

cent of Dutch Catholic women over thirteen years of age favoured birth control in some circumstances. This was not a sudden development; one historian
claims that there had been 'a steady simmering of unrest' from the 1950s and
the number of Catholic women using contraception had been rising during that
time.[86] In August 1963, the Dutch bishops proposed that the Vatican Council
should examine the question.[87] Pope John XXIII, who died in June 1963, had
already appointed a six-man commission to advise him on birth control, ahead
of international conferences on population in New Delhi, and a WHO conference in Geneva.[88]

The *Catholic Standard* published an English translation of Bishop Bekkers'
statement on its front page, without comment and it reprinted Bekkers' second
statement in August 1963.[89] The *Standard* also published a review of John
Rock's book, *The Time has Come*. Rock, a professor at the Harvard Medical
School, father of five, a devout Catholic of Irish-American background was
a leading expert on infertility, who played a key role in developing the Pill.
He sought to reconcile the Pill with Catholic teaching on fertility regulation,
by presenting it as a chemical refinement/advance on the rhythm method. His
book was highly influential, among obstetricians,[90] and more generally, but it
does not appear to have been reviewed in any Irish daily or Sunday newspaper,
though it is mentioned in a leading article in the periodical *Hibernia* in 1965.
In an article published in *Good Housekeeping* in July 1961, reprinted the following September in *Reader's Digest*, Rock described the pill as offering 'a
truly natural method of birth control – the one the body uses to prevent conception – so it should meet no cultural, and eventually overcome present limited religious, objections. This method is obviously much "natural' than wilful
intra-marital continence…'[91] Rock argued that if sexual relations were moral
during the infertile phase of a woman's menstrual cycle, they were also moral
when she was taking the Pill. Rock featured on the cover of both *Time* and
Newsweek, so his arguments would have percolated into every Irish provincial town. However, Boston Cardinal Richard Cushing stated that his opinions
'lack any official approval as authentic Catholic teaching….The entire chapter
on the teaching of the natural law in matters which pertain to the morality of
artificial contraception is over-simplified'.[92]

---

[86] Chris Dols and Marten van den Bos, '*Humanae Vitae*: Catholic attitudes to birth control in
the Netherlands and transnational church politics, 1945–1975', in Harris (ed), *The schism
of 1968*.

[87] *IT*, 16 May 1964.

[88] This commission originated in the Catholic University of Louvain. Harris et al.

[89] *Catholic Standard*, 5 April 1963, 23 August 1963.

[90] Holles St consultant and Master, Dermot MacDonald mentioned Rock as his inspiration.

[91] McLaughlin, *The Pill, John Rock and the Church*, p. 155.

[92] *Catholic Standard*, 11 October 1963.

On 15 May 1964, a 'specially contributed' leading article in the *Catholic Standard* was titled 'MATRIMONIAL ETHICS. English Hierarchy takes a stand'. It opened with the statement: 'The question of Birth Control has been a relatively simple one thus far'; 'theologians and Catholic doctors have been busy in meetings and in publications on this subject for some time. One stimulus they feel is the expectation that the [Vatican] Council will deal with the problem in the long-awaited Schema 13 which would set out the Catholic church's position on "the burning questions of the hour": nuclear weapons, race relations, the population explosion and family planning'. The *Standard* reported strong interest in England in the Catholic church's position on birth control. It referred to the recent disciplining of a Catholic woman doctor who had opened a family planning clinic on Merseyside, and extensive coverage on mainstream television and radio programmes.[93] The Archbishop of Bombay, Dr Roberts, who was then in England, had published a book of essays titled, *Contraception and Holiness*, where he stated that he could see reasons why a couple would decide in conscience to use contraception to preserve their marriage. He did not grasp the reasons for the traditional Church teaching on birth control and asked that it be reconsidered. This was one of a series of books published that year, questioning church teaching.[94]

The story of Dr Anne Biezanek, a 'Catholic Marie Stopes', whose clinic, dedicated to St Martin de Porres, provided the entire range of contraceptive devices to a working-class community on Merseyside, captured the attention of the English newspapers. She published a book *All Things New: the Declaration of Faith*, setting out theological arguments to justify her actions. She was denied Holy Communion in several churches, and on 31 May, she received Communion in Westminster Cathedral (many journalists were present) having given advance notice of what she would be wearing. She had been denied Communion in her local church. In the face of this avalanche, Dr Heenan, Archbishop of Westminster, had engaged in 'a pre-emptive strike by issuing a pastoral directive, stating that "contraception is not an open question" whether by "pill" or "contraceptive instruments"', 'for it is against the laws of God'.[95]

On 23 June 1964, Pope Paul VI addressed the College of Cardinals 'on the problem which everyone is talking about, birth control'. He described the matter as 'complex and delicate'....with 'multiple aspects, multiple competencies'.[96] But conservative forces were rallying. Cardinal Alfredo Ottaviani, Secretary of the Sacred Congregation of the Holy Office – the most senior

---

[93] *Catholic Standard*, 15 May 1964.   [94] Noonan, *Contraception*, pp. 512–4.

[95] Alana Harris, '"The writings of querulous women": contraception, conscience and clerical authority in 1960s Britain', *British Catholic History*, 32, no 4, 2015, pp. 557–85; *Catholic Standard*, May 15, 1964.

[96] Kaiser, *The encyclical that never was*, p. 87.

office in the Vatican, other than the Pope, gave an interview which appeared to rebuke the Archbishop of Westminster, Dr Heenan for his views. This story was reported in the *Irish Times*.[97] Dr Heenan, of Irish descent and a regular visitor to Ireland, had spoken about his hopes for a new pill that would determine the precise timing of ovulation. Cardinal Ottaviani urged the clergy and others to 'keep silent on the pill....until the Holy See has had time to study it'.[98]

The winter 1964 edition of the Irish Jesuit periodical *Studies*, which had an educated lay Catholic readership, published an article, titled 'The Pill', by Joseph Fuchs, a professor at the Gregorian university and a member of the papal commission. Fuchs referred to Rock's argument that the Pill was broadly similar to the rhythm method, adding that several US theologians had dismissed this. He also cited articles by a German, a Dutch and a Flemish theologian published in 1963/64 in European theological periodicals setting out a case for permitting the use of the Pill 'for the purpose of responsible birth regulation'; arguments similar to those advanced by Rock. Fuchs described the case for or against the Pill as a permissible form of family planning as 'a discussion ... a long way from leading to a common solution based on rational ground'.[99]

Although the *Standard* gave substantial coverage to these stories, it did so with an inference that the debate was not relevant in Ireland. It published many articles critical of birth control, including one on the failure of a family planning programme in Japan and the medical risks associated with the Pill. These stories were juxtaposed with articles on Ireland's falling population, emigration, rural depopulation and similar themes, at a time when the population was rising, emigration was falling and a marriage boom was underway.

The draft of Schema 13, the Church in the Modern World [later known as *Gaudiam et Spes*] which was published in autumn 1963 stated that 'Marriage is not instituted solely for procreation'; a decision as to family size was a matter for the married couple, to be made 'with full and conscious responsibility'.[100] This sparked a heated debate at Vatican II. Most Irish voices were firmly in the conservative camp, though Rafferty noted that Dr Philbin, bishop of Down and Connor, told the Council 'that the Church could not condemn contraception without addressing the problems of married couples'.[101] Cardinal Conway complained that the draft schema had 'serious defects'; it failed to discuss the commercialisation of sex and desecration of human love.[102] Cardinal Michael Browne, an Irish Dominican, argued that no useful discussion could be held about the problems of married couples. He was outvoted by a wide margin. When Cardinal Suenens (Belgium) demanded a complete re-examination of

---

[97] *IT*, 19 June 1964.   [98] *Catholic Standard*, 12 June 1964.
[99] Joseph Fuchs, 'The Pill', *Studies*, December 1964, pp. 352–71; quotation, p. 354.
[100] Noonan, *Contraception*, p. 508.
[101] Oliver Rafferty, *Catholicism in Ulster 1603–1983* (Hurst and Company, London, 1994), p. 253.
[102] *Catholic Standard*, 30 October 1964.

the theology of marriage, and warned that this was 'a new Gallileo case', he received a standing ovation.[103] With almost universal attendance at church and no evidence of widespread rebellion against Catholic teaching on birth control (though some Irish women were using the Pill), the Irish clergy were not facing the challenges that confronted the church in the Netherlands where, according to Cardinal Alfrink, marital difficulties was a major factor in people leaving the church.[104] Irish daily and Sunday newspapers gave very little attention to these stories; significantly less than British media.[105]

Work on the Vatican II Schema 13 overlapped with the deliberations of the Pontifical Commission on the Study of Population, the Family and Birth, established by John XXIII. Pope Paul VI expanded the membership to include a number of leading theologians. By the end of 1964, it had expanded further, with fifty-five members, including thirty-four laymen and women.[106] The membership was never publicly announced by the Vatican.[107] The expanded membership is one indication of the increasingly heated debate within the church. In November 1965, Vatican II approved a text on marriage, which reiterated the importance of conjugal love, and told couples to decide on the number of children but warned against using methods of birth control that were condemned by church teaching: the 'holy synod does not intend to propose immediately concrete solutions'.[108] In the spring of 1966, the Pontifical Commission was further expanded with the appointment of fourteen additional members – all bishops and cardinals, including the archbishop of Cashel, Dr Morris. Paul VI announced that the appointments were designed 'to give it more authority'.[109]

By this time, Irish theologians Denis O'Callaghan and Enda McDonagh were internationally recognised for their contributions on marriage and contraception. In 1966, Dr O'Callaghan presented a paper on 'The evolving theology of marriage' at the annual conference of the British CMAC. That paper, together with shorter contributions by Enda McDonagh and Fr Maurice O'Leary, chairman of the CMAC, were published in the British theological journal the *Clergy Review* in November. An introductory editorial, by Rev Charles Davis SJ, suggested that 'the present crisis over birth control is far greater than many at first thought'; he referred to 'the long delay in issuing the papal statement'. The contributions by O'Callaghan and McDonagh set the context for the debate in the 'new theology of marriage' – and the central place that this accorded to the sexual act. Dr O'Callaghan stated that the very fact that the topic was being discussed was 'evidence of a radical change in

---

[103] *Catholic Standard*, 6 November 1964.   [104] *Catholic Standard,* 6 November 1964.
[105] On media coverage in Britain, see Alana Harris, 'A Gallileo moment….' in Harris (ed), *The schism of '68.*
[106] Kaiser, *The encyclical that never was*, pp. 47, 66, pp. 103–5.
[107] *Catholic Standard*, 11 March 1966.   [108] Kaiser, *The encyclical that never was*, pp. 157–8.
[109] Kaiser, *The encyclical that never was*, pp. 168–9; *Catholic Standard*, 11 March 1966.

theological teaching'. He suggested that 'even Church authority must admit of a certain fallibility in its directive on concrete matters which depend to a large extent on human insight'. He highlighted 'real advances in the theology of marriage': specifically the emphasis on love, which went 'hand in hand with responsible parenthood ... Procreation is not something to be left to chance and to "providence"'.[110] These concepts were far removed from the belief that the primary purpose of marriage was the procreation of children or the views that Irish Catholics had reported to Bruce Biever.

Dr O'Callaghan suggested that 'the duty of responsible parenthood under-lines the need for some effective method of family planning which will be practicable for the generality of married couples'. He examined the dispute over contraception under three headings: principle, tradition and authority and suggested that 'the rational arguments against contraception as formulated at present do not compel assent'. He again rejected the argument that the Pill offered 'a middle way ... the extension or prolongation of the safe-period'. Under 'tradition', he suggested that teaching on birth control reflected an evolving doctrine. That left the question of authority as the sole justification for the current position. He emphasised that *Casti Connubii* was not an *ex cathedra* pronouncement. Progressives argued that by convening a papal com-mission, the pope 'had already in effect admitted the possibility of change'. He concluded that 'the question of the lawfulness or unlawfulness of contraception should not be regarded as definitely settled. The time-honoured arguments are not fully convincing, and tradition and authority should not be used to bolster up a position which cannot be proved rationally'. He dismissed the search for another Pill which would regulate ovulation, criticising the 'casuisty required to differentiate between the various uses of the different pills' as evidence of 'just how unreal was our sexual morality'.[111]

On 29 October 1966, when the O'Callaghan article was probably in the press, Paul VI in an address to a congress of Italian gynaecologists and midwives, described birth control as 'a very delicate question'. He informed them that the papal commission had completed its work, but its conclusions cannot be seen as definitive because 'they carry grave implications'. He announced that he was delaying a decision on family planning for some time. In his detailed account of the papal commission and the efforts of conservative Vatican clergy to block change, Kaiser claims that the pope was speaking 'bureaucratese', but members of the commission who read this statement understood that he would not accept their recommendations to amend church teaching on contra-ception.[112] An article in the Vatican newspaper *Osservatore Romano*, stating

---

[110] *Clergy Review*, li, November 1966, pp. 838–9.
[111] *Clergy Review*, li, November 1966, pp. 840–9.
[112] Kaiser, *The encyclical that never was*, p. 229.

that 'assent to an unnatural regulation of births ... would be an assent to moral irresponsibility' would appear to confirm that point of view.[113] On 22 October 1966, the *Irish Independent* reported that the Pope's decision would be delayed, and on 30 October, it gave a brief report of his statement.[114] This story was not covered in the *Irish Times* until 21 November, when the newspaper reported on an article in the Jesuit magazine *Civiltà Cattolica*, suggesting that the Pope's silence reflected 'the complexity and gravity of the case'.[115]

2.4   Family Planning in Ireland – A Moving Picture

The delay in determining Vatican teaching on contraception was not matched by a standstill in Irish public opinion. The new emphasis on private conscience, and the belief that papal teaching might change, contributed to a liberation of attitudes, which was fuelled by earlier marriages, a rising marriage rate and a more relaxed approach towards courtship and social life. These changes are evident in the media – especially women's magazines, and the women's pages in daily newspapers. There were a number of new Irish-published women's magazines: *Women's Way* first published in 1963, *Young Woman* (1967) and *Woman's Choice* (1968), indications of a growing market, especially among younger women.[116] Stopper noted how they deployed the power of personal testimonies, 'the comfort it gave women to hear individual stories from others going through the same difficulties – deserted wives, struggling mothers of twelve unable to access contraception', 'or unmarried mothers shamed into giving her baby up for adoption'.[117]

Archbishop's House did not have any influence over *Woman's Way* or *Woman's Choice*, in contrast to the newspapers. In 1967, Dr McQuaid's secretary told him that he had complained to the editor of *Woman's Way*, some years ago, about an editorial stating that marital problems should not be raised in the confessional. Clear noted that while the founding editor of *Woman's Way*, Sean O'Sullivan, was in favour of sex education and some form of birth control, though not the Pill, under his successor Caroline Mitchell, the editorial line was 'broadly in favour of birth control'.[118] Dr McQuaid's secretary pointed out that Caroline Mitchell was a Protestant, and 'several members of the editorial staff may be lapsed Catholics'. With the exception of columnist

---

[113] *Catholic Standard,* 12 November 1966.   [114] *II,* 22 October 1966.
[115] *IT,* 21 November 1966 Account given of Papal dilemma. Birth-control questions.
[116] Caitriona Clear, *Women's voices in Ireland: Women's magazines in the 1950s and 1960s* (Bloomsbury, London, 2016), pp. 1–11. Anne Stopper, *Mondays at Gaj's: The story of the Irish Women's Liberation Movement* (Liffey Press, Dublin, 2006), pp. 1–2, 34–7; Laura Kelly, 'Debates on family planning and the contraceptive pill in the Irish magazine, *Woman's Way,* 1963–1973', *Women's History Review,* 3, no 6, 2021, pp. 971–89.
[117] Stopper, *Mondays at Gaj's,* pp. 54–5.   [118] Clear, *Women's Voices,* p. 65.

Angela McNamara, 'all the articles dealing with matters of sex are very much astray morally'.[119]

Woman's Way sought to maintain a careful balance between conservative opinion, epitomised by Angela McNamara, and more liberal views. Although McNamara, who became Ireland's best-known agony aunt, upheld Catholic teaching in her column, her articles alerted readers to the existence of the Pill and the debate over its use. 'Artificial birth control. A growing threat to be overcome', November 1963, warned readers that oral contraception would 'shortly be launched on the British market in a very big way indeed'. The Pill was forbidden under 'Church Teaching'. Over one million American women were using the Pill; Britain was about to follow. 'Already the moral behaviour in all classes of society is being deplored'.[120] The same issue of *Woman's Way* reported on the new family planning clinic at Holles St, quoting from a speech by Dr Kieran O'Driscoll to a meeting of the IMA:

The moral aspects of birth control have been spoken of by the last three Popes, but their words did not receive the publicity they deserved. This subject has been buried under the carpet for too long. Theologians who previously favoured the large family now put the emphasis on welfare and education but cited the danger of viewing birth control beyond the context of Catholic teaching. Procreation and education were of equal importance and should be co-ordinated intelligently with the Church's directives.

At this time the Holles Street Clinic was only providing advice on the safe period.[121] In March 1964, Angela McNamara's letters' column included a query about the times of this clinic.

In March 1965, an unnamed marriage counsellor, who was described as a woman doctor, devoted a column in *Woman's Way* to 'Regulation of Family', in response to numerous letters from readers. She wrote that 'there are times when it is neither desirable nor suitable for a woman to bear a child, when either medical or economic reasons make it impracticable for her to do so. … It is obligatory for married couples to bring into the world the number of children that they can reasonably take care of. It is **WRONG** (as in original) to produce children in unlimited numbers in circumstances when neglect sometimes becomes inevitable'. She emphasised that the rhythm method was in line with Catholic teaching, and she was extremely positive about its success. The fact that she felt a need to state this is one indication of the level of knowledge and current attitudes in Ireland; it was just becoming possible to speak about limiting family size in a positive tone. She continued: 'Please do not jump to the conclusion that I am trying to advocate the control of all marriages by the rhythm method'; there were 'very many happy married couples who welcome

---

[119] DDA XXV/456/12/(1), 21 December 1967; Paul Ryan, *Asking Angela McNamara: An intimate history of Irish lives* (Irish Academic Press, Dublin, 2012).
[120] *Woman's Way*, 14 November 1963, p. 14.   [121] *Woman's Way*, 30 November 1963.

with real joy a succession of pregnancies'. The article ended with a quotation from Pius XII's 1956 address to Catholic midwives.[122]

There is evidence that attitudes towards frequent pregnancies were changing. One letter to Angela McNamara came from a woman whose neighbour, on being told that she was expecting her third child, said 'Ah well, it can't be helped'; her mother in law 'made the same sort of remark'.[123] In 1969, Dorine Rohan reported that 'the usual reaction one witnesses to a third or fourth pregnancy is at the worst, disappointment and depression, at the best ...a remark like "I don't mind too much". All the people I questioned on how they liked having large families...would have been able to do a better job with 3 or 4 children'.[124]

A 1966 series by Mary Leland, titled 'Whither Love', quoted the comments and experiences of various women: Mrs WK who regretted not knowing more about birth control when she married, and her disappointment at being pregnant after three months 'I just wasn't ready for it'. The mother of three small children, she and her husband were now using the rhythm method, which meant that 'I'm a black negligee girl only six nights of the month'. Leland reported that 'Talking to these people married and single, I sensed a kind of rage, mostly against the doctors or the priests, both of whom, it was felt had confused the issues of sex, contraception and marriage so inextricably that it was difficult to decide on the truth'. She described the strategies that women had adopted: 'they shopped around looking either for a sympathetic and realistic priest or a responsive and understanding doctor – often for both'. Wives continued going to confession locally; their husbands might seek a sympathetic priest in one of the Orders (a comment that suggests her respondents lived in cities or large town; Leland was based in Cork). One couple stocked up on literature that was banned in Ireland while on honeymoon abroad. Almost half of those that she talked to wanted contraceptive devices to be available from their doctors; but 'Nobody wanted them generally available from chemists'.[125]

When *Woman's Way* became a weekly publication in September 1966, it carried a series of three articles on The Pill. The first, by Rev Denis O'Callaghan, noted that 'Birth Control has been very much in the theological news in recent years. The crisis it constituted for Catholic conscience was referred to more than once in speeches during the Vatican Council'. The matter had been brought to a head by the new theology of marriage, with its emphasis 'on the intimately personal character of the sex act'. He summarised the current position as a 'three cornered battle' between conservatives, radicals and those holding moderate positions. 'In so confused a situation it would be too much to expect uniform directions from those who counsel or inform practice from even well-intentioned

---

[122] *WW* 1 March 1965, p. 21.   [123] *WW* 1 August 1964, p. 42.
[124] Dorine Rohan, *Marriage Irish style* (Mercier, Cork, 1969), p. 112.
[125] *WW*, 1 August 1966, Whither love?, p. 45.

partners'. He told readers that this 'state of uncertainty will reign until the whole question of the lawfulness of the Pill ....has been settled once for all'. He dismissed as wishful thinking those who hoped that a drug would be developed that could guarantee the safe period by determining the date of ovulation.[126] A second article by an unnamed doctor discussed the medical issues, including contraindications for taking the Pill. The third, by journalist Monica McEnroy, called for the Pill to be widely available. She denounced the fact that women had to rely either on celibacy or 'chance the "safe period"' as a 'national scandal'. She cited a medical consultant who spoke of the 'horrifying numbers of young married women being driven into nervous exhaustion and insanity by continual pregnancies' and asked 'when the Irish clinics [presumably those attached to maternity hospitals] are going to start dealing with married women patients according to their medical requirements and let us make our own decisions on the matter of Church rule'. She had received letters from women from all parts of Ireland who had asked their doctors for the Pill and been refused. One thirty-five-year-old mother of five was told that she would have to wait until they got permission from Rome. [This woman had high blood pressure so should not have been prescribed the Pill, irrespective of papal teaching.] McEnroy closed with the statement that 'The women of Ireland, especially the young married women, **must stop being afraid**....afraid of our husbands afraid of our bishops; afraid of our doctors, afraid of everyone'.[127] Rev Dr Bastable (UCD lecturer in Logic) wrote to McQuaid expressing concern that 'articles on marriage, particularly those by Monica McEnroy, are subversive of our standards of morality'. He was critical of coverage of the papal commission on birth control, and birth control generally.[128]

McEnroy's column was probably influenced by two articles published in the *Journal of the Irish Medical Association* in August 1966. One was a speech by Dr Alan Browne, of the Rotunda Hospital on the topic of Better Obstetrical Services. He spoke of the increasing numbers of young mothers who suffered mental illness and were becoming dependent on tranquilisers:

Our churches, our legislators, our educational authorities, our own profession and husbands have much to answer for to the mothers of Ireland if we do not face and surmount this problem. The mother of three or four children is running from the moment she gets out of bed until she falls into it again late that night in a state of exhaustion. She has no half-holiday, she has no time for hobbies, or relaxation in the shop, the bingo hall, or the tennis court.

He urged husbands to 'let your wife drive you to the office – leave her the car for the day'. Although his comments display an urban, middle-class perspective (car, office, woman driving), his message was clear.[129] The same issue of the

---

[126] *Woman's Way*, 9 September 1966.   [127] *Woman's Way*, 23 September 1966.
[128] DDA XXV/456/12/(1), 21 December 1967.   [129] *JIMA*, August 1966, p. 36.

JIMA included a paper by Dr Browne, titled 'A survey of unlimited reproduction' which reported on the incidence of grand multiparity: births to mothers of seven or more living infants. They accounted for 12.8 per cent of births in the Coombe in 1951–2, 10 per cent in 1964 and 11 per cent of births in the Rotunda in 1963. He concluded that 'the situation showed no tendency to decrease... over a ten-year period'. He reported that 'family planning advice was being given to only to a tiny proportion of patients seen at the Rotunda Hospital at their own request and in accordance with the principles of the Roman Catholic Church, but this was ineffective as a means of limiting reproduction'.[130] The *Journal of the IMA* in December 1966 carried a four-page advertising insert for the Organon drug Lyndiol, 'for the regulation of the menstrual cycle', which would appear to be the first such advertisement in the journal.

By the early 1960s, Michael Solomons, a consultant gynaecologist at Dublin's Rotunda Hospital was providing family planning to public patients at his gynaecological clinic in Mercer's Hospital, a general hospital, where he also held a consultant position. Many of the women had written to the International Planned Parenthood Federation in Britain, and were referred by them. The decision to use Mercer's rather than the Rotunda indicates a reticence about family planning in the Rotunda, perhaps because most patients and many nurses were Catholic. Solomons claimed that parents of prospective nurses would be reluctant to have their daughters train in a hospital that provided advice on contraception.[131] Solomons has been described to me as someone whose commitment to family planning was out of line with the general run of Dublin gynaecologists, including the consultants in the Rotunda – a hospital not trammelled directly by having a Catholic archbishop on the board but nevertheless constrained by the conservative culture of the times.

The Rotunda opened a 'Fertility and Marriage Guidance Clinic' in 1964. The Coombe, the last of the three maternity hospitals to provide family planning services, opened a 'Marriage Guidance Clinic' in 1965; the annual report noted that 'many patients either for medical or social reasons are anxious to avail of it'.[132] The National Maternity Hospital was determined to give some elementary family planning advice to the masses – Dermot MacDonald and Declan Meagher both recalled speaking to 50–100 women at the weekly sessions. Declan Meagher recalled only one question/comment at the many talks that he gave. One woman asked how many children were in his family. When he replied nine, she retorted that the family planning advice being offered did not appear to be very reliable! Initially, the Rotunda appears to have provided a personal service for a small number. Of the twenty-five women who

[130] *JIMA*, August 1966, p. 37.   [131] Michael Solomons, *Pro-Life*, pp. 17–21.
[132] Rotunda Hospital Clinical Report 1964, p. 59; Coombe Lying-In Hospital Clinical Report for the year 1965.

attended the Rotunda clinic in 1964, five were given advice on 'ovulation and timing of intercourse' and twenty were given prescriptions for the pill. The annual report for 1965 set out a series of medical criteria for prescribing the Pill for Catholic patients: 'heavy periods, irregular periods, painful periods, or PMS'; so broad that most women could probably qualify. Thirty-eight Catholic patients – apparently all those seen – were prescribed the Pill. In 1966, the Master of the Rotunda chaired a meeting attended by the consultant obstetricians, the Catholic chaplain, the matron and senior nursing staff to examine the possibility of establishing 'Marriage Guidance Clinics'. Clinics were established which were staffed by consultants on a voluntary basis and during the year a total of 320 women attended, but the report is much vaguer on contraceptive methods: 'Advice given at these clinics varied according to the needs of each case. Anovulants are prescribed in selected cases'. By 1967, attendance had risen to 597. The women who attended that year included a thirty-nine-year-old mother, with TB, who had undergone twenty-one pregnancies and given birth to twelve living children, women suffering from TB who were described as under-nourished, and a thirty-nine-year-old mother of ten, whose husband had deserted her on several occasions leaving her with no means of support.[133] In 1968 (when *Humanae Vitae* was published), 301 mothers attended the clinic. Solomons stated that they included 'women who had tuberculosis or whose children had tuberculosis, those with alcoholic or unemployed husbands and those whose husbands had deserted them during the course of their pregnancy. All of these women had ten or more pregnancies'.[134]

In October 1966, Michael Viney presented the television programme, 'Too many children', consisting of taped responses of mothers to various questions, followed by a studio panel consisting of a gynaecologist (Dr Declan Meagher of Holles St), social worker, Noreen Kearney, a priest (Enda McDonagh) and a psychiatrist. During the course of the programme, he remarked that 'any day now a pronouncement from the Pope may well take this whole issue a big step further'.[135] The uncertainties over papal teaching are evident in the pages of the *Catholic Standard*, where a woman correspondent, real or fictitious, a mother of four, described discussing the question of preventing a fifth pregnancy with her confessor and a doctor. Her pregnancies had been difficult: she mentioned various medical consequences. Her doctor advised against a further pregnancy, and a confessor approved her decision to use the Pill, which was warmly welcomed by her husband, but her conscience was deeply troubled. She asked 'why did the first priest give me permission'.[136]

---

[133] Rotunda Hospital Clinical Report 1965, p. 49; 1966, p. 75, and 1967, p. 69.
[134] Solomons, *Pro-life*, p. 21.   [135] Daly, *Sixties Ireland*, p. 146.
[136] *Catholic Standard*, 11 April 1967.

By 1966/67, the medical profession was less cautious about family planning, but divisions were becoming evident. A symposium on Family Planning was described as 'for many the highlight' of the 1967 annual meeting of the IMA. Over a hundred doctors were present; one speaker described it as 'the most important medical meeting he had ever attended'.[137] Professor McClure Brown of the Institute of Obstetricians and the Hammersmith Hospital described Irish doctors as 'impatient' at the delay in a papal decision; he doubted that all 12,000 prescriptions were given for medical reasons.[138] The *JIMA* reported that 'few could have expected the impact made by Dr Declan Meagher' from Holles St. 'an institution with the highest scientific standards, but in Irish Catholic eyes, it is also regarded as the centre of ethical orthodoxy'. He told the conference that the Holles St clinic was now prescribing the Pill; the *JIMA* reported that this 'will have a profound effect on the attitude of Irish doctors to those patients with family planning problems... the subsequent discussion revealed widespread support for the use of this contraceptive method of family planning'. However, the writer cautioned, that 'The one or two dissident voices raised represent a larger hard core of contrary opinion in the profession than this Meeting would indicate'.[139] The report of this meeting concealed as much as it revealed.

During the IMA meeting, Syntex Pharmaceuticals, manufacturer of the contraceptive pill, held a press conference, which was chaired by Dublin cardiologist Risteard Mulcahy, who emphasised that the event was not part of the official programme. The medical director of Syntex Pharmaceuticals reported that 10 per cent of English women, aged 16–45 and 3 per cent of Irish women were using the Pill. Forty-one Irish doctors were supplying Syntex with information about its use. The editor of the *JIMA*, Dr Henry Counihan, a cardiologist at Dublin's Mater Hospital, described the press conference as 'illegal'. In response to queries from journalists, he later explained that 'the sale of contraceptives in this country is illegal and a meeting advocating them is therefore illegal'. This story was covered in a number of British newspapers,[140] and it attracted attention in Archbishop's House. The Archdiocesan Chancellor dismissed the report in the *Daily Mail* on the grounds that the paper 'is a rag ... a most unreliable source'; he described the article reporting the numbers of Irish women on the Pill, as 'clearly mischievous, designed to exploit a situation on very meagre evidence – less evidence, I would think, than in fact exists'. He doubted whether it would have much impact in Ireland. He described a statement by Dr Kevin Feeney (Coombe) as 'not too bad – not carrying anything like the implications of Dr Kieran O' Driscoll's recent address to Holles St. At least, he advises the patients first to consult their confessors; and he does counsel against gossip, a most prolific source of misrepresentation (even of doctors) on this subject. His "first we

---

137 *IT*, 29 June 1967; II, 29 June 1967; *Daily Telegraph*, 29 June 1967.
138 *IT*, 1 July 1968.   139 *JIMA*, August 1967.   140 *IT*, 29 June 1967.

make sure that there are reasonable medical, social and economic reasons", is at worst, ambiguous. He seems to require, medical, social and economic reasons – all three, medical alone <u>might</u> in a given case, justify the administration of the Pill'. He suggested that Dr Counihan had raised 'a most interesting point', was it legal to speak in public about contraception in Ireland? He dismissed Risteard Mulcahy, who chaired the press conference as displaying 'a grossly naïve immaturity....certainly the worst "quote" of them all'.

The growing concern of the archdiocese is evident

There can be no doubt that considerable confusion exists on this subject; we do not have to wait for the *Daily Mail* to tell us this. But I do not think that fault for this can be laid at the door of the Bishops, or the priests, or the doctors. The confusion is, I fear, inherent in the situation which arose inevitable when the Pope, in his second 'admonitio' especially <u>counselled</u> a common norm (Pius XII), as an interim measure. The Holy Father must surely be aware of the present situation and yet he has not spoken.[141]

In 1967, Monica McEnroy alleged that 'the gap in Irish maternity services caused by the gap in family planning clinics is as wide as ever'. Nineteen Irish women died in childbirth in 1966; she claimed that this was an under-estimate. Over the past year, 'there has been a great deal of shadow-boxing'. 'A few private doctors' were now prescribing the Pill, but according to an unnamed commercial traveller (who presumably worked for a drug company), this was only happening in the cities. He claimed that there were 'whole districts where one dare not mention anovulants to the doctors'. She quoted another doctor who decried the 'false impression that any woman who wants the Pill can get it', and she described the experiences of women who were prescribed the Pill in an unnamed 'city centre clinic'. "'I was cross-questioned by the doctor on my religious attitude to taking the Pill. I was so furious I could have burst out crying I was afraid to say anything in case he would not give me the prescription.... what you have to go through before your get the Pill; you get put on it as a kind of compliment'". In what is possibly the first widely available article in an Irish publication to extend the contraceptive debate beyond the Pill, she noted that the current position discriminated against women 'who happen to be unsuited to the Pill'.[142]

A paper by Drs Meagher and MacDonald using data from the Holles St clinic provided the first authoritative evidence about fertility and sexual behaviour in Ireland. They emphasised that advice on birth regulation was 'an essential part of obstetric care', and 'responsible parenthood'. The group talks given in the hospital to recently delivered mothers were an 'attempt to overcome the lack of motivation which is the commonest obstacle to the success of the advice'. When the talks began the safe period was the only

---

[141] DDA 13/XX handwritten the Chancellery.   [142] *Woman's Way*, 11 August 1967.

method described, and explanatory leaflets were distributed. By 1966, more than 20,000 women had attended these talks, plus unspecified numbers of medical and nursing students. Initially, the women who attended the Family Planning Clinic were self-selecting, half were from working class families; 17 per cent had one child and 44 per cent had two to four children. Because the clinic was overcrowded, in February 1966, attendance was restricted to specific categories of women who had given birth in the hospital; women with serious medical conditions; those with high fertility and 'a distressing socio-economic problem', and mothers under thirty with five or more children. Only 30 per cent of women in the first two categories, who were given appointments, attended; two-thirds were accompanied by their husbands. A majority of those given appointments lived in Dublin city or county, so distance did not account for non-attendance, and the majority of those who failed to attend, did not respond to follow-up letters asking them to attend. Several of these women suffered from acute medical problems. The prognosis for a successful future pregnancy in the case of one woman with acute rhesus problems, who had failed to respond to five letters from the hospital was described as 'almost hopeless'. Another woman with five children born by caesarean section, who had developed renal failure requiring dialysis on her most recent pregnancy, failed to respond to letters addressed to herself and her family doctor.

The clinic collected some limited evidence about the frequency of sexual relations, probably the first such information collected in Ireland – 43 per cent reported once or twice a week; and female orgasm – 58 per cent reported always, and some data on peak libido. Of 107 women who were asked about previous attempts at family planning, 40 per cent had used coitus interruptus, 24 per cent had used the calendar method, 33 per cent had used no method and 3 per cent had resorted to complete abstinence. Meagher and O'Driscoll reported that 'the mean frequency of intercourse may be less than in other communities'. They noted that one of the strongest criticisms of the rhythm method is that it demands abstinence from intercourse at a time when libido may be at its highest; 'the high incidence of coitus interruptus... highlights the urgent need for adequate marriage guidance services'. The rhythm method required a couple to abstain from intercourse until a regular menstrual cycle had been determined, which might require celibacy for six months or more following the birth of a child. This 'imposes an intolerable strain on many marriages'. At the conclusion of this paper, they noted that the clinic now prescribed the Pill 'as a contraceptive for selected medical and social cases. It is our experience that the safe period is inadequate for serious medical and social cases'. They summarised their paper as follows: 'Responsible parenthood implies birth regulation. Advice on family planning should be freely available to all mothers. Lack of motivation is the commonest obstacle to effective advice. Fear of pregnancy is detrimental to marital harmony. Use of the infertile period demands long periods of abstinence. This imposes an intolerable strain on some marriages'.[143]

This article was challenged by a letter-writer to the *JIMA* who asked whether they also prescribed, condoms, IUDs and other devices, and 'if not why not?' He added, 'For a Catholic Hospital with the Archbishop as patron, serving a Catholic community, to adopt a policy directly opposed to the official view of the Catholic Church is startling. It surely deserves more attention than inclusion as an addition in brackets to an article on family planning'. In their reply, Drs Meagher and MacDonald stated that

During recent years the ethical basis for the prohibition of contraception has been seriously questioned by theologians. A Papal Commission was set up to examine the issue and has reported in favour of contraception in the exercise of responsible parenthood. The delay in the decisive Papal pronouncement appears to confirm that a state of doubt exists.

We do not advocate the 'Pill'. The issue for doctors in not the morality of taking the pill but rather the morality of refusing to provide it for patients who feel entitled, in conscience, to take it. It is our duty to treat patients; it is the patients who make the moral decisions. In this situation we have concluded that to deny the Pill to couples who need it, is at variance with the dictates of justice and charity.

In common with all Catholic doctors, we eagerly await the time when our moral responsibility in this matter is clearly defined.[144]

In February 1968, Rev Peter Flood, a Benedictine monk, who was obviously of Irish birth, but based in Ealing Abbey told Dr McQuaid that he had been in correspondence with the Master of Holles St 'an old student and friend'. Dr O'Driscoll had complained that the Church had not spoken, and Rev Flood had referred him to the Archbishop while pointing out that the papal commission was 'only a Commission and not part of the Magisterium of the Church'. He concluded that Dr O'Driscoll 'has not the training to appreciate the factors involved and I suspect is badly advised by someone'.[145] John Marshall, a member of the papal commission, appears to have kept the CMAC informed of the work of the Vatican commission, and Declan Meagher, who attended monthly 'pillar' meetings of the CMAC was privy to this information. John Bonnar, who was then based in Britain, has described being summoned to a meeting in Liverpool in the summer of 1968, which was attended by approximately thirty Catholic gynaecologists from Britain and Ireland, and by John Marshall and three theologians including Dr O'Callaghan. The doctors were told that Church teaching would change, and that this had been recommended by the commission, who had found no theological basis for a church ban on contraception. Furthermore, the changes went beyond approving the Pill and included approval for sterilisation.[146] It was not to be.

---

[143] *JIMA*, December 1967, Meagher and MacDonald, 'A hospital family planning service'.
[144] *JIMA*.   [145] DDA, *Humanae Vitae* files, 13 February 1968.
[146] Interviews with Declan Meagher, and with Dr John Bonnar.

3   'A Bitter Blow'

Humanae Vitae and Irish Society, 1968–1973

In 1968, Garret FitzGerald, then an economist and commentator on economic and demographic issues concluded that 'Ireland is currently undergoing a demographic revolution of unusual proportions'. Fertility had been falling at an annual rate of 2 per cent, which had now accelerated to 4 per cent. Many married couples were obviously controlling fertility; the boom in marriages was not followed by a corresponding boom in births.[1] There was an anticipation that the Vatican's position on contraception might change, which may explain inaction on the part of Archbishop's House. Although McQuaid's papers reveal concern about statements on family planning by various doctors, there is no evidence that he contacted the National Maternity Hospital when they began to prescribe the Pill and although he grumbled in private about the 1967 IMA meeting, he issued no public statement and did not contact the participants. The archdiocese was holding its fire, pending a decision from Rome.

Orthodoxy reigned however in areas that were under the Archbishop's control, such as issuing an *imprimatur* – permission to publish. Denis O'Callaghan's article 'Authority Conscience and the Pill', which he submitted to the *IER* in November 1967 was yet another reiteration of his views on the modern theology of marriage and the implications for a papal ban on contraception. It included the phrase, 'The Pope confesses his own perplexity; the procrastination and the almost self-contradictory character of some of his remarks is evidence of the dilemma in which authority finds itself.' Having refused an *imprimatur* for publication in *IER*, the Archbishop took steps to ensure that this article would not be published in the *ITQ*. In a letter to Dr Lennon, Bishop of Kildare and Leighin, who approved articles in the *ITQ*, he said that 'in my opinion, he [O'Callaghan] called into doubt the divine law concerning contraception, failed to observe the direction of the Sovereign Pontiffs, in particular Paul VI, and was calculated to increase the confusion now lamentably affecting both priests and laity'.[2] The Archbishop also expressed concern over a newspaper article by the Cork priest, Dr James Good, and more

[1] Contrasting trends in marriage and fertility, *IT*, 2 October 1968.
[2] DDA *Humanae Vitae* Public Affairs, 377, 2 February 1968.

muted concerns about an article by Enda McDonagh on Christian marriage in an ecumenical context, where Dr McDonagh stated that 'the goals whether expounded by the Lambeth Conference or the Vatican Council are the same' – responsible parenthood, 'whatever number of children can be provided for', describing Catholic teaching on the means of family limitation as 'at present under study'.[3]

Senior Irish clergy welcomed the publication of *Humanae Vitae* which reiterated traditional teaching on contraception. International reaction exposed deep divisions among Catholic clergy and laity in many countries. In Ireland, despite evidence that attitudes were changing, the storm was contained more effectively than elsewhere. Archbishop's House had received advance notice of publication together with a copy, and Dr McQuaid spoke at the opening of a press conference on 29 July, publication day. The main speaker was Dr Cornelius Cremin, Professor of Moral Theology at Maynooth. He emphasised the need for 'sincere external and internal obedience' to the magisterium of the Church and concluded by stating that 'whatever may have been people's views up to this the teaching of the Church was now unquestionable'.[4] In a letter to the Papal Nuncio, later that day, the Archbishop reported that the press conference that lasted two hours and forty minutes 'had exceeded beyond my expectations'. The questions, 'with one exception were searching and very respectful'.[5] But *Hibernia*, reviewing the media coverage reported a 'mixed reaction', adding that it was 'curious that the only priests who wrote to the press were priests well known for the championship of the papal teaching', whereas, in Britain, the media featured a range of views. *Hibernia* suggested that there had been 'no real change in the style of exercise of church authority in Ireland since the Vatican Council'. It also claimed that there had been a poor public reaction to the press conference called by the Archbishop.[6] One letter in the *Irish Independent* commented on the 'relative calm with which the document has been received'.[7] But an editorial in the *Irish Press* suggested that the encyclical would 'stimulate rather than stifle the debate'.[8]

The archdiocesan press office received many requests for Dr McQuaid, or a priest from the archdiocese to appear on British television programmes, including the leading BBC current affairs programme *Panorama*. There were also requests from foreign journalists, and for permission to film a baptism in Dublin's Pro-Cathedral (refused). While the press office, having checked with the Archbishop declined most requests, in a few exceptions the Archbishop identified a suitably orthodox priest. It proved difficult to control international media. There was consternation when it emerged that an agreed interview with

---

[3] Enda McDonagh, 'Christian marriage in an ecumenical context', *The Furrow*, January 1968, p. 10.
[4] *IP*, 30 July 1968.   [5] DDA/XX/6, 29 July.   [6] *Hibernia*, September 1968.
[7] *II*, 7 August 1968.   [8] *IP*, 30 July 1968.

an Irish priest, who supported the encyclical, would be followed by a panel discussion that included a priest opposed to papal teaching. McQuaid's position on the encyclical is summarised in the sentence. 'Doctrine must first be emphasised, before compassion'.[9]

The most prominent dissenter among the Irish clergy was Cork theologian Fr James Good who described *Humanae Vitae* as 'A major tragedy for the Church'. He suggested that the 'understanding of marriage problems put forward in this document appear to be out of date and inadequate'; the conclusions regarding birth control were 'unrealistic and incorrect'. He had no doubt that they would be rejected by a majority of Catholic theologians and laity; 'as a teacher of theology, philosophy and medical ethics, I cannot see my way to accepting the teaching on contraception put forward in this document'.[10] In a second statement, some days later, he said that 'while I accept the Pope's ruling of today, I believe that the conclusion drawn is incorrect. The manner in which the statement was made must be regretted after the public had been prepared for the opposite decision by a panel of experts and theologians etc. for the past two years'. He claimed (correctly) that a majority of priests and bishops on the Papal commission 'favoured a different line of thought'. He concluded that 'the Pope was in an impossible position, and he decided on the status quo and those of us in the church who think otherwise must do our utmost to convince the clergy and through them the bishops of our views on this great problem. To those burdened with huge families and low incomes this encyclical is a bitter blow'.[11] Dr Good received 300 letters and telegrams in response – it is not clear how many came from Ireland.[12] He was barred from preaching in public and hearing confessions and was removed from his position as professor of Catholic Theology (a chair funded by the Hierarchy) at UCC.[13] Dr Denis O'Callaghan writing in *The Furrow* in November 1968 did not give the encyclical a clear endorsement,[14] though he avoided the full glare of publicity, perhaps because the article appeared in a theological journal, not the national press, and although John Horgan summarised the contents in *The Irish Times*, O'Callaghan's argument was couched in language that would have been impenetrable to most readers.

The timing of the encyclical had major implications for coverage in the Irish media. An encyclical issued in 1964 or 1965 would have received much more respectful treatment, but by 1968, the RTÉ current affairs programme, *Seven Days*, and dedicated woman's pages in Irish newspapers, staffed by a new generation of female journalists, did not confine themselves

---

[9] DDA/XX/14, 7 August 1968 HV Public Affairs.   [10] *IP*, 30 July 1968.
[11] Fr James Good, statement issued 29 July 1968, DDA/XX/8/2(i).
[12] DDA box marked *Humanae Vitae*, unlisted material Fr Good to Fergus O'Rourke.
[13] *IP*, 19 October 1968.
[14] Denis O'Callaghan, 'After the encyclical', *The Furrow*, November 1968, pp. 633–41.

to reporting uncritically the views of churchmen, politicians, or medical professionals. *Seven Days* featured a debate between Dr Cremin and Ballyfermot GP Patrick Leahy who claimed that the Pope had 'no compassion'. Dr Leahy described the problems facing mothers with six, seven or ten children, or mothers with cardiac conditions. The programme featured a young mother, who had given birth to two children in rapid succession, and was now on the Pill, with the 'permission' of her confessor and a Catholic gynaecologist. She felt that she could no longer continue taking the Pill and described herself as 'disappointed and disillusioned'.[15] Micheline McCormack in the *Irish Press* reported the comment of one young mother that she met at a bus stop – 'Sometimes it is difficult to cope with a load of children. Still if they come, they come'. A mother of two told her, 'I don't see how he could have made a different decision and I agree with it'. She quoted the views of two gynaecologists: Dr P. F Denham, 'a disaster for Christianity' and Eamon de Valera: 'What the Pope says goes. We will obey him'.

On 12 August, the *Irish Times* informed readers that they could publish only a fraction of the letters that they received about the encyclical and would concentrate on those that made a fresh contribution. Most contributors were critical. *Hibernia*'s summary of the provincial papers reflected wider acquiescence. The encyclical received extensive coverage and was the subject of many editorials. *The People* (Wexford) reported the dissenting views of Fr Good and a number of international theologians, including Hans Kung but advised that 'In Ireland we cannot allow ourselves to be swayed by the attitudes of theologians no matter how learned or respected they might be. The decrees of the bishops must be regarded as morally binding, if not intellectually acceptable'. The *Kilkenny People* highlighted the dilemma that the encyclical presented for practising Catholics and expressed regret that 'his teaching should differ from the firmly held convictions of so many bishops and of the major theologians'. The *Limerick Weekly Echo* canvassed public opinion – a mother of fourteen said that she did not need the pope to tell her that birth control was wrong, whereas a newly-wed couple described the papal ruling as 'out of the question' for them. The *Donegal Democrat* approved of the ruling, likewise the *Connacht Telegraph*, the *Derry Journal*, and *The Kerryman*, which published the entire encyclical.[16]

Despite the apparent evidence of strong support for papal teaching, Dr Cremin, writing to McQuaid, expressed the 'fear that our own task is far from ending with the Press Conference'.[17] In September, Fr Gerry Watson, Professor of Classics at Maynooth published an article in the *Irish Times*, titled, 'Priest and Conscience', which argued that 'Mature Catholicism' demanded, an 'intellectual assent to the Church's teaching and not simply a passive acquiescence to

[15] *IP*, 30 July 1968.   [16] *IT*, 5 August 1968.   [17] DDA, 16 August XX/33.

commands imposed from above'. He indicated that many priests felt that their freedom of expression had been curtailed since its publication; 'they did not find the arguments of the Encyclical intellectually convincing. But they found themselves bound not to contradict publicly the Pope or their own particular bishop'. Many were aware of the crisis that married couples faced and advised them in private that they should consult their conscience. Professor Watson summarised the more sympathetic and qualified responses of the Catholic hierarchies in the Netherlands, Belgium and Germany and expressed the hope that the October meeting of the Irish Hierarchy would 'issue a statement proving that they too respect the maturity of the Irish laity'.[18]

The statement that issued following the meeting of the Hierarchy on 8–9 October left little room for an informed conscience. It opened with a reminder that 'The Second Vatican Council' teaches that 'a religious submission of mind and will must be given to the authentic teaching of the Pope even when he is not speaking *ex cathedra*'[19]. It continued: 'This Encyclical contains the authentic teaching of the Pope. We are confident that our people will accept it as such and give it that whole-hearted assent which the Second Vatican Council requires'. The papal teaching 'merely reaffirms what the Church has always taught'. Conscience 'must be conformed to the Divine Law, submissive to the teaching authority of the Church'. Despite some recognition of 'the delicate and personal problems and intellectual difficulties' that Church teaching might present, especially for doctors, the message from the Irish Hierarchy was uncompromising.[20] The editorial in the *Irish Independent* welcomed the compassionate tone but commented that 'Of its nature this painful controversy has involved a questioning of the very elements essential to sustaining the encyclical: whether its teaching is in fact authentic at every point, whether an informed conscience can in fact be rendered submissive'.[21]

Although there were dissenters, the responses in Ireland were much more muted than in other western countries. Rev F. Browne, director of post-marriage counselling for the Dublin Archdiocese, reported that his conversations with priests working in parishes indicated that many women had ceased taking the Pill; many were silent; some were awaiting further clarification from the archdiocese. He suggested that the matter should be discussed at a conference of the clergy.[22] According to Dorine Rohan, all the priests that she had spoken to had expected some relaxation in papal teaching, but 'for many in pastoral work it relieves them of the unenviable onus of decision which they had to carry when married people sought their advice'.

[18] *IT*, 10 September 1968, 61.
[19] 'The Bishops of Ireland "Statement on *Humanae Vitae*"', *The Furrow*, 19, no 11, 1968, p. 6.
[20] *II*, 10 October 1968, p. 1.   [21] *II*, 10 October 1968, p. 16.
[22] DDA/XX/17/1, 28 September 1968.

Many priests in the confessional felt so strongly about the suffering and distress caused in marriage by the Church's ruling, that they advised some mothers who sought their advice to take the Pill. Others left it to the person's own conscience. Many people who could not get permission from one priest looked around until they found a more sympathetic confessor! Similarly with doctors. Many feel now that there will be an increase in the 'clientele' of non-Catholic doctors, while the Catholic doctors feel in conscience they cannot prescribe the Pill....one priest engaged in marriage counselling told me that he dealt with many cases where the marriages were breaking up because the couple were abstaining completely.... because of fears .... of another child. One priest reported that 'sleeping in the sitting room – this happens more often than one would expect'.[23]

The number of women taking the Pill is estimated to have fallen from 17,000 to over 15,000, following the publication of the encyclical but this proved only a short-term reaction. By 1973, an estimated 19,000 Irish women were using the Pill.[24]

Archbishop McQuaid received letters for and against the encyclical, including a number of obsequious letters from diocesan clergy. They provide unparalleled insights into Irish Catholic marriages of that era. All correspondents received a personal reply from his secretary: one dissenter was advised to read 'the entire document of the Holy Father and then have it explained to you by a reliable person who can set forth your obligation in conscience to accept that teaching'.[25] One man expressed his support for the Archbishop: 'Now is a time to stand and be counted'.[26] A UCD academic requested 'that prayers be said for those in turmoil at the recent Papal Encyclical. In the various statements, no such request was emphasised. Are your flock not worthy of this? Rather there was jubilation without this practical charity. It was called "a most compassionate document"! I beg of you to lead us in a day of prayer'.[27] A 'young Irish Catholic mother' expressed

my gratitude and admiration....a source of consolation to both my husband and myself and it will be our support and guide in the education of our nine children in these matters. My only regret is that the statement was so long delayed and that the direction and guidance given by our priests, even here in Dublin was so divergent.

A single woman, an 'ordinary member of the laity', offered 'sincere congratulations'.[28] A former pupil of the Archbishop now living in Boston in a 'liberal' parish, where the parish priest 'has guitars in the sanctuary, Protestants in the pulpit and the national Catholic Reports in the church porch', was happy 'to see that Ireland is still the Island of Saints and Scholars'.[29] One man wrote on behalf of himself and his wife. They were in their forties, parents of three children and did not plan on having any more children. They had used the

[23] Dorine Rohan, *Marriage Irish style* (Mercier, Cork, 1969), pp. 92–3.
[24] Daly, *Sixties Ireland*, p. 149.   [25] DDA/XX/11.   [26] DDA/XX/8/6.   [27] DDA/XX/8/8.
[28] DDA/XX/8/11, XX/8/13.   [29] DDA/XX/8/16.

rhythm method successfully, but it had left them with little sexual satisfaction, and tended to 'leave the act devoid of real love'. Their primary complaint was that 'Catholics in other parts of the world are in fact practising contraception with what is in fact the permission of their priests and bishops …how can there be different rules?' They could not accept the encyclical as binding.[30]

An unnamed, correspondent – probably a medical doctor from Cork, wrote to Cardinal Conway, explaining that in the first fourteen years of his marriage, he and his wife had 'fully accepted' church teaching, and nine children were born. He described the burden of raising nine children 'without any help in the home as really unsupportable for my wife who went on the Pill'. He had 'reluctantly accepted her decision' but having discussed the matter with Catholic theologians in Ireland and the USA, he became convinced that he was mistaken in his conservatism. This letter prompted, what can only be described as an unsympathetic response from Cardinal Conway, stating that he could not comment on the home situation 'because I do not know why there is no help in the home',[31] a comment that reveals much about the Cardinal's limited vision of Irish family life. A male journalist, whose letter to UCC academic Dr Fergus O'Rourke (see below) has somehow come into McQuaid's papers, explained that he was a

[f]ather of four, quite well spaced, thanks not to Rhythm or artificial means, but through the trying and strenuous fact of abstaining, a way I would not recommend for my worst enemy if I had one. I think it is dehumanised and soul-less, heartless and the greatest encouragement to couples to give up religion or faith and rely instead on pure and godless reason. My wife is still a staunch believer, and accepts, as I knew she would, this new document, but for my part, I could not believe in a God that is a sadist, and cannot accept that *Humanae Vitae* is definitive…[32]

3.1   The Doctors

In 1968, the medical profession was the only group providing advice or access to family planning, however limited. The 1935 Criminal Law Amendment Act still applied, and there is no indication that it was widely ignored or defied, and the sections of the 1929 Censorship of Publications Act relating to the provision of information about contraception remained unchanged. So, the response of the medical profession was critical. Shortly after the encyclical was published, the Master of the National Maternity Hospital Dr Kieran O'Driscoll issued a statement 'stating that the recent Papal Encyclical is accepted by the staff in this hospital as a clear directive against the use of the Pill to prevent contraception in any circumstances'. He felt that he had a duty to dispel any

[30] DDA *Humanae Vitae* misc. 380, 25 August 1968.
[31] Loose material box marked *Humanae Vitae*, unsigned letter dated 1 August 1968.
[32] DDA Loose material in box marked *Humanae Vitae*, September 1968.

misunderstanding.[33] But a group of twenty-one Catholic doctors – obstetricians, psychiatrists, research scientists and general practitioners – issued a statement expressing anxiety lest the encyclical be interpreted 'with a rigidity', which they believed was 'scarcely justified'. 'Every effort should continue to be made to meet the difficulties that constantly arise when medical practitioners are called on to assist married couples in the exercise of responsible parenthood'.[34] The signatories included Professors of Psychiatry, Ivor Browne (UCD) and Thomas Lynch (RCSI); obstetricians, John Boyle and Donal O'Brien (Coombe); J.B. Kearney, R.C. Sutton, Robert O'Donoghue and T.C. O'Connor (Cork); Professor Eamonn O'Dwyer (UCG); pathologists, Dermot Hourihane (TCD) and Robert Towers (St Vincent's hospital); John Casey anaesthetist (Cork); Risteard Mulcahy, cardiologist (St Vincent's and the Coombe), W.E. O'Dwyer, Professor of Medicine (RCSI), Liam O'Connell, presumably a GP; Pauline O'Connell, Denis O'Sullivan genito-urinary surgeon Cork and Dr Marie O'Sullivan presumably a GP.[35] The number of Cork signatories is noticeable, as is the absence of consultants attached to the National Maternity Hospital, though it is unclear whether Drs Meagher and MacDonald, who ran the Holles St clinic, agreed with Dr O'Driscoll's stance. Archbishop McQuaid wrote to Ivor Browne, the first name on the list, asking him to explain this statement, but there is no evidence that he replied.

Dr Anthony Clare[36], a young psychiatric registrar, criticised the efforts of his medical colleagues to find a *via media*. He reported that two prominent gynaecologists, Karl Mullen and Raymond Cross, had stated that women taking the Pill for medical reasons faced no difficulties in continuing with that course of action, and he examined the debate as to how far the medical case could be extended. Maynooth theologian Dr Cremin had ruled out use of the Pill for medical reasons where a woman had a kidney complaint or heart disease – conditions that would deteriorate during pregnancy. He quoted Fr Denis Faul, of the Armagh archdiocese – 'Doctors have now got completely explicit guidance on what they knew and should have been following anyway. A doctor can no more prescribe the Pill as a contraceptive than he can procure an abortion or directly sterilise a patient'. Dr Clare concluded that there were only two options open to the medical profession: complete obedience, as expressed by Dr O'Driscoll, or the stance taken by the secretary of the Italian Catholic Doctors' Association: – that any doctor who accepted the rhythm method as the only method of birth regulation would be acting against his professional conscience. In a 1966 survey of final year medical students at UCD, 40 per cent

[33] *II*, 3 August 1968.   [34] *IT*, 3 August 1968.   [35] *IP*, 3 August 1968.

[36] Brendan Kelly and Muiris Houston, *Psychiatrist in the Chair: the official biography of Dr Anthony Clare* (Irish Academic Press, Dublin, 2020) does not discuss his involvement in this debate.

of Catholic students had indicated a willingness to prescribe the Pill to Catholic patients who requested it; 88 per cent of the sample and 79 per cent of Catholic students expressed the hope that the Catholic church would alter its teaching on birth control, though only 60 per cent expected this to happen. He concluded that 'many [doctors] who fundamentally agree with Pope Paul will continue to prescribe the Pill with scrupulous consideration to their patient's physical, mental and moral position, and will appeal to conscience to justify their course of action'.[37]

The divisions within the medical profession were evident in the Guild of St. Luke, SS Cosmas and Damien. When the encyclical was published, the general secretary Dr Raymond Magill, issued a statement accepting it without reservation, without first securing the approval of other officers. Shortly after Magill's statement was published, the Master-General Dr R. O'Donoghue (a signatory to the letter cited above), informed the media that 'the statement.... did not, as claimed, represent the view of the Irish Guild', because the branches had not been consulted. A definitive statement would be issued following a full meeting.[38] In a letter to members, summoning a special meeting Dr Magill explained that he had been unable to contact other officers. He argued that

a refusal to make a statement, under the circumstances, amounted to a tacit rejection of the Encyclical.... Once the Pope had issued his Encyclical, our job was merely to obey his orders....Our personal disappointments and bewilderment is really of no importance at this crisis in Church affairs; our job merely is to help the ordinary people of this Country who will be even more bewildered and disappointed and who acutely need our help now. I do feel all Doctors should very carefully weigh the consequences of their statements at this moment, considering the effects their words have on the lay-folks' difficulties, rather than use statements to vent a personal displeasure and disappointment.

When the Guild met, they failed to agree a statement. A compromise motion was proposed, welcoming the encyclical,

and especially its definite affirmation on responsible parenthood. It is the experience of the Guild that family planning contributes positively to the integrity of family life, enriching it in depth and consolidating fidelity.

The Guild in the spirit of loyal allegiance to the Papal pronouncement recommends that members should advise married couples who have 'serious motives for spacing out births' to have recourse to the infertile period in their approach to responsible parenthood.

The Guild, nonetheless, feels constrained to point out that the failure rate for family limitation by this method is high. Consequently, it not only endorses the Holy Father's appeal to men of science to strive 'to provide a sufficiently secure basis for a regulation of birth founded on the observance of natural rhythms' but proposes that this be made the special concern of the Guild everywhere and immediately.[39]

---

[37] *IT*, Doctors and the Pill, 7 August 1968.   [38] *IT*, 3 August 1968.   [39] DDA/XX/27.

Although one member described this as 'a statement that might be acceptable to the conservative theologians', it was 'shot down by our Clerical colleagues'.[40] Dr Collier, bishop of Ossory, reported to Monsignor Horgan that the guild had met the previous night and

> both sides admitted that it went better than we expected. At least we were on speaking terms at the end...... the gist of what we agreed upon was that '"doctors do their best and follow their conscience, informed by the teaching of the Church"'... 'the appeal to "follow one's conscience"...came up again and again, and it was as clear as the proverbial pikestaff that for many of them this meant "ignore the Papal teaching". The statements of some foreign Hierarchies have given support to this mentality, and I can see that it is at the core of our present trouble in the Guild'.

He suggested that it would be advisable to issue 'a good, clear and full statement on what "following one's conscience" really means in this instance'.[41]

The divisions over *Humanae Vitae* appear to have marked the end of the Guild. Dr Conor Ward, a consultant paediatrician, told me that it never met again in Newman House. The medical profession was caught in a three-way division: between those who accepted papal teaching; those who sought a compromise, involving more flexible definitions of medical cases and conscience, and those who abandoned all efforts at compromise. The moderates hoped that although the Pope would not undermine his authority 'by changing his encyclical. He may however allow a wide interpretation of paragraph 15 particularly in the face of mounting opposition' and fears of a schism within the Church.[42] Paragraph 15 permitted the use of 'illicit methods' for medical reasons – the double-effect argument, that Anthony Clare had suggested was unworkable. An opinion poll of doctors quoted in the *Irish Medical Times* showed that of the 538 who took part, 65 per cent disagreed with the papal ruling and 91 per cent said that it would not lead to major changes in their advice to patients.[43]

3.2   Bargy Castle

The most public Irish response to *Humanae Vitae* was a meeting at Bargy Castle in Wexford in September 1968. The idea appears to have originated in the divisions within the Guild of St Luke, SS Cosmas and Damien. The event was organised by Dr Fergus O'Rourke, Professor of Zoology at UCC. The list of suggested invitees included priests, doctors and academics. The letter of invitation said that 'it is intended to discuss all aspects of the encyclical in a tranquil atmosphere without any danger of a leak of information'. The draft

[40] DDA 16/9/69.
[41] DDA XX/35. D. Collier, St Kieran's College Kilkenny, to Horgan, 3 October 1968.
[42] DDA *Humanae Vitae*, 16/9/68 re preparations for Bargy Castle meeting.
[43] Daly, *Sixties Ireland*, p. 149.

programme for the two-day event included sessions on the obstetrical, psychiatric, sociological and demographic implications of the encyclical. Sunday was left for ethical considerations, including the natural law. Each topic would be introduced by an expert, with most of the time dedicated to discussion.

Attendance was limited to fifty, though this was slightly exceeded. Garret and Joan FitzGerald only heard about the planned event at the last moment and were admitted. Many invitees, including Dr Kieran O'Driscoll, and Rev. Denis O'Callaghan did not attend, though Rev Enda McDonagh was present as were Fr James Good, ESRI Director Michael Fogarty and his wife; several of the twenty-one Catholic doctors who had signed the dissenting letter, plus a number of UCD academics (including two historians, former colleagues of mine, and their wives). The media was represented by John Horgan, T.P. O'Mahony and Louis MacRedmond – three journalists who had reported on Vatican II and religious affairs.

Vincent Grogan, Supreme Knight of the Knights of St Columbanus, sent a report of the conference to Dr McQuaid, the Archbishop of Cashel, Dr Morris and the Bishop of Limerick Dr Henry Murphy, which was published in the Catholic journal, *The Furrow* and subsequently reproduced in *The Irish Times*.[44] It noted that the numbers using the Pill had increased significantly in Ireland 'while the encyclical was being awaited'. This had happened 'in a context of discussion and theological doubt'. Evidence given at the conference indicated that the 'the encyclical had created great problems for a significant number of people regarding the Church, in relation to authority and developing ideas about the nature of the Church'; the encyclical contained 'apparent inadequacies and inconsistencies.... More was in question than simple obedience'. Those attending believed that the encyclical was 'not the only element to be taken into account in the formation of a conscience'; there was a need to encourage discussion, and concerns that 'undue stress' would be placed on 'absolute and unquestioning obedience'; 'both clergy and laity participants saw the need for increasingly personal decisions in faith based on informed conscience as part of progress towards authentic Christian maturity'. The medical doctors present rejected the recommendation that the rhythm method was an effective method of birth control; the married couples agreed that rhythm or abstinence could result in 'a deterioration in the quality of the life of the family as a whole'. Many of those present were not convinced by the encyclical's condemnation of contraception as intrinsically evil, though Grogan reported that one attendee was of the opinion that 'a case could be made on natural law grounds against the use of contraceptive methods'.[45] The wives who were

[44] *IT*, 4 November 1968.
[45] Bargy Castle Meeting, *Humanae Vitae*, *The Furrow*, 19, no 11, November 1968, pp. 565–8. For a description of the meeting, see Garret FitzGerald, *All in a life. An autobiography*, (Gill & Macmillan, Dublin, 1992), pp. 83–4.

present drafted a short report, stating that in their experience the use of the 'unreliable rhythm is potentially destructive of Christian marriage....damaging, not only to the relationship between husband and wife, but also through the tensions thus created to the family as a whole'. They concluded that 'married life can best be safeguarded and fostered, and the mutual love of the spouses strengthened, by methods of family planning, which do not impose the kind of strain imposed by the unreliable rhythm method'.[46] There is no indication that this document was shown to Dr McQuaid or members of the Hierarchy.

When Michael Fogarty, director of the ESRI, was invited to Bargy Castle, he asked whether the organiser had succeeded in getting 'a reasonable balance of people for and against and a clear enough understanding among them of the sort of results that such a Conference might produce?' He believed that there was 'a very large grey area in the encyclical [which].... could be large enough to allow all but a small margin of practical problems to be coped with'. His query as to 'the sort of results that such a Conference might produce' was pertinent. Although Bargy Castle was the first significant initiative by Irish Catholic laymen and women to interrogate Catholic teaching on fertility control, it is difficult to identify any long-term outcome.

In November 1968, the UCD Medical Society organised a debate on contraception that received extensive coverage in the *JIMA*. Declan Meagher said that family planning presented doctors with serious responsibility; part of the problem (large families) was due to the success of the medical profession in reducing foetal and infant deaths. He described family planning as 'an exercise in social and preventive medicine which must consider couples in the whole context of their medical and social environment'. Doctors should be educated in family planning; some couples found the rhythm method 'impractical or impossible and believe that it seriously harms their marriage to abstain....' He expressed the opinion that 'no one has a right to impose his version of morality on another, provided a third party is involved;.......which is more artificial to take a pill to prevent ovulation or to take a pill to precipitate ovulation? Yet, there is every indication that this latter measure would be welcomed by the Church authorities as natural, or as perfecting the safe period'. Having listened to couples who had used the Pill he concluded that 'their experience does not support the woeful predictions commonly made about the evils of contraception', that it leads to 'marital infidelity promiscuity, divorce abortion'. Similar warnings were given when the safe period first became known.

John Marshall, responding to Dr Meagher's paper, expressed concerns over a recent survey of family doctors in England and Wales showing that whereas 94 per cent of non-Catholic doctors would raise the question of family planning with a woman, who had a medical condition, and three children, only

[46] Joan FitzGerald papers, my thanks to John FitzGerald for showing this to me.

63 per cent of Catholic doctors would do so. He believed that doctors had a responsibility in such circumstances to advise a couple to avoid pregnancy; 'those who say the infertile period will meet all their needs [are] living in cloud cuckoo land. Equally those who say that this method of contraception is of no value are speaking from ignorance, not knowledge, from prejudice, not scientific detachment. For those for whom the infertile period does not provide an adequate answer, the doctor has a special responsibility. He cannot unload his responsibility on to the Pope'. Enda McDonagh expressed the hope that the medical profession and the Catholic church would tackle this problem together.[47]

When Dr McQuaid blessed and opened a new department for teaching obstetrics and gynaecology at UCD, located in the National Maternity Hospital, he said that 'we have received the assurance that in the essentially human sphere of fatherhood and motherhood, the teaching of this hospital will be rightly based on the objective moral law which is the law of God'. He referred to the authority of *Humanae Vitae* and condemned 'the peculiar ignorance of intelligent men, uneducated in theology and philosophy....[who]refuse to allow the teaching authority of the Church to intervene in the moral question of applying to human persons the techniques of medicine'.[48] The *Irish Times* devoted an editorial to this speech. It claimed that 'an assurance has been given that there will be no teaching on the medical aspects of contraception in the new joint teaching unit' despite the fact an estimated 25,000 women were using the Pill as a contraceptive and an increasing number of couples were using other means. It asked whether one-third of newly qualifying doctors would be 'passed fit to practice medicine without any knowledge of contraception at a time when the practice of various means of birth control is increasing among all sectors of the Irish community?... The doctor must be aware of his patient's moral convictions at least as much as his own'.[49]

The Dublin Diocesan Press Office complained to the editor of the *Irish Times*, Douglas Gageby about the omission of a paragraph from the Archbishop's statement, and Gageby agreed that the speech should be printed in full. He indicated that Dr David Nowlan, the newspaper's medical editor, continued to have reservations, and his views would accompany the text. The paragraph, whose omission Dr McQuaid had highlighted stated that 'We can, therefore, be confident that the medical teaching here imparted will be genuinely scientific. It will, on that account have due regard to the most modern, attested techniques of medicine. Equally, it will apply those techniques with full respect for the human person and for the law of God'.[50] Dr Nowlan emphasised that patients should have a 'free and fully informed choice' with respect to family planning.

[47] *JIMA*, Vol 62, no 382, April 1969.   [48] *IT*, 5 November 1971.   [49] *IT*, 9 November 1971.
[50] *IT*, 'What the Archbishop Said', 20 November 1971; DDA/XX/100/1.

He accepted that the person who lectured on family planning to the medical students in Holles St 'covers as much ground as he can and that he covers it with medical objectivity', but the students received no clinical training on many aspects of the subject. Dr Nowlan concluded that 'With much emphasis on the moral aspects of the problem as still seem evident, it is doubtful that most fully qualified experts in family planning would recognise that the new teaching unit can provide full and unprejudiced clinical teaching in contraception for prospective doctors'.[51]

A letter to the *Irish Times*, signed by Kieran O'Driscoll, the outgoing master who was about to take up a new chair and by Professor Eamon de Valera, and Declan Meagher, O'Driscoll's successor as Master, refuted claims that the unit would not teach about the medical aspects of contraception: 'We wish to answer by stating that no such assurance has ever been sought or given. To inform, however, is not necessarily to advocate, and the public will recognise that the doctor is also entitled to respond in the dictates of conscience'.[52] This statement is ambiguous about teaching on contraception in Holles St. A group of medical students, who were then in residency, wrote that they had received comprehensive lectures from the UCD Pharmacology Department on the physiological and biochemical aspects of the contraceptive pill and a lecture on family planning which covered contraception.[53]

Irish doctors were poorly informed about the medical aspects of family planning, and ignorance was not confined to graduates of the National University of Ireland. Dr Austin Darragh, a graduate of Trinity College Dublin (1954), writing in the *Irish Medical Times (IMT)* stated: 'It may come as a shock to laymen to learn that doctors up to the present day have not had the benefit of any adequate sex education in Irish medical schools, so when a patient turns to his physician for help it is often a case of the blind leading the blind'.[54] Obstetrician Andrew Curtain, who graduated from Royal College of Surgeons in Ireland in 1972, cannot recall any teaching about contraception in the RCSI or during his clinical training in the Coombe Hospital. Patricia Crowley, an obstetrician who graduated from UCD in 1975, received some theoretical lectures in the Pharmacology and Therapeutics course on the how the combined Pill worked and the risks of thromboembolism, but no specific teaching on the risks/effectiveness of different methods of contraception. Clinical lectures in Holles St. emphasised the risks associated with high parity births, and Professor de Valera lectured on the female menstrual cycle and how that could be applied to 'natural family planning'.[55]

---

[51] *IT*, 20 November 1971.   [52] *IT*, letter 13 November 1971.
[53] *IT*, letter 12 November 1971.
[54] *IMT*, 2 April 1971. Available at DDA/XX/129/15.
[55] Email communications from Drs Crowley and Curtain 2021.

The debate as to how far a doctor's conscience should determine clinical practice was very active at this time, with the liberalisation of abortion in the UK; increasing demands for contraception by single people; male and female sterilisation and the use of amniocentesis and other diagnostic tools to detect foetuses with serious medical conditions. Ian Donald, a leading British gynaecologist, and inventor of ultrasound, who emphasised that he was not a Catholic, dismissed the current training for doctors about how to address these issues, as 'inadequate'.[56]

3.2.1   The First Family Planning Clinic

In 1970, the journal *World Medicine*, published a cover story article titled 'A Land of Saints and Hypocrites'. It described the Republic of Ireland as having 'the most stringent anti-contraceptive laws in the world', although 'the law is flouted daily', with sales of 20,000 packets of the contraceptive pill every month; 'with a few brave exceptions, supporters of a change in the law are afraid to stand up and be counted'.

The result is unashamed hypocrisy: doctors refusing family planning advice in their hospital clinics but generally prescribing the Pill in their private practices; priests, depending on how their consciences are affected by the social tragedies in crowded city slums, making wildly different interpretations of the meaning of the Encyclical; and Catholic women "shopping" for contraceptives north of the border.

The article, by an unnamed medical doctor, reported that 'a surprisingly large [number] in Dublin, continued to prescribe the Pill with no scruples about their own, or their patients' moral propriety. ....Other medical practitioners – even at consultant level – are willing to prescribe the Pill, but not willing to stand up and be counted as "Pill men"'. The cover of *World Medicine* featured a photograph of a black door with the sign 'Fertility Guidance Centre: Hours 7–8 pm Tuesday and Friday' and a telephone number. Ireland's first family planning clinic, located outside a hospital opened on 25 February 1969, six months after the publication of *Humanae Vitae*, in Merrion Square, close to Government Buildings, and the private rooms of many of the city's consultant doctors. Consultant pathologist, Dr Robert Towers, who was secretary to the Fertility Guidance Centre (FGC), explained that they had chosen a prominent address to prevent comparisons being drawn between the clinic and 'a back-street abortionist'. It received start-up funding from the International Planned Parenthood Federation (IPPF) who paid for the renovation of the premises and trained the medical staff. Otherwise, it relied on donations and voluntary contributions from clients. The seven founding directors included gynaecologist

[56] *IT*, 1 February 1972.

Dr Michael Solomons; GPs Dr James Loughran and Dr David Nowlan – medical correspondent of *The Irish Times*, and pathologists, Robert Towers, and Dermot Hourihane, who were among the twenty-one Catholic doctors who had written a public letter dissenting from the papal encyclical, plus a nurse, Marie Mullarney, and a social worker. The founders followed the example of the Dublin maternity hospitals, in avoiding the term 'family planning'. The proposed clinic had emerged from a 'study group' established by Dr James Loughran a GP in the north Dublin village of Skerries, which included doctors, theologians, nurses, social workers and members of the public. There were a growing number of reports about the medical risks associated with the contraceptive pill for women with high blood pressure and other medical conditions. Doctors were becoming aware that the Pill could not meet all contraceptive needs, especially cases where there were strong medical contraindications against a future pregnancy. The clinic was established as a non-profitmaking registered company to protect the individuals involved. Clients were advised about a variety of contraceptive measures; they were measured for diaphragms but initially these were not supplied; women had to order them from England and face the consequences of possible seizure by customs. Intra-Uterine devices (IUDs) were fitted by a family planning clinic in Belfast. Most packages addressed to the clinic from overseas were opened by customs officers, and some of the literature that they ordered failed to arrive.[57]

The clinic opened without publicity, fearing that it would be picketed. It cannot be a coincidence that *Irish Times* medical correspondent, David Nowlan, a board member, does not appear to have written about the clinic for almost six months after it opened. In the early months, the clinic saw only four to six patients a week, in two weekly evening sessions, but attendance rose as its existence became known. Most clients heard about it through word of mouth. In the first nine months, 140 women attended. Women's magazines were the second largest source of information.

3.3   Pandora's Box: Contraception, *Humanae Vitae* and Irish Society

Given the changes that were underway in Ireland by the late 1960s – earlier marriages, so more relaxed attitudes towards young people's social (and sexual) lives; increasing numbers of media discussions over fertility control, the Pill, and the sexual revolution that was underway in many parts of the western world, there was no possibility that the status quo could be sustained with regard to contraception. Journalist Dorine Rohan noted that the delay in issuing a papal verdict on family planning had promoted debate.

---

[57] *World Medicine*, 10 February 1970.

Married couples have discussed it, practised it, rejected it, condemned it, welcomed it, questioned it, prayed about it, and avidly awaited the Pope's decision. The reactions in Ireland .... have been varied, but nobody is without strong and fiery feelings on the subject. As somebody remarked, 'it has become as popular a subject as the weather'... Anger, sadness, astonishment, relief have been felt and expressed in every sphere of the community. The fact that it has taken five years for the Pope to make his decision makes it all the more agonising for married couples to accept, and without doubt will be one of the major reasons why many who have been practising birth control will not return to the fold.[58]

Contraception featured frequently in personal advice columns in women's magazines, and in the women's pages of daily and Sunday newspapers. They published letters from women, and occasionally from men, revealing their personal dilemmas and difficulties in securing information and access to contraception. Journalism helped to bridge the information gap, in published articles, and private correspondence with readers. Rohan claimed that

Coitus interruptus is a fairly widely used form of contraception in Ireland...It is also a mortal sin. Due to its relative low rate of success the 'rhythm method', the only form of birth control permitted to date by the Roman Catholic church is not much relied upon, although a priest in the Catholic Marriage Advisory Centre told me that 'for those who persevere with it is quite successful' ... apart from anything else it is quite a complicated business, and many appear to abandon it in the early stages for various reasons.... many women told me that the priest told them to abstain altogether. They said that they never got round to finding out if it worked or not, as their husbands 'got fed up waiting'.... Even those who did persevere with it, whom I spoke to said they were nervous wrecks wondering whether they had 'got caught or not'.[59]

In June 1970, *Woman's Choice* presented a special report on the FGC clinic. It reported that they received letters daily about birth control.

The letters come from women who, if they are Catholics, have come to terms with the Papal Encyclical *Humanae Vitae*, or if they are non-Catholics want more than just instruction on the safe period or the rhythm method....Others simply want to call a halt to the baby a year pattern and some never want it to begin.....

Since this magazine was born, we have become increasingly aware of the enormity of Ireland's birth control problems. The implications are far-reaching. The heartaches the hardships and problems that follow go way beyond the difficulties of yet another mouth to feed.

It is more than a financial burden. Irish women feel the strain, so do housing facilities; schools, teachers; opportunities both social and occupational. And while the Government admits the special position of the Church in this country, it conveniently allows a certain amount of flexibility and law-bending to make birth control possible.

Is this enough? We know that many women are terrified to approach their doctors on the subject because they cannot anticipate the consequences and if he refuses, they may not have the courage to try again somewhere else.

[58] Rohan, *Marriage Irish style*, p. 92.   [59] Rohan, *Marriage Irish style*, pp. 78–9.

Woman's Choice described the Fertility Guidance Clinic as 'the only place in Ireland where a woman can have answers to *all* her questions'. By the summer of 1970, there was a six weeks' waiting list for appointments; a social worker described this as 'eternity for the woman who finally plucks up the courage to dial our number and wants to come the following day'. The clinic was running five sessions a week, including one morning and one afternoon session. They were also answering up to 150 queries a week.[60]

The men and women who founded FGC wanted to provide family planning services for working-class women, especially those with large families. That had also been the objective behind the Holles St Clinic, but as Meagher and MacDonald reported, they proved a difficult group to attract. Of the initial 140 patients attending FGC, only 11 held a card entitling them to free GP services, cards held by roughly one-third of the population. Dublin working-class couples were dissuaded from limiting their families, because the Dublin Corporation housing policy gave additional points for each child, as did other local authorities. Máirín de Burca, who was actively involved in the Dublin Housing Action Committee, noted that until 1971, families living in smaller Corporation maisonettes received information with their rent books informing them that they could transfer to a larger house after three years if they had four children, or after four years, regardless of family size – an obvious incentive to have more children in a short time.[61]

FGC was more successful at attracting younger middle-class women. A majority of clients opted for the Pill; just over one quarter was fitted with a diaphragm, others were referred elsewhere to be fitted with an IUD, and a small proportion opted for the rhythm method.[62] The large number who sought prescriptions for the Pill indicates an unwillingness to approach their family doctor or they may have been refused a prescription. *World Medicine* quoted the clinic secretary, Mrs Yvonne Pym: 'I am inundated with inquiries from country districts where women sometimes feel out on a limb. Often there is only one doctor in the place, and they are frightened to ask him for family planning advice because they know that he's anti-family planning. Some inquirers even ask for replies to be sent under plain cover to a friend's address'.[63] Her comments are confirmed by the women's magazines; readers frequently wrote seeking the name of a sympathetic doctor or confessor. By the autumn of 1970, arrangements were in place for FGC patients in the Cork area to have follow-up visits in that city. Attendance increased six-fold during 1970; the rise was particularly marked after the clinic was featured on a RTÉ *7 Days* programme. By the end of that year, a second clinic had opened in Mountjoy Square with a view to attracting more

---

[60] *Woman's Choice*, 9 June 1970.   [61] *Hibernia*, 4 September 1980.
[62] *IT*, 23 March 1970.   [63] *World Medicine*, 10 February 1970, 'Dublin's Lonely Outpost'.

working-class clients.[64] The outbreak of violence in Northern Ireland made women reluctant to travel to Belfast, and in 1971 the Dublin clinics began to fit and check IUDs.[65]

Many letters published in women's magazines asked: 'Please tell me if there is anyone, or anywhere, in Dublin where I can get advice on family planning'. This letter came from a married woman, who had given birth to three children in four years of married life; 'both he and I now agree that we must have a little time not only for ourselves but for the children we already have'. This woman was 'afraid of taking the contraceptive pill and feel that the rhythm method is too risky to start for a while. I would not mind trying it a year from now – but I want that year without any risks at all'. The standard response was to publish contact details for the FGC,[66] though the fact that initially sessions were only held in the evening limited access for those living outside Dublin. One woman who was referred by *Woman's Choice*, was aged thirty-seven, mother of five children, the youngest two years old. 'My husband and I still love each other very much, but we have tried not to sleep together since the last baby was born as we do not want any more children. We do not like having to live like this'. She was willing to use contraception. The magazine advised her to attend the FGC and suggested that her husband might accompany her.[67] Another woman living in a rural area, 'not too far from Dublin', was married for twelve years and the mother of six children. She and her husband did not want any more children but 'The doctor I go to says that abstinence is the best method of birth control and refuses to give me the Pill, although he says he will help my husband and I to understand the rhythm method. My friends have told me that this is not very effective and have told me to take the Pill, but I am afraid to do so as it is a sin. Is there anything I can do? I really do not want another baby for a long time'. She was advised to visit another doctor – one recommended by her friends, or FGC.[68]

FGC tried to circumvent Irish law by not charging for its services – clients were asked to make a donation and the clinic did not distribute, import, or manufacture contraceptive devices. But in March 1970, *Hibernia* reported that 'many small packets containing two small tubes of spermicidal jelly' had been seized in recent weeks by Customs and Excise staff, despite being addressed to the users in plain wrapping and supplied on a prescription issued by FGC. *Hibernia* claimed that this infringed the rights of citizens and suggested that the 1935 Act did not preclude possession of contraceptives for personal use.[69] Gerard Goldberg, a Cork lawyer, claimed that while the 1935

---

[64] *IT*, 26 March 1971.   [65] *Annual Report FGS* 1971; McCormick, p. 357.

[66] *Woman's Choice*, 9 December 1969.   [67] *Woman's Choice*, 13 January 1970.

[68] *Woman's Choice*, 24 February 1970; Laura Kelly, 'The contraceptive pill in Ireland, c. 1964–1979: activism, women, and doctor-patient relationships', *Medical History*, 64, no 2, 2020, pp. 195–218.

[69] *Hibernia*, 6–16 March 1970.

Act listed penalties for those who sold or distributed contraceptives, it made no reference to importing contraceptives for personal use; foreign visitors were permitted to bring contraceptives for personal use, if they declared them to customs.[70]

3.4   A Right to Family Planning?

Contraception became a political issue when the Irish Family Planning Rights Association (IFPRA) – an embryonic organisation, without officers or a constitution – convened a meeting in Dublin's Buswells Hotel, across the road from the Oireachtas in October 1970. Their goal was to establish the right to responsible family planning. The meeting passed a resolution demanding the repeal of the 1935 Criminal Law Amendment Act.[71] The FGC had adopted a policy of 'don't rock the boat'[72] but the seizure of contraceptive supplies posted to clients threatened that stance. The IFPRA meeting was chaired by Dr Jim Loughran. He pointed out that Ireland had voted in favour of a UN declaration two years earlier which stated that 'Couples have a basic human right to decide freely and responsibly on the number and spacing of their children and a right to adequate education and information in this respect'. Speakers outlined the current legal position; journalist and midwife, Monica McEnroy claimed that the campaign was designed to prevent abortion clinics opening in Ireland in future. The attendance included representatives of the Church of Ireland and Presbyterian congregations. Michael Melville, an airline pilot, who was an instigator of the meeting, wrote on two occasions to the Catholic Hierarchy inviting them to send a representative, or alternatively, provide a statement on the attitude of the Catholic church to the use of birth control by non-Catholic couples, but he didn't receive a response.[73]

Senator Mary Bourke (the future Mary Robinson), who represented Trinity College in the Seanad, gave notice at the meeting that she would introduce a private members bill, drafted by IFPRA, seeking the repeal of the existing laws.[74] IFPRA held its first annual general meeting in January 1971 – its aim to rescind the laws on contraception which 'denies the fundamental human right of access to information about, and the means of family planning'. The committee, chaired by economist and demographer, Brendan Walsh included several medical practitioners; Fianná Fail senator Neville Keary (a member of the Church of Ireland); barrister and future chief justice Ronan Keane, Michael Melville and Christopher Morris, who was active in campaigns against compulsory Irish and corporal punishment in schools. [There appear to have been

---

[70] *IT*, 9 April 1970.   [71] *IT*, 23 October 1970; Brendan Walsh Papers, IFPRA folder 1.
[72] *II*, 27 October 1970.   [73] DDA XV/30/36 Minutes of the Hierarchy, 12–14 October 1970.
[74] Ferriter, *Occasions of sin*, p. 410.

an overlap between campaigners for an end to corporal punishment, and advocates of family planning.][75] The *Irish Times* reported that the general feeling was that the Association 'should maintain an image of respectability and responsibility'. Proposals for action included a test case challenging the seizure of contraceptives for personal use by customs officials and publishing information that might contravene the 1929 Censorship of Publications Act. The primary goal was to change public opinion by writing letters to the media and targeting three key groups: 'the poor women of Ireland' 'the conservative doctors of Ireland' and politicians. Brendan Walsh told the meeting that the Association was 'advocating an idea the time for which had come'.[76]

In November 1970, the Medical Union of Ireland organised a meeting on the subject 'Family Planning – the Doctors' Dilemma', with a panel consisting of Dr Denis O'Callaghan, Senator Mary Bourke and three doctors.[77] This would appear to have been Dr O'Callaghan's most public forum since the publication of *Humanae Vitae*. He told the audience that it wasn't possible to give 'a simple and universally agreed oral answer' to the question; any decisions must be made by the parents (i.e. the couple); the doctors' role was to give advice. He presented a positive gloss on the encyclical, describing it as 'a milestone in the developing theology of marriage' and told his audience that 'the more balanced theological interpretation is found in many of the explanatory statements issued by Bishops Conferences in the Catholic world, [though presumably not in Ireland] and it is almost universal in present day moral theology…. This interpretation accepts the moral values inherent in the practice of the infertile period but admits the rightness of some method of birth control other than infertile period in difficult cases where the welfare of the family and the marriage relationship is at stake. In these situations, the individual circumstances are crucial, and it is not easy to give guidance in general term.' He concluded that 'it is pity that so much energy has been used in debating the details of birth control method, which is not of that great moral significance. Method or technique is important but will not in itself guarantee the quality of family life, and it is here that the moralist should be primarily interested'.[78]

The combination of the nascent IFPRA meeting and the Irish Medical Union debate would appear to have roused Dr McQuaid to action. He requested a copy of Dr O'Callaghan's speech and began working on a statement addressed to priests of the archdiocese. He was particularly exercised by 'the action of three Maynooth Professors' – McDonagh, O'Callaghan and Watson. His

[75] Mary E. Daly, 'The primary and natural educators? The role of parents in the education of their children in independent Ireland', in Maria Luddy and James Smith (eds), *Children, childhood and Irish Society 1500 to the present* (Four Courts, Dublin, 2014), pp. 65–81.

[76] *IT*, 27 January 1971.

[77] *II*, 17 November 1970.   [78] DDA Humanae Vitae Box 402.

confidant Dr Cremin expressed concerns about 'doctrinal confusion' among the Maynooth divinity students, which he saw as evidence of 'drift in the Faculty'.[79] In the first draft of his letter, the Archbishop reprimanded doctors, professors of theology and journalists for commenting on the topic and reiterated that the bishop was the sole authority on this matter:

If medical doctors undertake to issue declarations relating to moral law, they are gravely obliged to inform themselves accurately regarding objective moral law....The proper function of journalists is to report facts truthfully. If journalists venture into the area of the doctrine of the moral law, they too are gravely obliged to understand correctly, and to state accurately, the moral law....Professors of moral theology are gravely bound to instruct the students, only in accordance with the mandate of the authority that has appointed them. That mandate requires that they accept and teach only what the authority in the Church teaches....In a Diocese there is only one teaching authority – the Bishop....

In order to correct this confusion, he repeated 'the objective moral law concerning the regulation of birth: every action which, either in anticipation of the marriage act or in the accomplishment of that act, or in the development of the natural consequences of that act, proposes, either as an end or as a means, to make procreation impossible is gravely unlawful.'[80]

This uncompromising statement prompted concerns among senior staff in Archbishop's House. The Chancellor Dr Sheehy and Dr Curtin expressed strong reservations. Jerome Curtin described the text as 'objectively very good' before noting that 'statements of the Catholic Hierarchies can be cited rather against it'. He was concerned that 'good people, who comprise 99% of marriages, who have come to a working way of solving their difficulties, even by the mistaken judgement of using the pill, will be completely upset'.[81] Dr Sheehy shared Dr Curtin's fear that 'the statement as it stands would upset the "good people" to no positive advantage'. He cautioned that 'Certain sections of the text are, I feel, liable perhaps even likely to provoke controversy – and controversy of a kind which has nothing to do with the central point....for example "The proper function of journalists is to report facts truthfully" Not all journalists would agree that this adequately defines their role – I could see a sub-leader in the *Irish Times*, "Dr McQuaid on the function of journalists"'.

Journalists, always a touchy group, would not, I think be alone in these days in challenging a Bishop's definition as to the role and function of a particular profession. Doctors could easily do the same. So could Professors of Moral Theology. Whether they be right or wrong, a challenge of this kind could serve only to weaken the statement on the moral law regarding the regulation of births. This is a risk which I think Your Grace ought not to take.[82]

[79] DDA/XX/90/3, 21 November 1970.   [80] DDA Humanae Vitae Box, 387.
[81] DDA 382, 20 November 1970.   [82] DDA 399, 22 November 1970.

McQuaid's frustration at this advice is evident; 'To which I say: it would be easy to keep silence, if so many doctors, journalists and priests had not made <u>objectively</u> wrong statements. I state the objective law; I leave the subjective worries to the confessors. And my function is to state the law.'[83] A revised statement, which was read at all masses in the archdiocese omitted explicit references to journalists, doctors and theologians, referring only to statements in the media. It emphasised that the bishop was the only teaching authority in a diocese; although conscience was a judgement made by an individual, for that judgement to be right, it must be consistent with the moral law (presumably as laid down by the bishop). It closed by calling on all 'to accept the doctrine of the moral law that the Church unfailingly affirms'.[84]

The Archbishop displayed little sympathy for confessors, let alone conflicted married couples. At a meeting organised by the IMA, one doctor told the story of the mother of ten living children, who had had four spontaneous abortions. She had no knowledge of the safe period, and no interest in learning about it, because her alcoholic husband insisted on his conjugal rights at all times – her doctor had no hesitation in prescribing the Pill. Fr. Michael Browne, director of the Irish branch of the CMAC who was present, described this woman's treatment, by her husband as 'no more than repeated acts of rape'. He noted that 'women [who were taking the Pill] shop around for a confessor'.[85]

3.5   *Chains or Change*: The Irish Women's Liberation Movement

Brendan Walsh's belief that the time had come for reforming the laws on contraception appeared to have been confirmed in the spring of 1971. On 3 March, Senator Mary Robinson placed a private members bill on the order book of the Senate to repeal the relevant sections of the 1935 Criminal Law Amendment Act and the 1929 and 1945 Censorship of Publications Acts.[86] Three days later, Ireland's most-watched television programme, *The Late Late Show*, was the occasion for the launch of the Irish Women's Liberation Movement and the publication of a pamphlet, *Irishwomen: Chains or Change*, which ended by listing five reasons why Irishwomen would be better off living in sin than getting married.[87] The IWLM identified five priorities: justice for deserted wives, widows and unmarried mothers, equal pay, equality before the law, equal educational opportunity and contraception.[88] However Stopper points out that 'contraception was not even listed in the booklet's table of contents – it

---

[83] DDA 382, November 1970.   [84] *IP*, 30 November 1970.

[85] *Woman's Way*, 22 January 1971.

[86] Olivia O'Leary & Helen Burke, *Mary Robinson. The authorised biography* (Lir/Hodder & Stoughton, London, 1998), p. 58.

[87] *IT*, 'Women's Liberation', 9 March 1971.   [88] *Chains or Change*.

was hidden under the heading "Incidental Facts'" and it simply outlined the current position in Ireland. She concluded that the IWLM founders, who were mostly journalists, 'must have felt they had more freedom to express their views in the newspapers, through their journalism'.[89]

On 10 March, Senators Mary Robinson and John Horgan attempted without success to have their Criminal Law Amendment Bill, given a first reading, which would enable the Bill to be published. Resolutions urging repeal of the anti-contraception legislation were tabled at both the Fianna Fáil and Labour annual conferences.[90] Labour passed the resolution by an overwhelming majority. Conor Cruise O'Brien presented the case for repeal in terms of sectarianism and the rights of the individual conscience. But dissenting voices referred to the 'rotten society' that would inevitably follow a relaxation of the laws – venereal disease, free love, and wife swapping.[91] Several Fianná Fail Cumainn tabled counter-resolutions urging no change in the law[92] – an indication of a developing battle. In the event, that 1971 Ard Fheis ended early in chaos, because of the fallout from the previous year's Arms Crisis (where Lynch sacked two influential members of Cabinet), and the topic was not debated, though it appears that Lynch had planned to give a commitment to amend the laws and the Constitution, in order to make them more amenable to Ulster Protestants.[93]

3.6   Contraception and Public Morality: A New Message from the Catholic Hierarchy

The threat that the Oireachtas might repeal the existing laws, or that a successful challenge might be brought in the courts, prompted the Catholic Hierarchy to action. The bishops, at their spring meeting in Maynooth issued a statement expressing their sympathies with public disquiet 'regarding the pressures being exerted on public opinion repealing the laws on divorce, contraception and abortion'. They warned that these questions 'go far beyond purely private morality or private religious belief. Civil law on these matters should respect the wishes of the people who elected the legislators and the bishops confidently hope that the legislators themselves will respect this important principle'.[94] The Dublin Synod of the Presbyterian Church called on the government to amend the laws in relation to the import and sale of contraceptives, and the Church of Ireland Archbishop of Dublin Dr Buchanan issued a statement to the effect that contraception was a matter for private conscience not state control. He quoted

---

[89] Stopper, *Mondays at Gaj's*, pp. 76–7.
[90] *IT*, February 16, 1971.   [91] *Irish Times*, 1 March 1971.
[92] UCD Archives (UCDA) P 176/350 FF papers national executive 26/4/1971; *Irish Press*, 20 February 1971.
[93] *Sunday Independent*, 14 March 1971.   [94] *The Furrow*, April 1971, pp. 244–5.

the statement by the Lambeth Conference – the supreme body of the Anglican Church – on responsible parenthood.[95] A long article by the *Irish Times* medical correspondent Dr David Nowlan, titled 'How ten Catholic countries deal with contraception' revealed a wide range of legal and administrative arrangements; some countries provided family planning programmes, others were totally opposed to them. In Italy, although the law prohibited contraception, the Pill and condoms were widely available – the Pill as a 'cycle regulator', the condom as a means of preventing the spread of venereal disease.[96] This article indicated that Ireland was an outlier among Catholic countries.

Dr McQuaid made a personal contribution to this debate in a pastoral letter, which was read at masses throughout the archdiocese on 28 March 1971 (Sunday). The IWLM staged a walkout in several churches as a protest;[97] many men and women who were not members of the IWLM also walked out. He presented his pastoral as an attempt to address the 'confusion' which was being spread by 'the frequent and inaccurate use of terms such as *planne*d or *responsible* parenthood'. He reiterated that 'any [such] contraceptive act is always wrong in itself', so it was impossible to speak of a right to contraception – a comment that appears to be a direct challenge to the IFPRA. The new element in this message was the reference to public morality – this was targeted at politicians and the emerging debate over the repeal of the current laws. He alleged that access to contraceptives would threaten moral standards, especially among the young. Politicians should be aware of the social consequences arising from any alteration in the laws. He dismissed the argument that the law should be changed in order to promote a united Ireland, 'It would indeed be a foul basis on which to attempt to construct the unity of our people'.[98]

Dr McQuaid received many letters in response to this pastoral – significantly more than after the publication of *Humanae Vitae*, or his statement in November 1970, which would appear to indicate that the Irish debate had developed more slowly than elsewhere. The majority were supportive, even enthusiastic about the pastoral letter. The Archbishop had tapped into a cohort of men and women who were confused and outraged by changing sexual morality. A married man from a middle-class suburb expressed his admiration:

my wife and I, in common with tens of thousands in this Diocese and throughout the country, thank God for one archbishop willing to express with such authority, certitude, clarity and courage the principles of which our people need to be reassured.

In today's terrifying situation of daily pressures, some malicious and some simply irresponsible, to replace Christian standards and traditions by the illusions of a progressive and emancipated humanism, God has been good to us in guiding Your Grace's hand.[99]

---

[95] *Irish Times*, 22 March 1971.   [96] *IT*, 25 March 1971.
[97] Nuala Fennell, *Political woman: a memoir* (Currach Press, Dublin, 2009), p. 61.
[98] *Irish Times,* 29 March 1971.   [99] DDA/XX/82/3.

One woman described his letter as 'a breath of fresh air'[100] A public health nurse expressed gratitude that 'we in Ireland still have men with your courage', adding 'I regret I am not a married woman'. She suggested holding a mass meeting on Mother's Day to protest against the introduction of legislation repugnant to our Catholic religion.[101] A male Dublin solicitor reported said that he had 'felt an overwhelming sense of pride…. One could hear a pin drop'.[102] The father of a young family in Kilkenny wrote that

I don't want to see them grown up [sic] in the kind of Ireland these people have in mind. Make no mistake about it, in this matter you have the backing of the overwhelming majority of Irish families who have their faith, their children, and their country, and who don't want to see everything they cherish sold out shamelessly by these arrogant agitators who claim to speak for them as a cloak for their own ends.[103]

The father of a young family with a north Dublin address claimed that most of the young men in his office agreed with the pastoral; 'Catholics, both legislators and non-legislators can no longer claim to be in doubt as to what to do'.[104] A woman who wrote on behalf of herself and her husband, asserted that 'This is no time for compromise or pacification, regarded rightly by the people as a sign of weakness'[105] One woman, who was expecting her first child, despite having been told by doctors that she would be unable to have a baby, wrote that

The people who advocate artificial birth control seem to do so from a very selfish motive.…The ordinary housewives and mothers of this country have been confused by the comments and controversy that surround this subject. A loving and gentle husband who regards the marriage act as a mutual act of love and not just something for his own personal gratification is the best 'contraceptive' any woman could have.

McQuaid pencilled – 'what a charming letter.'[106]

One couple, who wrote on at least two occasions, stated that

We were beginning to despair and there seemed no answer to the mounting wave of propaganda. But Sunday was such a wonderful day…. How happy we were and how urgently we sought out the few who we know would feel the same as we did. ….I cannot help feeling that there must be some very strong influence behind all this – some connection perhaps with our entry into the EEC – some condition of membership which is being kept from us.[107]

A woman who said 'Good for you' gave a long account of her family history. She had given birth to twelve boys and two girls and lost five other babies – three in one year; one child was born with a club foot; the baby was epileptic. Her last child, delivered by caesarean section, was born when she was almost

[100] DDA/XX/82/5.   [101] DDA/XX/82/8.   [102] DDA/XX/82/12.   [103] DDA/XX/82/19.
[104] DDA/XX/82/20.   [105] DDA/XX/82/25.   [106] DDA/XX/82/26.   [107] DDA/XX/82/27.

forty-six years old.[108] A woman, 'just one of the many ordinary women of Ireland who is appalled at the prospect of legalized contraception in Ireland... just a grandmother', wondered how to organise against the spread of contraception; she suggested something modelled on 'the campaign of Prayer for the silent Church'.[109] A parent of two young teachers reported that they 'constantly complain about the lack of direction from the Bishops on major issues. I wish you could have seen the look of happiness on their faces'.[110] A man, with an address in an affluent Dublin neighbourhood, who described himself as a practising Catholic, claimed that he was

disturbed by the failure of the Catholic Hierarchy, with the exception of yourself, to take up the issue of the proposed change in the laws relating to contraception. A small group of dissident and immoral persons, which unfortunately appears to include some priests, is trying with the aid of the news media that is totally sensational and biased (sick) to give the impression that this change in the law is desirable.[111]

A woman who was expecting her sixth child phoned Archbishop's House: she was 100 per cent in agreement with the pastoral letter. 'If contraceptives are freely available, we will have the permissive society in no time. Promiscuity is also inevitable'. She had phoned because she believed that he 'would only hear from the protesters'.[112] One nun who was attached to a convent secondary school told him that

Due to the public statements of some priests which seem to contradict the traditional teaching of the Church, especially in the matter of artificial contraception, an alarming situation is developing.

Parents and others with whom I am in contact (some my own past pupils) are very, very perturbed at these developments. The heartrending complaints I get from time to time would draw a tear from a stone.

Both parents and teachers are appalled at the recent statements of Father Gerard Watson at a meeting of the Irish Family Planning Rights Association. They find themselves placed in a very embarrassing position by the questioning of their children and pupils, on his statements.

She had appealed to Dr Newman, the President of Maynooth College, 'to devise some means of getting priests and theologians to keep their theological speculations for private debates and discussions. The introduction of theological speculations to the public by the various communications media is very confusing and damaging to the Faith'. She wondered whether the Archbishop would appeal to the Pope to give an 'ex cathedra' ruling on contraception.[113] That was probably a step too far even for Dr McQuaid.

Some correspondents denounced stories published in the *Irish Times* by John Horgan, a journalist and senator who was co-sponsor of the bill to repeal the

---

[108] DDA/XX/82/28.   [109] DDA/XX/82/34.   [110] DDA/XX/82/36.
[111] DDA/XX/89/15.   [112] DDA/XX/90/1.   [113] DDA/XX/94/4 1–2.

law on contraception. One reported that women teachers in Cabra (a convent school), 'were furious at the Kenny woman [journalist Mary Kenny]' and others. RTÉ's Saturday night *Late Late Show* was also denounced. A recurrent theme was the wish for guidance and authority: what to think and what to do. This is summarised in an admiring letter from Maynooth College: 'in this time when confusion is being used as an instrument of policy, what so many Catholics hunger after is a clear, reasoned, unequivocal statement of doctrine'.[114] The letters suggest that the deference to clerical authority identified by Bruce Biever remained strong, though the number of dissenters had increased.

3.7   Catholicism and Contraception: The Dilemma for Many Irish Couples

Critics adopted quite a different tone. A young woman, writing from the middle-class suburb of Foxrock, who was soon to be married, asked

Why Father is the Dublin pastoral so negative, offering nothing for daily life....For the past year especially in local churches we never hear any sermon that we can carry away with us. ....why does His Grace frequently speak of contraception for example? .... Well I do think in conscience and using God-given reason that planned children are the only children that should be brought into the world.[115]

A young couple (known to me) told the Archbishop that, 'in all conscience we must say to you that we cannot support the views you hold on this subject and we request you not to be guilty of the worst form of divorce i.e. divorce from your people'.[116] A woman wrote of her

sense of despair....I do not belong to any group or organisation, nor have I ever written to anyone ....I have the gravest fears that should the Catholic church in Dublin continue on this course it will soon cease to have any meaning for me, for my children and for a large number of my friends.

A mother of three from south Dublin, wrote to protest

most strongly....I object to your attempt to use the criminal law of this state to enforce the opinions of one church on all of the community. I reject the argument that condemns contraception and allows the use of the safe period, the intention of which is to avoid conception. I object to the emotional tone of the letter and to its being read out before a mass congregation which included children of a sensitive age. I don't know what my nine- year old daughter made of references to "animal acts".

Another young married woman failed to see how reforming the laws on contraception would remain

---

[114] DDA/XX/83.   [115] DDA/XX/82/106.
[116] DDA/XX/89–9-. They went on to become parents of five children.

"A curse upon our country".... The sexual act between married couples should be spontaneous, thus resulting in a happy union. ....To say that "planned" or "responsible parenthood", is an "insult to the Catholic faith", and "gravely damaging to morality" is too much for any intelligent person to accept. To make reference to the "sexual conduct of other countries" implies that the Catholics in other parts of the world, have been led astray by laws which permit contraception, and we know this to be untrue. How can the Church in this country really condemn the woman who tries to elevate herself to a dignified level of womanhood. I think therefore the time has come when both Church and State must allow the women of Ireland to decide for themselves on this very personal issue.

One of the few anonymous letters came from a woman who had to spend six months of every pregnancy in bed.

The rhythm method does not work for me and speaking as a trained nurse I assure you we made no mistakes. We tried total abstinence, but my husband does not agree with this and says this is not a marriage.

After a major operation two years ago, her doctors instructed her that she should not have any more children; she was still attending hospital following that operation. She described the 'mental and spiritual anguish of a Catholic mother placed in this predicament'; she could not use oral contraception because of medical contraindications:

but for the fact that Cardinal Heenan spoke at that time and said keep going to the sacraments I don't know what I would have done ...... [he] spoke with compassion and some glimmer of hope to people like me placed in such dilemmas......I struggled and prayed my way through each day until yesterday....Your pastoral letter yesterday had an appalling effect on my husband he told me after Mass that he was sorry but that he shall not attend Mass anymore and had come to this decision having listened to your pastoral letter!!

I appreciate your point of view, but could you not have some compassion or appreciate that there may be some exceptions to the rule!!.... How am I going to bring up my five children good Catholics when the basic example of a good father attending his religion is now gone?....in total despair I now need your prayers very badly indeed.... Please do not turn any more people away from the church with statements that have no love of Christ in them.[117]

The Catholic church was fighting on several fronts: trying to control dissent among laity and clergy and confronting the threat that legislation might be introduced to remove the prohibition on contraception and perhaps the constitutional ban on divorce. The emerging debate over minority rights in light of the crisis in Northern Ireland was an additional complication. A minority of correspondents mentioned legislation. One, a supporter of McQuaid's pastoral, addressed the rights of religious minorities:

If Protestants feel they have a right to buy contraceptives and that the State should grant them this right then allow them this right to be exercised, not publicly through clinics,

---

[117] DDA/XX 89/90.

hospitals and chemists but through their own Church bodies, Church Halls or whatever arrangements they wish for themselves exclusively.[118]

A married couple, well known in Dublin's theatre circles, who may not have been Catholics told him that

We recognise your position as pastor but feel this is a matter of secular government which attempts to redress the limitations of the civil liberties of a minority of this country. We find offensive your use of the pulpits of the diocese for furthering your view which is not shared by a significant number of your community.[119]

A Protestant man with an address in Sligo was

absolutely outraged by your pastoral letter, and object in the strongest possible terms to your remarks which I consider narrow bigoted unchristian and "bent".... I object to your obvious intention of trying to interfere with the process of civil law and most of all I object to having your doctrine which I neither support or believe rammed down my throat by law especially after the public utterances by my own archbishop.[120]

This 1971 McQuaid letter and the statement issued by the Hierarchy have a significance that goes well beyond the question of contraception. A scholar who examined the political influence of the churches on government policy in several countries – including Ireland – suggested that 'churches ironically gain their greatest political advantage when they appear to be above petty politics – exerting their influence in secret meetings and the back rooms of parliament rather than through public pressure or partisanship. A church's ability to enter these quiet corridors of power depends on its historical record of defending the nation – and thus gaining moral authority within society and among politicians'.[121] Writing about Ireland, she stated that 'Much of the church's direct influence relied on institutional access, and it was both preemptive and hidden'; for decades, the church had 'extraordinary political and cultural influence, and could, in many policy areas, effectively veto policy initiatives. Furthermore, these vetoes were commonly covert and did not impinge on public awareness'.[122] These statements were arguably the most overtly political pastorals since the 1922 statement by the Hierarchy denouncing the republican side in the Irish civil war or the 1931 'red scare' pastoral. This recourse to an uncompromising public statement; the warning to legislators, suggests a loss of confidence by the Hierarchy in their capacity to achieve moral authority through more covert means. If the Archbishop was in contact with the government with respect to proposed changes to the 1937 Constitution or contraception, they were not recorded in his papers or in government files. The position

---

[118] DDA/XX/82/31.   [119] DDA/XX/89/9.   [120] DDA/XX/89/14.

[121] Anna Grzymala-Busse, *Nations under God. How Churches use moral authority to influence policy* (Princeton University Press, Princeton, 2015), p. 2.

[122] Grzymala-Busse, *Nations under God*, p. 73.

of the Catholic church as a voice of the Irish nation was coming into question because the definition of the nation was being questioned because of the violence in Northern Ireland – both in terms of geographical boundaries and its religious complexion. The Irish Catholic church was also facing an unprecedented level of dissent from the laity, and some clergy. While the threat in 1922 to excommunicate those fighting on the anti-Treaty side in the civil war alienated some republicans from the Church, the overwhelming majority of the anti-Treaty side did not identify as an anti-clerical party or movement, indeed the contrary. That was not the case with respect to contraception.

The letters quoted above were private. A parallel debate in the media revealed growing unease with church teaching and a search for ways to remain a practising Catholic, while using a reliable form of contraception. One woman, with an address in Cork, described how 'the safe period or nursing my children not being safe for me and with five children I plucked up courage and after making my confession, decided to ask the priest's advice…I explained my problems, a two-room flat, ever-present fear of eviction, my husband in casual employment'. The priest told her 'to go home and get my husband to agree that in no circumstances would we do anything to control our family….I approached another priest who was kind but who gave me the usual rigmarole about a large family being lucky'.[123] Another woman began 'I don't know how to start this letter to you'. She had been married for nineteen years and was the mother of two living children but had experienced two stillbirths. The couple didn't want any more children. Her husband was unwell following major surgery, and he was 'being treated for his nerves', only working half the year. She was also 'being treated for my nerves, but I would say it was losing the babies that made my nerves as they are; I worry a lot over the two that I have. I always fear that something might happen to them'. Her husband was 'very considerate and I think it would kill me if I was to have another baby. I just couldn't cope with it. We didn't have intercourse since the last baby, and she is four now. It is hard to keep on saying no all the time and it is not every man that would put up with it. I get desperate at times so could you please help me. I am nearly 39 now and my periods are very irregular but is there any safe time I could be sure of. Please help me it was my husband who asked me to write to you'.[124]

A number of letters highlighted the dilemma that many women faced in confession. A young woman about to marry but not yet in a position to start a family because the couple was saving to buy a house wrote that 'for the first time in my life I have been refused absolution in confessions. I told the priest that I had started to take the Pill (to see if it agreed with me) and that I intended using it for the first 12 months of my marriage. After being refused

[123] *Woman's Way*, 18 June 1971.   [124] *Woman's Choice*, 26 January 1971.

absolution, I felt condemned and rejected. I was told that I should either follow the rules of the Catholic Church or go my own way'. The editor of the
problem page reassured her that they had consulted a priest and 'not many
would have refused you absolution in these grounds'; she was given the name
and address of a sympathetic confessor.[125] Another wrote that following the
birth of her child, she visited the FGC where she was given a prescription for
the Pill.

My problem began when I went to Confession and told the priest…and explained my
reasons and my circumstances. He advised me to go off the Pill and work the safe
period etc. and said it was against the Pope's teaching for him to tell me it was o.k. to
go ahead and continue taking it. I left the Confessional feeling thoroughly mixed up
and felt I just couldn't go to Holy Communion although he gave me absolution as I still
felt I wasn't doing any great wrong taking the Pill. Since then, I have drifted from my
religion, often not even going to Mass.[126]

A mother of ten children, the youngest two weeks old, wanted to avoid another
baby: 'I'm afraid my doctor here is not so understanding. I have spoken to him
about it, but he does not seem to mind. Before my last baby was born, I had
trouble with my nerves and I do not want to go through that again.'

A husband wrote that

Our local curate is very much against birth control by use of the Pill, but I am really
worried about my wife and don't really know where to get help. She has had four babies
in four years; one of them has died on us which has upset us both terribly….since the
baby's birth and death we have not had intercourse and I miss it and I believe it is bad
for her too because we were used to a very good sex-life. Our second and third children
were conceived while were practising the rhythm and temperature methods and the last
was the result of coitus interruptus. Now I am determined to use proper contraceptives,
either the Pill or anything else the doctor recommends…my wife is anxious going to
confession.[127]

3.8   The Doctors

Woman's Choice concluded that maternity hospitals 'have no wish to get
involved. Patients with many children are allowed home with inadequate
information on even the "safe period"'.[128] Many women were unwilling to
ask their doctor for a prescription for the Pill, fearing refusal. One woman
explained that her family doctor had known her since she was a child, and she
was uncomfortable discussing contraception with him.[129] Some gynaecologists who advised patients to delay a subsequent pregnancy, gave them no

---

[125] *Woman's Choice*, 10 August 1971.   [126] *Woman's Choice*, vol 4, no 3, October 1971.
[127] *Woman's Choice*, 4.47 and 4.51, 1972.   [128] *Woman's Choice*, 13 July 1971.
[129] *Woman's Choice*, 6 July 1971.

advice as to how to achieve this. One mother of three children, all born by caesarean section – the oldest three years old – 'desperately want[ed] to avoid becoming pregnant for at least another three years. I was told after the first that I should space my family, but the doctor did nothing to help me plan and I had no way of getting any other help, although a neighbour told me about the rhythm method, and I tried this after the second baby. Now I won't sleep with my husband until we have done something about this'[130] There were helpful and sympathetic doctors; *Woman's Choice* supplied their names by post; one correspondent wrote that her doctor had promised to help them get contraceptive supplies.[131]

The medical profession remained divided. Little more than a week after McQuaid's pastoral, the *Irish Medical Times* reported the findings of a survey showing that of the 1,198 of an estimated 2,700 doctors registered in Ireland who had responded, 73 per cent were in favour of legalising contraceptives, and almost two-thirds of those in favour (62.7 per cent) were opposed to making them available only on prescription. Most doctors wanted access restricted to family planning clinics, pharmacies and medical suppliers. Those who were opposed to making contraception available made it clear that their opposition reflected Catholic Church teaching.[132] The *IMT* also published a letter from a doctor in Cork, who reported 'several instances of really deserving cases who failed to find a doctor who would prescribe the contraceptive pill, such as two women recently who had 3 and 4 still born infants due to haemolytic disease caused by rhesus incompatibility; and another case, not at all uncommon in this city, of a 46 year old woman expecting her 23rd baby and she happened to be suffering from pulmonary TB'. He asked, 'What advice can be offered to patients, unsuited for the safe period or the Pill'?[133]

Woman's Choice published a questionnaire about contraception, which attracted over 600 responses. Asked whether a change in the current law would be 'a curse on the country', 20 per cent said yes, 78 per cent said no and 2 per cent were undecided. Only 27 per cent were in favour of contraceptives being freely available in pharmacies; most feared that uncontrolled access, not on prescription 'would have disastrous effects on younger single people'. 64 per cent of respondents were in favour of making contraceptives available only on prescription. Those most in favour of change were women with one or more children. 27 per cent of respondents were using a contraceptive device.[134]

---

[130] *Woman's Choice*, 7 December 1971.
[131] *Woman's Choice*, 4 No 15, either 21 or 28 December 1971.
[132] *II*, 8 April 1971; *IT*, 9 April 1971.
[133] *Irish Medical Times*, 2 April 1971 at DDA/XX/129/15.
[134] *Woman's Choice*, 20 April 1971 and 6 July 1971.

3.9   Clerical Dissent

The Catholic clergy had remained remarkably quiescent in the immediate
aftermath of the publication of *Humanae Vitae*, but some were showing signs
of dissent. Denis O'Callaghan expressed concern that doctors were being
forced to prescribe the contraceptive pill for some women, who might have
health conditions giving rise to medical risks, because it was the only reliable means of contraception available.[135] Two Maynooth professors, Fr Gerry
Watson and Fr Enda McDonagh, addressed public meetings organised by the
IFPRA. Fr Watson attracted front page headlines in the *Irish independent*, the
daily newspaper with the largest sales, following a speech in Dun Laoghaire,
where he stated that what was right for Catholics in the rest of the world could
not be wrong for Catholics in Ireland. Those who wanted the ban on contraceptives removed were 'not Godless people, nor were they a minority or a pressure group'.[136] In the same week, sixteen 'prominent priests' from Northern
Ireland and the Republic, members of the recently established Association of
Irish Priests expressed regrets that so many statements 'have been couched, in
the main, in extreme terms'. They emphasised that opinion varied throughout
the church. Most signatories were members of religious orders; they included
Fergal O' Connor, OP a lecturer at UCD, his fellow-Dominican theologian
Austin Flannery, Michael Sweetman, SJ, Cathal O'Flanagan, a member of the
Franciscan Order, Des Wilson a curate in Belfast who became well known for
his work during the Northern Ireland conflict, and members of the Maynooth
Mission to China, and the Passionist and Marist Fathers. Three signatories
were attached to the Dublin archdiocese. Their statement noted that while
uncontrolled access to contraception would give rise to social and moral problems, 'there are other evils already with us which should also be the concern
of Christian moralists', such as bad housing, land speculation and lack of educational opportunities.[137]

When *Humanae Vitae* was published an editorial in the *Irish Press* suggested that the encyclical would 'stimulate rather than stifle the debate'.[138] By
1971, a public debate on family planning was underway, and the status quo
was being challenged, as was church teaching. Conservative Catholics were
disturbed by fears of moral disruption and the debate about the primacy of
personal conscience. They craved the dogmatic certainties of Dr McQuaid's
1971 Lenten pastoral, whereas many couples were distressed by their efforts
to control family size while observing church teaching, and by the apparent
lack of humanity in McQuaid's pastoral. The FGC principle of 'don't rock
the boat' was being challenged by proposals for a private members bill; by

[135] *Irish Press*, 17 March 1971.   [136] *II*, 28 April 1971.   [137] *II*, 26 April 1971.
[138] *IP*, 30 July 1968.

the IWLM, and growing breaches of the 1935 Act, and the crisis in Northern Ireland prompted a debate about minority rights and laws that reflected the views of one religious community.

3.10   Minority Rights and the Northern Ireland Crisis

The greatest pressure for change came from north of the border. The Northern Ireland protests introduced the language of civil rights into Irish public life: specifically, the argument that Irish Protestants should have legal rights that were compatible with the teaching of their church. References to discrimination against Northern Catholics prompted reflections on possible discrimination against Protestants in the Republic. In September 1969, shortly after the outbreak of violence in Northern Ireland, Canon E.P.M. Elliott, who was based in Belfast, wrote an article in the *Church of Ireland Gazette*, titled 'Protestant Fears'. He quoted the Cameron Report into the disturbances in Northern Ireland – 'A sense of continuing injustice and grievance among large sections of the Catholic population of Northern Ireland'[139] – before listing the grievances of Protestants in the Republic: the 'special place' accorded to the Roman Catholic church in the 1937 Constitution, mixed marriages, divorce, and restrictions on birth control. He concluded that, 'it seems reasonable to suggest that the restrictions in the Republic are "discrimination on the grounds of religious profession, belief or status"'.[140] An editorial in the *Irish Press* on 30 November 1970, coinciding with Dr McQuaid's statement on contraception, noted that contraception 'is not merely a matter of theological responsibility'; it was 'bound up with the other matters which those who support the continuing Partition of this country point to as an interference with liberty of conscience and thus becomes a matter of political as well as theological concern'.[141] At a meeting organised by the IFPRA in 1971, which attracted a capacity crowd of 200, Conor Cruise O' Brien, urged the government to refute the allegation that 'Home Rule is Rome Rule'.[142]

An editorial in the *Church of Ireland Gazette* following the publication of *Humanae Vitae* had expressed 'sadness and apprehension'; it suggested that the encyclical 'is bound to be a stumbling block' for couples in a religiously mixed marriage,[143] but it expressed no opinion on the legal aspects. The Church of Ireland and the Presbyterian Congregation were represented at the first IFPRA meeting in January 1971. In March, the Dublin Synod of the Presbyterian

---

[139] *Disturbances in Northern Ireland. Report of the Commission appointed by the Governor of Northern Ireland.* Published in Belfast, 1 September 1971.
[140] Protestant Fears part 2. The practical issues, *Church of Ireland Gazette*, 19 September 1969.
[141] *IP*, 30 November 1970.   [142] *IT*, 31 March 1971.
[143] *Church of Ireland Gazette*, 9 August 1968.

Church called on the government to amend the laws relating to the import and sale of contraceptives and the Church of Ireland Archbishop of Dublin Dr Buchanan issued a statement to the effect that contraception was a matter for private conscience not state control, quoting the 1968 Lambeth Conference – on responsible parenthood.[144] He emphasised that 'Contraception is not the same as abortion or divorce. Each is a distinct issue. ….My conviction is that a positive approach to all these personal moral issues is better than all the prohibitions in the world'.[145] In April, an editorial in the *Church of Ireland Gazette* pointed out that members of the Church were unable 'without resort to subterfuge or criminal practice, to conduct their private lives in marriage along lines that are sanctioned by their Church'.[146] When a motion on contraception was debated at the General Synod in May, several speakers went to considerable effort to refute claims that a more liberal contraceptive regime would inevitably mean greater sexual promiscuity (the argument advanced by the Catholic Hierarchy in spring 1971).[147] The General Synod unanimously adopted a motion welcoming efforts to change the law on contraception. The Irish Council of the Mothers' Union issued a statement

While we welcome the benefits of science in other aspects of life, including the help given to childless couples, so we welcome the possibility of relieving women of the fear and dread of bringing children into the world for whom they feel they cannot provide.

While we realise the Government's responsibility in protecting our young people from the dangers involved in the open sale of contraceptives we would however, press the Minister to alter the present laws so that all forms ….should be legally available, with proper safeguards, to those married couples whose conscience permits their use.[148]

The rights of Irish Protestants proved more persuasive to politicians than the needs of Irish couples. In the early 1970s, there was, what in hindsight appears to have been a highly unreal flurry of speculation that major changes in the constitutional relationship between the two Irelands were imminent. This prompted much heart-searching over unionist attitudes towards an independent Ireland. It led to a debate about Article 44 in the 1937 Constitution, which referred to the 'special position' of the Roman Catholic Church; the constitutional ban on divorce, and legislation prohibiting contraception. In December 1969, Taoiseach Jack Lynch gave a long interview on the RTÉ Current Affairs Programme, *Seven Days*, where he spoke about divorce and contraception in the context of Northern Ireland. He stated that 'The use of contraceptives is a matter of conscience.[149] But Lynch failed to confront the fact that the law restricted the rights of women and men to exercise their conscience on this

---

[144] *Irish Times*, 22 March 1971.   [145] *Church of Ireland Gazette*, 26 March 1971.
[146] *Church of Ireland Gazette*, April 1971.
[147] *Church of Ireland Gazette*, 21 May 1971 and *IT*.   [148] *IT*, 1 June 1971.
[149] *IT*, 29 December 1969.

matter. There is no evidence that Lynch's government had any intention of amending the law at this time, rather the contrary. He ensured that all questions were referred to the Minister for Justice Micheál Ó Moráin. When Garret FitzGerald, now a TD asked whether the government planned to amend the laws, Lynch gave a flat 'no', telling the Dáil that he had been misrepresented: his statement did not mean that it was possible to import contraceptives for personal use.[150] A note prepared for the Minister for Justice, in preparation for a response to this question, advised him that

Whatever is said in supplementaries, it is suggested that it would be better to avoid taking the position that there is not a genuine difficulty. There does seem to be a genuine difficulty – it does not arise from the Taoiseach's statement but from the facts of the situation- namely that, since it is impossible legally to obtain contraceptives (i.e. either to buy them or to import them), those whose religion or conscience permits them are being deprived of the opportunity (and therefore, on the practical level, of the right) to do what their religion or conscience allows.[151]

There is no indication that the government was prepared to address this 'genuine difficulty', and they appear to have contemplated restricting divorce to those whose religion permitted it, as opposed to extending it to all citizens as a right.[152]

When Senator Mary Robinson made a second attempt in 1971 to introduce a private members bill to repeal the laws prohibiting information and access to contraception, she presented the case for legislation in terms of human rights.[153] John Horgan, a co-sponsor, argued that the bill should be taken on grounds of 'legal urgency, social urgency and political and constitutional urgency'. Many people were breaking the law by importing contraceptives for personal use 'because it [the law] interferes with what they consider to be their human rights'.[154] Mary Robinson highlighted 'the many statements made by the Taoiseach and Dr Patrick Hillery [Minister for External Affairs] about the necessity to create a pluralist society and not to discriminate on the basis of religion'. She referred to 'religious and moral partition' – the need to change attitudes, if 'we are serious about the North'; offering couples 'the possibility in their own privacy of following their consciences in relation to family planning'.[155] When Labour TD Noel Browne and his colleague Dr John O'Connell sponsored another private members' bill in 1972, they spoke about the rights of a minority in a pluralist society – the religious minority and Catholics who believed that they had the right to use contraception – arguing that by publishing the private members' bill the government could demonstrate their

---

[150] Dail Debates, 21 April 1970.   [151] NAI DT 2003/16/34 Criminal Law Amendment Act.
[152] Daly, *Sixties Ireland*, p. 335.   [153] Daly, *Sixties Ireland*, p. 185.
[154] Seanad Debates 31 March 1971, col 1354.   [155] SD, 7 July 1971, columns 966–7.

commitment to a '32-county non-sectarian State'. In his 1972 book, *Towards a New Ireland*, which was written in response to the crisis in Northern Ireland, Garret FitzGerald stated that 'The Republic's laws on censorship and contraception are highly contentious issues with Northern Protestant opinion... It seems sensible, therefore to initiate changes in the Republic... as part of a programme designed to show Northern Protestant opinion that the will to reunification on an acceptable basis is genuine'.[156]

3.11   Legislate or Wait: 1971–1973

By the spring of 1971, it was widely rumoured that the government was in the process of drafting legislation on contraception. This was specifically stated by Dr Robert Towers, a founding member of FGC, in an article in the *Irish Medical Times*.[157] During his St Patrick's Day visit to the USA, Jack Lynch hinted that changes on divorce and contraception were being contemplated in order to assist Irish reunification, though when he was pressed by journalists who met him at Dublin Airport on his return, Lynch, ever evasive in his views – not just on contraception – told reporters that no draft legislation was being prepared, though the matter would be studied closely.[158] By the time that McQuaid's Lenten pastoral appeared, the Fianna Fáil parliamentary party and the government were committed to discussing contraception, and there were further reports that a government bill was in preparation.[159] (This may have prompted McQuaid to issue his pastoral letter.) *Irish Press* journalist T.P. O'Mahony suggested that the ban on contraception should be removed 'for its own sake, without any reference to wooing the people of the North'.[160]

In April 1971, the IFPRA and Senator Robinson submitted a draft of their private members' bill to the Taoiseach. Robinson's first private members' bill had provided for the repeal of the relevant sections in the 1929 Censorship of Publications Act and the 1935 Criminal Law (Amendment) Act, leaving the sponsors open to the accusation that they were in favour of making contraceptives available to all and via slot machines. The 1971 bill provided for controlled access both to contraceptives and to literature on the subject. The sale and distribution of contraceptives would be confined to hospitals, clinics controlled by a local authority, health board, a clinic relating to human fertility operating under the control of a medical practitioner and premises operating under the control of a registered pharmacist or any other premises permitted by the Minister for Justice. Three of the four forms of contraception would only

---

[156] Garret FitzGerald, *Towards a New Ireland* (Torc, Dublin, 1973), p. 152.
[157] *IMT*, 19 March 1971, copy found in DDA/XX/129/15.
[158] *IT*, 18 March 1971; *II*, 22 March 1971.   [159] *IT*, 22 March and 29 March 1971.
[160] *IP*, 17 March 1971.

be available on a doctor's prescription; chemists would be expected to exercise discretion with respect to the fourth item, condoms, but the Bill did not restrict contraception to married couples, on the grounds that the state did not attempt to control sexual relations between consenting adults aged 17 or over.[161]

In a memorandum to government Minister for Justice, Des O'Malley suggested that the government should oppose this bill, but before announcing this, they should make a statement in Dáil Éireann to the effect that they would wish to remove restrictions limiting the freedom of married couples to use contraceptives, **if this could be done without serious damage to the social environment,** [my bold] but there were serious difficulties. This became the dominant government argument. It echoed statements by the Catholic Hierarchy highlighting the adverse social consequences of any relaxation. The memorandum stated that the Church of Ireland was opposed to contraceptives on public sale and wanted them confined to married couples, whereas 'many other persons including the sponsors of the Seanad Bill' were in favour of contraceptives being available to anybody who wanted them, or at least those over a specified age – though Robinson's bill had no age limit.[162] The Department of Justice tried to ensure that this memorandum should be treated as secret – which would preclude other ministers and departments being consulted outside Cabinet – but the Taoiseach's Department insisted that normal procedures should apply; memoranda should be circulated to all Ministers ahead of Cabinet meetings. Although this item appeared on the agenda at the next four Cabinet meetings, consideration was postponed, and it was withdrawn on 6 July 1971 until further notice.[163] Repeated deferral of an agenda item generally indicates divisions within the Cabinet. It also suggests that Lynch was not willing to push the Cabinet to take a decision. Family planning did not return to the agenda for almost a year.

The debate on a first reading of Mrs Robinson's bill took place on 7 July 1971, without advance notice being given to the sponsors. The chair of the Seanad, Tommy Mullins, opposing the Bill, explained that it was being taken because 'it has become such a nuisance every time the Seanad meets'; he described the Bill as 'unacceptable in its present form' but did not give any reasons for this statement.[164] He took advantage of standing orders relating to a first reading, to prevent further debate, though some members protested. Asked whether the government was planning its own Bill, he replied that 'The Government are considering the question and when the time arrives will take appropriate steps to deal with the matters concerned'.[165] The Department of

---

[161] *IT*, 26 May 1971.
[162] NAI DT 2003/16/34 Criminal Law Amendment Act, Dept of Justice memo, 16 April 1971.
[163] NAI DT 2003/26/34.   [164] SD, 7 July, col. 968.
[165] SD, 7 July 1971, col. 969.

Justice memorandum was removed from the Cabinet Agenda on 6 July, the day before this Seanad debate.

By July 1971, the law relating to contraception was the subject of a High Court challenge, brought by Mary McGee. The resort to a legal challenge reflected trends in Ireland and in the United States. In 1963, Mrs Gladys Ryan, a Dublin housewife challenged the addition of fluoride to drinking water in Dublin; the 1965 Supreme Court ruling, rejecting her case became a landmark case in the exercise of citizen's rights.[166] In the USA where the attorney representing birth-control pioneer Margaret Sanger had explained that reforming the law was 'a matter of educating judges to the mores of the day', major reforms in access to contraception were achieved through the courts. In 1965, the US Supreme Court case *Griswold v. Connecticut* dismissed laws preventing the sale or distribution of contraceptives; *Eisenstadt v. Baird* (1972) established that single people had the same right to contraceptives as married couples.[167]

While the Government may have welcomed the High Court case as an opportunity to postpone a difficult decision, the 1972 Church of Ireland Synod revealed growing impatience at government inaction. The Role of the Church Committee was 'disturbed by the reaction of the Government to the Resolution of the General Synod 1971 (and similar resolutions from the Presbyterians, Methodists, Society of Friends, and Dublin Council of Churches) welcoming the efforts being made to amend the legislation [on contraception]. Not merely has the Government failed to take positive action itself, but it has seen to it that Dáil Éireann refuse leave to introduce a Private Members Bill'. They criticised a statement by Minister for Foreign Affairs Patrick Hillery where he suggested that the Protestant minority in the Republic was 'satisfied'.[168]

This statement may have prompted the re-appearance of contraception on the Cabinet agenda. Minister for Justice Des O'Malley suggested that the government should take a decision and make an announcement *before* the High Court had passed judgment. He indicated that it would be prudent to expect the court case to fail, but he believed that the law prohibiting the advocacy of contraception would be found unconstitutional. He set out several options for legislation including making the Pill available as a contraceptive on prescription and enabling people to secure other contraceptives by mail order. The case for making other contraceptives (which should be read as a reference to condoms) available on prescription had been examined and rejected. The options were therefore: to permit unrestricted sales from designated premises or to make provision that customs officers would have no duty to seize contraceptives. The laws prohibiting the sale of contraceptives should be removed in the case

---

[166] Ruadhán MacCormaic, *The Supreme Court* (Penguin Ireland, Dublin, 2016).
[167] Reed, 'The birth-control movement before Roe V. Wade', pp. 44–5.
[168] *Church of Ireland Gazette*, 26 May 1972. Hillery statement made on 23 September 1971.

of substances available on prescription, and 'there could be a nominal though unenforceable prohibition on sales to persons under a specific age'. If changes were to be made, he would favour the second option.

Mr O'Malley warned that 'An objection to a big change all at once is that it would be liable to be looked on as an official declaration of the arrival of the Permissive Society'.[169] A subsequent memo suggested that it would be difficult to enforce the law that chemists should only supply contraceptives (condoms) on prescription. Requiring a prescription would be seen as rationing by price – limiting access to those who could afford to pay a doctor, though the extension of the General Medicine Scheme in 1971 would reduce the impact of that argument. On 12 June 1972, the Cabinet authorised the Minister for Justice to prepare a proposal for legislation to control the sale and distribution of contraceptives, in the event that the High Court decided in favour of the plaintiff.

The draft heads of this bill provided for amendments to the 1935 Act, so that it would not be an offence to import contraceptives, unless they were for sale; a customs officer would not be under a duty to seize imported contraceptives, whether they came by post or in a person's possession, if he was of the opinion (determined by matters such as the quantity) that they were not for sale or distribution. The prohibition on sales of contraceptives would not apply to any drug or preparation sold on prescription. Advertisements for drugs or preparations in a book, pamphlet or periodical would not be unlawful under section 17 of the 1929 Act, provided that they were not available to the general public. References to 'the unnatural prevention of conception' in section 16 of the Censorship of Publications Act 1929, and sections 7 and 9 of the Censorship of Publications Act 1946 would be deleted.[170] The introduction of this legislation would appear to have been dependent on the outcome of the McGee case. The High Court rejected her claim that the seizure of contraceptives by a Customs Officer was unconstitutional. In a brief judgement, the President of the Court determined that the 1935 Act was not inconsistent with the Constitution.[171] This removed pressure to legislate until the Supreme Court had ruled on this matter.

The only immediate outcome of this debate over minority rights was the deletion in December 1972 of Article 44, referring to the 'special position of the Roman Catholic Church' with over 80 per cent of those who voted in favour of the change, but there was no opposition to the referendum and consequently no serious discussion of the role of the Catholic church in Irish society. The government took advantage of the pending Supreme Court case to postpone the thorny issue of whether to legalise contraception and under what terms, despite substantial evidence that a growing number of Irish people were seeking more effective means of limiting pregnancies, and that demand for reliable

[169] NAI DT 2003/16/34, 30 May 1972.   [170] NAI DT 2003/16/34, 12 June 1972.
[171] NAI DT 2003/16/34, 2 August 1972.

contraception extended beyond the Pill. During the late 1960s and the early 1970s, most western countries removed legal restrictions on contraception, and at times, there appeared to be a prospect that Ireland would do likewise. That did not happen. Church and state had reframed their argument against change, focussing on the potential damage that a more liberal regime would inflict on Irish society. The misery that many Irish couples endured because of lack of access to reliable contraception was discounted.

4   Contraception
Access and Opposition, 1973–1980

The year 1973 promised change. Ireland became a member of the EEC on
1 January. A general election saw a Fine Gael/Labour government take
office, following sixteen years of Fianna Fáil governments. The report of the
Commission on the Status of Women, published in July recommended major
reforms with respect to employment, pay and welfare, including an end to the
ban on married women employed in the public service. It also recommended
that 'information and expert advice on family planning should be made available through medical and other appropriate channels to all families throughout
the country. Such advice should respect the moral and personal attitudes of
each married couple'. The Department of Health should determine how the
requirements with respect to family planning should be met.[1]

4.1   The McGee Case

In December 1973, the Supreme Court delivered its verdict in the McGee case,
ruling that it was legal to import contraceptives for personal use, but the Court
did not strike down the restrictions on the sale, wholesale importation and
distribution of contraceptives. The judgment was based on the safety of Mrs
McGee's life and health, and 'the security and wellbeing of her marriage and
family'. It emphasised the right of a married couple to privacy – a judgment
that was very much in line with the 1965 US Supreme Court decision *Griswold
v. Connecticut*, which formed the basis for the 1973 US Supreme Court decision on abortion, *Roe v. Wade*.

In his judgment, Mr Justice Brian Walsh determined that

The sexual life of a husband and wife is of necessity and by its nature an area of particular privacy. If the husband and wife decide to limit their family or to avoid having
children by use of contraceptives it is a matter peculiarly within the joint decision of
the husband and wife and one into which the State cannot intrude unless its intrusion
can be justified by the exigencies of the common good. The question of whether the
use of contraceptives by married couple within their marriage is or is not contrary to

---

[1] *Commission on the Status of Women*, (Dublin, 1973) para. 574.

the moral code or codes to which they profess to subscribe, or is not regarded by them as being against their conscience, could not justify State intervention. Similarly the fact that the use of contraceptives may offend against the moral code of the majority of the citizens of the State would not *per se* justify the intervention of the State to prohibit their use within marriage. The private morality of its citizens does not justify intervention by the State into the activities of those citizens unless and until the common good requires it.[2]

This judgment did not wholly reject the Catholic Hierarchy's argument that legislation should uphold public morality, but it set a high threshold. It drew a distinction between the constitutional rights of married couples and single people. The rights of married couples were strengthened by Article 45 of the Constitution, where the state promised to uphold the institution of marriage. On that basis, it would appear that the constitution could uphold the right of married couples to contraception. But while the judgment vindicated the rights of married couples to use contraceptives, it did not enable them to do so, other than by importing contraceptives for personal use.

The ruling created a legal and political vacuum that continued until the 1979 Family Planning Act came into effect in the autumn of 1980. During these years, access to contraception increased significantly, though unevenly. Contraception became a major battleground between those seeking to preserve a traditional Ireland, and those who favoured change; divisions that included attitudes towards minorities, and a united Ireland. The increasing availability of contraception, despite no change in the law, plus the fact that politicians in all parties were divided on the issue, gave oxygen to strident grass-roots groups that linked contraception with abortion. Although this opposition is often interpreted as evidence of the continuing authority of the Catholic church, the tactics were new: graphic images of aborted foetuses, mass letter-writing campaigns to the media and politicians, lay leadership, female activism and close links with international anti-abortion groups. The conservative forces that emerged during the 1970s provided the momentum behind the campaign for a Pro-Life Amendment that was launched following the enactment of the 1979 Family Planning Act.

4.2   Changing Behaviour and Attitudes

Sociologist Máire Nic Ghiolla Phádraig reported that a survey carried out in 1973/4 of attitudes to contraception and abortion among 2,400 Irish Catholics showed that most respondents reacted 'in terms of moral judgements, seeing these actions as right or wrong'. Almost 2/3 viewed contraception as always or generally wrong; just over one-quarter regarded contraception as right;

---

[2] McGee v. Attorney General 1973.

95.4 per cent determined that abortion was always or generally wrong.[3] In the 1970s, Ireland was divided into three groups: those who were determined to use contraception and make it available; those determined to combat change, and a middle cohort that opted for a quiet life.

The first groups to challenge the ban on contraception – the Irish Family Planning Association (IFPA, formerly the FGC) and the IFPRA – adopted a non-confrontational approach. In March 1971, however, the Irish Women's Liberation Movement (IWLM) travelled by train to Belfast, where they purchased contraceptives and dared Irish customs officials to confiscate them when they alighted in Dublin. Journalists and photographers had advance notice of the 'contraceptive train' and gave it massive publicity; later that evening, the women appeared on the mass-audience Saturday night *Late Late Show*.[4] Their antics probably served to entrench conservative opinion. Journalist and feminist Mary Maher who had just given birth to her second daughter 'remembers watching it all on television in Holles St Hospital with a sinking heart. This type of protest would, she feared, alienate the very women they were hoping to attract'.[5] *This Week* alleged that the IWLM had contemplated sending a woman to Belfast to be fitted with a coil and then declare it 'to doubtless red-faced Customs men', on her return, but they feared that such 'sensational publicity' would only result in their being labelled as 'cranks'.[6] Earner-Byrne and Urquhart suggest that the episode 'also reinforced the somewhat exaggerated notion of the North's liberalism'.[7]

The IWLM soon split between those who wished to concentrate on left-wing causes such as housing and Northern Ireland, and a mainstream movement focussed on measures to assist widows and deserted wives and secure the rights of married women with respect to the family home. Second-wave feminism played a limited role in extending access to family planning until the late 1970s, though it may have encouraged women to control their fertility and seek reliable contraception. In 1969, Students for Democratic Action, a left-wing movement, called for legislation to legalise divorce and contraception, as part of a slate of demands that included housing and limitation on garda powers.[8] In the 1970s and later decades, students' unions played a major role in providing access to contraception and challenging legal restrictions.

Long before the Pill became available, contraception was seen as encouraging pre-marital sex, a point of view that was not limited to Ireland. The late 1960s brought what Cook, writing about Britain, has described as 'a transformation of sexual mores', involving an open acknowledgement, even

---

[3] Máire Nic Ghiolla Phádraig, 'Social and cultural factors in family planning', *The Changing Family* (Family Studies Unit, UCD, Dublin, 1984), p. 83.
[4] Anne Stopper, *Monday at Gaj's*, pp. 167–8.   [5] *Magill*, April 1979.
[6] *This Week*, 5 March 1971.
[7] Earner-Byrne and Urquhart, *The Irish abortion journey*, p. 58.   [8] *IT*, 14 January 1969.

celebration of sexual activity among single people.[9] In Ireland, the recorded rate of 'illegitimate' births (many women went to Britain) began to rise in the late 1960s and it continued to rise. Irish women's magazines published letters from single women who wished to have sex with their boyfriend or were under pressure to do so.[10]

In 1974, the south-city IFPA clinic reported that 43 per cent of clients were unmarried and 53 per cent were under twenty-four years. A survey by Emer Philbin Bowman indicated that while three out of five single women attending this clinic were planning to marry, in the near future, the remainder had no such plans. Although the proportion of single women who were sexually active was rising, she concluded that it was lower than in Britain or the United States, and age of first intercourse was higher. Nevertheless, Ireland was experiencing – albeit more slowly – changes in sexual behaviour found elsewhere, and lack of access to contraception was not a deterrent. Most of the women who attended the IFPA clinic were well-educated and from middle-class backgrounds; all but 6 per cent were sexually experienced and had been sexually active for an average of 2.2 years before attending the clinic. At this time, opinion polls showed that only 20 per cent of respondents and 21 per cent of young married women were in favour of contraceptives being available to single people.[11]

Although opinion polls suggest that support for legalising contraception grew during the 1970s, most respondents wanted some restrictions. A 1971 opinion poll in *Woman's Choice* – which would not have been representative of the wider population – showed that 61 per cent would welcome a change in the law but 64 per cent believed that contraceptives should only be available on prescription.[12] A more representative poll that year showed that only 29 per cent of women and 35 per cent of men approved of the sale of contraceptives. The only group where a majority favoured legalisation were men aged 25–34. By the spring of 1974 however, a majority in all socio-economic groups except farmers supported Mary Robinson's Private Members' Bill (see Chapter 5). Support for change had almost doubled since 1971 among those aged 35–44: from 36 per cent to 62 per cent, but only 30 per cent of those over fifty-five years favoured reform.[13] A 1973 article by Heather Parsons reported that 'Most women don't particularly care what the law says'. Although a majority of the women that she interviewed did not want to have any more children they feared that more liberal contraception would lower moral standards.[14]

[9] Cook, *The long sexual revolution*, p. 295.
[10] *Woman's Choice*, 17 June 1969; 23 September 1969 and many other editions.
[11] Emer Philbin Bowman, 'Sexual and contraceptive attitudes and behaviour of single attenders at a Dublin family planning clinic', *Journal of Biosocial Science*, 9, 1977, 427–45.
[12] *Woman's Choice*, 13 July 1971.   [13] *Hibernia*, 3 October 1975.
[14] *Woman's Way*, 1 June 1973.

By the autumn of 1975 however, it would appear that support for reform had fallen, and the proportion of 'don't knows' had increased from 3 per cent to 16 per cent; most of these appear to have previously favoured change. 47 per cent were in favour of contraceptives being sold through chemist shops and 37 per cent were against. Pollsters attributed the fall in support to Taoiseach Liam Cosgrave's vote against his government's family planning bill (see Chapter 5). Support among married women of child-bearing age was unchanged at 68 per cent. A majority (52 per cent) of farmers and their family members continued to oppose the sale of contraceptives, with only 30 per cent in favour.

The polls indicate a regional and an urban/rural divide; 53 per cent of those polled in the more rural Connacht and Ulster were opposed to legalising contraceptives. Munster – a key middle-ground showed the highest proportion of undecided. Among those in favour of change, 55 per cent wanted contraceptives available only on prescription, 37 per cent wanted access restricted to married couples, 12 per cent wanted open sale to married couples and 13 per cent open sale to adults.[15] Another poll published in the *Sunday Press* in November 1975, which is noteworthy for the absence of undecided responses, showed 52 per cent of married women and 53 per cent of married men favouring contraceptives being available.[16] There was little change between 1975 and 1977, when 47 per cent of those polled were in favour of making contraceptives legally available and 37 per cent were opposed. In Dublin city and county, the margin was 60–40 per cent, but Dublin and urban Ireland (53 per cent in favour) were the only areas with a majority favouring change. Rural Ireland recorded a significant proportion of undecideds.[17]

4.3   Clinics and Condoms

There is no evidence that contraceptives (other than the Pill) were widely available before 1970, but the publicity given to the IWLM 'contraceptive train' and an RTÉ television programme, where a chemist in Enniskillen (Northern Ireland) described the range of contraceptives that he carried, and the journalist bought condoms, which were duly confiscated at the border by a customs officer, alerted people to this possibility.[18] Although the Supreme Court ruling only applied to married couples, government files indicate a concern that the Court would give a similar ruling in favour of the rights of single people, and this fear may have blunted the enforcement of laws relating to the import of

---

[15] *Hibernia*, 3 October 1975.
[16] *Sunday Press*, 16 November 1976; R.S. Rose, 'An outline of fertility control, focusing on the element of abortion in the Republic of Ireland to 1976', (Stockholm Ph.D. thesis), p. 101; copy in. Barry Desmond Papers, UCDA, box 352.
[17] *Magill*, October 1977.
[18] NAI DT 2003/16/34 for description of the RTÉ programme.

contraceptives. Some consignments imported from Northern Ireland for distribution in family planning clinics or by mail order were seized and the gardaí carried out occasional raids on Dublin's Well-Woman Clinic. But there was no sustained witch hunt, despite repeated demands from the anti-contraception lobby groups. In 1975, *Hibernia* (no fan of the status quo) reported that somebody working in family planning in Northern Ireland regarded the services available in Dublin as comparable to Northern Ireland.[19] That would not be true of provincial Ireland.

4.3.1   Irish Family Planning Association

In 1973, the Fertility Guidance Clinic changed its name to the IFPA, and it became an associate member of the International Planned Parenthood Federation (IPPF), which gave them access to IPPF resources and funding.[20] IFPA became a full member in 1975. The Minister for Industry and Commerce refused them permission to register as a charity, so they established a limited company.[21] The Pill remained the most popular method of contraception among IFPA patrons; in 1975 and 1976, over two-thirds of clients in Synge Street opted for oral contraception. The Mountjoy Square clinic which catered to a higher proportion of older married women – some were referred by the Rotunda Hospital – recorded higher numbers supplied with the cap and IUDs, though the Pill remained the most popular method.[22] In 1976, the IFPA reported that a growing number of clients were young married women who wished to continue in paid employment after marriage. Over half attended on the recommendation of a friend; only 10 per cent were referred by their doctor.[23] Consultation fees ranged from £1.50 to £3 depending on the client's income; for fitting an IUD, the fees were £6–£8. Medical card holders were treated free of charge.[24] In 1977, the IFPA saw more than 35,000 clients. There were no appointments, so clients often had to endure a long wait, though women who were having IUDs inserted were given priority.[25]

The IFPA's most significant long-term contribution was training doctors, nurses and social workers in family planning and providing a range of new services, including sterilisation (see Chapter 7), and clinics dealing with human sexuality and personal relationships. They supplied speakers to women's groups, student societies and other fora. In January 1973, they hosted an international conference on 'Family planning and young People', organised by the

---

[19] *Hibernia*, 3 October 1975.   [20] IFPA annual report 1973.
[21] IFPA annual report 1973.   [22] Statistics from IFPA annual reports.
[23] *II*, 3 June 1976.   [24] *IT*, 8 November 1973, Linda Kavanagh the story so far.
[25] Richard Kevin O'Reilly, 'Population dynamics and family planning in Dublin', Ph.D. University of Connecticut 1981, pp. 85–87.

IPPF, which was targeted at journalists and broadcasters communicating with young people. They authored papers on sex education for youth magazines. In 1975, IFPA clinics were recognised by the Joint Committee on Contraception of the Royal College of Obstetricians and Gynaecologists and the Royal College of General Practitioners (both UK-based but with many Irish members). The first training course was held in October 1975. Nurses who worked in IFPA clinics were awarded certificates in family planning; in the autumn of 1975, they held two training seminars for public health nurses – more than seventy attended. These seminars 'had the added significance of being recognised by the Department of Health as a legitimate post-graduate educational exercise for staff in the Public Health Service'. Nurses were reimbursed for travel expenses and the course fee.[26] The training course for doctors failed to gain similar recognition. Junior hospital doctors had to attend in their very limited free time,[27] and they presumably had to pay. Andrew Curtain worked in the Mountjoy Square clinic while he was a junior doctor in the Rotunda; he was denounced from the altar in the Pro-Cathedral. The IFPA information sessions for social workers provided practical information about family planning; Alan Shatter, a solicitor and future Cabinet Minister, advised on the legal position. The IFPA engaged with emerging women's groups, seeking speakers on topics such as family planning or the menopause. In 1979, they highlighted their success in 'winning a foothold in some of the AnCo[28] training and re-training programmes for women', and they had made initial contacts with the health education section of Eastern Health Board, which enabled them to set up workshops on human sexuality and contraception for wider audiences.[29] By the mid-1970s, they were devoting increased resources to communication, 'because of the increasing volume of anti-pill and pro-Billings information and mis-information that was appearing in the press'. They determined not to reply to 'each assault, but to issue from time to time, sensible and correct factual information in the form of press statements'.[30] The National Archives holds a copy of *Facts on Contraception – an answer to the Irish Family League* published by IFPA, which has a date stamp of 11 February 1974.[31]

4.4   Family Planning Services

In 1972, a year before the Supreme Court Judgment, some members of the IFPRA, having taken legal advice, set up a limited company, Family Planning Services (FPS), to distribute non-medical contraceptives, mainly condoms. The initial capital was provided by the Joseph Rowntree Foundation, an English

---

[26] NAI DT 2006/133/215.   [27] Information from Dr Tim Gleeson.
[28] An Co – An Comhairle Oiliúna was the state training agency.
[29] IFPA 1979 annual report.   [30] 1975 annual report.   [31] NAI DT 2005/7/345.

charity. The first chair was Trinity College Dublin geneticist Professor David McConnell, who became involved having attended an IFPRA public meeting in Dun Laoghaire; another founding member was statistician Robert Cochran. They began with a PO Box, inviting clients to donate £1 for six condoms plus a brochure. FPS subsequently opened a clinic in Pembroke Road, which was led by Dr Derek Freedman.[32] Frank Crummey who worked full-time with FPS in the early years, claimed that they 'decided to distribute condoms and other contraceptives as blatantly as possible to see, yet again, how far we could push the laws'. In his memoir, Crummey described how he and his four daughters 'had a regular post-Mass ritual on Sundays of answering letters from women in response to ads I had personally placed in *Woman's Way* magazine advertising free condoms'. Supplies from the London Rubber Company were shipped to Northern Ireland; he collected them twice a month.[33] In order to circumvent the law customers were invited either to make a donation, or become associate members of the company. FPS had over 20,000 clients in the first year; 40 per cent were referred by the IFPA clinics,[34] which did not supply non-medical contraceptives. FPS supplied bulk order to doctors and saw its future role as a wholesaler to colleges, clinics and similar outlets.[35] Cloatre and Enright state, correctly that 'FPS became a mass condom distribution network, starting from a small operation that was initially heavily reliant on volunteers. The profits from supplying condoms enabled FPS to become more professional and open a clinic.'[36]

In Ireland, as opposed to Britain, where 'many wives shied away from the issue, leaving responsibility for birth control in the hands of their husbands',[37] women generally took the initiative in seeking contraception. In 1973, more than 85 per cent of FPS clients were women. Many were mothers of large families in their late 30s and early 40s (too old to be on the Pill); just under half had a Dublin address.[38] Those who worked with FPS or the Galway family planning clinic described early visitors to their clinics as 'edgy .... ashamed .... uncertain of themselves ... embarrassed'.[39] An American doctoral student who carried out research in the IFPA and FPS clinics in the late 1970s commented that

---

[32] Interview with Dr David McCullough 24/1/2011. Brendan Walsh Papers, Folder 1.

[33] Frank Crummey, *Crummey v. Ireland. Thorn in the side of the establishment* (Londubh Books, Dublin, 2010), pp. 95–6.

[34] Keith Wilson-Davis, 'The contraceptive situation in the Irish Republic', *Journal of Biosocial Science*, 1974, pp. 487–8.

[35] Brendan Walsh Papers, Folder 2.

[36] Emilie Cloatre and Máiréad Enright, '"On the perimeter of the lawful": enduring illegality in the Irish Family Planning Movement, 1972–1985', *Journal of Law and Society*, 44, 4 December 2017, pp. 474–7.

[37] Fisher, *Birth control, sex, & marriage*, p. 5.

[38] Brendan Walsh Papers, Folder 2 FPS.

[39] Cloatre and Enright, '"On the perimeter of the lawful"', pp. 479–80.

purchasing contraceptives from a woman 'has never been easy for some men ... Clinic personnel would often remark that married customers, more often than not having bolstered their courage for the event with pints of Guinness stout at the nearby pub, would be stopped short by the crowded waiting room'. He described the FPS clinic as 'more attractive though smaller.... There are obvious attempts to make the clients as comfortable as possible and the choice of a location may well have reflected that'. Many clients worked in nearby offices; and purchases took place 'away from the gaze of the women in the waiting room'.[40] In contrast to the IFPA, FPS did not cater to poorer clients with medical cards.

4.5   Beyond Dublin

The IFPA and FPS played a critical role in expanding family planning beyond Dublin. In 1974, the IFPA was approached by a Cork-based group called Le Chéile (together), who were interested in setting up a clinic. They put them in touch with a medical group already in existence, in the hope that they would work together.[41] IFPA provided technical advice and financial support to the Cork clinic that opened in early 1975, chaired by gynaecologist Edgar Ritchie. When clients were asked how they learned about this clinic, the most common response was from a pastoral letter written by Cornelius Lucey, the Bishop of Cork, read at all masses, denouncing the family planning clinic at 8 Tuckey Street![42] The Cork clinic did not initially affiliate with the IFPA, but it changed its mind in 1977.

A clinic opened in Navan in 1975, directed by Dr Mary Randles. When she moved to the town, she was shocked by the many women who were mothers of very large families '14, 16 and 18 children'. Women were coming to the GP practice that she ran with her husband, seeking letters that they could show to their confessor, stating that they had a medical reason for using contraception. She refused these requests, 'I wanted women to decide for themselves if they wanted contraception and I encouraged them to get their other half to pay for it'.[43] Her clinic handled postal queries, including a 'striking number' from counties that were some distance away, probably because people preferred to receive packages with a Meath, rather than a Dublin postmark. Although Dr Randles, like many other doctors who were actively promoting family planning, was extremely concerned about women with large families, most clients of the Navan clinic were women in their twenties – those about to marry or

---

[40] O'Reilly, 'Population dynamics and family planning in Dublin', pp. 87–92.
[41] IFPA annual report 1974.   [42] Professor Tom O'Dowd.
[43] *II*, 13 May 2021. The Randles couple also campaigned against corporal punishment in schools; many of those who were actively promoting contraception were opposed to corporal punishment.

mothers of 1–2 children, who viewed family planning as a 'financial and social necessity'. Many doctors were slow to refer patients, 'and quick to voice disapproval of patients who request Family Planning', which 'occasionally instils a sense of guilt in the woman but happily this is not normally the case'. It proved difficult to publicise the Navan clinic; women found it difficult to obtain the phone number and information on opening times; women's magazines remained the most useful source of information.[44] The IFPA also provided support and advice to groups who were planning to establish clinics in Galway and Limerick.[45] By 1978, IFPA was providing administrative and financial support to a clinic in Bray, near Dublin and moves were afoot to establish a federation of Irish family planning clinics, with an appropriate structure.[46] The clinics remained heavily reliant on voluntary support; medical devices, such as IUDs or diaphragms were brought from Britain or Northern Ireland in personal luggage. One doctor who had worked with the Cork clinic before taking up an appointment in Wales carried supplies whenever he made a visit home[47]; non-medical contraceptives came from FPS. But the growing numbers attending the various clinics masked the fact that poorer women with large families – the original target group – continued to be under-represented.[48] In 1978 however, the IFPA reported that the proportion of clients from lower income groups presenting in Mountjoy Square had risen from 26 per cent in 1975 to 49 per cent.[49]

4.6   Student Unions

Student unions were the main providers of non-medical contraceptives to younger people, especially young men. By the mid-1970s, Trinity College Students' Union was supplying contraceptives and an abortion referral service for students. The UCD Students' Union Shop began to sell condoms in 1975, a decision that prompted the resignation of the engineering students' representative, who claimed that he was required to sell them.[50] Many of the early clients were members of staff, and the shop was also visited by a plain clothes woman garda who asked to buy condoms, in an effort at entrapment. She was asked for a donation.[51] UCD Student's Union probably installed the first slot machine for condoms in Ireland; it was removed on a number of occasions by the authorities.[52] In 1975, the Vice President of the Union of Students of Ireland was co-opted to the IFPA information and education committee;

[44] *Family Planning News*, autumn 1975.   [45] IFPA annual report 1975, 1977.
[46] Annual report 1978.   [47] Information from Professor Tom O'Dowd.
[48] *Family Planning News*, autumn 1975.   [49] IFPA annual report 1977.
[50] *II*, 13 November 1975.   [51] Information provided by Joe Little, then a UCDSU officer.
[52] My brother, who was working on his thesis in the UCD Library on a hot summer day in the late 1970s, saw the then-registrar Maurice Kennedy, accompanying two porters who were carrying the condom machine. That machine was still in the Registrar's office in the mid-1990s.

an IFPA representative addressed the annual meeting of USI welfare officers, and they produced a leaflet that would be distributed with condoms by student unions.[53] In 1978, IFPA set up an information and advisory session for the UCD Students' Union.[54] However student unions were not all in agreement on contraception, and it proved a divisive issue at several USI conferences.

The establishment of family planning clinics in Galway and Limerick reflected the fact that both were university towns. The first family planning service in Limerick was established in the new National Institute for Higher Education (NIHE) – now University of Limerick. Many of those involved were the wives, often English-born, of NIHE lecturers.[55] NIHE provided the expertise and impetus to establish a clinic in the city, with the active assistance of socialist politician Jim Kemmy. A public meeting in 1975 with over fifty in attendance was addressed by three representatives of the IFPA. *Family Planning News* commented that: 'The members of the medical profession in Limerick have a reputation for conservatism but this image too is changing, and some young doctors have already begun to show an interest'.[56]

A Galway clinic opened in 1976 in a highly contentious environment. In 1974, Galway Corporation passed a resolution condemning contraception; this was seen as a response to the fact that UCG sociology lecturer and Labour Senator, Michael D. Higgins, a future President of Ireland, had voted in favour of Mary Robinson's family planning bill. The Galway Family Planning Association was founded by Michael Conlon a recent graduate of UCG (now Galway University) and a member of Official Sinn Féin. Membership was drawn from students and others associated with the university. The Students Union allocated the proceeds of its 1976 Rag Week to the proposed clinic, prompting an outraged response from the mayor – Fianna Fáil councillor Mary Byrne, and local newspapers. This decision was reversed by an emergency meeting of the Students Union – which saw students who were members of religious congregations, Opus Dei and Fine Gael student politicians pitted against Official Sinn Féin and liberal voices. A clinic promoting natural family planning opened in the city, but the family planning clinic found it impossible to rent space and was forced to compromise by introducing a mail order service, supplying condoms in return for 'donations'.[57] When the Galway clinic eventually secured premises in the summer of 1977, it had to contend with protests, including groups reciting the rosary outside the door. Women and university staff were strongly represented among company shareholders. John Cunningham's excellent short history notes that divisions soon emerged among the founding members between those who supported a traditional clinic,

<hr />

[53] IFPA annual report 1975.   [54] IFPA annual report 1978.
[55] Thanks to Dr John Logan for this information.
[56] *Family Planning News*, autumn 1975.   [57] *II*, 18 April 1977.

led by trained medical professionals, and left-wing feminists who favoured a more self-directed model, including counselling for LGBT clients and abortion referral. Most patrons simply wanted reliable contraception.[58]

By the end of the decade, the family planning clinics claimed to have almost 100,000 clients.[59] Services that started on a voluntary basis were becoming commercial. By 1977/78, FPS had an estimated annual turnover of £100,000, which was similar to the estimated cost of prescriptions for the contraceptive pill for GMS patients. In 1977, 160,000 prescriptions were issued to panel patients; if each prescription ran for six months, this would indicate at least 80,000 GMS patients on the pill.[60] Condoms were also being imported from Northern Ireland and sold in public houses or door-to-door. (My mother once helped a young woman, who was travelling with a toddler and a heavy suitcase on the Belfast to Dublin train, by carrying her case past waiting customs officers; she only discovered the contents when the woman thanked her!). The rather acrimonious battle for exclusive rights to sell Durex in Ireland in 1980, between FPS and a commercial company is an indication that contraception had become a major business.[61]

Access remained difficult for couples in rural or small-town Ireland. When Wilson-Davis surveyed Irish women in 1973, only 3 per cent from an agricultural background had used the Pill and only 5 per cent of those who had controlled their fertility had used condoms, jellies or chemical methods. In rural and small-town Ireland, 'everyone knows everyone else and no one knows people better than the postman ... anyone in a rural area who wished to obtain them [contraceptives] would have to write to one of the Dublin clinics and it would soon become known in the area that X was receiving packets in brown envelopes from Dublin'. In 1974, FPS reported that 10 per cent of the packages posted to country areas did not reach their customers.[62] Journalist Nell McCaffrey wrote of 'moral police officers ... in the person of the village postmistress or postmaster. The package would sometimes arrive, steamed open, clumsily resealed and empty'.[63] There might only be one general practitioner, in remote areas, so if he (and it was generally a man), was unwilling to prescribe the Pill, a woman had no alternative other than a long trip to a family planning clinic. This was difficult; most women did not have access to a car and would find it difficult to take a day away from the family home or farm.

---

[58] John Cunningham, 'Spreading VD all over Connacht', Reproductive rights and wrongs in 1970s Galway, *History Ireland*, 19, no 2, March–April 2011, pp. 44–7; see also Cloatre and Enright '"On the perimeter of the lawful"'.

[59] *Magill*, January 1979; Brian Trench, 'The contraceptive backlash'.

[60] *Hibernia*, 3 August 1978.   [61] *Hibernia*, 4 September 1980.

[62] J Keith-Wilson, 'Some results of an Irish family planning survey', *Journal of Biosocial Science*, 6, 1974, pp. 437–40.

[63] Quoted in Ferriter, *Occasions of sin*, p. 422.

4.7   Legal Challenges

In December 1973, customs officers seized a consignment of pamphlets on family planning, addressed to FPS director, Dr David McConnell, at Trinity College Dublin. He claimed that this was the first such occurrence and feared that 'a clampdown had been authorised'.[64] The Supreme Court Judgment did not address the 1929 Censorship of Publications Act. On 20 December 1973, the day after the judgment was issued a summons was served on the IFPA and FPS for breaching the 1929 Censorship of Publications Act and the 1935 Criminal Law Amendment Act by selling contraceptive devices and supplying a booklet about family planning.[65] The cases were brought by a man, who had written to FPS using the names of his daughters aged 9 and 11 years, enclosing a postal order. He received condoms and spermicidal jellies in return. He sent a similar letter (all were typed at his place of work in Dublin Corporation) to IFPA (then FGS), seeking an IUD. They informed him about the price and enclosed a booklet: *Contraception. A Guide for Parents and Prospective Parents,* written by Drs Jim Loughran, Robert Towers and David Nowlan.[66] The sixteen-page booklet had two main sections: 'Effective Family Planning Methods' gave short descriptions of the pill, IUD, diaphragm and sterilisation; 'Less Effective Family Planning Methods', discussed the rhythm method, withdrawal, condoms, foams and jellies and abstinence. The booklet gave names and addresses for clinics and other relevant organisations, including the two IFPA clinics,[67] CMAC branches and others providing advice on Catholic-approved methods.[68] The judge dismissed both cases, arguing that FPS was not selling contraceptives, though it requested donations, and the booklet did not advocate any method of unnatural prevention of conception. The IFPRA met the legal costs incurred by IFPA and FPS in this case.[69]

The IFPA booklet was initially only available through its clinics, but in 1972–73, it went on sale in Dublin bookshops, and copies were distributed by FPS. It was advertised in *Woman's Way*. An estimated 10,000 copies were distributed. The original version had no diagrams or illustrations, but feedback revealed that many couples found it easier to understand the information in diagrammatic form, so the booklet was revised.[70] In December 1976, a notice appeared in the *Iris Oifigiúil* – the government publication that contained official notices – banning the booklet under the 1946 Censorship of Publications Act, not on the grounds that it advocated contraception, but alleging that it was indecent and obscene. IFPA and FPS first heard of the ban when they were contacted by journalists. FPS responded by holding a

[64] *Hibernia*, 18 January 1974.   [65] *IT*, 11 January 1974.   [66] *IT*, 20 February 1974.
[67] Crummey, *Crummey v. Ireland.*, pp. 104–5.   [68] *IT*, 20 February 1974.
[69] IFPRA Annual Report 1974 NAI TD 2005/7/345.   [70] *IT*, 6 May 1977.

meeting that was 'half press conference, half protest', where they planned to distribute copies of the banned publication. They gave advance notice to the Gardaí. Crummey claimed that a garda who was given a copy, asked to keep it for personal use.[71] The ban was warmly welcomed by conservatives. One woman, who wrote to the Taoiseach, claimed that she had been chosen by her friends to express their gratitude at the ban; she also complained about contraceptives being available in UCD and Trinity. The Pro-Fide Movement with an address in Dublin's Abbey Street, which would appear to be the address of the CTSI bookshop, attacked the booklet. The Holy Ghost Fathers wrote to the Minister for Justice expressing concern at the IFPA challenge to the censorship board. Leslie Quelch of the League of Decency, an inveterate correspondent, claimed that if the challenge was successful 'it will discredit the function of the Board'. He described the IFPA as 'the most savage and damaging lobby society has had to confront... an attempt to foist on the people of Ireland a culture and a way of life alien to the religious beliefs and moral standards of our people'.[72]

The IFPA challenged the prohibition, as did Frank Crummey a member of FPS, and his wife – the latter on the grounds that it deprived them of information that they needed to plan their family. These cases were combined in a High Court hearing. The judgment, delivered by Mr Justice Hamilton (a future chief justice), found in favour of the appellants on the grounds that they had not been given notice of the ban and an opportunity to refute the claim that the booklet was indecent or obscene.[73] Solicitor Alan Shatter noted that this was the first court challenge to the Censorship of Publications Acts, and it applied to any banned publication.[74] It is not surprising that the Censorship Board appealed the decision to the Supreme Court.[75]

The Supreme Court unanimously dismissed the Appeal, quoting the evidence given to the High Court which described the publication, as 'a 30 page booklet.... a simple guide to contraception and fertility...produced by responsible and qualified people'. The booklet 'espoused no cause: it advocated no course of conduct, it simply made available the basic facts, with necessary diagrams, on which persons, so minded could exercise their options....therefore it could not be said, as it could if this was a plainly pornographic production, that the board was justified in not giving the publishers an opportunity of meeting in advance the case for issuing a prohibition order'. Mr Justice Kenny highlighted the fact that the authors were three registered medical practitioners, 'The decision to prohibit the sale and distribution on the ground that it was indecent and obscene involved the very serious implication against them that each of them had committed a criminal offence'.[76]

---

[71] Crummey, *Crummey v. Ireland*, pp. 103–6.   [72] NAI, TD 2007/116/273.
[73] *IT*, 2 July 1977.   [74] *IT*, 18 July 1977.   [75] *IT*, 11 July 1978.   [76] *IT*, 28 July 1978.

While the IFPA pamphlet was banned (temporarily), despite having been in print and widely distributed for several years, a 1977 booklet by Janet Martin, former woman's editor of the *Irish Independent*, titled 'The essential guide for women in Ireland', was not subjected to censorship, despite containing a chapter on family planning, perhaps because the ban on the IFPA publication was under appeal.[77] Imports of contraceptives were occasionally seized; as noted earlier, there were often customs officers to meet the Belfast train at Dublin's Connolly station. In 1978, customs officers in Dundalk prevented the import from Northern Ireland of a consignment of contraceptives.[78] FPS determined to present a constitutional challenge. Robert Cochran, FPS director, stated that the company had never concealed the fact that they were selling contraceptives. They were a non-profit organisation, which supplied many family planning clinics. The Galway clinic chose to be joined in the legal challenge.[79] News of a potential threat to FPS commonly resulted in a queue of clients seeking supplies.[80] In November 1978, the Contraceptive Action Programme – a left-wing feminist group – opened a shop Contraceptives Unlimited. All proceeds would go to support the court challenge. There would be no age limit on purchasers though 'very young teenagers' would be referred to a family planning clinic.[81] The shop was designed as a publicity device; the lease only ran until the New Year.

4.8   Second-Wave Feminism and Family Planning

The role of second-wave feminism in expanding access to contraception in Ireland is complex. Tara Keenan-Thomson claims that 'The furore created by *Humanae Vitae* dominated public discourse on women's roles in the late 1960s, …. it helped bring to a culmination an emergent feminist consciousness that had been quietly fomenting since the middle of the decade'.[82] It is difficult to reconcile that statement with Emer Philbin-Bowman's survey that showed that only 34 per cent of single women attending a Dublin IFPA clinic in 1974 'broadly supported the aims of the women's movement'. Six per cent believed that the movement was too aggressive; the remaining two-thirds 'were either completely uninterested or unaware of being discriminated against (24%) or were happy to see equality end with equal pay (34%)'. Those most supportive of feminist causes were women who had no immediate plan to marry, if ever.[83]

---

[77] *IT*, 3 June 1977.   [78] NAI DT 2008/142/221; *IP*, 10 September 1978; *IP*, 1 September 1978.
[79] *IP*, 22 September 1978.
[80] Cloatre and Enright, '"On the perimeter of the lawful"', p. 483.
[81] *IP*, 28 November 1978.
[82] Tara Keenan-Thomson, *Irish women and street politics, 1956–1973* (Irish Academic Press, Dublin, 2010), p. 115.
[83] Emer Philbin Bowman, 'Sexual and contraceptive attitudes', p. 442.

The report of *the Commission on the Status of Women* recommended that information and advice on family planning should be available through medical and other appropriate channels to families (not defined) throughout the country. The advice should respect 'the moral and personal attitudes of each married couple'; 'medical requirements arising out of the married couples' decisions on family planning should be available under control and through channels to be determined by the Department of Health'.[84] The Commission appears to have given considerable thought as to whether contraception came within their terms of reference, and efforts were made to dissuade them from considering the matter. In November 1970, Elizabeth Lovatt-Dolan, a member of the Catholic Women's Federation, informed Archbishop McQuaid that 'my information is that as yet the Commission had not had evidence from the Fertility Guidance Clinic, and I gather the Commission is having second thoughts about receiving evidence at all, having regard to their terms of reference'.[85] The Report of the Commission stated that they had received submissions from IFPRA and the FGC. In order to demonstrate that family planning came within their remit, they noted that 'the subject of family planning and the status of women comes within the programme of work with which the United Nations *Commission on the Status of Women* (which can be seen as the parent/progenitor of the Irish Commission), concerns itself', and they cited the 1968 UN Conference on Human Rights in Tehran and the 1969 UN Declaration on Social Progress and Development.[86]

Contraception was a divisive issue for most sections of Irish society, and women were no exception. Stopper has described contraception as 'one of the IWLM's most delicate and important demands'; she claims that the founders 'were aware of the complexities entangled in the contraception debate and they knew that they would have to tread more carefully with this issue'.[87] Council for the Status of Women (CSW) was established in 1973 as an umbrella group for women's organisations, with a mission to campaign for the implementation of the recommendations of the *Commission on the Status of Women* and to advance women's rights '*through established means*'. The membership included long-established organisations such as the Irish Countrywomen's Association (ICA), and explicitly feminist organisations.[88] The CSW did not make a submission to government on the 1974 contraceptive bill or following its spectacular defeat on the second reading. They eventually held a special meeting on family planning in the autumn of 1975 where member organisations were asked for their views – but the questions were carefully framed, in

---

[84] *Commission on the Status of Women*, para 574.   [85] DDA XX/96/1, 24 November 1970.
[86] *Commission on the Status of Women*, paras 569–571.
[87] Stopper, *Monday at Gaj's*, pp. 173–4.
[88] Connolly, *The Irish women's movement*, pp. 98–100.

terms of regulation/restriction, rather than access, presumably in the hope of placating conservative organisations.

1. Does your organisation think that legislation is necessary or desirable to control contraceptives?
2. Does your organisation think that we should urge this upon the government and the media?

Nineteen organisations favoured legislation, two were against and one abstained. Six did not attend that meeting – presumably to avoid having to express an opinion. There was considerable divergence between the nineteen that favoured legislation. Adapt – The Association for Deserted and Single Parents – believed that contraceptives should only be available at health centres and family planning clinics. The Single Women's Association wanted a clamp down on the existing freedom to import contraceptives and illicit sales, but they had no objections to methods approved by the Catholic church. The Dublin University Women Graduates Association (DUWGA) argued that severe restrictions would tend to encourage a black market; contraceptives should only be available in pharmacies, to people over the age of 16 (the age of consent). Faced with such widely diverging views, the CSW did not issue a statement.[89] Linda Connolly suggests that 'This provides an indication of the conscious sensitivity of the CSW to the conservative values of Irish society, the need to be more cautious to avoid de-mobilisation and also the ideological orientation of the majority of its constituent organisations and members'.[90] It also reflects a lack of leadership on this issue.

The ICA was Ireland's largest women's organisation with approximately 1,000 guilds (branches), the majority in provincial towns and villages. Journalist Monica McEnroy, who was active in the IFPRA, complained that they would rather write letters to the newspapers about 'black spots on tomatoes' than express a point of view on contraception.[91] When the ICA surveyed its guilds in 1974 about the entire range of recommendations in the report of the *Commission on the Status of Women*, many reported that they had decided 'not to discuss' contraception; the matter should be 'left to conscience', or 'left to individual couples' – avoiding the fact that legislation was necessary if many couples were to exercise their preferred options. One guild in county Cavan recorded that 'members felt it was up to each couple to satisfy their own conscience in relation to this matter. We felt that a lengthy discussion on it would prove embarrassing to some'. Another replied, 'yes provide no method is adopted that contravenes the law of God or runs counter to nature'. Iniscarra, county Cork balloted its members: fourteen wanted 'no change'; two favoured

---

[89] UCDA Gemma Hussey Papers, P179/40.
[90] Connolly, *The Irish women's movement*, p. 147.   [91] *II*, 27 October 1970.

making contraceptives available without restrictions; nine favoured making them available with restrictions; three wanted them available for financial or medical reasons only, three only through family planning clinics, one only on doctor's prescription and two to married couples only and with a requirement to produce a marriage certificate; and twenty-seven endorsed the recommendations of the *Commission on the Status of Women*. Another Cork guild reported that 'members adopted a conservative attitude and seem content with the status quo'. Most guilds that favoured making contraceptives available wanted them confined to married couples. But many preferred to remain silent. The ICA position is consistent with opinion polls showing that farmers were the most conservative social group.[92]

The ICA conducted another survey in 1978 through a questionnaire drawn up by the CSW which was published in their magazine *The Countrywoman*. This captured the views of individuals, not guilds, though only 1,158 members replied. Seventy-eight percent favoured some form of National Family Planning Service; 28 per cent of those who were not in favour of such a service would support a natural family planning service; 25 per cent wanted a service without discrimination available regardless of marital status and 62 per cent (and 80% of those aged under forty-two years) wanted more information on different forms of family planning. Respondents with large families and those on low incomes were most interested in getting more information.[93] The small proportion of members who responded makes it difficult to determine the significance of these findings.

4.9   Well Woman and the Contraception Action Programme

The Well Woman Clinic which opened in 1978 was the first feminist-centred clinic, offering a range of medical advice and assistance including family planning and abortion referral. The clinic was picketed and subjected to occasional visits by the gardaí, but the publicity – plus advertisements in magazines such as *Magill* and the best-selling *Sunday World* (provided without charge in the early years), and on Ireland's expanding network of pirate radio stations – attracted many callers. Directed by Anne Connolly, a former officer of the Trinity College Student's Union, initial funding came from the Marie Stopes Clinics. They had decided to open a clinic in Dublin and asked Connolly to become the director. She had reservations about the links with Population Services International, which controlled the Marie Stopes Clinics, and she disliked the commercial ethos. Population Services

---

[92] NLI, Irish Countrywomen's Association (ICA) Papers, 39866/4 Questionnaires Commission on the Status of Women.
[93] NLI, ICA papers, 39865/1.

International sold sex toys and had engaged in some ethically dubious sterilisation practices in developing countries, but their organisational processes and expertise proved invaluable.[94] Connolly insisted that the clinic would be an autonomous company, and within a year they had broken all links with Marie Stopes.[95] Well Woman reflected the spirit of second-wave feminism: teaching women about their bodies and how to care for their health. No stirrups were used when conducting gynaecological investigations; those attending were described as clients, not patients and women were given their charts to read in the waiting room. Marital status was irrelevant. Well Woman provided treatment for pre-menstrual tension, menopause, postnatal problems, psycho-sexual counselling and artificial insemination, initially from a husband, later using donor sperm, plus a wide range of contraceptive methods, including male sterilisation. Their success highlighted major shortcomings in existing medical services for women. They were open about providing contraception to single women and confidential pregnancy tests.[96] It was the first Irish clinic to offer the morning after pill and a post-coital IUD.[97] Most controversially, it acknowledged that it offered non-directive counselling and referrals for women seeking abortions, plus a check-up after a termination. The advertising slogan – 'for people who wanted to choose' – consciously echoed the 'women's right to choose' slogan often used in campaigns for abortion rights.

The clinic was staffed by trained doctors, nurses and receptionists.[98] Despite the strong feminist ethos, it never ran a service that didn't pay. The business model assumed fifteen fee-paying clients to three who were seen free of charge, indicating that a majority were middle class.[99] Those attending had to pass the gauntlet of women on their knees saying the rosary. Condoms were sold from a machine in the reception area. They dispensed and sold the pill at a much lower price than pharmacies but could not dispense it free to GMS patients. Some non-paying clients travelled long distances with the clinic's name and address. Many were pregnant single women, who felt that they could not tell their parents. Many married women who were referred for abortions did not inform their husbands. Well Woman provided referrals for amniocentesis and genetic counselling, and they hosted the first meeting of the Rape Crisis Centre – which developed as a separate entity.[100] Reflecting the real dilemmas that many Irish women faced, they often referred clients to a sympathetic priest, generally a

---

[94] Interview with Anne Connolly, 22 August 2015.
[95] *IT*, 8 May 1982, The Saturday Interview.
[96] Anne Connolly interview; pregnancy tests were only available through laboratories and required samples to be submitted by a doctor. Jesse Olszynko-Gryn, 'The feminist appropriation of pregnancy testing in 1970s Britain', *Women's History Review*, 28, no 6, 2019, pp. 869–894.
[97] Anne Connolly interview.   [98] *Irish Press*, 30 July 1978.
[99] Anne Connolly interview.   [100] Dr Áine Sullivan, interview 19 August 2013.

member of the Society of Jesus, whose headquarters were across the street.[101] In 1982, Connolly noted that they had never been prosecuted, though gardaí carried out several raids. On at least one occasion, having completed their formal duties, they sought advice about contraception.[102]

It took approximately nine months to establish the Well Woman clinic. Many landlords refused to rent space. Recruiting nurses proved relatively easy, and the initial staff had all trained with IFPA. It proved more difficult to recruit doctors. Two junior doctors who were training in gynaecology were informed by a consultant that they must choose between working with Well Woman and a specialist career, so Well Woman decided to recruit doctors who were planning careers in general practice, because this presented fewer problems.[103] Dr Áine Sullivan was approached at a seminar on the menopause and asked to consider working with Well Woman, which she did for several years.

Well Woman's reliance on medical professionals and its strong business model contrasted with the Contraception Action Programme, which was launched in 1976 by Irish Women United (IWU), a radical feminist movement that championed a wide range of issues, including divorce, free childcare, equal pay, and equality in education. Their contraception campaign specifically targeted working-class communities. The IWU activists were young, many in their teens.[104] The CAP campaigned for free contraception, and they opened a shop Contraception Unlimited – the first to sell condoms and other non-prescription contraception openly, initially in Harcourt St, but later in the popular Dandelion Market, off St. Stephen's Green. They distributed condoms in Dublin working-class communities such as Ballymun and Ballyfermot. This campaign drew support from other women's groups (and from FPS), but it was led by IWU.[105] CAP members in Cork sold condoms from market stalls and in working-class housing estates.[106] Anne Speed, one of the founding members, claimed that they didn't get the support they had expected from established left-wing parties, such as the Communist Party and Sinn Féin and from other women's groups.[107] CAP operated without any medical involvement – they also campaigned for abortion rights and were involved in establishing the Rape Crisis Centre.

In 1977/78, CAP conducted a survey in Ballinteer, a rapidly expanding south Dublin suburb, with many young families; 540 married women, 86 per cent aged from 21 to 40 completed questionnaires. Sixty per cent had one or more children aged under five; 47 per cent were using some form of family

[101] Áine Sullivan interview.   [102] *IT*, 8 May 1982.   [103] Anne Connolly interview.

[104] Connolly, *The Irish women's movement*, p. 90; Laura Kelly, 'Irishwomen United, the Contraception Action Programme, and the campaign for free, safe and legal contraception, c. 1975–81', *IHS*, 43, no 164, 2019, pp. 269–97.

[105] Kelly, 'Irishwomen united', p. 284.

[106] Cloatre and Enright, '"On the perimeter of the lawful"', p. 495.

[107] Pat Brennan, 'Women in revolt'; *Magill*, April 1979.

planning; one-third had attended a family planning clinic. Only 18 per cent believed that family planning provided by GPs was adequate. Among those who were dissatisfied with their GP's service 39 women explained that their GP only provided the pill; 27 claimed that he/she would not advise on all methods; 34 found their GP unsympathetic to personal problems; and 115 said that the GP had insufficient time to discuss family planning. 93.7 per cent wanted a family planning service in their local health clinic; 57 per cent believed that it should be free, though 32 per cent believed that those who were ineligible for free medical care should pay.[108]

4.10   The Doctors

There must be an end put to the spread of family planning clinics throughout the land. Indeed, some of those already opened should be closed for they are a disgrace and a slur on the medical profession. They represent a signal failure of Medicine as a caring profession and the fact that they exist at all shows that the doctors to whom people should be able to turn for help – the GPs etc… have been found wanting.

Clinics must be closed. …The medical profession must assume its responsibilities and provide for the needs of the community in terms of both service and the adequate training of doctors – those already in practice and those to come.[109]

Although some doctors were involved in establishing family planning clinics, the medical profession played a peripheral role during the 1970s when access to non-medical contraception was rapidly expanding. Many doctors adopted an ostrich-like attitude towards contraception, and there are numerous reports of women who were reluctant to ask their GP to prescribe the Pill, for fear of being refused. Women on GMS panels could find it difficult to switch to a more amenable doctor. One Donegal mother of three wrote to *Woman's Choice* because her doctor had refused her a prescription. She was advised that if his conscience would not permit him to prescribe, he should refer her to a colleague; alternatively, she should contact a family planning clinic in Derry (Northern Ireland). Another reported that her doctor told her to consult her priest before he would consider prescribing. *Woman's Choice* had failed to identify a sympathetic doctor in her area, so she was referred to an IFPA clinic. Another woman, coming to the end of her supply of the Pill, but unable to travel to Dublin, asked for the name of a local doctor 'who would prescribe without questioning or making it a big issue'. Another woman preferred to seek a prescription from a doctor that she did not know. Some women, who had been prescribed the Pill at their post-natal visit to a maternity hospital, and needed a renewed prescription, found that no local doctor would oblige. One woman dreaded applying to her doctor for a prescription

---

[108] Ballinteer Family Planning Survey – copy on NAI DT 2008/148/219.
[109] *JIMA*, March 27 1976 Forum: 'Professional Negligence' by Dr Michael Flynn.

'as I only got it out of him the last time after a verbal battle. I feel I couldn't go through this again'.[110]

By the mid-1970s, women's magazines were advising many correspondents to consider non-chemical methods of contraception. Women holding a medical card could have an IUD fitted free of charge by a family planning clinic, but GPs might charge a small fee.[111] The greatest difficulty was finding a doctor who had been trained in fitting IUDs. By 1979, the IFPA claimed that approximately 100 doctors had completed their training course.[112] One married woman, who had an IUD fitted when living in England, went to her doctor for a check-up 'but all I got was a lecture on the wrong I was doing so we parted on bad terms'.[113] A young woman who had experienced two difficult pregnancies reported that

I asked my gynaecologist for the pill and he refused and said he didn't approve of it and has never given it to anyone for a long period. He did however give it to me to regulate my periods for two months…I suggested that what I really had in mind was having an IUD fitted and he was shocked, and I wondered what I said wrong to get him so angry. He said if that's what I had in mind that he couldn't help and would not tell me of any doctor who would do this for me. I then went to my family doctor who delivered me into this world, and he would not help me either. So it seems that no one who knows my record of two difficult deliveries wants to help me and I have no alternative but to turn to strangers for help

She had two month's supply of the Pill 'and after that it's at the mercy of God'.[114] One of the most revealing letters came from a thirty-year-old woman who had given birth to seven children in nine-and-a-half years. She had a long talk with a priest who advised her to use contraception, but her doctor would not prescribe the Pill because of her medical history. A friend in England sent her some 'sheaths, but when they arrived, we found we both don't know to use them. Both of us had never seen them before until now'. She was referred to FPS for advice and future supplies.[115] A mother with four children under six years of age asked whether she would need a doctor's letter, or proof of marriage to obtain condoms from FPS. Some couples who were using condoms were keen to remain in good standing with the Catholic church and the magazine received several requests for names of sympathetic priests, who would act as confessors. One woman, who had obtained condoms begged for help 'because I couldn't bear to be denied the sacraments and it would also worry my husband, who is a loving partner and father.…'[116]

[110] Woman's Choice, 29 March 1973, 19 April 1973, 17 May 1973, 13 September 1973; 22 November 1973.
[111] Woman's Choice, 18 October 1973.   [112] Magill, January 1979.
[113] Woman's Choice, 4 October 1973.   [114] Woman's Choice, 3 January 1974.
[115] Woman's Choice, 7 November 1974.   [116] Woman's Choice, 12 June 1975; 21 August 1975.

Family planning remained a divisive issue for the medical profession. In 1974, the Consultative Council on General Medical Practice in Ireland recommended that married couples should be allowed to use the contraceptive of their choice and the Oireachtas should legislate accordingly. The IMU delegated the question to a committee, which Rose claimed 'effectively crushed' the issue.[117] In 1977, the IMA annual conference approved a resolution advocating free contraception – including IUDs, by fourteen votes to ten, but approximately fifty members who were present abstained, and an even greater number chose not to attend that session.[118] More than fifty doctors signed a letter to the IMA President protesting against this vote being taken; they noted that 80 per cent of the membership was Catholic.[119]

The annual reports of the Dublin maternity hospitals give some indications as to what, if any family planning was provided. The services in hospitals outside Dublin remain a mystery, because they did not publish annual clinical reports. Dublin gynaecologists were mainly concerned with older women who had given birth to numerous children; in such cases, an additional pregnancy could present medical risks and unacceptable social pressures. In 1971, the Coombe hospital elected a new Master – James Clinch. A Catholic who was raised in Britain and a graduate of Trinity College, as a junior doctor in Cardiff, he was involved in setting up a family planning clinic in the main maternity hospital, when family planning was belatedly provided under the NHS. As Master, he held a weekly family planning clinic for women who had given birth in the hospital. He prescribed the Pill, and he fitted the IUD, which was a medically appropriate form of contraception for older mothers of large families, though its use was controversial. Over time, somewhat to his surprise, many older mothers were referred to him by the sisters in charge of post-natal wards, and the hospital's social worker, who had initially been hostile to his clinic. The Master of a Dublin maternity hospital has exceptional authority, so he opened this clinic without seeking or receiving approval from the hospital board or fellow consultants. When Dr Clinch's term ended in 1978, the clinic was discontinued.[120] The Rotunda operated a low-profile family planning clinic for post-natal mothers. They prescribed the Pill, and women who required other forms of contraception were referred to the IFPA clinic in nearby Mountjoy Square.[121] When Dermot MacDonald succeeded Declan Meagher as Master of Holles St, his first report, for 1977, reinstated a heading 'Family Planning Service'. It reported that the service had been reorganised, with one full-time nursing sister providing an

---

[117] Rose, 'An outline of fertility control, focusing on the element of abortion in the Republic of Ireland to 1976', pp. 43, 47 56. UCDA Barry Desmond Papers, box 352.
[118] *IP*, 15 April 1977.   [119] *JIMA*, 18 June 1977.
[120] Information supplied by Dr James Clinch.   [121] Information from Dr Andrew Curtain

educational programme in the post-natal wards. Mothers were interviewed; all methods of family planning were explained 'with particular reference to their advantages and disadvantages – their risks, success rates and failures rates' and 'all devices' were displayed during these talks – which would appear to suggest that advice was not confined to 'natural methods'. Appointments were made for women to attend CMAC or ovulation methods clinics elsewhere but not apparently with the IFPA. Women with 'particular medical or social indications' were given out-patient appointments, but only 43 per cent turned up – defaulters were contacted. Only 19 of the 128 mothers who were identified in 1977 as having 'particular indications' had serious medical needs; the remaining 110 had social needs – 'in the broadest sense'. At the follow-up clinics, 'All methods were discussed with each couple or with each mother at the clinics. Natural methods alone were chosen by 38 couples (73%), 10 selected other methods and 4 were undecided. A postal advisory service has also been established'.[122] The high proportion opting for natural methods suggests that those who were interested in other methods went elsewhere; alternatively, the information presented may have directed women towards 'natural methods'. The tone of the 1978 report was different. 'The emphasis is on natural methods', though all methods were explained, and devices displayed. All women were given an explanatory leaflet about 'natural' methods.[123] In 1976, Patricia Crowley, then a senior house officer, was reprimanded by a nursing sister for prescribing the pill to a young mother in her twenties, who had recently given birth to her second child; her eldest was one year old.[124]

4.10.1   Opposing Voices

The opening of family planning clinics and the growing (if limited) availability of contraceptives prompted a conservative backlash. There is a widely held opinion that Vatican II had only a limited influence on Irish Catholicism, but as Donnelly shows, the liturgical reforms prompted a wave of new religious devotions among conservative Irish Catholics that were centred on Mariology. Many of those who were active in these devotional movements joined campaigns against contraception.[125] The Nazareth Family Movement originated in a meeting of people who were campaigning to have the rosary recited nightly on television. They expressed shock at the 'wave of pornography sweeping the country', and the hostile response to Dr McQuaid's 1971 pastoral letter. However, the Dublin archdiocese was concerned about their links with

---

[122] Holles St 1977, p. 68.   [123] Holles St 1978.   [124] Dr Patricia Crowley informant.
[125] James S. Donnelly, 'Opposing the modern world: The cult of the Virgin Mary in Ireland, 1965–1985', Éire-Ireland, 40, no 1&2, 2005, pp. 183–245.

devotion to 'Our Lady of All Nations' – a movement that originated in the Netherlands, which promoted a range of prophecies.[126]

The number of such movements increased during the 1970s. Several expressed belated opposition to the decision of the 1972 referendum which removed article 44 of the 1937 Constitution relating to the 'special position of the Roman Catholic Church', and they were horrified by the Supreme Court Judgment in the McGee case. One woman from Galway who claimed to be writing on behalf of an unnamed organisation of mothers, protested at the prospect that Mary Robinson's 1973 bill would be passed. This unnamed group also objected to the imminent opening of a Russian Embassy in Ireland 'as we consider it will also be injurious to the welfare of our children'. This was not the only letter to link the new Russian Embassy with legalising contraception; another woman who claimed that enacting Mary Robinson's 1973 bill would turn Ireland 'into a Second Soddom and Gomorrah', claimed that the Russians 'are already here, as witness all the strikes', before going on to complain that the Russians had secured cheap surplus EEC butter'.[127] Activists targeted elected politicians, and national and local newspapers. They were highly critical of RTÉ, the national broadcaster, and Conor Cruise O'Brien, the Minister responsible for overseeing broadcasting, who was known to favour access to contraception. The League of Decency, headed by T.B. Murray, wrote several letters to Taoiseach protesting at the appearance of pro-contraception speakers on RTÉ and the failure of the RTÉ director-general to address their grievances.[128]

4.11   International Links

By the early 1970s, the Irish campaign against contraception had developed links with anti-abortion movements in Britain and the USA, and their discourse increasingly conflated abortion and contraception. In 1971, Dr John Kelly, chair of the Right to Life Commission in Indiana, came to Ireland to give a lecture. He was prompted to do so by a letter from his daughter, a student at UCD, who claimed that 'abortion is more of a problem in Ireland than is spoken of'. The Irish Right to Life Society was led by Mrs Mavis Keniry.[129] In January 1973, Fr Paul Marx, OSA, a leading US anti-abortion campaigner, who was touring Britain, paid a short visit to Ireland, which was organised by the British Society for the Protection of the Unborn Child (SPUC). He told an audience of student nurses that 'You have in Ireland, a group which

---

[126] DDA XXI/94/5/1.   [127] NAI TD 2004/21/461.
[128] NAI DT 2005/7/349, October–December 1974.
[129] DDA XX/103/1. Dr Kelly was involved with the La Lèche group that promoted breastfeeding. Mrs Keniry was a midwife.

promotes contraception. I say right now that that leads to abortion'.[130] The American influence is evident in the many letters to the Taoiseach enclosing gruesome pictures of aborted foetuses, which originated in the USA.[131] There were demands for a referendum to overturn the McGee ruling; in hindsight the seeds of the campaign for a constitutional amendment to affirm the rights of the unborn can be detected by 1974.

Many anti-contraception groups were led by women. Ireland was by no means unique in generating a divided response to second-wave feminism. The opening sentence in Marjorie Sprull's book about American feminism states that 'There were two women's movements in the 1970s: a women's rights movement that enjoyed tremendous success, especially early in the decade and a conservative women's movement that formed in opposition and grew stronger as the decade continued'.[132] In Britain, the 1967 abortion act and decriminalisation of homosexuality resulted in the emergence of counter-movements with prominent female leaders such as Mary Whitehouse and Nuala Scarisbrook. A similar split occurred in the United States, where powerful women, such as Phyllis Shlaffly championed the role of women in the home and opposition to abortion, securing significant political influence.

The Irish Family League (IFL) was founded in May 1973 by Maire Bhreathnach and Mavis Keniry, with Miss Mary Kennedy – an indefatigable letter-writer to newspapers as secretary. The League was founded at a seminar organised by Hamish Fraser, an Englishman and former communist who became involved in ultra-traditional Catholic causes, including opposition to Vatican II. Fraser was concerned at 'the penetration of traditional Irish Catholic society by secularist pressures – both domestic and external'. The IFL's mission was 'to combat divorce, contraception, abortion and euthanasia and defending the rights of parents and the family'. In a tribute to Fraser, after his death, Mrs Keniry noted that he collected the first subscriptions, printed the first IFL pamphlets, organised three seminars with speakers from the USA, UK and Europe and visited the USA to seek financial support.[133] The IFL presented an apocalyptic vision for Ireland. Legislation permitting contraception in 1974 would, they claimed be followed by abortion in 1978, euthanasia in 1980 and a dystopian 1984. They circulated a four-page stencilled leaflet

---

[130] *Irish Independent*, 17 January 1973.

[131] NAI DT 2005/7/347 *Life or Death*, published by Illinois Right to Life Committee Chicago.

[132] Marjorie J. Sprull, *Divided we stand. The battle over women's rights and family values that polarized American politics* (Bloomsbury, 2017), p. 1.

[133] *Hamish Fraser. A memorial volume. Fatal Star* (edited and introduced by Geoffrey Lawman, The Neumann Press, Long Prairie, Minnesota 1987), pp. 288–9. I am indebted to Patrick Maume for informing me of the origins of the Irish Family League and lending me his copy of this rare volume – only 400 copies were printed, and for alerting me to Fraser's role in the Irish anti-contraception movement.

(the quality of most early publications was primitive; material originating in the USA stands out for that reason), titled *Our Way of Life is in Danger* to all Ministers, TDs and Senators. It warned that the Supreme Court was in danger of exceeding its functions.[134]

The League combined opposition to contraception with sympathy for militant republicanism – a combination that has generally been overlooked. They prepared a dossier on the Dublin family planning clinics, and a 'Who's Who' of those working in that field, which they sent to all TDs and Senators, with a list of newspapers and magazines described as giving undue publicity to illegal contraceptive services. *Is contraception the answer*, a booklet published by Veritas, the CTSI publisher, asked, 'Is it not monstrous that there should be men and women who consider themselves patriots, yet have the impertinence to insist that Ireland can hope to enjoy unity only if she is prepared to renounce her treasured Christian heritage, in favour of the decadent norms of her ancient enemy?' Linda Kavanagh, a journalist with *Woman's Choice*, claimed that the brochure was initiated by the IFL though they were not mentioned on the pamphlet. The IFPA published a rebuttal titled *Facts on Contraception. An answer to the Irish Family League.*[135] They sent copies to TDs, Senators, and medical practitioners; groups that had been supplied with copies of *Is Contraception the Answer.*

The Cork-based Mná na hÉireann (women of Ireland) led by Úna Mhic Mhathúna, and Áine Uí Mhurchú – married women with young families, was established in 1973 with a mission 'to uphold the dignity and rights, moral and civil of Irish women'. They were opposed to changes in the law relating to abortion and divorce and to married women working outside the home. They wished to retain Article 41 of the 1937 Constitution – relating to women in the home and they campaigned for 'a living wage for the head of each family to enable them to live as befits the dignity of man', ensuring that women were not forced by economic pressures to work outside the home. They were also opposed to the establishment of state-run nurseries (there is no evidence of such plans) and state-supported family planning clinics. Mná na hÉireann alleged that Mary Robinson was 'a Trinity College nominee to the Seanad and is therefore not an elected representative of the people, and should not be allowed to impose her views on the Irish public'.[136]

When journalist Mary Leland interviewed Mná na hÉireann, the secretary of that organisation taped the interview and took copious notes. Leland commented that 'They believe that the press and radio are under the influence of the "handful" of people, promoting a stream of pro-contraception propaganda, who are backed

---

[134] NAI DT 2005/7/347.
[135] IFPA annual report 1974. There is a copy of the pamphlet on NAI DT 2005/7/345.
[136] Mary Leland interview, *Irish Times*, 24 November 1973.

by capitalistic vested interests'.[137] The Irish Right to Life Society told Kavanagh that they believed that the media were not honest, and 'preferred to carry on in their own quiet way'. Kavanagh reported that 'When given the opportunity of putting across their point of view, [they] seem reluctant to do so'. Researching this story was 'almost like trying to write an article on the activities of the Special Branch [the garda national security section]. After going round in circles for days, you still find that you haven't got very much further'. They refused to grant her an interview as they felt it would be 'unethical' that it should appear in a magazine that was in favour of contraception.[138] Dr Andrew Rynne, a prominent advocate and supporter of family planning, claimed that it was very difficult to gain any information as to the number of members, their aims, objectives and frequency of meetings. 'It is sometimes hard even to be sure who their leaders are, or how they reach a consensus about their various policies. Some guilds and leagues avoid all publicity; their leaders are not contactable by telephone and are not willing to give statements to the Press, much less to the author of a book. Influence rather than information seems to be the preferred tactic of their founders'. He described their working methods as 'Individual silence ...coupled with collective sloganeering'.[139]

Kavanagh described the SPUC as the only organisation that was 'forthright and helpful'. Its leaders – Mr and Mrs Desmond Broadberry – parents of eighteen children – had campaigned against the 1972 referendum to remove article 44 from the constitution. Mrs Broadberry was an enthusiastic advocate of the Billings method.[140] The Irish League of Decency, founded in 1974 by J.B. Murray, was determined to prevent the passage of the Fine Gael/Labour Government's contraceptive bill, believing that it would result in the complete demoralisation of society. *Woman's Choice* reported that the sixty individuals who attended the League's inaugural meeting were almost all in their 'senior years'.[141] Their aim was 'to arrest the decay so evident in our modern society.... To end, or at least curb permissiveness with all its attendant evils (e.g. promiscuity, contraception, divorce, broken marriages and loss of souls); to stamp out pornography, excessive drinking and drug-addition, indecent films, plays books and magazines and to endeavour to restore the dignity of women and respect for them by men, and encourage those who are straying from their God to return to him'. Murray claimed that the organisation was open to all creeds and classes. Taoiseach, Liam Cosgrave received a small number of letters from members of the Protestant community, emphasising that not all Protestants were in favour of making contraception readily available, one intriguing feature of Irish moral conservatism

---

[137] *Irish Times*, 24 November 1973.
[138] Kavanagh, *Women's Choice*, 10 January 1974.
[139] Andrew Rynne, *Abortion. The Irish question* (Ward River Press, Dublin, 1982), pp. 44–8.
[140] *Woman's Choice*, Lynda Kavanagh, The anti-contraception lobby, 10 January 1974.
[141] *Woman's Choice*, 4 May 1974.

is the almost complete absence of Protestant voices. This contrasts with the USA where much of the momentum in the Pro-Family, Pro-Life came from Protestant churches; perhaps because in the United States, conservatives did not oppose birth control, confining their campaign to abortion and other life-style issues.[142]

4.12   'Natural' Family Planning – A House Divided

Information about Catholic church-approved methods of family planning only became widely accessible in the 1970s. In 1973, when Keith Wilson-Davis carried out a survey of married women aged 15–44, asking about their attitudes to contraception, 62 per cent of those who reported using family planning had used, or were using the safe period.[143] The first Irish CMAC conference was held in 1969. By the following year, there were eleven centres in Ireland, north and south.[144] In 1971, the director of the Dublin archdiocesan marriage advisory bureau reported a steady attendance of 10–12 couples each week at classes on the temperature method. He was not sanguine about its popularity; only a small number of Dublin doctors were 'genuinely interested'; 'a smaller number again' recommended the method to patients and coached them. It was 'exceedingly difficult to find the kind of doctor who has such a degree of conviction about this method as would encourage him to help people here at the bureau; it was too restrictive and too complicated for the average person and doctors found it easier to prescribe the pill.' He suggested that the church should establish classes in working-class suburbs like Ballyfermot and Crumlin, because couples found it difficult to travel into the city centre. He advised that classes should be given by married women; it did not require medical qualifications.[145] The Bishop of Cork, Dr. Cornelius Lucey, closed the local branch of the CMAC in 1972 because a medical counsellor with CMAC had told an audience at UCC that 93 per cent of attendees sought advice on family planning. He established a new programme overseen by an advisory council of priests, who would lead all training courses.[146]

Nurses were a key group in promoting 'natural' family planning. By the 1950s, the Irish Nurses Organisation (INO) had fully subscribed to 'Catholic social teaching' and they supported the Catholic church and the Irish medical profession during the debate on the future of the Irish health service.[147]

---

[142] Sprull, *Divided we stand*, pp. 235–61, especially p. 250.

[143] Keith Wilson-Davis, 'Irish attitudes to family planning', *Social Studies*, vol 3, no 3, 1974, p. 270.

[144] Marshall, *Fifty years*, pp. 73.4.

[145] DDA/CSWB/Agencies AB8/B/XIX, 27 April 1971.

[146] Murray, 'The best news Ireland ever got'; *Catholic Standard*, 19 January 1973.

[147] Mark Loughrey, *A century of service. A history of the Irish Nurses and Midwives Organisation, 1919–2019* (Irish Academic Press, Newbridge, 2019), pp. 103, 107.

In 1969, the *Irish Nurses' Journal* reported on a 'teach in' at the National Maternity Hospital, attended by nurses and midwives from all parts of Ireland. The article expressed some disappointment 'with the methods advocated' but qualified this with the statement that the 'enthusiasm with which these well-tried methods were explained, and the attention paid to them by the patients whom we met left us in no doubt as to the value of these methods'. The article, which included a chart showing the safe period, reported a remarkable, and unproven 96 per cent success rate for the temperature method, and a success rate of 84 per cent for the calendar method.[148] The removal of the marriage bar for public service employees meant that a growing number of married nurses and midwives were working in Irish health services, and some became instructors and advocates for 'natural' family planning. In 1974 *The World of Irish Nursing*, the official journal of the INO nominated two members – a religious sister who was a midwife tutor in the Lourdes Hospital Drogheda (run by the Medical Missionaries of Mary), and a nurse from the regional hospital in Limerick to serve on the Natural Methods Family Planning Council.[149] The goal was to spread information about 'natural' methods and provide the necessary back-up, including research and education. I suspect that this Council was short lives; it has left no trace. The failure to provide substantial support for 'natural' family planning – both information and training – suggests that the Irish Hierarchy was either arrogant or complacent. Alternatively, they feared that couples who tried 'natural' methods and found them wanting would adopt more reliable methods, as happened elsewhere.

The INO took a firm stand against contraception. In 1974, they ran a seminar on contraception and abortion – which attracted a capacity audience. Ita Leydon, a nurse tutor at St James' Hospital wrote that the seminar had revealed 'the great need which is felt by nurses for information and guidelines on these controversial but very importance aspects of modern life'; many nurses were 'quite confused even on basic issues such as the various forms of contraception; whether the pill and IUD were abortifacients; somebody asked "who or what is Billing". Many are asking what the church says, what do doctors think and above all what should nurses do'. She gave a list of recommended readings, including *Humanae Vitae*, John Billings, *The Ovulation Method*, and other works of proven orthodoxy.[150]

A policy statement drafted by the INO in 1978 acknowledged that couples had a right to plan their families. It recommended methods that were based on 'the natural cycle of fertility' – that is those permitted by the Catholic church.

[148] *Irish Nurses Journal*, 8 August 1969.
[149] *World of Irish Nursing*, 3, no 4, April 1974, p. 54.
[150] *World of Irish Nursing*, April 1974, p. 56.

The use of 'any IUD, any medication or any interference which hinders the normal development of a pregnancy was a denial of the basic right to life'. This statement expressed concern at the apparent lack of follow-up of women who were prescribed the Pill; it recommended that comprehensive counselling, accurate instruction and follow-up support by trained personnel should be available, and it welcomed the WHO study on the Billings method taking place in Ireland (discussed later in this chapter).[151] Loughrey has highlighted 'the frequent references to Catholic teaching by Catholic commentators' in INO publications.[152]

4.13   Billings

The role of the CMAC in promoting 'natural' family planning was overtaken by others with a more evangelistic fervour, who promoted the Billings Method. This was named after the Australian neurologist John Billings, who with his wife Evelyn developed a method of detecting ovulation by monitoring changes in cervical mucus. One Irish source[153] has told me that Billings was asked to carry out his research by the Australian primate, Irish-born Cardinal Mannix. It was widely known that changes in cervical mucous were linked to ovulation, and scientists had been working to devise a method of fertility control based on this. The first studies were carried out in 1945.[154] The names of the other scientists who contributed to this research feature only in scholarly publications. Billings published his first research in 1964.[155] He was active in the Australian CMAC, but they parted company in 1970, and he continued to receive considerable support from the Australian Catholic church. It appears that the Australian CMAC was uncomfortable with the passionate confidence of Billings advocates, and they were sceptical of claims that the method could be easily understood by 'the simple and the poor'.[156] There appears to have been a similar division in Ireland. The CMAC was more cautious in its claims, and they advised couples to use as many indicators as possible: calendar, temperature and mucus – a combination known as the sympto-thermal method.[157] Billings claimed that multiple methods resulted in anxiety and confusion.[158]

According to John Bonnar, 'The main advance of the Billings method was to teach women themselves to detect changes in the cervical mucus',

---

[151] *World of Irish Nursing*, 7, no 5, May 1978, p. 7.
[152] Loughrey, *A century of service*, p. 120.   [153] Dr Niall Tubridy.
[154] David Nowlan, *IT*, 24 September 1971.
[155] J.J. Billings, *The ovulation method* (Advocate Press, Melbourne, 1964); Jane Quinlan, *The Billings method*. Information, books charts and stamps (Cork, 1976).
[156] Katharine Betts, 'The Billings method of family planning: an assessment', *Studies in Family Planning*, 15, no 6, November–December 1984, pp. 253–4.
[157] Marie-Therese Joye SRN.   [158] Betts, 'The Billings method', pp. 253–4.

whereas the temperature method required training, and an instrument. Billings described his method as going back to nature, escaping 'the tyranny of the thermometer' with women training other women to detect changes in their body. It was in tune with second-wave feminism in dismissing professionals, promoting self-awareness of the body, self-screening (i.e. checking the breast for possible changes), and female networks. Evelyn Billings was a critical figure in this process. Apart from the 'back to nature' message, Billings claimed to expand the days of safe sex – enabling couples to have sex *before* ovulation, which was discouraged by the temperature method, and he claimed that his method was effective for women with irregular menstrual cycles. One scholar concluded that its success rested on the institutional power of the Catholic church and fears about the medical risks associated with the contraceptive pill.[159]

According to NAOMI – the National Association for the Ovulation Methods in Ireland, Billings was introduced into Ireland in 1971 by Fr. Dermot Hurley, an Irish Columban priest, and former head of the CMAC in Fiji, who met Dr Billings in Melbourne. In an article in the *Irish Times*, Fr Hurley suggested that this was the magic solution. He quoted a comment by Evelyn Billings that 'there will be little need for family planning clinics in five years' time' – because it would supplant barrier and chemical methods and it was taught woman to woman – and not in a clinical setting. According to Fr Hurley, Dr Billings, a father of nine, feared that it was so effective that 'if it were universally adopted' the birth rate might plummet.[160] *Irish Times* medical correspondent, Dr David Nowlan, poured cold water on these claims – citing a 1970 WHO report which concluded that it was not a reliable guide to detecting fertile or infertile periods; 'unless Dr Billings has stumbled on something quite new.... this method is not as successful as he claims'.[161]

The disagreement was about scientific evidence and effectiveness, but it was also ideological. In an article published in the *Irish Times*, Dr Billings presented a dystopian picture of other contraceptive methods. He dismissed the Pill, injections, and the IUD as 'a failure', claiming that many manufacturers of the Pill had ceased production and virtually all had abandoned research to develop new anovulants. He alleged that surgical sterilisation resulted in a high incidence of psychological consequences plus the risk of autoimmune disease. He gave an encyclopaedic and grim list of the medical side effects of the Pill, before going on to extol the mucous method of detecting fertility, and its success in developing, (we would now say Third World), countries where women were maintaining charts of their menstrual cycles using coloured stickers – red

[159] Betts, 'The Billings method', p. 254.   [160] *IT*, September 24 1971.
[161] *IT*, 24 September 1971.

for a menstrual period, green for 'dry days' when it was safe to have sex, and white with a baby picture for fertile days.[162] Dr Nowlan, a director of the IFPA, claimed that Dr Billings' article had 'very little basis in known fact and virtually every statement in it is either wrong or misleading'.[163]

At a conference on 'Population and Ecology' held during the 1973 Eucharistic Congress in Melbourne, the method was acclaimed as the solution to overpopulation – low cost and capable of being used by women who were illiterate. The first report of the method's effectiveness was conducted in Tonga in 1972. This trial involved 282 couples over nine months; 82 pregnancies resulted, but 50 women 'broke the rules', and it was claimed that 28 deliberately became pregnant – so only three pregnancies were attributed to method failure.[164] This became the standard approach in Billings trials. When couples found it too difficult to abstain from sex for the many days required each month, the resulting pregnancies were classified as breaking the rules – not as evidence that many couples found the method unacceptable.

Dr John Marshall reported that the Tonga study showed a pregnancy rate of 25 per cent per year, according to the Pearl formula, which was commonly used by scientists studying contraception. He described this as 'unacceptably high'.[165] Marshall conducted a study of 166 women in Britain and Ireland who were using the temperature method, having been instructed by the medical correspondence section of the British CMAC. They were asked to record a mucous chart. He concluded that this method was unsuitable for 30 per cent of the women; he reached no conclusions as to method's effectiveness.[166]

Cork appears to have been first Irish centre to promote Billings. This may be a consequence of the fact that Dr Lucey had closed the CMAC. In 1972, a clinic was opened in the Capuchin Friary by OMAS – the Ovulation Method Advisory Service, led by Sr Anne Healy SRN, who had learned the technique in New Zealand. Jane Quinlan, the wife of a UCC professor Senator Patrick Quinlan, was a prominent advocate. By 1974, there were six centres in Cork.[167] A 1974 article in *The Furrow* reported that in Cork, the method was taught one-to-one by a doctor; there were 300 users. It was being taught by a doctor in Wexford, by a 'lady doctor' in Donegal and at the Social Services Centre in

---

[162] Billings, 'New dilemma for family planners', *IT*, 24 September 1971.

[163] Nowlan, Some reasons for doubt, *IT*, 24 September 1971.

[164] M.C. Weissman, L. Foliaki, E.L. Billings and J.J. Billings, 'A trial of the ovulation method of family planning in Tonga', *Lancet*, ii, 1972, 813.

[165] John Marshall, 'The prevalence of mucous discharge as a symptom of ovulation', *Journal of Biosocial Science*, 7, 1974, p. 50.

[166] Marshall, 'The prevalence of mucous discharge', p. 55.

[167] *The ovulation method of natural family planning*. Based on a lecture by Dr Billings – no date, NLI accession stamp is 22 October 1974.

Stanhope St Convent in Dublin.[168] DOMAS – the Dublin Ovulation Advisory Service claimed to have been in existence since 1971,[169] which might be an example of Dublin/Cork competition. Dr Maeve Fitzgerald, a lecturer in anatomy at UCG, lectured on using cervical mucous to detect ovulation, as part of an extra-mural programme in 1972. Her lecture was published in the *JIMA*. She suggested that the method was no more difficult than looking for blood on a toothbrush and claimed to have taught it since the early 1960s. She conceded that 'a high level of commitment on the part of the woman and her husband is essential' but claimed that there had been no failures among couples who adhered to the method.[170]

In 1975, Conor Carr, a consultant obstetrician in Portiuncula Hospital Ballinasloe, issued a 'cautionary word' to *JIMA* readers about this method. He was conducting a study with women, who were using either the temperature or calendar method, and he described the results as 'far from encouraging general adoption of the method'.[171] In a follow-up article, he stated that 'to date the promotion of the use of the Billings Method has been conspicuous by two characteristics namely firstly the enthusiasm of the promoters and secondly the almost complete lack of statistics on the clinical results'. In his small trial with 104 post-natal women, 'virtually all private patients', 6 of the 44 who *completed* charts (from an initial 104), became pregnant within six months. He pointed out that 'the impression is generally given that this is a method which is easy to use and to teach' – his statistics suggested otherwise. By 1976, advocates of the Billings method were urging users to undergo 'prolonged individual instruction and detailed follow-up over several months'. Dr Carr suggested that the onus was on those running Woman to Woman clinics with prolonged instruction to produce statistics showing their failure rates.[172] This article provoked critical responses from fellow doctors; one Billings advocate suggested that it should have been titled, 'How not to teach the Billings method'. Dr Kevin Hume – a colleague of Dr Billings, who visited Ireland on several occasions, – described the Carr survey as an example of 'what NOT to do'. Dr Carr countered that Dr Hume had given twelve references in his article, only one contained 'real statistics'.[173]

The Billings method attracted little publicity in Ireland in the early 1970s. The teaching and evangelisation was led by women, and while some were medical professionals, many were not. In 1976, Jane Quinlan published a book on the method complete with charts and colour-coded stamps.[174] A revised edition in 1979 indicated that Cork OMAS was now affiliated with NAOMI – a

---

[168] Desmond Morrison, 'Natural methods of family planning', *The Furrow*, vol 25, no 10, September 1974, pp. 322–3.
[169] *II*, 20 January 1978.   [170] *JIMA*, July 1972.   [171] *JIMA*, 8 March 1975.
[172] *JIMA*, 10 April 1976.   [173] *JIMA*, 18 September 1976.
[174] Jane Quinlan, *The Billings method*.

national association, 'which co-ordinates the work of local centres ensures the standard of teaching in its affiliated centres and helps to promote the method throughout the country'. The first edition of Quinlan's manual appears to have been sold as a self-help manual, though OMAS Cork replied to letters from users. The 1979 edition cautioned that 'No one can assume that she can follow the method by reading the booklet or hearing about it from someone else. Though the method might seem easy, personal instruction from someone very familiar with it is the best way to learn and gain confidence.... Instructresses give this personal attention at centres of instruction. It is very necessary for a woman to return to the centre with her charts for follow-up interviews, which are private and confidential, until she understands the method.'[175]

In 1975, John Bonnar, an internationally recognised scientist and author of early scientific papers on the contraceptive pill, was appointed Professor of Obstetrics and Gynaecology at Trinity College Dublin. In 1977, he became a principal investigator on a World Health Organisation (WHO) study of the effectiveness of the Billings method. Ireland was one of five area studies. Bonnar estimated that 20,000 Irish couples were using 'natural' family planning which, if accurate, was approximately half to two-thirds of the number using the pill. Ireland was vital to the success of Billings because the method had failed to attract support in western Europe. The WHO trial initially planned to include Italy, but they failed to find sufficient couples who were willing to participate (the trial sought 200 couples in each country), so Dr Bonnar was asked to lead a trial in Ireland.

The *Catholic Standard*, which had given very little coverage to family planning, led its first issue in 1977 with this story. They commented that this research

still of a confidential nature.... may affect the whole future of the Billings methods. Ireland is rapidly becoming a richer, more urban society and if it can be shown there is good success rate in Ireland using these methods it may influence other countries to adopt them. But it can be safely predicted that by mid-1978 Ireland may be a word often used by international Family Planning experts. It will be the industrialised model for the success or relative failure of the 'natural' Family Planning methods.

It reported the views of an unnamed Dublin Professor, undoubtedly John Bonnar, that 'the richer a society becomes, the more sophisticated, the higher the failure rate for the rhythm method. In rural areas and more simple societies the failure rate is much less'.[176] On another occasion, Dr Bonnar reflected that 'the development of the ovulation method seems to have started further south in Cork, Wexford, and perhaps less urbanised areas.... The Rhythm [calendar

---

[175] Quinlan, *The Billings method*, Revised edition 1979 Compiled by Ovulation Method Advisory Service (OMAS) (Cork) affiliated to NAOMI Box 33 Brian Boru St Cork.
[176] *Catholic Standard*, 7 January 1977.

method] is something that we would very much like to bury'.[177] In 1977, what claimed to be the first WHO-backed diploma in natural family planning methods was introduced in Cork – targeting doctors, nurses and specialist health educators.[178] The women chosen to instruct Irish participants in the WHO study were members of three groups: OMAS (Cork), the Family Life Centre, based at the Marian Shrine at Knock, and the CMAC.[179]

The 1977 Christmas edition of the *Catholic Standard* reported that the natural family planning agencies, involved in the WHO study, were 'actively co-operating in order to bring effective natural family planning methods within the reach of every Irish woman'. It listed centres throughout Ireland where 'natural' family planning instruction was available. Some gave a priest as the contact point, but many gave the name of one or more women – often nurses, sometimes a nun. The majority of laywomen mentioned were married. But the coverage was patchy; some counties listed only one centre.[180] A conference organised by the recently founded Council of the Ovulation Method of Ireland, estimated there were between seventy and ninety centres, eleven in Dublin.[181] In 1978, a documentary by the Radharc team of Catholic priests, titled 'Australia is leading the field', reported on the Billings method.[182] Despite the hype about Australia and Billings, a 1978 study showed that just over 1 per cent of Australians surveyed were using the method.[183]

An article in *Hibernia* by John Feeney titled 'John Bonnar's Billings Boom' claimed that 'It was the smack of professional acceptability that seems to have persuaded the Church to back the Billings method so forcefully…. Under the aegis of Professor John Bonnar TCD, the Billings method has been adopted all over the country. Since last year, 101 Billings centres set up in Southern Ireland and 11 in Northern Ireland. The centres were based in church halls, convents, or Catholic schools'. An estimated 40,000 women received instruction in 1977. Feeney offered two explanations for this success: women who did not have access to a car could attend a local centre, and it attracted women who were abandoning the Pill because of reported health risks.[184] Dr Bonnar highlighted the need for women aged thirty-five and over – where there were strong medical contraindication to the Pill – to find an alternative method of family limitation.[185] Both Mavis Keniry, who headed DOMAS/later NAOMI, and Bonnar associated Billings with feminism and the growing demand for natural childbirth.[186] Feeney claimed that 'Billings is the prime contraceptive method in Ireland today', before asking 'the vital question – does it work'.

[177] *II*, 29 December 1977.   [178] *II*, 15 December 1977.
[179] *Catholic Standard*, 19 February 1977.   [180] *Catholic Standard*, 23 December 1977.
[181] *II*, 16 May 1977 – Dr Robert Doyle Wexford President.
[182] *Catholic Standard*, 20 January 1978.   [183] Betts, 'The Billings method', p. 261.
[184] *Hibernia*, 19 October 1978.   [185] *Catholic Standard*, 23 December 1977.
[186] *II*, 17 February 1978; 3 May 1978.

He claimed that Dr Bonnar sounded 'considerably less sure of that today than he did a year ago; "the Irish results have not been so marvellous"'.[187] Bonnar believed that the method was most effective where couples were determined not to have additional children and were strongly motivated to accept the necessary abstinence; he also advocated combining Billings with barrier contraception – a pragmatic approach to overcome the long periods of abstinence that was incompatible with Catholic teaching.[188]

The WHO trial was conducted in India, New Zealand, El Salvador, the Philippines and Ireland. A total of 869 couples initially enrolled, but only 725 continued beyond the 'teaching phase'.[189] The selection criteria 'minimized the risk of including women with irregular cycles'. After sixteen cycles, almost half had discontinued the method, 23.6 per cent did so due to pregnancy.[190] The Irish trial recruited approximately 200 couples. Bonnar concluded that women with more than twelve years of education had the greatest difficulties in engaging with 'natural' family planning; right-wing Catholics also faced difficulties. Farmers' wives and daughters were most in tune with 'natural' family planning, including Protestant nurses in the Adelaide Hospital, many of them from farming families.[191] I can only conclude that right-wing Catholics were ill at ease with examining their bodies, and women from a farming background understood the rhythm of fertility and sterility in livestock. While Billings has commonly been associated with Catholic users, there is international evidence that it was used by Muslim, Hindu and Protestant couples;[192] including some members of the Church of Ireland (see Chapter 5).

Princeton demographers Trussell and Grummer-Strawn concluded that the 'efficacy of the ovulation method is high if used consistently and correctly but the ovulation method is very unforgiving of imperfect use' – deviation from the rules. Failure to adhere strictly to the rules brought a 28 per cent risk of pregnancy per cycle. Their analysis of the WHO data revealed an overall pregnancy rate of 20.4 per cent per year among those in the trial.[193] Most pregnancies occurred because the subjects broke the rules. The highest proportion of risk takers was in New Zealand, followed by Ireland; the greatest recorded success rates were in the Philippines where almost half the participating women were illiterate. Betts concluded that educated women were more likely to blame the

---

[187] *Hibernia*, 19 October 1978.   [188] *Magill*, June 1979.
[189] James Trussell and Laurence Grummer-Strawn, 'Contraceptive failure of the ovulation method of periodic abstention', *International Family Planning Perspectives*, 16, no 1, March 1990, pp. 5–15.
[190] Betts, 'The Billings method', p. 259.
[191] Interview with Dr Bonnar, the Charlemont Clinic, 29 April 2014.
[192] Hanna Klaus, Miriam Labbok and Diane Barker, 'Characteristics of ovulation method acceptors: a cross-cultural assessment', *Family Planning*, 19, no 5, September–October 1988, 299–304.
[193] Trussell and Grummer-Strawn, 'Contraceptive failure of the ovulation method', p. 5.

method for their pregnancy.[194] Trussell and Grummer-Strawn concluded that 'the ovulation method cannot be regarded as a reasonable contraceptive choice for all women or couples'; most would find it difficult to abstain for nearly half of each menstrual cycle. They quoted a comment by Josef Roetzer, who pioneered the sympto-thermal method of periodic abstinence: '"natural conception regulation" is not contraception but a way of life'.[195] A study carried out in Los Angeles of two groups, one using the sympto-thermal method and one using Billings, concluded that Billings had a higher failure rate.[196] About half the women who joined the WHO study completed the study in a non-pregnant state.[197] The key issues about Billings, and other 'natural' methods, are captured in John Feeney's interview with Dr Bonnar, where the latter wondered whether 'the method can work in a society where there is a strong impetus, through the media, for a high rate of intercourse in young married couples. In other words, he claims that woman are not prepared to abstain for at least eight days – and in some cases up to 17 – per month to make the method work.'[198]

By the late 1970s, opponents of changes to Irish laws on contraception had seized on Billings as the solution to the problem. *Gift of Life*, a pamphlet published by an advisory committee of the Knights of Columbanus, probably in early 1979, demanded state support to promote 'natural' methods of contraception. In 1978, NAOMI united the various local groups, and they appointed retired Holles St consultant Arthur Barry as their president. He warned that the organisation could expect no co-operation from doctors, because doctors could not make money by advising women to go to their centres.[199] It is significant that these groups, which had been led by women, selected an elderly male gynaecologist as their president.

The 1970s is the decade when family planning became more widely available in Ireland and a topic that was widely discussed, and family size among younger couples fell significantly. This happened in a legal vacuum and had very uneven access to contraception. The decade also saw the emergence of pressure groups who were determined to prevent any easing of the laws, and the first strong group to promote Catholic-approved methods. The lay leadership and the large numbers of women who were involved in Billings, and in groups who opposed any change in the laws, indicate a change in Catholic church involvement in socio-political campaigns, with the Hierarchy taking a less prominent role. The efforts to introduce legislation permitting access to contraception during the 1970s, discussed in Chapter 5, took place against the background of these grass-roots activities, in favour and against change.

---

[194] Betts, 'The Billings method', p. 259–61.
[195] Trussell and Grummer-Strawn, 'Contraceptive failure of the ovulation method', pp. 14–15.
[196] Betts, 'The Billings method', p. 258.
[197] *Fertility and sterility*, Proceedings of Conference in Dublin, June 1983, edited R.F. Harrison, J. Bonnar, W. Thompson, 1983.
[198] *Hibernia*, 19 October 1978.   [199] *II*, 14 May 1979.

5 'Against Sin'[1]
An Irish Family Planning Bill, 1973–1979

Irish politicians were followers rather than leaders when it came to reforming contentious social legislation, but for a brief period, in the early 1970s, it appeared that constitutional and legal reform on divorce and contraception was imminent. If that had happened, Ireland would have been in line with international trends. During the 1960s and early 1970s, many countries repealed or amended long-standing laws on contraception, abortion, and homosexuality. In 1968, the United Nations International Conference on Human Rights in Tehran adopted a resolution that 'couples have a basic human right to decide freely and responsibly on the number and spacing of their children and a right to adequate education and information in this respect'. Ireland voted for the resolution,[2] which was affirmed at the UN General Assembly the following year, as part of the Declaration on Social Progress and Development. This stated that a country's national welfare and medical services should provide 'education, training of personnel and the provision to families of the knowledge and means necessary to enable them to exercise their right to determine freely and responsibly the number and spacing of their children'. When this was debated at the UN, the Irish delegation claimed that the phrase 'and means' presented difficulties, but they were overruled. Ireland abstained on the vote on this article, but voted in favour of the Declaration.[3] In 1972, the Consultative Assembly of the Council of Europe called on member states to authorise the sale of contraceptives, establish family planning advice services, encourage the integration of family planning in general medical services and ensure that young people receive suitable sex education; family planning should be included in all medical/para-medical education.[4] These were uncomfortable occasions for Irish

---

[1] NAI DT 2009/16/123 Family Planning Bill 1978. 'There is no specific provision confining the sale, etc. of contraceptives to married persons. As you are aware, there are good reasons for this. It is hoped, however that in general, the Bill, without saying so, is and appears to be "against sin"'. Parliamentary draftsman to Sec D Health.

[2] *Commission on the Status of Women*, para 570.

[3] General Assembly resolution 2542 UN Doc/A/7630; *Commission on the Status of Women*, para 570.

[4] *IT*, 30 June 1973.

delegates, given a wish to establish a stronger international presence and they added to domestic pressures for change, as did the recommendation of the 1973 *Commission on the Status of Women* that information and expert advice on contraception should be available.[5]

When Ireland became a member of the EEC on January 1, 1973, she was the only member state that prohibited contraception. A 1971 article in the short-lived periodical *This Week* noted that when Belgium, 'a predominantly Catholic country entered [the EEC] she changed her contraception laws which mirrored Ireland's up to that time in order to fall into line with other EEC countries'. Ireland, Spain and Portugal were the only countries in western Europe with stringent laws restricting contraception; the only eastern European countries with similar restrictions were Albania and Bulgaria.[6]

Contraception featured to a minor extent in the general election campaign of February 1973. In the closing days, the Women First page of the *Irish Times* submitted a list of questions to all the political parties; one question asked whether they planned to reform the laws on contraception, and if so, to outline the proposed changes. Fianna Fáil responded that they had already indicated that they were reviewing the current laws but did not propose to make any further statement pending the Supreme Court judgment on the McGee case. Labour replied that it was party policy that contraceptives would be made available through health centres. Sinn Féin declared that every woman was entitled to control her own body; they proposed to establish a network of free family planning centres. The most interesting response came from Fine Gael, which had entered an agreement with Labour to form a coalition government if both parties received sufficient electoral support. The agreed programme for government did not mention contraception, though both parties gave a commitment to introduce legislation to end all discrimination against women, and legislation 'to deal with the plight of the widowed, orphaned and deserted'. Fine Gael supplied the *Irish Times* with a copy of a speech by Garret FitzGerald, a member of the party's frontbench, which addressed several issues of interest to women, but said nothing about contraception.[7]

The election brought sixteen years of Fianna Fáil government to an end. A Fine Gael Labour Coalition took office, with Liam Cosgrave as Taoiseach and Labour Party leader Brendan Corish as Tanaiste and Minister for Health. During the campaign, some Labour candidates gave commitments that if the party was in government, they would seek changes in the laws relating to divorce and contraception. But as Meehan notes, Labour was not united on contraception; in 1972, three members of the party voted against a private members' bill

---

[5] *Commission on the Status of Women*, para. 574.
[6] *This Week*, 5 March 1971.   [7] *Irish Times*, 27 February 1973.

sponsored by two Labour TDs – Noel Browne and John O'Connell.[8] Fine Gael was even more divided and had given no commitment to legislate. In 1971 when Jack Lynch appeared to be committed to reforming the law on contraception, Fine Gael leader Liam Cosgrave indicated that he was opposed to any change.[9]

5.1   McGee, Sunningdale and Contraception

On 19 December 1973, the Supreme Court determined that a married couple had the right to use contraceptives. The ruling was given on 19 December, ten days after the Sunningdale Agreement, which appeared to offer a solution to the Northern Ireland crisis. The major unionist and nationalist parties in Northern Ireland and the British and Irish governments agreed to the introduction of a power-sharing executive and measures to recognise 'an Irish dimension'.[10] The Sunningdale Agreement prompted what proved to be unrealistic hopes of major political and constitutional change in Ireland.[11] Liberalising the laws on contraception was seen as contributing to that process. Senators Robinson, Horgan and West had tabled a new bill in November 1973, prompting yet another statement from the Catholic Hierarchy urging legislators to take account of the common good – a common good that ruled out amending the laws.[12] An editorial in the *Church of Ireland Gazette* pointed out that '*en route* to this argument they lay down the "clear teaching of the Catholic church"'.[13]

In contrast to previous private members' bills on contraception, this bill was given a first reading on 14 November, which meant that it was printed. Responsibility for family planning was moved from the Minister for Justice to the Minister for Health – making it a matter of health not criminal behaviour. Contraceptives would be sold in pharmacies and other outlets licenced by the Minister, and imports would be controlled. The 1935 Act would remain in existence, with these modifications. The remaining provisions counteracted the unlicensed sale, importation or distribution of contraceptives. The sections of the Censorship of Publications Acts relating to literature about family planning would be amended. The Bill did not restrict access to contraceptives to married couples, or by age. The proposers expressed the hope, rather optimistically, that the legislation would not be

---

[8] Ciara Meehan, *A just society for Ireland? 1964–1987* (Palgrave Macmillan, Basingstoke, 2013), p. 124.
[9] *Sunday Independent*, 14 March 1971.
[10] Noel Dorr, *Sunningdale: The search for peace in Northern Ireland Sunningdale* (RIA, Dublin, 2017).
[11] Dorr, *Sunningdale*, pp. 381–3.   [12] *Irish Times*, 29 November 1973.
[13] *Church of Ireland Gazette*, editorial 7 December 1973.

treated as a party-political matter: that senators and deputies would be free to vote as they wished. In October 1973, they sent a copy to Minister for Justice Patrick Cooney.[14]

On 1 February 1974, shortly before an expected second reading, the Role of the Church Committee of the Church of Ireland wrote to all senators and to the Minister for Justice, reporting the recent Synod decisions on contraception and stating that, 'We believe that an urgent examination of certain issues which infringe personal rights and freedoms is essential, and that the state should not endeavour by legislation to regulate matters which ought to be governed by individual consciences'. They highlighted a statement by Protestant gynaecologists, which was published as an appendix to the 1972 report of the Role of the Church Committee, recommending that all means of contraception should be available on prescription. The fact that the contraceptive pill was 'not without risk' for women aged over 40, and might be 'positively dangerous' for some, 'provides a convincing argument' for making all forms of contraception available. Sterilisation should be available (discussed in Chapter 7), and sterilisation and contraception 'should be considered separately from abortion'. The Church of Ireland submission included a consensus statement from an ad hoc group of Northern Ireland Catholic and Protestant gynaecologist that met on four occasions.

In the absence of family planning, fear of unwanted pregnancies may lead to refusal of marital rights. This could result in marital disharmony even infidelity. Therefore, family planning in this broad context is a positive good. From the medical point of view, planning for the protection of an ailing mother's life and health is also a positive good. It has been suggested that some methods of family planning, by obviating the risk of pregnancy, give women a sexual freedom that may increase the incidence of v d and divorce; we have no evidence that this is so in this community. Every method of family planning should be available to all couples without legal restriction. It is recognised that the acceptance of any particular method is a matter for the conscience of the people concerned.[15]

On 4 February, three days after the Church of Ireland letter, the Presbyterian church wrote to all members of Seanad Éireann, reiterating a statement by the Presbyterian General Assembly which affirmed that 'family planning is in itself a good thing in itself'... 'The decision to use contraceptives within marriage should not be regarded as in itself wrong. Nevertheless, the decision to use them should not be taken lightly or inadvisably'. The Society of Friends wrote to senators on 15 February.[16] These three letters issued shortly before the second reading of the Robinson Bill suggest that the main Protestant churches had mounted a co-ordinated campaign.

---

[14] NAI DT 2011/17/789; SE 21 February.   [15] *Church of Ireland Gazette*, 8 February 1974.
[16] Seanad Debates, 20 February, cols 217–221.

The momentum was not one-way. The volume of letters on contraception received by the Department of the Taoiseach in the 1970s would appear to have exceeded the number about Northern Ireland, though some writers addressed both topics. The majority of writers were opposed to reforming the law. There was a flurry of letters in the winter of 1973 and spring of 1974 – prompted by the Robinson Bill and the Supreme Court Judgment. Senator Mary Robinson was a bête-noir; one woman who wrote to Liam Cosgrave 'on the eve of the Feast of the Holy Innocents' (28 December) told him that 'The time of Herod is still with us and his sword is still unsheathed against the helpless innocent. Mary Robinson and Co. are now taking his place to deal out death to these most helpless of all humanity – unborn babies'; contraception was 'in reality abortion'. A midwife employed by the Southern Health Board, who claimed to have elicited opinions – presumably among her patients, assured him that 99.5% of the general public, young and not so young, are 'entirely against Mrs Robinson.... let her take her pills and appliances if she has need of them and let us lead our youth as best we can'. She suggested that Mrs Robinson had 'no experience of the world, give her another 10 or 20 years and she will be in a better position to "dictate"'.

Some correspondents enclosed medals, scapulars, or Mass offerings. Many referred to papal infallibility, and other theological arguments. These letters display little awareness of, or respect for minority opinion, and the potential impact on Ulster unionists of rejecting the legislation on contraception. Some correspondents were either unwilling or incapable of distinguishing between the respective spheres of church and state. One nurse warned that if contraception was legalised, 'it will surely bring the wrath of God on Catholic Ireland'. A man with an address in Killarney told the Taoiseach:

I was disgusted to see that Mary Robinson and her pals succeeded in having this introduced in the Senate; at a time when our people in the North are murdering one another, thousands dying in Ethiopia, what an indictment to say we in the south are concentrating our attention in a predominately Catholic society on such a degrading subject.

He was appealing to Mr Cosgrave, 'as a fellow Catholic'.[17] Alice Glenn (a future Fine Gael TD) who styled herself Chairman of SOS – Save our Society – informed the Taoiseach that her organisation was conducting a fact-finding canvas nationally, but as yet only had results from Dublin constituencies. She reported that in the average household, 75 per cent of people of all ages, were against the sale or general availability of contraceptives. In areas dominated by young married couples with 1–3 children and heavy mortgage payments, opinion was divided 50:50. She concluded that over 70 per cent of the electorate opposed the sale or general availability of contraceptives, and

---

[17] NAI DT 2004/21/461, November–December 1973.

they were prepared to subject the question to a referendum if necessary. She gave no indication as to how this information was compiled, though she may have canvassed Fine Gael branches. Alice Glenn emphasised that 'the electorate considers that this matter transcends politics, and they are not at all worried about how it affects North South relations'. SOS sent the Taoiseach two pages of signatures from Cork members – many gave addresses at the County Hospital in Mallow. They informed Liam Cosgrave, a dedicated horseman, who hunted regularly that 'a large number of the signatures are from followers of the Duhallow Hounds, including the honorary secretary, members and subscribers and farmers'.[18]

On the other hand, an Irishman with an address in Birmingham claimed that rejecting the Robinson Bill 'would be a political disaster as far as the North is concerned …. a slap in the face for our Protestant fellow countrymen'.[19] One woman with an address in affluent Dublin 4, expressed amazement

at the way in which the Northern Ireland Protestants have allowed us to reach to them, dictate to them and condemn them for their discrimination without, except in a very mild way and in only a few cases telling us to have a look at our own sins. Over the past four years the Catholics, North and South, have given the impression that they are always sinned against, never the sinner….They tell you that they want unity by reconciliation but in actual fact they mean by domination. We have a Family Planning Bill…of course it will not be passed because of the self-righteous hypocrisy that goes on here. …The 26 counties is a land of Pharisees.

The Corrymeela community in Northern Ireland, whose mission was to promote reconciliation between Catholics and Protestants, passed a resolution urging legislators

to resist the attempt being made to retain the moral teaching of a single Church as part of the law of the land, and to treat with caution the unproven assumption that the controlled availability of contraceptives leads to a general lowering of moral standards. Liberalisation of the law in this respect should not be seen primarily as a gesture towards Northern Protestants but as recognition of the dignity of the individual and his right to decision, and as a step towards a more open honest and caring society in Ireland.

Paradoxically, they explained that they did not propose to publicise this resolution. A more bizarre reference to the Northern troubles came from a man who claimed that 'Satan wages the war in the North among other reasons, in order to force the introduction of all the lewd aspects of the British welfare state upon the Republic, knowing well that worse will follow if he succeeds. Our precious Catholic heritage is being held up for barter'. He enclosed a copy of the secret message from Our Lady of Fatima.[20] A doctor with an address

---

[18] NAI DT 2005/7/348.   [19] NAI DT 2004/21/461, November–December 1973.
[20] NAI DT 2005/7/345 and 346.

in Mr Cosgrave's Dublin constituency asked 'where is the honesty in con-demning violence in the North or anywhere – if we legislate for contraception in the South.... For contraceptives are abortifacients and abortion is murder of the innocents...married couples have no more right to commit murder than the unmarried have.'[21]

The most interesting letter came from a Redemptorist priest, who began by congratulating Mr Cosgrave on the recent Sunningdale Agreement. He agreed with the Catholic bishops 'that the "contraceptive mentality" and the "permissive society" are socially undesirable. Yet I believe that a change in the present laws is necessary. I think that that this is true not for the sake of the minority but for all strands of the population'. Over the past year, he had conducted Missions in cities and rural areas. 'Everywhere I have met women, in their thirties or early 40s, with 5, 6, or more children and in desperate situa-tions. For many of them have husbands who will not or cannot practice absti-nence or the safe period. Many of them cannot face the prospect of another child. Many are afraid to take the pill or have been forbidden by their doctors. For such women I do not believe that to use a contraceptive would be a sin, it would be at worst the lesser of 2 evils I do not believe that the state should forbid them'. He wished to see contraceptives made available 'in a controlled way'. He closed the letter by flattering Mr Cosgrave that he was 'now a very strong man' who should use his political strength to enact legislation permit-ting contraception.[22]

5.2   Government Legislation: The 1974 attempt

A memorandum for government, drafted by the Attorney General Declan Costello, in response to the Robinson Bill, determined that the attitude that was 'most widespread in the country' was that the law should be changed to make contraceptives available subject to restrictions on sales and advertisements. The government must decide whether to allow a free vote. He recommended that legislation should be drafted limiting contraceptives to married couples, with sales restricted to pharmacies. Wholesalers and pharmacists would be permitted to import supplies subject to licence; advertisements would be pro-hibited. The principle underlying government legislation should be that contra-ception was a matter of private conscience for married couples. While making them available could lead to undesirable social consequences (presumably making them accessible to single people), and should therefore be prohibited, this would be difficult to implement. Access should be controlled by requiring married couples to secure a certificate from a doctor stating that they were mar-ried: the 'doctor would not be prescribing but merely certifying the status of

[21] NAI DT 2005/7/34721, March 1974.   [22] NAI DT 2004/21/461, November–December 1973.

the applicant'.[23] These proposals drafted in November 1973 bear an uncanny resemblance to the 1979 Act. They capture the underlying dilemma facing successive governments: how to make contraception available to married couples, but not to single adults. Although a growing minority of single men and women were using contraception – and a greater number were sexually active – public opinion was divided between those who opposed any relaxation of the laws, and those who wanted contraception to be available to married couples; there was minimal support for making contraception available to single people.

The Attorney General presented two options: drafting a government bill along the lines outlined above or initiating a discussion in the Dáil setting out the case for and against changing the law and giving members the freedom to propose amendments or draft legislation. The government would then introduce legislation that reflected Dáil opinion. [The only comparable precedent was the 1935 Criminal Law Amendment Act, discussed in Chapter 1.][24] It acknowledged the difficulties that any government faced in legislating on contraception. Conor Cruise O'Brien, Minister for Posts and Telegraphs, who was in favour of reform, wrote to Labour leader Brendan Corish, warning that the tactics to be followed when Robinson's bill was tabled, required 'careful consideration'. Although Labour had voted in favour of legislating for contraception, the party was divided. He suggested that deputies and senators should be given a free vote. If the government took the initiative and introduced legislation, it would be 'likely to incur odium from two sides – those who object and those would object if – as seems likely the Government measure was more hedged around with restrictions than Mrs Robinson's'. If the Government was seen to be 'under fire in this way', he feared that the opposition 'would certainly be tempted to put on a whip. .... and see that the Government initiative was defeated.... Fianna Fáil would reckon the dividends in rural areas of opposing the legislation would outweigh potential damage in the cities', and the government's prestige would suffer. There was 'no adequate reason for us to run the risk at all'.[25] This proved to be a remarkably accurate prediction. He sent a copy of this document to the Attorney General.

The first reading of the Robinson Bill on 14 November confirmed that the government would have real difficulties enacting legislation. The Leader of the House, Fine Gael Senator Michael O'Higgins, announced that the government would not oppose a first reading, but it was 'a matter for individual Senators' to determine whether to support or oppose it. He was opposed to a first reading and stepped aside from his role as Leader of the Seanad for the day. He warned

---

[23] NAI DT 2011/17/789 Family Planning Bill, 14 November 1973.
[24] It is not dissimilar to what happened in 2017–18 when an Oireachtas Committee drew up recommendations for legislation on abortion, which was adopted by the government.
[25] O'Brien to Corish, 7 November 1973, NAI DT 2011/17/789.

that 'if we enact legislation of this sort, however sincere and well intentioned our motives, this generation of Irish politicians will be called to account at the bar of history to answer the charge of our children and their children that we were the ones who publicly discarded the standards and values which, with conviction, I believe were the true standards and values which were treasured by Irish generations of the past'.[26] In January 1973, he wrote to the Taoiseach apologising if his decision to table an amendment to the second stage of the Robinson bill had embarrassed him or the Government; he understood that he was free to vote as he wished. On 12 February, the *Irish Times* reported that the government was considering introducing its own legislation.

When the second reading of the Robinson Bill came before the Seanad the following day, Senator O'Higgins (acting in a personal capacity), introduced an amendment designed to prevent the second reading. He questioned the argument that it was a function of the Senate to 'regulate and regularise the position as a result of the Supreme Court decision'. He claimed that the bill was 'not sanctioned by public demand'. It 'was undesirable in terms of the common good, but in a predominantly Catholic State.... the common good will not be divorced from moral values'. He countered arguments that the law should be changed in order to improve north–south relations and recognise minority rights, suggesting that the 'Home Rule is Rome Rule' argument was motivated by political expediency. The rights of those who viewed contraception as morally wrong should not be disregarded.

Senator Robinson spoke of 'regularising the position' in the light of the Supreme Court judgment.

As the law now stands, any person, married and unmarried, and with no age limit, can use contraceptives, manufacture contraceptives, distribute contraceptives, and since the recent judgement in the Supreme Court, import contraceptives... However, none of these people can inform themselves fully on the subject. As the law now stands, they cannot acquire responsible literature describing the various forms of contraceptives, warning them of the potential danger of the contraceptives they are importing from abroad, warning them of the conditions which make it unsafe to use the pill and generally advising them in a full manner on the whole question of family planning.

She claimed that 'people might rightly say that the country might be flooded with literature and with these devices'.[27] Plaintiffs might take other legal cases, resulting in 'a series of decisions which chipped in a piecemeal fashion, at other aspects of our law, leaving an unregulated and unco-ordinated situation and one which gradually liberalised – probably more than many legislators would wish – the law relating to family planning'.[28]

---

[26] Seanad Debates (SD), vols 76 no 1, 14 November 1973, cols 6–9.
[27] SD, 20 February 1974, vol. 77 no 2, cols 207–8.   [28] SD, 20 February, col 211.

Minister for Justice, Patrick Cooney, criticised the tone of the Senate debate. The Supreme Court had determined that married couples could not be denied access to contraceptives by law: 'there is nothing that the Oireachtas can do to undo what the Supreme Court have done'. Debating the merits or otherwise of contraception was no longer relevant. The government was finalising work on a bill that, while respecting the decision of the Supreme Court, would impose restrictions on the importation and overall access to contraceptives.[29] The Robinson Bill was defeated on a second reading. The government indicated that they would allow a free vote on their bill. Senator O'Higgins wrote to the Taoiseach indicating that this decision had largely resolved his difficulties.[30]

The decision to introduce a government bill may have been influenced by a public opinion poll. On 18 February, *Irish Times* journalist John Cooney reported that Keith Wilson-Davis, who had recently carried out an opinion poll on contraception (see Chapter 4) had received a phone call from Nicholas Simms an advisor to Minister for Posts and Telegraphs Conor Cruise O'Brien (his father-in-law), asking his views as to whether contraceptives should be made legal in Ireland. Keith-Wilson allegedly reported that 57 per cent of married women favoured repeal. He was contacted the following day seeking additional information. It was originally intended that Labour Senator Brendan Halligan would quote this data during the debate on the Robinson Bill.[31]

On 19 February, the Cabinet authorised the Minister for Justice to proceed with drafting a bill, prohibiting the sale and importation of abortifacients (there were claims that IUDs were abortifacients), and confining sales of contraceptives to licensed chemists. Unmarried persons would be prohibited from importing or buying contraceptives. Manufacture would be prohibited except under licence; advertisements would be controlled.

On 22 January, Noel Reilly, Secretary of the IMA, informed the government that the Central Council of the IMA had considered the proposed Family Planning Bill [this suggests some advance knowledge of a government bill] and decided that 'irrespective of the views of individual registered Medical Practitioners on the matters....it would not...be appropriate for Registered Medical Practitioners to be required to sign prescriptions as envisaged in terms of Section 3 of above Bill'. He suggested that the bill should be changed to provide that sales, etc, of non-medical contraceptives should be in compliance with 'conditions which may be prescribed by the Minister for Health'.[32] The Minister could include a clause stipulating that only married couples could buy contraceptives, but the medical profession would play no role in enforcing that regulation. The IMA executive had expressed the view that 'the onus should not be on doctors to prescribe all the family planning needs of the country, and

[29] SD, 21 February 1974, cols 238–54; 381–4.   [30] NAI DT 2005/7/345.
[31] *IT*, 18 February 1974.   [32] NAI DT 2011/17/789, 22 January 1974.

particularly not to have to prescribe those contraceptives which are fundamentally non-medical'.[33] This decision was published in the *JIMA*, together with the resolution that the Central Council had conveyed to the government.[34] The omission of any reference to married couples in the Robinson Bill reflected a belief that this would be unenforceable. Officials cautioned that it was impossible to determine, in the event of a case taken by a single person, whether the Supreme Court would rule against granting single people access to contraception. They also warned that it was impossible to police the importation of contraceptives for personal use.

The draft government bill followed the lines set out in February, with two changes – the Minister could permit a married couple to import contraceptives for personal use, if they were unable to secure supplies locally, and contraceptives could be sold or supplied in hospitals, clinics, or by local authorities. A pharmacist who breached the legislation – presumably by supplying single people – would have his/her licence revoked. A memorandum by Wally Kirwan – an official in the Department of the Taoiseach with special responsibility for Northern Ireland, emphasised that 'If this Bill were introduced – it would be the subject of some considerable opposition. It is an attempt by the State to regulate private morals, and no very clear definition of public interest. Whatever we may think personally ... it can I think, do no good to North-South relations'[35] Another memo submitted to Cabinet noted that

given the approved 'heads' the Bill was generally satisfactory. From the point of view of relations with Protestants in Northern Ireland it proposes to liberalise our laws sufficiently in my opinion, to meet what would be likely on the available evidence to constitute their wishes regarding the laws to apply in a future united Ireland. The safeguards it contains for morality and what a large body of opinion of all denominations regards as the quality of life in Ireland are generally satisfactory. It is to be noted that the Bill provides that licences may not be granted by the Minister for the import, sale or manufacture of contraceptives, which he is advised by a Committee to be established, is also an abortifacient. It is almost impossible to know how many Protestants in Ireland or in Northern Ireland favour the legality of abortion. The number may not be so large as to provide any basis for a claim that our laws should not rule on this matter. ...even if there were any such basis it would clearly be impossible to secure any political support.[36]

The liberal momentum inspired by the Sunningdale Agreement was counterbalanced by the Attorney General. As a High Court judge Declan Costello had dismissed the McGee case, which was then appealed to the Supreme Court. He wished to include a provision making it unlawful for an unmarried person (other than certain exempted persons, such as doctors, gardaí and licensees such as pharmacists) to possess contraceptives, and to permit a

---

[33] *JIMA*, January 1974.   [34] *JIMA*, February 1974.
[35] NAI DT 2005/7/341, 15 March 1974.
[36] NAI TD 2005/7/341 Family Planning Legislation, 14 March 1974.

member of the gardaí to ask an individual, suspected of possessing contraceptives, whether he/she was married and to indicate the date and place of the marriage. This file reveals a disturbing tendency to intrude into personal lives to an unprecedented extent. It even suggested that married couples might lend their marriage certificates to single or widowed persons, to enable them to buy contraceptives! Minister for Justice, Patrick Cooney, rejected these extreme proposals.[37]

On 19 March 1974, the Cabinet, chaired by Taoiseach Liam Cosgrave, approved the text of a government bill subject to minor amendments. This decision was unpopular with many members of the Fine Gael party. The Cork North-East constituency executive reported that it was the unanimous wish of a large annual general meeting that the bill should be shelved. They criticised the Minister for Justice for failing to discuss the proposed legislation at a parliamentary party meeting before it was announced. They appealed to the Taoiseach 'You, and you alone in the Fine Gael party is [sic] the man whom friend, and foe alike have implicit trust in. Do not let Ireland start on the slippery slope to a Permissive Society. Act while there is still time. Posterity will revere you for your actions'.[38]

Introducing the bill, Patrick Cooney gave the measure a deliberately conservative gloss. He highlighted the fact that it would regulate imports of contraceptives, which had become widely available following the Supreme Court judgment:

I have had clear evidence that as a result of it a black market exists and is growing in the illegal sale of contraceptives in this country. They can be imported as I have said without let or hindrance and this is being done. Orders for contraceptives are being solicited by mail order firms from outside the State and these orders are being solicited indiscriminately. The firms concerned apparently are using street or telephone directories. It has been rather irately brought to my notice that one firm is enclosing a sample of its wares with the order form.[39]

As to the argument that it would be impossible to restrict access to married couples, he suggested that 'It is a well-recognised principle of jurisprudence that to set out a prohibition in a statute is in itself a deterrent notwithstanding difficulties of enforcing it or of adducing proof to enable the sanction behind the prohibition to be imposed'. He claimed that restricting access to married couples was 'in accord with popular opinion'.[40]

Fianna Fáil had managed to avoid a vote on contraception at the 1974 Ard Fheis.[41] When the government Bill came before the Dáil, the party imposed the whip and opposed the legislation. Justice spokesman Des O'Malley said

---

[37] NAI DT 2005/7/341 Family Planning Legislation.   [38] NAI DT 2005/7/347, 31 March 1974.
[39] Dáil Debates (DD), 274 no 3, 4 July 1974, col 273.   [40] DD 274, no 3, 4 July 1974, col 288.
[41] *IT*, 18 February 1974.

that contraception was a matter of public morality: 'in any ordered society the protection of morals through the deterrence of fornication and promiscuity is a legitimate legislative aim and a matter not of private but of public morality'. He suggested alternative approaches that would meet the Supreme Court ruling, such as making contraceptives available through the health boards.[42] The decision to oppose the bill reflected the views of party members, and probably a majority of TDs, but Fianna Fáil also detected an opportunity to inflict damage on a divided government. Fine Gael deputy Oliver J. Flanagan, who belonged to the morally conservative wing of the party, described it as 'an evil bill' and denounced 'organised pressure groups' who were campaigning for the laws to be changed.[43]

When the second reading was debated in July 1974, the Sunningdale Agreement had collapsed, and there was no immediate prospect of establishing a Council of Ireland. Nevertheless, Conor Cruise O'Brien put on record that all the main Protestant churches supported reforming the laws on contraception; rejecting the bill would damage relations between Catholics and Protestants. He claimed that in Northern Ireland, the topic was 'a highly emotionally-charged one with very important social and demographic connotations and it bulks large among the motives given in the North for aversion from the Republic.' If the measure was defeated, he feared that 'repercussions in the North will be serious'. Fine Gael deputy Paddy Harte, who lived one mile from the Border with Northern Ireland, also spoke about the impact of a defeat on North–South relations.[44]

The Bill was defeated on the second reading by seventy-four votes to sixty-one; the Taoiseach Liam Cosgrave voted with the majority. He had not informed Cabinet colleagues or even Fine Gael Ministers in advance, though in hindsight several argued that this was implicit in the decision to permit a free vote (the only occasion such a decision was taken by that government). One correspondent, who wrote to him in January, expressing fears that he was about the change his position on contraception, was reassured that this was not the case.[45] A further six of Fine Gael's fifty TDs followed the Taoiseach into the 'no' lobby; others would probably have done so if they had been aware of Mr Cosgrave's position. One Labour deputy was absent, probably deliberately. Meehan has described the result as 'a disaster for the coalition'.[46] Cosgrave received many letters congratulating him on his stance.[47]

---

[42] DD, 4 July, col 305. In 1985, Des O'Malley was expelled from Fianna Fáil for voting in favour of Barry Desmond's bill liberalising access to contraception.
[43] DD, 11 July, col 932–3.   [44] DD, 11 July, cols 912–18; cols 1206–13.
[45] NAI TD 2005/7/344, Contraception resolutions and miscellaneous correspondence.
[46] Meehan, *A just society*, pp. 127–8.   [47] NAI DT 2005/7/349.

5.3   Private Members' Bill, 1974–1976

The three university senators introduced yet another private members' bill in December 1974. Speaking on the first reading, Senator Robinson warned that there would be 'strong adverse reaction from people outside this country, from many citizens living in this country, and obviously from citizens of Northern Ireland', if the Seanad did not permit publication.[48] It passed a first reading, with the support of Fianna Fáil Senators. More than two years elapsed before it received a second reading in December 1976. By then two of the sponsors, Senators Robinson and Horgan had joined the Labour Party, and the bill was introduced with the permission of the Labour Party, and apparently with their support. It replicated many elements of the 1974 government bill: making the sale, import, manufacture of contraceptives subject to licence by the Minister for Health, and subject to the conditions set by the Minister, and imposing controls on advertising. The proposed change to the Censorship Acts also replicated the government bill. However, reflecting Labour Party views, it promoted a role for the health boards in family planning.[49] The other major divergence was the omission of any provision restricting contraception to married couples. Senator Robinson quoted a ruling by the US Federal Supreme Court to the effect that it would be unconstitutional in the USA 'under similar constitutional provisions' to Ireland, to confine access to married couples.[50] The Seanad adjourned for Christmas without voting on the measure, but not before Fianna Fáil had issued a statement indicating that they viewed legislation as a matter for government.

When the debate resumed, the Minister for Health and Labour Party leader Brendan Corish addressed the Seanad. Although Labour, alone of the three main parties, had voted in favour of legislation, they were treading warily. Corish suggested that the three main political parties should consult on the matter. If these talks proved successful, an all-party committee of both houses might be established to extend the consultation with a view to securing agreement on legislation. He would issue an invitation to Fine Gael and Fianna Fáil in his capacity as leader of the Labour Party (not Tanaiste or Minister for Health) – an indication of the Jesuitical manoeuvres that contraception had fostered within the coalition. This speech prompted Noel Browne (his former party colleague), to dub Corish 'Pontius Pilate'.[51] When a vote was taken in the Seanad on 5 May 1977, the second reading was narrowly defeated by twenty-three votes to twenty.[52]

There was no prospect of all-party talks because a general election was imminent. When the election was called, the Women's Political Association

---

[48] SD, 17 December 1974, col 116.   [49] SD, 16 December 1976, cols 1083–87.
[50] SD, 16 December 1976, col 1081.   [51] SD, 9 February 1977, cols 94–5.
[52] SD, 5 May 1977, col 802.

asked all TDs and Senators to complete a survey indicating their views on legislating for contraception. While all the Labour deputies who replied favoured the introduction of comprehensive family planning services provided by the state, only 31 per cent of responses from Fine Gael and a mere 12 per cent from Fianna Fáil concurred; 80 per cent of Fianna Fáil respondents, said 'no' as did 56 per cent of Fine Gael politicians. The response rate was low; sixty-five TDs and thirty senators declined to respond, including Liam Cosgrave, Brendan Corish, Frank Cluskey (Coalition spokesman on Social Welfare), Gene Fitzgerald, Fianna Fáil spokesman on Women's Affairs, and Charles Haughey, Fianna Fáil spokesman on Health. The questionnaire covered a wide range of issues relating to women's employment and welfare in addition to divorce and contraception. The only deputy to assent to all the proposals was 1916 veteran and Fianna Fáil TD Dick Grogan, who was not standing for re-election.[53] During the course of the campaign, Corish gave a commitment that the party would introduce legislation, if returned to office, but he emphasised that there would be a free vote, and he proposed to consult the other parties. Fianna Fáil leader Jack Lynch gave a commitment to introduce legislation to **control** [my emphasis] the distribution of contraceptives. The party would consult widely before the bill was drafted. Charles Haughey, the spokesman on Health, who had recently rejoined the front bench, emphasised that the consultation was not designed to reach a consensus, but to gauge public opinion. It was 'a fundamentally important national issue' that contraceptives be available to married couples.[54]

5.4   'An Irish Solution': The 1979 Family Planning Act

5.4.1   Consultations

Fianna Fáil won the general election in June 1977 by a landslide. The margin of victory meant that they were in a position to pass legislation on contraception, even if a number of TDs abstained or voted against the government. There is no evidence that contraception had any impact on the outcome of the election, which was won on promises of tax cuts and increased public spending. The new government approached legislation on family planning precisely as Lynch had indicated. In October 1977, Charles Haughey, Minister for Health, brought a memorandum to government setting out the key issues and outlining his plans to consult interested parties. The government gave its approval, requesting a further submission when the consultations had been completed.[55] The key issues identified were as follows:

---

[53] *IT*, 2 June 1977.   [54] *IT*, 27 May 1977.
[55] NAI DT 2009/16/123 Health (Family Planning Bill), 1978.

(i) To what extent should public authorities, and in particular health boards, be involved in providing advice on family planning?

(ii) What changes, if any, should be made in the present law on the sale of contraceptives?

(iii) To what extent, if any, and in relation to what group or groups of the population should contraceptives be made available under the health services?

Consultations were not limited to those topics. Over the following twelve months, the Department of Health met a wide range of organisations and interest groups including the Medico-Social Research Board, the Irish Medical Association, the National Health Council (NHC), the Pharmaceutical Society of Ireland (PSI), the Irish Pharmaceutical Union (IPU); the major churches; Health Boards, the Irish Nurses Organisation (INO), the Association of Social Workers, Irish Family Planning Association, Irish Family League, Irish Congress of Trade Unions, and organisations promoting the Billings method. They received written submissions from the Natural Family Planning Centre Cork, NAOMI, Parent Concern, the Society to Outlaw Pornography, the Irish Council of Civil Liberties, the Family Centre Knock Shrine; Christian Counsel, the Congress of Secondary School Parents Association, the Cork Federation of Women's Organisations, Cherish (an organisation representing single mothers), and the Union of Students in Ireland. The IFPA was only included in the consultation because they requested a meeting; no other family planning groups were contacted and neither was the Institute of Obstetricians and Gynaecologists.[56]

The minister attended many of these meetings. There were two rounds of consultation with some interest groups: before the bill was drafted, and a second following publication.[57] The invitation to these meetings acknowledged that the current position where contraceptives could be imported without restriction (if a person claimed that they were for personal use) was unsatisfactory, but legislating would be difficult.

5.5   The Health Sector

The first consultative meeting was with the IMA on 26 January 1978. Mr Haughey told the delegation that it was appropriate to begin with the

---

[56] NAI DT 2009/16/123 Office of the Minister for Health, Memo for Government, 23 October 1978.

[57] I am extremely grateful to Barry Desmond, Minister for Health, 1982–7, who had copied the records of these meetings for his personal use and gave me permission to consult them in the UCD Archives. His files do not contain the written submissions, and I have not located these in the National Archives. Unless otherwise stated, the material cited below comes from the Barry Desmond papers, unlisted, Box 210.

doctors.[58] They indicated that doctors generally would accept 'their proper role' if legislation was enacted. The law should be changed, but it 'need not be extensive'. GPs should be the primary providers; the role of Health Boards should be limited to infertility and problem cases, such as psycho-sexual issues. IMA Secretary Noel Reilly emphasised that the main decisions were political and social. Medical practitioners would not accept the role of arbiters of moral consciences. They would not take decisions based on age or marital status, but legislation should not provide that persons could demand contraception as of right – this request was presumably designed to enable doctors to opt out of providing contraception. The delegation highlighted the need for training in family planning. The IMA favoured regulating volun-tary bodies providing contraception, and they wanted contraception removed from the criminal law. Mr Haughey referred to differences of opinion among the IMA membership and asked whether a confidential survey of members would provide a truer picture of opinion than was currently available; he offered the Department's assistance with this if the IMA wished.

The discussions with the NHC coincided with the Council's AGM.[59] It was common practice for the Minister for Health to meet the NHC on such occasions however Mr Haughey was 'indisposed', so the meeting took place between the NHC Council and officials. In 1977, the AGM of the NHC had unanimously passed a motion in favour of legislation controlling the sale, importation and manufacture of contraceptives. They published a modified version of this resolution in their annual report, substituting the words 'respon-sible outlets' for 'pharmacies'.[60] The Department sought their views about the role of Health Boards in family planning. They replied that family plan-ning was a matter for a couple and their GP. Health boards should provide services, where doctors were unwilling to do so. Nurses should be trained to promote natural family planning. Contraception should be decriminalised, but limited to married couples, though this would prove difficult to enforce. Asked whether control of contraceptives should be the responsibility of the medical profession or the state, one delegate suggested that it was a matter for both parties. The representative of An Bord Altranais, the body responsible for the

---

[58] Delegations: Minister, Dr Joyce, CMO; Mr Hensey, Secretary of the Department, Dr O'Rourke and Frank Foley. IMA President Dr Healy, Drs Sean Boyle, Ray Hawkins, Hugh Raftery and Noel Reilly and Mr Byrne.

[59] The Council was established under the 1953 Health Act to advise the Minister on such general matters affecting the health or incidental to the health of the people, as might be referred to them by the Minister. The Council was also free to comment as they saw fit, on matters relating to the health service, though not on questions of pay or conditions. The Council was established in response to pressure from the medical profession for an organisation that would liaise with the Minister for Health: Minutes of NHC 14 June 1974 speech by Tanaiste (and Minister for Health), and Minutes 21 November 1975. Lenus website, accessed 19 March 2018.

[60] Minutes, 27 August 1976; 25 March 1977; accessed 19 March 2018.

registration and regulation of nurses and midwives, indicated that all nurses and midwives should have comprehensive training and knowledge of family planning methods. Although the Bord had included a section on family planning in their training programmes in line with EEC directives, they had not expressed any views on the merits of contraception.

There was broad agreement within the NHC that family planning and contraception were 'basically social problems and as such were matters for politicians'. There was a consensus that GPs, public health nurses and midwives should be trained to enable them to provide advice on contraception and legislation should be amended. The extent to which contraception should be provided under the Health Acts required detailed examination but did not require separate legislation. One member of the NHC, Dr de Courcy Wheeler, a GP based in the Midlands, who was not present, submitted a statement. He was in favour of condoms being available without prescription because this might prevent vd and abortion; he also favoured male and female sterilisation, and he believed that abortion should be available on 'strong medical grounds', which appeared to refer to non-viable foetal abnormalities and genetic reasons. This is the first mention that I have seen in the Irish debate on contraception, of the value of condoms in preventing disease; Dr de Courcy Wheeler's views were out of line with the majority.

A meeting with a joint delegation of the Pharmaceutical Society of Ireland and the Irish Pharmaceutical Union took place later that day.[61] The IPU acknowledged that there was 'wide division' among members, and some 'possibly a substantial number' would not provide contraceptives and would lobby against any involvement by pharmacies. They suggested that Health Boards should supply the best methods of contraception to each individual if GPs were unable or unwilling to do so. IPU members would only sell condoms if sales were restricted to pharmacists. It would be impossible to implement restrictions based on either age or marriage. Free contraception should be restricted to necessitous persons' – these were not defined.

The Pharmaceutical Society had established a sub-committee to consider the matter. When their Council had reviewed their report, it would be forwarded to the Department. There was a spectrum of opinion within the Society on the involvement of the Health Boards; some believed that they should only give advice others suggested that they should fit appliances that required medical intervention. The PSI agreed with the IPU that pharmacists could not implement restrictions based on age or marriage, though they would 'exercise

---

[61] The Pharmaceutical Society of Ireland, established by Act of Parliament in 1875, is the statutory body that oversaw the education, examinations and registration of pharmaceutical chemists, and the enforcement of regulations relating to the Pharmacy Acts. The Irish Pharmaceutical Union, now Irish Pharmacy Union, is the representative body for community pharmacists in Ireland.

responsible control'. They wanted free contraception to be restricted – one delegate said that 'contraception should not be provided as a social service'. They asked the Department about the consequences if pharmacists refused to supply condoms. The Secretary of the Department of Health reassured them that this would not affect contracts where a pharmacy supplied medicines to General Medical Service (free healthcare) patients. The President of the PSI suggested that doctors should be permitted to opt out of fitting IUDs; the department's chief medical officer concurred, though he noted that with increasing evidence about the side effects of the contraceptive pill, there was 'greater pressure' to fit IUDs. Both the NHC and the pharmaceutical delegation agreed that while some pharmacists or doctors might not wish to supply contraception, 'there would be enough to provide any necessary cover'.

The Irish Nurses Organisation wanted nurses to play a major role in promoting natural methods of family planning, with health boards providing training. The general secretary explained that the INO considered that contraception should be restricted to married couples. Asked about single people who put themselves at risk of pregnancy, she replied that the answer was 'a proper education for living'. The INO was concerned about nurses who might have conscientious objections to advising on contraception. They suggested that this difficulty would be eased if health boards only gave advice and instruction on natural methods. Asked how a health board would know whether a client was married or single, they replied that the majority of those attending local clinics would be known to the nurses. Asked whether violence or alcoholism in a marriage, might justify contraception, the INO countered that insufficient attention was given to the dangers associated with the Pill. As to the additional costs involved in having condoms only available on prescription, a delegate said that 'this would be the cost of protecting a better way of life'.[62]

The most liberal views within the health sector were expressed by the Irish Association of Social Workers. They favoured a family planning service provided by the health boards and family-planning clinics – the latter should receive public funding. Health boards should provide comprehensive training in family planning; all forms of contraception should be available free of charge with no restrictions based on marital status or age. They rejected an age limit, because that would rule out providing contraception to young, mentally handicapped girls. One delegate expressed the view that sexual activity cannot be controlled; it was a reality. Asked about conscientious objectors, they said that they would be few, and in such cases, a client could be referred to another social worker.[63]

---

[62] 21 June 1978, Miss Meehan, Mrs Monaghan, Mrs Courtney and Miss Taaffe with the Department represented by O'Rourke and Foley.

[63] 21 June 1978, Miss Roantree, Miss Torode, Miss Garland and Mr Goodwin. The Minister was not present; the Department was represented by Mr O'Rourke and Mr Foley.

One of the most significant consultations took place between the minister and the regional health boards. The CEOs of all eight health boards were present plus some members from each board. The large meeting may have been inhibiting because there was a widespread unwillingness to express opinions. A summary compiled by the Department noted that seven of the eight health boards believed that they had a specific role with respect to family planning, but five suggested that this should be limited to providing training and advice. Two favoured providing comprehensive family planning services; one argued that family planning clinics should be under their control. There was a consensus in favour of restricting sales to married people, though one member of the Southern Health Board favoured including couples in stable relationships. All acknowledged the difficulties that restrictions would impose; some supported restriction by age; one wanted to control access by granting or refusing people a purchase license. Most delegates believed that contraceptives should only be available on prescription. Two wished to provide free contraception to GMS patients, but a member of the SHB argued that 'contraceptives like cosmetics should not be supplied free'.

The chair of the Eastern Health Board, which included Dublin and surrounding areas, told the Minister that members had agreed that the board should give advice on family planning; legislation was a matter for parliament. This was the extent of common ground among EHB members; his personal opinion was 'a moral conservative view'. Another member, social worker Noreen Kearney commented that the Health Board had a responsibility to the less well-off people who could not access family planning services. A GP suggested that Board's role should be mainly educational: they should not run clinics or deal directly with the public, only through medical practitioners.

The chair of the Midland Health Board resorted to platitudes. 'His was a common-sense point of view but he was satisfied that the Minister had common sense enough to deal with this matter in a common-sense way and in the best interests of all the people'. Another member, a doctor, did not wish the MHB to provide a family planning service. Doctors would have nothing to do with condoms – they were a social matter and for legislators. The vice chair, a doctor, acknowledged that he was in the minority: he would welcome legislation providing for the sale and distribution of contraceptives through health boards, clinics and GPs. Limiting access to married couples might create a black market.

The Mid-Western Health Board favoured a service that would not include sterilisation or abortion and would respect conscientious objections. Contraception should be restricted to married couples, and under licence. However, a doctor, who was a Board member, said that it was unfair to limit access to married couples. Another representative, a pharmacist suggested that provisions already existed that would enable the Minister to issue licenses providing for the sale of all contraceptives, similar to the controls governing the supply of contraceptive pills. He favoured restricting access by age rather than marital status, with measures to prevent purchase by those under 16 years.

In 1972, the North-Eastern Health Board, which included two Ulster counties with a significant Protestant minority, had passed a unanimous resolution requesting the government to introduce legislation governing the sale, importation, regulation, and control of contraception. One delegate, Dr Rory O'Hanlon, FF TD, a GP and a future Minister for Health, was opposed to clinics; he believed that contraception was a matter for family doctors. He claimed that there was a consensus that access should be restricted to married couples, though he was aware of the difficulties that this entailed. An unidentified member of the NEHB explained that he was interested in civil rights and foresaw difficulties in such restriction. He would prefer restriction by age.

Sean McEniff (FF), vice chair of the North-Western Health Board, suggested that family planning should be provided through community care, GPs and hospitals, but not health board clinics. A meeting of the NWHB had divided 50/50 on whether access should be limited to married couples and whether contraceptives should be provided free to married GMS patients. One group felt that contraceptives should be available only on prescription.

The chair of the South-Eastern Health Board reported that it had proved difficult to secure consensus, and this was also true of 'ordinary people'. There were no young people on the Board, and none 'of the few ladies who attended the board meeting' had commented on the issue. He was reporting the views of middle-aged males. Majority opinion was opposed to health board clinics; GPs should confine advice to married couples; contraceptives should only be available on prescription; and GPs should determine who should be supplied free of charge. Another member of the SEHB 'could not see why the Church should depend on the legislature and the Health Board to prop them up on morality'. Health boards had a responsibility to meet medical needs. He believed that primary responsibility for contraception remained with GPs, and he described the current situation, where anybody could import and make available any kind of contraceptives as 'invidious'.

Mr Baker, FRCS, who reported the views of the Southern Health Board stated that they wanted to confine their role to providing advice, though some members wanted the Board to exercise control over existing clinics. The majority were of the view that IUDs were abortifacients and should not be available. Changing the law and determining who should have access to contraceptives were matters for legislators. The Western Health Board concurred that such details were a matter for legislators. They saw the Health Boards as 'natural implementers'; family planning services should be comprehensive and acceptable to the eligible classes. Services delivered through health boards should be limited to families (i.e. married couples).

Mr Haughey told this meeting that he did not plan to initiate a general discussion. He asked whether natural family planning should receive as much encouragement as artificial methods. Some of those present wanted more emphasis placed on natural methods, others wanted both options available. One doctor noted that in some parts of rural Ireland, GPs might only encourage natural methods, which discriminated against GMS patients. When Mr Haughey queried whether the choice of doctor available to GMS patients did not meet such a case, this doctor replied that 'there may be no other doctor in the area'. Noreen Kearney (EHB) suggested that health boards could use social workers to provide advice and education on family planning. Mr McEniff, NWHB, commented that 'it seemed that no-one felt that condoms would be generally available', though it might be worth noting that he lived close to the border with Northern Ireland. Mr Haughey concluded by noting that this meeting might be setting headlines for less controversial aspects of health legislation.

5.5.1   The Churches

At their spring meeting in 1978, the Irish [Catholic] Episcopal Conference announced that they had accepted the Minister's invitation to a consultative meeting. They also issued a statement reiterating that contraception was morally wrong, but that did not mean that the State was bound to prohibit access to contraception. They continued to highlight the social consequences that would ensue if contraceptives became available.

The issues which we have been raising are issues of public morality, affecting the well-being of our whole society. No responsible person wishes to see multiplied in our country the social evils to which we have called attention. The problem facing the legislator is precisely this, to decide whether, or to what extent new legislation can provide safeguards against such evils, and whether or how these safeguards can be made effective.[64]

They claimed that 'there is a whole area within which it seems difficult to separate procedures which are primarily abortifacients from those which are primarily contraceptive.... Legalisation of such procedures would seem to leave a dangerous legal opening towards abortion'. They recommended that the health service should promote natural family planning and carry out further research in that field.[65]

The Catholic Hierarchy reiterated these views in more forceful terms during their ninety-minute meeting with the Minister and officials. Dr Cahal Daly, Ardagh and Clonmacnoise (a future Archbishop of Armagh) stated that: 'if

---

[64] Statement from the Irish Bishops' Conference on Proposed Legislation Dealing with Family Planning and Contraception, *The Furrow*, August 1978, pp. 525–7.
[65] *IT*, 5 April 1979.

there is to be new legislation it should be minimal and restrictive and should not be separate from a total service in support of the family. It should be seen as part of the national ethos'. He conceded that restrictive legislation was difficult to sustain and there would be continuing pressure to repeal these restrictions. 'Nevertheless …incorporation of restrictions in legislation is not pointless. It indicates the legislative intent and the state's commitment'. Restricting outlets 'seems to offer the best likelihood of success' but 'even this has problems'.

The bishops expressed unequivocal opposition to involving the health boards in family planning. They warned this would give rise to social difficulties, even if their role was limited to advice. Requiring health boards to provide family planning 'would seem to be in effect projecting the country immediately and needlessly into a situation of nation-wide availability, with … unpredictable social and moral consequences …Contraceptive advice and services would thus not only become universally available; overnight, they would be given a totally new and spurious aura of official approval and medical respectability. Contraception would be officially introduced into provincial areas, where there has been no demand in public opinion'. They alleged that taxpayers would object to public money being spent 'fitting devices'. Contraception was not a medical problem – associating it with the health boards was 'fraught with danger'. It would be morally wrong to impose statutory obligations on health board personnel. Many would have conscientious objections, and the conscientious rights of staff must not be infringed. They claimed that the effect of providing family planning through health board clinics would be 'more far-reaching than if similar promotion was being done privately'.

Cahal Daly argued that 'A major progression from virtually nothing to ready availability would have serious moral, medical and social consequences, as happened elsewhere.' When the Secretary of the Department suggested that it would be difficult to exclude the health boards from an advisory role; family planning services seemed 'a normal development in maternity services', Dr McNamara (Bishop of Kerry, later Archbishop of Dublin) said that agencies other than health boards would not give the same official status to contraception. He warned of the social consequences that would follow the introduction of a comprehensive family planning service. When the Minister suggested that providing contraception to single people would be better than abortion, Dr Daly countered that the McGee judgment was based on the family.

The bishops expressed concerns about some existing family planning clinics, especially those that referred clients for abortions. It would be 'utterly objectionable' if they were given any role providing family planning. The Secretary of the Department suggested that this was one argument in favour of involving the health boards. Dr Lennon (Bishop of Kildare and Leighlin) who would appear to have been the most moderate member of the delegation expressed the view that the philosophy of the IFPA was 'wrongly based even if some of the people involved were genuinely concerned'. Dr McNamara wondered whether their activities could be curtailed. When Dr Daly inquired about sterilisation, Mr Haughey indicated that he did not propose to legislate on that matter – he gave a similar reply to other delegations.

Mr Haughey reassured the bishops that there was no question of providing for abortion. Further research might be necessary on the question of abortifacients. He was considering whether the State should encourage the promotion of natural family planning and research in that field, 'since it had certain advantages over artificial methods'. The legislation would differentiate between making information available by proper sources and commercial exploitation through advertising. He referred to the question of restricting access, whether to married people, or by age. It would not be compulsory for doctors and other health professionals to provide family planning services. He had already made it clear that no officer of the Department was to be required to deal with family planning matters if they did not wish to do so.

The Minister mentioned that he had found the representatives of the CMAC 'somewhat reluctant to talk about contraception'. Dr Lennon explained that their main role related to marriage preparation courses and training marriage counsellors; they had only recently begun to train family planning tutors. He claimed that the thirty-two CMAC centres were too remote for many people. Cahal Daly said that the CMAC was mainly in contact with the middle class; they had little impact on lower-income groups. The Department raised the possibility of making an annual grant to the CMAC. The bishops countered by referring to Dr Bonnar's work (see Chapter 4) and the interest that he was promoting in natural methods. They suggested that funding might be given for research in this field, 'in support of marriage and the proper status of women'. They wanted to exclude condoms from the legislation, arguing that they had no medical function and did not need medical intervention and they pressed their case against IUDs, arguing that there were 'various definitions of abortion'. Asked how contraception should be provided, Dr McNamara suggested that there might be special clinics, providing a very restrictive service. The Minister suggested that there might be legal difficulties if medical practitioners had to be involved in making condoms available.[66]

Mr Haughey met representatives of the Church of Ireland some weeks before he met the Catholic Hierarchy.[67] Their submission stated that family planning and contraception were matters for married people. They would have to consider condemning any bill that provided for access by single people.

---

[66] Barry Desmond Papers Box 210, 2 June 1978; *II* 3 June 1978, *IP* 3 June 1978.
[67] Meeting on 29 May 1978. The delegation consisted of Dr McAdoo, Professor Alan Browne, Mrs McClatchie and Canon Willoughby. Mr Haughey was accompanied by the Secretary of the Department and Mr Foley.

They favoured extending existing family planning clinics and expanding the services offered. Health Boards should draft information leaflets giving details of doctors and clinics providing family planning services. Sales outlets should be restricted; there should be a schedule listing which types of contraceptives were only available on prescription. If doctors and pharmacists had access to information, they saw no need to advertise contraceptives. They were opposed to IUDs on the grounds that they were abortifacients; abortion should only be permitted in exceptional medical cases.

The Archbishop of Dublin, Dr McAdoo, emphasised that the standing committee of the church had only examined the question of family planning – contraception for married couples. Canon Willoughby reiterated that most members of the church favoured that stance. Gynaecologist, Professor Alan Browne, was more equivocal, though he favoured 'some control'. Mr Haughey suggested that it would prove difficult to restrict contraception to married couples. Some single people put themselves at risk, would contraception not be better? The delegation rejected that argument on the grounds that, 'to answer yes meant that they approved or condoned premarital sexual relationships'. If single people were given access to contraception, the Church would consider whether 'this was helping young people to live a decent life and whether such legislation made it even more difficult to live a Christian life'. It is clear during this exchange and elsewhere that the government was uncertain how the Supreme Court might respond to a constitutional challenge by a single person, similar to the McGee case. Professor Browne noted a growing problem where tests were revealing serious deformities in foetuses, and mothers were seeking abortions. The delegation was informed that abortion was only relevant insofar as some contraceptives 'claimed to be abortifacients'.

Mr Haughey asked every delegation about their views on natural methods. Mrs McClatchie, a member of the Church of Ireland delegation, expressed strong support, while acknowledging that the Billings method 'does not always work'. She regarded it as useful in spacing children in marriages where an additional child 'would not be a problem'. Professor Browne described Billings as 'very good when there is full commitment from a couple'.

The Methodist church argued that all contraceptive methods should be available, ideally to those in stable relationships, but the law should not discriminate against single people.[68] One delegate stated that unwanted children were not desirable. Health boards should provide a comprehensive service, including education on human relations; contraception should be free for medical card holders. They were opposed to slot machines and newspapers advertisement and appear to have been divided as to whether condoms should be

---

[68] 17 April 1978, Rev. A. Mears, Miss Margaret Burns and Mr John Bailey, met the Minister, Secretary and Mr Foley.

available only on prescription. One member suggested that this would create unnecessary work for doctors, but another believed that it would give them an opportunity to give advice (presumably on responsible sexual behaviour and family planning).

The views expressed by the Presbyterian delegation were closer to those of the Church of Ireland.[69] They favoured research into natural methods; opposed single people having access to contraception but recognised that it was impossible to prevent some access. They would like to see restraints to protect young people. Ideally, contraceptives should only be available on prescription and through doctors or pharmacies; free contraception should only be provided to medical card holders if there were medical reasons for doing so. Although they were concerned about abortifacients, they indicated that the Presbyterian General Assembly was unlikely to exert pressure on the government with respect to IUDs.

The views of the church delegations had much in common. All favoured restrictions. Three of the four wanted contraception confined to married couples, while recognising that this would prove difficult, and there was significant support for restricting access by means of doctors' prescriptions, and positive attitudes towards natural family planning. The Catholic Hierarchy indicated a reluctant acquiescence towards restricted access. Their opposition to a major role for the health boards was significant because that was being considered by the Department of Health. [This was Labour Party policy so it would have been discussed during the term of the previous Minister for Health, Brendan Corish.] The demand by the Hierarchy for government support to promote natural methods gave the Minister a possible carrot that might mitigate their opposition. The Hierarchy's preference for groups associated with the ovulation/Billings method rather than the CMAC is interesting.

5.5.2   Advocacy Groups; Civil Society

Family planning clinics were not included in the consultation process, but when the IFPA requested a meeting, they were facilitated.[70] Mr Haughey suggested that they should treat the discussion as confidential – if that was said at other meetings, the Department note-taker failed to record it. The IFPA expressed the view that contraceptive services should be available nationwide, and not restricted to married couples. Family doctors should be the primary source of advice, and contraceptive services should be available through the health boards. The IFPA saw its future role in providing education and training in family planning, and problem cases, such as psycho-sexual counselling and

---

[69] 17 April 1978, Rev McConnell, Rev McDowell, Dr Hazel Morris and Mr McWilliams.

[70] Dr George Henry, Dr David Nowlan, Dr P Dowding, Mrs Marie Mullarney and Mrs Jones.

contraception for those who felt unable to discuss the matter with a family doctor. Dr George Henry highlighted the problem for women over thirty-five years in accessing contraception because, in many parts of Ireland, the Pill remained the only option. When they broached the topic of sterilisation, Mr Haughey replied that there was no law prohibiting sterilisation and he did not propose to include it in his bill. He asked whether IUDs were abortifacients. Dr Henry denied that they were. There was 'even less justification for describing the mini-pill as an abortifacient' (as several of the anti-reform groups were wont to do). He highlighted the medical risks when IUDs were fitted by untrained people. Asked if they provided information on natural methods, the IFPA confirmed that they did, but not on Billings because it demanded a lot of time. On the question of contraception for single people, Mr Haughey commented that 'the ordinary person's reaction was contraception may be OK for married but not for the unmarried'. Dr David Nowlan (*Irish Times* Health correspondent) stated that doctors would not prescribe condoms, and they would resist restrictions based on marriage or age. Dr Dowding suggested that it would be more responsible if single people used contraception, to which the Minister remarked that other groups had also argued that contraception for unmarried people was the lesser of two evils.[71]

Department of Health officials met supporters of the Billings method: the chair and secretary of NAOMI; representatives of the Family Life Centre at Knock Shrine, and Dr John Bonnar and a public health nurse from Limerick, who was involved in the WHO project. NAOMI wanted health boards to provide extensive education in natural methods, with at least one trained co-ordinator. Other forms of contraception should be restricted to married couples, available only on prescription from chemist shops with 'purchasers signing a register as for poisons'. The legislation should list the permitted forms of contraception, which should not include IUDs. When Professor Bonnar suggested that there was an obligation to provide contraceptives 'for the deprived section of the community', the other delegates objected. He expressed the view that 100 centres for natural methods would not cater to all needs. Asked what should be done in cases where natural methods would not work, a woman delegate said that this would be legislating for bad marriages. Dr Bonnar noted that while the well-to-do could find a solution, there was a responsibility to provide other means of family planning for poorer women 'if natural family methods were insufficient'. He asked the Department what would be done about IUDs. The assistant secretary replied that it was not proposed to legislate for the termination of pregnancies. Dr Bonnar suggested that there was no need to make IUDs available: diaphragms condoms, the Pill and natural methods would be adequate for Irish needs.

---

[71] 24 April 1978.

Mr Haughey joined this meeting at a late stage, having been detained in Dáil Éireann, and it became a duet – in almost perfect harmony – between the Minister and Professor Bonnar. Both are enthused about natural family planning. Mr Haughey described it as 'complementary to his own wish to develop a positive attitude to health'; he would like to see it developed further. 'His general approach would be that natural methods should have at least as much prominence as artificial methods and he was prepared to assist financially'. Dr Bonnar noted that 'the [Billings] method gave a woman confidence in her own ability to control her fertility', to which the Minister replied that 'it was the development of this personal responsibility for her own welfare that made the general concept worthy of support'.[72]

The submission by the Irish Congress of Trade Unions was drawn up by ICTU's women's advisory committee. It suggested that family planning should be seen as an extension of community care, provided by trained staff, through the health boards and community care centres. Contraceptives should be supplied on medical advice, regardless of status, age, or circumstances, free for GMS patients and those suffering from chronic disease. They were opposed to condoms available only on prescriptions. Mai O'Brien explained that members had initially held divergent views, but their submission was unanimously approved by the committee. She told the Minister that the contraceptive pill was sold door to door in certain areas; the poorer section of the community had no access to contraception. When Mr Haughey stated that the health boards preferred that family doctors should be the primary providers, she claimed that many doctors were not familiar with the range of family planning options, or were not interested, and they often took the easy way out by prescribing the Pill. Mr Haughey mentioned that he had recently spoken to the La Lèche League (which supported breast-feeding) and asked whether ICTU had any views on that subject. Mai O'Brien cited a recent article showing that breast-feeding was confined to high-income mothers; it did not suit working mothers.

The most revealing comment during this meeting came when Ruarí Robert ICTU general secretary confirmed that Congress had not discussed family planning. He described it as 'a controversial issue... he would see no reason to divide membership on an issue that was not primarily a union matter'. Mr Haughey stated that one of the major issues that had to be addressed was whether contraception should be confined to married people. The Women's Committee rejected this partly on grounds of equality, and partly because of difficulties in enforcement. Fintan Kennedy suggested that there was no precedent for such a restriction. The delegation agreed with the Minister's

---

[72] The file does not give the date of this meeting.

suggestion that controlling access through a doctor-based service might be the best option.[73]

The meeting with the Irish Family League followed a predictable pattern. They called on the Minister to outlaw all means of artificial contraception on medical, moral, social, and demographic grounds. They expressed grave concern that the Supreme Court was emerging as a Third House of the Oireachtas; a constitutional amendment should be enacted to curb the power of the court. They saw no need for legislation. Mr Haughey explained that his job was to legislate: a total ban presented difficulties in light of the Supreme Court judgment. A total ban would require changing the constitution. He told the Irish Family League 'that he now thought that he understood their point of view' [shades of Charles de Gaulle speaking to white settlers in Algeria] and thanked them for 'expressing it so cogently'. One delegate told him that 'this was one of the most crucial debates that the country had ever faced: it ranked with the treaty and the neutrality issues'. If money was available, it should not be spent on contraception, but on married mothers and on the forthcoming Children's Year.

Barry Desmond's Papers do not contain the complete set of minutes of the consultative meetings, or all the submissions received. The submission by the Women's Representative Committee, established by the government in 1974 to implement the recommendations of the Commission on the Status of Women, favoured making contraception available without restrictions on age or marital status – they described such restrictions as unconstitutional, unworkable and undesirable. They regarded family planning as a medical not a legal matter. The health boards had an important role to play in providing access; contraceptives should be available through health centres and community care centres under 'proper medical supervision' and on prescription through pharmacies. They advocated strict control of advertising, and the need for those involved in family planning to receive appropriate training.[74]

The records of these meetings indicate extensive support for legislation to provide for contraception. Although many delegates recognised the difficulties of restricting access on the basis of age or marital status, a majority favour restrictions and there was broad agreement that contraceptives should only be available from pharmacies or healthcare providers. Many speakers drew a distinction between family planning, which was seen as desirable, and apparently applying only to married couples – and contraception.

---

[73] 10 July 1978. Delegation Fintan Kennedy, Ruari Roberts, Mai O'Brien, Brid Horan and Carmel Dunne. Minister Haughey, Mr O'Rourke, assistant-secretary and Mr Foley.

[74] *IT*, 18 October 1978. The committee was chaired by Labour TD Eileen Desmond, with representatives of ICTU, the Federated Union of Employers, the Council for the Status of Women, and the ESRI.

These consultations ended any prospect that the health boards would provide a comprehensive family planning service: the health boards were divided in their views and reluctant to undertake this role. The medical profession was determined to protect the primacy of the family doctor, and the Catholic church was utterly opposed to health-board involvement. The submissions from nurses, pharmacists and doctors combined concern for public morality with a determination to protect professional interests and, in the case of doctors and pharmacists a determination to reserve the primary role in contraception for private providers. Women constituted a small minority of those attending these meetings and the majority were members of groups who opposed access to contraception: the INO, the Irish Family League, NAOMI and the Knock Family Life Centre.

5.6   Legislation

A summary of the consultations given to Cabinet stated that 'the majority view was that any legislation should provide for a more restrictive situation in relation to the availability of contraceptives than that which exists at present'. The most commonly expressed view was that access should be restricted to married couples, 'if only to demonstrate the expressed views of a majority of people in the country, and to avoid the conclusions being drawn, in the absence of such a restrictive provision that the availability of contraceptives to young and unmarried people had the approbation of the State'. The IFPA, Irish Association of Social Workers, and ICTU were singled out as favouring contraceptives being freely available to all who sought them. However, many deputations, including ICTU wanted all forms of contraceptives, including condoms to be available only on prescription. The memorandum suggested that 'If such a provision was contained in the legislation, it seems that it would meet with the general approval of those who felt that the legislation relating to contraception should be restrictive'. The majority view was that the health boards should not provide contraception, but opinion was not unanimous, and there was some divergence of opinion as to whether contraception should be free for GMS patients. Delegations that expressed fears that legislation permitting the sale of contraceptives would pave the way for abortion had been given an assurance that a specific provision would be included indicating that nothing in the legislation should be construed as permitting abortion.

The outline scheme for legislation presented to Cabinet placed the provision of advice, information and contraceptive devices 'firmly in the context of Family Planning' – that is regulating births within marriage. It proposed to give 'equal if not greater emphasis.... to natural as opposed to artificial methods', including a provision that advice information and instruction on natural methods 'should be made readily available to all families willing to avail of them'. Contraceptives should be available only on prescription and '**primarily** [my emphasis] to married couples but also, both for medical reasons and in circumstances considered appropriate by the registered medical practitioner, to other persons'. Making all contraceptives, including condoms available only on prescription, was a means of restricting access. Informal discussions with representatives of the medical profession indicated that 'The view of those consulted was that Family Planning should be undertaken in the context of family medicine, and while they are not anxious to be involved in the prescription of condoms, they see that such involvement could be acceptable to the majority of the profession in a situation in which family planning, in broad terms, is being made its responsibility'. Family planning would be provided by, or under the supervision of doctors: GPs or through services arranged by the health boards or other agents. If the Billings method could be shown to be effective, 'it would diminish many of the difficulties currently associated with legislation on family planning'.[75]

The draft bill, approved by Cabinet in December 1978 adopted a conservative tone. It obliged the Minister to **provide** 'a comprehensive natural family planning service', and to **control** the provision of family planning services involving the supply and use of contraceptives [my emphases]. No restrictions or regulations were imposed on providers of natural family planning; other methods could only be provided with the Minister's consent, where this was in the public interest and the Minister was satisfied that there was a particular need. Early drafts referred to contraceptives being available 'primarily to married couples', but this phrase was omitted presumably because it might be open to constitutional challenge. The more ambiguous term, 'bona fide family planning' – an implicit, but not explicit reference to marriage – was substituted.[76] The Bill was widely criticised by liberals and conservatives. USI, by a two-thirds majority passed two motions committing the organisation to fight for contraceptives to be available freely through the health service with a comprehensive education programme, and opposing legislation that restricted access on any basis. The Knights of Columbanus urged that the Bill be changed to include a ban on the distribution of contraceptives, and they called for a free vote in the Oireachtas.[77]

5.7   Further Consultations

On 4 January 1979, the Council of the IMA issued a statement that it could not recommend to its members that they should prescribe 'non-medical' contraceptives. The *Evening Herald* speculated that Mr Haughey might be forced

[75] NAI DT 2009/16/123 Health Bill (Family Planning) 1978.
[76] NAI DT 2008/148/217 1978 Family Planning Bill Memo for Government, 8 December 1978, *IT*, 15 December 1978.
[77] *IP*, 5 January 1979; *IP*, 15 January 1979.

to abandon the bill in the light of the IMA's stance; he was asking doctors to be the final arbiters in cases where unmarried people sought contraceptives, which might leave doctors open to prosecution.[78] The IMA statement resulted in 'an emergency meeting' between the Minister and the IMA Council. The chair of the IMA told Mr Haughey that the Council had passed a motion seeking an amendment to the section that placed sole responsibility for issuing condoms on doctors, because Council felt that doctors should not be exclusively concerned with non-medical contraceptives.

Mr Haughey sought to sway the IMA by arguing that doctors should 'accept this element of health care and with the same integrity as they have long undertaken other aspects of health care'. If they failed to do so, he feared that the health service 'would become the domain of commercially-oriented bodies to the serious disadvantage of the community'. The IMA agreed that there was a need for family planning, and he would appeal to them to help provide that service. Doctors who wished to opt out on grounds of conscience were free to do so. One delegate said that she 'saw nothing demeaning in prescribing condoms'; if doctors failed to do so foreign commercial interests would move in, with intolerable consequences, but another described prescribing condoms as 'demeaning'. Doctors would only consider medical circumstances; restrictions on the basis of marriage were a matter for the courts. Several doctors suggested that there would be parts of Ireland where no doctor was willing to prescribe contraceptives. One doctor stated that the bill was too narrow for those in casual relationships who wanted contraception. Another noted that the IMA objections could be resolved if responsibility for the sale of condoms rested with the pharmacists, 'who are reported to be prepared to sell them'. He believed that pharmacists should be free to sell to all comers, but Mr Haughey countered that this would mean unrestricted access. He did not think that the medical profession was in favour of this, and he would regard it as unacceptable.

Mr Haughey acknowledged that doctors did not like having to prescribe condoms. 'As Minister he was required to undertake tasks that he did not like, but that was part of his job as Minister.... Similarly authorising condoms was part of an overall Family Planning Service which is surely a matter for doctors'. Family planning services were particularly the concern of family doctors, and he was entitled to ask doctors to undertake them. In cases of GMS patients, the doctor would be paid for each consultation, but patients would have to pay for condoms. He gave a commitment to discuss the question of educating doctors in family planning with the Association.

One doctor suggested that it was the doctor's role to advise on the best method of family planning, and this might be condoms. Dr John Bonnar

[78] *Evening Herald*, 5 January 1979.

suggested that 'under the Bill', the decision as to using condoms might be taken by the doctor rather than the married couple. He flattered the Minister, suggesting that there was already some international interest in the bill, as a measure that might help to stem teenage pregnancies – though he failed to explain how this might happen.

Mr Haughey suggested that an ad hoc group with representatives of the medical profession, health boards and the Department could play a useful role in developing a comprehensive family planning service. His words had some impact. One delegate explained that he had come to the meeting with an open mind, but was conscious that many doctors were opposed to prescribing condoms. Having heard the Minister speak about the purpose and spirit behind the Bill, he now supported it completely. The tone of the closing contributions was conciliatory. The IMA Chair said that they had examined the bill as printed, but not in the context in which the Minister had presented it, 'emphasising the role of the doctor in the community'. While the Council had been very definite in their views, they might wish to look at it further. IMA Secretary Noel Reilly told the Minister that the Association remained bound by the decision of Council and only Council could overturn that decision.[79]

Following this meeting, Mr Haughey stated that he would not amend the bill, and he maintained that position. When the IMA Council met on 1 March, one day after the introduction of the Second Stage,[80] they maintained their opposition, '[D]espite a persuasive and revealing letter from the Minister for Health'. However, *Irish Times* medical correspondent David Nowlan noted that this could not affect the working of the legislation, because members were free to decide whether to issue prescriptions for condoms. The IMA, by a substantial majority maintained its belief that they should not be the sole providers of condoms, but there was no consensus about alternative outlets.[81]

The INO supported the measure and welcomed the emphasis on natural methods, though they had concerns about the omission of any reference to marriage – the Minister informed them that this would present legal problems.[82] The legislation did not give nurses a central role in providing family planning, but pharmacists were crucial, hence the importance of a meeting with the IPU and the PS. The Pharmacological Society noted that pharmacists had a role to advise patients with respect to prescriptions, but the Bill did not appear to allow for this, unless they confined themselves to advice on natural methods. Mr Haughey agreed in principle with this interpretation. Pharmacists were opposed to non-pharmacists issuing contraceptives; it was agreed that

[79] Barry Desmond Papers Box 210.
[80] Fine Gael Health spokesman, John Boland, suggested that the second reading was deliberately timed to begin on the day before the IMA Council meeting. DÉ, 28 February 1979, col 347.
[81] *IT*, 2 March 1979.   [82] Barry Desmond Papers Box 210, 27 February 1979.

this would be discussed when regulations were being drafted. They were concerned that doctors might issue prescriptions for condoms permitting indefinite repeat supplies; Mr Haughey said that he envisaged time-limited prescriptions but acknowledged that the views of doctors must be respected.

The Pharmaceutical Union reported on a survey showing considerable opposition to selling condoms. About 73 per cent of members replied; 56 per cent indicated that they were prepared to dispense non-medical contraceptives; 40 per cent were not; 28 per cent would sell non-medical contraceptives without prescription and 60 per cent were opposed. The IPU expressed concern about the absence of a reference to married couples, and the possibility that doctors might issue prescriptions for condoms with no time limit or maximum quantity. They wanted prescriptions for condoms to be presented in a distinct form. Mr Haughey stated that a special form would be necessary, indicating that the contraceptives were being used in accordance with the Act.[83]

When he introduced the Second Reading, Mr Haughey emphasised that it was 'the result of careful and earnest consideration of a difficult situation …. a sincere attempt to meet that situation in a reasonable and acceptable manner'. His speech included the much-quoted phrase that it 'seeks to provide an Irish solution to an Irish problem'.[84] He drew a distinction between family planning and contraception and between family planning and abortion. Family planning services were defined as including information, instruction, advice or consultation; the provision of contraceptives was covered in a different section of the bill. Any individual or service providing family planning must include information on natural methods. The legislation sought to end mail order supplies. Individuals could import a limited quantity for personal use; larger quantities could only be imported under licence.[85] Opposition speakers John Boland (Fine Gael) and John O'Connell (Labour) claimed that there was a weariness, or deja-vu about the legislation. They criticised the onus placed on doctors; Dr O'Connell noted the absence of a definition of 'bona fide family planning'. Summing up the debate which stretched over several weeks, Mr Haughey noted that almost every deputy disliked some aspect of the bill; 'the views of the different Members of the House are so varied that it is utterly and totally impossible to conceive of any Bill I could bring into the House which would receive universal approval….The House is simply reflecting the views of the community it represents'. In face of criticism that the measure was sectarian, he noted that 'this Bill is far more in keeping with the views of the majority of the churches in this country, than more liberal proposals made by deputies during the debate',[86] a view confirmed by his consultations. Haughey's biographer Gary Murphy

[83] Barry Desmond Papers Box 210, 12 March 1979.
[84] DD, 28 February 1979, vol 312 no 3, col 335.   [85] DD, 28 February 1979, cols 321–35.
[86] DD, 25 April 1979, col 1477.

has recently revealed that on the night before he introduced the bill in the Dáil, Mr Haughey visited Archbishop's House 'to get the Catholic Church's final approval for his proposals from the Archbishop of Dublin, Dermot Ryan'.[87]

Fianna Fáil had eighty-two seats and a massive parliamentary majority. The second reading was passed by sixty-six votes to forty-nine. Allowing for those who were absent on official business, it appears that up to five FF deputies were missing, including Minister for Agriculture Jim Gibbons, an enemy of Haughey, who strongly opposed the measure. A statement issued on behalf of the Taoiseach noted that he had discussed the matter with Mr Gibbons, who had made clear that his objections were 'on grounds of personal conscience'. Having considered the matter, the Taoiseach would not insist on Mr Gibbons voting for this Bill.[88]

The often-tendentious contributions revealed the wide spectrum of opinion in the main political parties. John Boland, Fine Gael spokesman on health described the bill as 'unworkable…unenforceable and consequently unacceptable',[89] but his views differed widely from several party colleagues. The most accurate summary came from Labour TD John Horgan, who had sponsored several private members bills. He claimed that the Minister 'has borne more ridicule and more abuse on a sustained basis than I can remember any Minister having to put up with justifiably in this House'.[90] In his closing speech, Mr Haughey claimed that he 'sought to tread the middle ground',[91] but that space was characterised by a failure to define 'bona fide family planning', and other ambiguities. The legislation was widely condemned by conservatives; some called on the President not to sign it into law.[92]

The 1979 Family Planning Act ended almost a decade of legislative stalemate. The Act has been widely derided, generally by citing the phrase, 'an Irish solution to an Irish problem', but consultations with key interest groups suggest that it went as far as politically possible at this time. John Whyte noted that it was enacted without triggering a confrontation between church and state,[93] but Girvin claims that the Minister 'conceded every demand made by the bishops', except the inclusion of a specific clause confining contraception to married couples.[94] In 1983, journalist Gene Kerrigan described the legislation as

---

[87] Gary Murphy, *Charles Haughey* (Gill Books, Dublin, 2021), p. 346. Murphy discusses the bill in pp. 343–9.

[88] NAI DT 2009/136/192. The statement noted that this was the first time that this had arisen with respect to a bill introduced by a Fianna Fáil government, and Mr Lynch had decided to establish procedures for dealing with such eventualities in future.

[89] *DD*, 26 June 1979, col 1078.   [90] *DD*, 26 June 1979, col 1083.

[91] DD, 26 June 1979, col 1088.   [92] NAI DT 2009/115/95.

[93] John Whyte, *Church and state in modern Ireland, 1923–79* (Gill & Macmillan, Dublin, 1982), p. 416.

[94] Brian Girvin, 'An Irish solution to an Irish problem. Contraception, Catholicism and change', *Contemporary European History*, 27, no 1, 2018, p. 22.

'a genuine attempt to accommodate to the old values *and* the new, an impossible task, breeding a piece of legislation ignored in practice and condemned on all sides'.[95] Omitting definitions of 'family planning' or 'bona fide family planning purposes' was a deliberate attempt to placate conservative interests, without outlawing potential access for single people. The privileged treatment of natural methods and the promise of public money were designed to placate conservatives. The medical profession was wooed by emphasising the central role of GPs as opposed to a public health service. The 1979 Act should be seen as 'gesture politics' or political theatre. Few of those who were involved with legislation believed that contraception would be confined to married couples or 'bona-fide family planning', whatever that meant, but it perpetuated the fantasy that Ireland could stem the sexual and contraception revolution, and perhaps even find a solution in 'natural family planning'. Its enactment, the first major breach in Ireland's legislative moral wall, stimulated the campaign for a constitutional amendment affirming the rights of the unborn.

[95] *Magill*, September 1983.

6   The 1983 Pro-life Amendment

It is impossible to discuss family planning without reference to abortion. In Ireland, those who opposed even a minimal relaxation of the ban on contraception generally predicted that it would lead to the introduction of abortion. This was partly a matter of timing; the Irish debate on contraception got underway shortly after Britain reformed its abortion law in 1967 and at a time when other countries were making legal abortion more accessible. Ireland *was* different. Hesketh notes that in Britain and the USA, 'the issue [of abortion] became salient as a result of the activities of pro-abortion groups who were campaigning to liberalise abortion legislation... In Ireland, by contrast, the issue was politicised as a result of the activities of *anti* -abortion groups'. Unlike other countries where abortion legislation moved 'from restrictive to permission' the Irish campaign was 'anticipative' – initiated to prevent the introduction of abortion.[1]

From the 1920s, and probably earlier, many Irish women in crisis pregnancies travelled to England. PFI – pregnant from Ireland – was a widely used abbreviation in British medical and social services. After 1967, a growing number of pregnant women travelled, not only to conceal a pregnancy but also to terminate one. Britain's new abortion regime presented doctors and nurses who were opposed to abortion with ethical dilemmas, and first-hand knowledge of the workings of the British abortion act. Doctors and nurses moved freely between Britain and Ireland, and many Irish obstetricians underwent specialist training in the NHS. Almost all Irish consultant obstetricians were members of the British Royal College of Obstetricians and Gynaecologists,[2] and the MRCOG was a recognised professional pathway to consultant status. An Irish Institute of Obstetricians and Gynaecologists, affiliated to the Royal College of Physicians of Ireland (RCPI), was founded in 1968, and the Institute developed an Irish post-graduate training programme and qualification in obstetrics.

---

[1] Tom Hesketh, *The second partitioning of Ireland. The abortion referendum of 1983* (Brandsma Book Ltd, Dun Laoghaire, 1990), pp. 1–2.

[2] Professor Eamon de Valera, son of the Irish politician underwent post-graduate training at the Royal Post-Graduate Medical College (Hammersmith Hospital) but did not sit for the MRCOG reputedly for political reasons.

The ethical dilemmas presented by the new British legislation were probably a factor in these developments.

For more than a decade following the introduction of the British 1967 act, there were mass protests in Britain and repeated, though failed efforts to restrict its workings. Some of those who were active in the campaign were born and educated in Ireland, notably Dr Peggy Norris. These Irish expatriates played a key role in initiating an Irish anti-abortion movement. The 1973 US Supreme Court judgment *Roe* v. *Wade* had a considerable impact on the Irish debate because this judgment was issued shortly before the Irish Supreme Court ruled on the McGee case. Both judgments presented a direct challenge to conservative legislation, and they were in advance of any change that their respective legislatures would have enacted. Both relied on the issue of privacy. Similarities between the two judgments prompted claims that the Irish Supreme Court might issue a ruling permitting abortion.

Abortion in Ireland was prohibited under sections 58 and 59 of the 1861 Offences against the Person Act. Some lawyers have argued that the Act permitted abortion in limited circumstances. The UK Parliament passed the Infant Life Preservation Act 1929, permitting a termination after twenty-eight weeks (then regarded as the threshold of viability), for the purpose of preserving the life of the mother. The Bourne case in 1939 clarified that abortion was also permitted before twenty-eight weeks in similar circumstances. Whitty notes that there was no legal clarification in Ireland as to when an abortion was permitted; the exceptions allowed by the Catholic church – ectopic pregnancy and a hysterectomy in cases of cancer of the uterus – were not formally authorised by Irish law. The law did not recognise the principle of 'double effect', which was the justification used by the Catholic church.[3]

Illegal abortion was not unknown in Ireland, though this history has only begun to be uncovered in recent years. Cara Delay claims that the Irish story is broadly similar to elsewhere in Europe.[4] Pauline Jackson argues that the 1938 Bourne judgment, making it legal to carry out abortions in Britain in limited circumstances to protect the health of the mother, marked the start of Irish women journeying to Britain for abortion.[5] Ferriter notes that there were no prosecutions for illegal abortion in Ireland between 1938 and 1942, suggesting that women were travelling to Britain, and the twenty-five prosecutions between 1942 and 1946 would appear to indicate that wartime travel

---

[3] Noel Whitty, 'The law and the regulation of reproduction in Ireland 1922–1992', *University of Toronto Law Journal*, 43 no 4, autumn 1993, pp. 851–888.

[4] Cara Delay, Pills, potions and purgatives: women and abortion methods in Ireland, 1900–1950, *Women's History Review*, 2019, 28, no 3, pp. 479–99.

[5] Pauline Jackson, 'Outside the jurisdiction: Irishwomen seeking abortion', in Chris Curtin, Pauline Jackson and B Connor (eds), *Gender in Irish society* (Galway University Press, Galway 1987), pp. 203–23; Pauline Jackson, 'Abortion trials and tribulations', *Canadian Journal of Irish Studies*, 18, no 1, July 1992, pp. 112–20.

restrictions resulted in an upsurge in illegal abortions. If that was the case, the heavy custodial sentences for carrying out abortions issued in 1943/44 appear to have significantly reduced the incidence. There were only twelve prosecutions between 1947 and 1956. The high-profile prosecution in 1956 of Mamie Cadden, who was charged with murder when a woman on whom she was performing an abortion died – not the first client of Cadden's to die – may have deterred clients and illegal abortionists.[6] Delay suggests that Cadden was atypical: in Ireland, 'it was far more common for women to attempt to induce miscarriage by trying physical harm methods or consuming herbs, purgatives or pills': methods 'that were less likely to result in hospital visits'. Most known cases of surgical intervention happened in Dublin. They involved a small number of providers, including the notorious Cadden, and it is probable that most cases of illegal abortion were undetected and not prosecuted.[7] The Infant Life Preservation Act 1929 was not extended to Northern Ireland, and neither was the 1967 Abortion Act, but therapeutic abortions were carried out in cases where the mother's life was threatened.[8]

During the debate on the British Abortion Bill, opponents claimed that if it passed, the NHS might face a shortage of nurses, because many Irish nurses worked in the NHS.[9] In June 1968, the official journal of the INO published a statement by the Archbishop of Westminster, setting out guidelines for Catholic medical professionals in relation to the British Abortion Act.[10] In 1971, the journal of the Irish Guild of Catholic Nurses published a guide for Catholic nurses with respect to abortion. This stated that student nurses and midwives who had conscientious objections should not be involved in abortion cases; nurses should be prepared to take a job in another hospital or move to a different department.[11]

In 1972, the distinguished Scottish gynaecologist Ian Donald – he developed ultrasound as a technique for obstetrical diagnosis – gave the Charter Day lecture in Holles Street, titled 'Naught for your comfort', where he described the changing culture of obstetrics in Britain: 'an Irish postgraduate, unless he [sic] is prepared to ditch his religion or keep it secret may find it hard to get beyond the Registrar stage and even harder to obtain a consultant post'. He spoke about the demands for genetic counselling, artificial insemination by donor and in-vitro fertilisation (Louise Brown, the first successful IVF baby was born in 1968). 'The Irish Sea is only a couple of dozen miles or so wide, but can you retain your island status as England maintained her separateness from Europe until now?' This lecture was published in the *JIMA*; an editorial in the next issue claimed that it was the first article about

---

[6] Ferriter, *Occasions of sin*, pp. 253–6.   [7] Delay, 'Pills, potions and purgatives'.
[8] Earner Byrne and Urquhart, *The Irish abortion journey*, pp. 38–41, 69–73.
[9] Keith Hindell and Madeleine Simms, *Abortion law reformed* (Owen, 1971), p. 162.
[10] *Irish Nurses' Journal*, 1, no 6, June 1968.   [11] *Irish Nursing News*, Spring 1971.

the 1967 Abortion Act to appear in an Irish medical journal. The editorial noted that 'the title of Professor Donald's address has a prophetic ring to it. It is inevitable, that sooner or later a pro-abortion lobby will emerge'. It noted that 1,210 women from Ireland had abortions in Britain in 1971 – one in approximately 40 births, almost equal to the number of babies under one year old, who died in 1970.[12]

In 1974 the executive of the Institute of Obstetricians and Gynaecologists quoted a recent editorial in the *British Medical Journal*, which stated that 'it is inevitable that the Health Authorities should prefer for appointment to certain posts those who see abortion as properly part of clinical gynaecological practice', adding that 'what this implies is that a young doctor may find some difficulty in taking up a career in gynaecology in the NHS if he [sic] is fundamentally opposed on ethical grounds to abortion in the terms of the Act'. The Institute noted that it was 'of increasing urgency that satisfactory training programmes be organised for Irish graduates in the future'.[13]

A number of British gynaecologists, who were opposed to abortion, took consultant positions in Ireland. Conor Carr, an English public schoolboy and Cambridge University graduate (both his parents were Irish-born doctors), decided in 1966 to move to Ireland because he was not willing to conduct abortions. He became a consultant at Portiuncula Hospital in Ballinasloe.[14] Many Irish doctors undertaking advanced training in Britain opted to work with consultants who were known to be anti-abortion, such as Professor Hugh McLaren in Birmingham (a Scottish Presbyterian), a founding member of SPUC and a regular speaker at SPUC meetings, as was Ian Donald.[15] Both were regular visitors to Ireland. Dr Julia Vaughan, who chaired the Pro-Life Amendment Campaign (PLAC), became involved in the anti-abortion campaign in England in the 1970s when she was working there as a registrar.[16] One Irish consultant gynaecologist stated that he had been a member of both SPUC and LIFE (when he worked in England), though he left the former organisation because of its increasing stridency.[17] Abortion clouded the discussions on family planning at the Institute of Obstetricians and Gynaecologists. The minutes of the executive council of the Institute contain several statements emphasising that abortion must be distinguished from family planning.[18]

[12] *JIMA*, May 1972 and June 1972.
[13] Royal College of Physicians of Ireland (RCPI). Minutes Institute of Obstetricians and Gynaecologists 27 April 1974.
[14] Conor Carr, *The lucky twin, an obstetrician's tale* (no publication details given), pp. 1 and 7. My thanks to Brian Casey for alerting me to this book.
[15] Hindell and Simms, *Abortion law reformed*, pp. 95–6.
[16] *Magill*, July 1982, Blackmail on Abortion, Pat Brennan.
[17] RCPI Institute of Obstetricians and Gynaecologists, Abortion file.
[18] Institute of Obstetricians and Gynaeologists Minutes of Executive Council, 1 June 1973.

Abortion gave rise to 'a highly emotional debate' at the 1974 IMA conference. A motion condemning abortion was proposed by the Mayo branch, and
despite efforts to refer it to council, it was passed by thirty-four votes to twelve.
Most members chose to be absent from the debate, which was the strategy
commonly adopted when the conference debated motions on contraception.
But the *Catholic Standard* warned that 'What did emerge publicly for the first
time was the fact that a minority of doctors do approve of abortion in Ireland
and that the climate of opinion is such that a spokesman for the pro-abortion
point of view spoke freely' – the 'spokesman' in question was presumably
paediatrician Barry O'Donnell, who drew a distinction in his speech between
therapeutic abortion and abortion on demand.[19]

Groups such as Mná na hÉireann, the Responsible Society, and the Irish
Family League branded all family planning clinics as abortion clinics, and they
invoked the IUD to support their argument that contraception and abortion
were inextricably linked. From the early 1970s, successive Taoisigh received
letters from Britain, the USA and Australia from men and women of Irish birth
or descent, alleging that Ireland was about to legalise abortion. Politicians were
bombarded with gruesome pictures of bloodied foetuses and strident press-
cuttings about abortion clinics, as part of the anti-contraception campaign.[20]
Some correspondents berated them for permitting Irish women to travel to
Britain for abortion.[21] In 1973, Fine Gael TD Oliver J. Flanagan, a staunch
opponent of legalising contraception, sent Taoiseach Liam Cosgrave – who
shared his views – copies of brochures on the British Abortion Act, produced
by the UK Abortion Law Reform Association, to which Cosgrave sent a char-
acteristically direct response. 'Frankly I do not know why you should think
that I would be interested in reading it as of course there is no question of
legalising abortion here'. Anti-abortion lobbyists bracketed contraception with
abortion, divorce and euthanasia.[22] There is a sense that Ireland was viewed by
some international anti-abortion groups as a test case for holding the line on
the 'permissive society'.

The Irish anti-abortion campaign was originated by activists in Britain and
the United States. In January 1973, Fr Paul Marx paid his first visit to Ireland.
This American priest founded the Human Life Centre at St John's University
in Minnesota in 1972, a year after he had published *The Death Peddlers: war
on the unborn*, which argued that the United States was 'on its way to abortion
on demand'. He was in Britain when the US Supreme Court judgment *Roe* v.
Wade was published and he travelled to Ireland, apparently at the suggestion
of Liverpool gynaecologist Dr Peggy Norris, and under the auspices of the
(British) Society for the Protection of the Unborn Child (SPUC), though his

---

[19] *Catholic Standard*, 4 May 1973.   [20] NAI DT 2010/53/201, 12 November 1973.
[21] NAI DT 2010/53/241.   [22] NAI DT 2005/7/347.

itinerary appears to have been organised by the Irish Family League. Fr Marx gave two lectures in Cork one to a large group of teenage girls, and one to student nurses. Both meetings were hosted in institutions run by the Sisters of Mercy. He illustrated his lectures with graphic slides, and jars containing aborted foetuses preserved in formaldehyde. According to the *Irish independent*, the 500 schoolgirls who attended his talk were shown forty slides, 'many of baby just aborted'; a jar containing a twelve-week-old, aborted foetus circulated among the audience. The principal of one school whose pupils were present, expressed serious misgivings about these graphic displays, and a Cork diocesan priest, Fr Thomas Clancy, claimed that the shock session was 'a mistake', but the Sisters of Mercy justified the event. There is no evidence that the Irish authorities questioned his right to import or display anatomical remains. Fr Marx claimed to be shocked by how little had been done to educate the Irish on abortion. He mentioned that there was 'one embryonic group in existence: the Irish Right to Life Society'. He cited statistics on the number of women with Irish addresses having abortions in England. Speaking to reporters at Cork airport, he claimed that the Irish government would be open to the charge of allowing itself to be used as an agent for the British 'abortion business' if steps were not urgently taken to educate boys and girls on the implications of abortion. His visit attracted considerable media coverage; it was obviously designed by SPUC as a means of generating interest.[23]

This was the first occasion that Irish people and media were exposed to high-profile shock tactics, and they proved highly effective. In an uncanny prediction, *Irish Press* columnist, T.P. O'Mahony expressed the wish that 'If abortion ever comes before the Irish people as a legislative issue, it is to be earnestly hoped that the consideration of it will be free of the kind of scare tactics employed in Cork on Tuesday. That hope, however, is likely to prove ill-founded.'[24]

Fr Marx returned to Ireland in November 1973 a visit that may have been timed to coincide with Seanad debates on a private members bill on contraception. The Supreme Court judgment in the McGee case was also imminent. On this occasion, he travelled with three jars containing aborted foetuses, which he displayed to the media at Dublin airport, and at lectures in Maynooth College, UCD and elsewhere. This trip extended to twenty meetings that were arranged by the Irish Family League. He claimed that Ireland was 'the most odd and difficult' of all the countries that he had visited. 'There is an ostrich attitude here and a hypocrisy which is inconsistent to the situation ... blinding

---

[23] 'A cry from the womb', *Catholic Standard*, 19 January 1973; 'Baby in bottle shocks Cork girls, *Irish Independent*, 17 January 1973; "Education on abortion urged", Irish shocked anti-abortion campaigner', *II* 18 January 1973; *Irish Press*, 18 January, 'Cork churchmen in contraception clash'; T. P. O'Mahony, 'Scare tactics and abortion'.

[24] *Irish Press*, 18 January 1973, 'Cork churchmen in contraception clash'.

people's ability here to recognise the truth'.[25] Official figures show that in 1970, 261 women with Irish addresses had abortions in England; the numbers rose steadily in the following years. By 1980, 3,320 abortions were performed on women who gave Irish addresses; in 1990, the figure was 4,064 and these numbers underestimated the numbers travelling to Britain because some women gave British addresses. In 1980, Dr Andrew Rynne concluded that it was 'probable that if we allow for underreporting of addresses that abortion and single birth rates are equal'.[26]

Janet Martin, women's editor of the *Irish Independent*, attended one of Fr Marx's rallies. She paid a modest entrance fee of 40p, as did approximately 300 others. Fr Marx claimed that Irish newspapers had suppressed letters written by schoolgirls who had attended his talk in Cork. He deliberately blurred the line between contraception and abortion: "'you've the abortion … I mean family planning clinics right here in your city. I won't go into the details.'" – a blurring that was highly political, given that the Seanad was about to debate a bill on contraception. He claimed that those who had campaigned for legal abortion in the United States were now campaigning to legalise euthanasia, and he asserted that women who underwent abortions would have complications in later pregnancies. [This was true of backstreet abortions; there is no evidence of this when abortions were carried out by medical professionals.] He urged the audience to join the Irish Family League and to place anti-abortion posters in supermarkets. The meeting concluded with a film about abortion that ended with images of Hitler's death camps.[27] Mary Kennedy, secretary of the Irish Family League wrote letters to the newspapers, thanking all who had applied to join the IFL as a result of Fr Marx's visit, promising to contact them shortly.[28] Fr Marx's emotional campaign was undoubtedly instrumental in launching an anti-abortion movement that attracted support from a large cross-section of Irish society. He returned to Ireland on many occasions, targeting nurses and secondary schoolgirls, sometimes school boys. [On one occasion when I was scheduled to give lectures to approximately 800 secondary school students, as part of a Leaving Cert revision programme, one teacher from a Dublin convent school lamented that many of her pupils had decided to go to listen to 'that priest with foetuses in jars', though I recall that the lecture theatres were full.]

An Irish branch of SPUC was allegedly founded in 1973 by Mr and Mrs Desmond Broadberry, parents of eighteen children. Mr Broadberry first came to public notice as a defender of Article 44 in the Irish Constitution (repealed 1972)[29]; he made several appearances on the *Late Late Show*. It appears that

---

[25] *Irish Press*, 7 November 1973, 14 November 1973, p. 23.   [26] Rynne, *Abortion*, pp. 22–3.
[27] Janet Martin, An evening with Fr Marx, *II*, 19 November 1973.   [28] *II*, 29 November 1973.
[29] *Women's Choice*, 10 January 1974 – Linda Kavanagh.

the Irish Hierarchy had determined that linking contraception with abortion offered the best means of opposing any relaxation of the laws on contraception. Opposition to contraception did not carry the same emotional resonances. In 1974, Cahal Daly, bishop of Ardagh and Clonmacnoise, and one of Ireland's leading theologians, wrote a long piece titled: 'The lobby for contraception. What we can learn from England'. He drew extensively on *Abortion Law Reformed*, by Madeleine Simms and Keith Hindell, which examined the British campaign. 'Reflecting on the methods and tactics used in the Irish campaign I have been amazed to note the similarity between them and those of the abortion campaign in Britain'. Campaigners made abortion the subject of public debate by 'bombarding the newspapers and specialist journals with articles and letters. They worked on women's organisations, encouraging reaffirmation for the reform; they initiated a series of opinion survey which established that both the public and the doctors supported reform, and they lobbied MPs and supplied lists of speakers for television and radio progammes'. He claimed that 'few would deny that the above description could fit the Irish campaign for contraception or contraceptive law reform'.[30] This description also fitted – even better – the campaign in the early 1980s for a pro-life amendment.

The Irish Hierarchy upped their campaign against abortion in 1975. In his New Year's Day sermon archbishop of Dublin, Dermot Ryan claimed that abortion was responsible for the loss in one year, 'of more young Irish lives than perished in five sad years of the Northern conflict'.[31] The *Catholic Standard* devoted much greater coverage to abortion than to contraception. In February, it reported that a private members' bill at Westminster might bring an end to Irish women having abortions in Britain, and it carried an editorial and articles about abortions in other countries – including allegations that aborted foetuses were turned into soap. Peggy Norris addressed the Irish Hierarchy's emigrant conference urging them to assist women, who saw abortion in England as the solution to an unplanned pregnancy. She asked them to adopt a non-judgemental approach: 'clergy can help considerably; and have a duty to change the attitude of your community. You must remind the Christian community that not only have we to accept the frailty of human beings, but we must be prepared to help people who get into difficulties'. The laity also had a responsibility to change attitudes.[32] Bishop of Galway Eamonn Casey outlined plans to establish an organisation to provide counselling and other supports that would assist single mothers to keep their babies.[33]

The publication of a pastoral letter, *Human Life is Sacred*, in May 1975 was part of this process. The first thirty-four paragraphs – almost half of

---

[30] *Catholic Standard*, 15 March 1974.   [31] *Catholic Standard*, 3 January 1975.
[32] Galway Diocesan Archives, Browne Papers B11/250.
[33] *Catholic Standard*, 11 April 1975.

the document – were concerned with abortion. The opening sentence read: 'Human life is sacred even before it is born'. Paragraph 2 referred to 'respect for the unborn life'. Paragraph 4 informed the reader that the commandment, 'thou shalt not kill', 'unconditionally forbids the taking of innocent life from its beginnings in the womb', and it referred to 'the first moment of conception'. Paragraph 6 noted that 'abortion [was] now discussed in many countries almost as if it raised no problem at all'. A sub-section, titled 'Abortion is killing the innocent', went into considerable detail about the procedure. This was followed by sections on 'Rights of the Unborn', 'Consequences of Abortion', 'Legalization increases demand' – a reference to the position in the UK, 'Yes to Life' and 'The quality of life'.[34] The remainder of the pastoral discussed issues such as euthanasia, care of the elderly and paramilitary violence – which was arguably of more immediate concern than abortion in 1970s Ireland. The sections on abortion read as if they were written for a British Catholic congregation. The *Catholic Standard* claimed that Cahal Daly was assisted in writing this pastoral by Peggy Norris.[35]

There was a significant gap between rhetoric and action. Journalist John Feeney noted that two years after Bishop Casey indicated that a support service for unmarried mothers who might be contemplating abortion was a priority for the Hierarchy it had not yet been established. A report by Fr Andrew Kennedy of the CMAC had recommended setting up a national anonymous advice service, but the bishops rejected that proposal in favour of a regional network of telephone helplines, commonly manned by priests. Feeney noted that callers had no guarantee of anonymity or professional advice. Fr Kennedy wished to publicise the service in shopping centres and other public places, but the bishops preferred a more low-key approach. By March 1977, CURA had been launched, initially operating only within the Archdiocese of Armagh. Feeney claimed that a group of professional social workers and counsellors, 'despairing of the bishops', were preparing to launch another twenty-four-hour helpline, which was also open to women who had undergone abortion and suffered psychological consequences. This service would be led by psychiatrist Dr Dermot Walsh.[36]

Irish family planning clinics were careful to distinguish between contraception and abortion because they were conscious that they were operating in a legal vacuum and might be subject to legal challenges. They received requests for information and referrals for abortions in Britain. One doctor has described scribbling a UK phone number on a scrap of paper (often torn from a newspaper), without further details; placing it on the table and leaving the room;

---

[34] *Human Life is Sacred.* Pastoral letter of the Archbishops and Bishops of Ireland to the clergy, religious and faithful (Veritas Publications, Dublin, May 1975), pp. 5–19.
[35] *Catholic Standard,* 16 July 1976.   [36] *Hibernia,* 18 March 1977.

he would not hand it directly to a woman. In 1973, the *Catholic Standard*, citing social workers, claimed that 'at least ten doctors in Dublin, will, as a normal practice refer patients to medical contacts in Britain abortion operations.... a package abortion-tour racket is operating with the connivance of a doctor, who brings girls on weekend abortion trips to the North of England'.[37] The only group known publicly to provide abortion referrals at this time was the Students Union of Trinity College, and, in a more low-key manner, the UCD Students' Union.

In 1975, the IFPA held an extraordinary general meeting to determine whether they should have a policy on abortion. They concluded that the number of women with Irish addresses reported as having abortions was probably a serious underestimate. Many women were undergoing abortions without prior counselling, or post-abortion support, so the IFPA decided that it should offer counselling to women who were considering abortion, who would all be seen by a doctor. They organised a one-day seminar for staff on counselling women in pregnancy.[38] The annual report for 1978 recorded that the medical committee was concerned at reports from doctors working in the clinic that a growing number of women were attending for pregnancy tests [it was not possible to buy a self-testing pregnancy kit] and then seeking abortions. Many were not practicing any form of contraception. The committee agreed that 'these patients, who were often very distressed, should be thoroughly counselled by the doctor undertaking the particular clinic session'. This counselling would involve providing information on organisations that helped women 'who find themselves in the unfortunate situation. In the event of the patient persisting in her intention to have the pregnancy terminated there was little that the doctor could do in preventing her from travelling to England regardless of how she was counselled'.[39] It is unclear, probably deliberately so, whether the IFPA was providing referrals; if not, there were other outlets. Magazines, such as *Women's Choice*, received many requests for information phone numbers and addresses but they were careful not to supply such information, at least in public, referring correspondents to charities that assisted women in crisis pregnancies such as Ally and the Catholic Protection and Rescue Society of Ireland. In 1975, *Women's Choice* published an article describing abortion and the associated risks.[40]

The Well Woman Clinic, which opened in 1978, offered an abortion referral service that became widely known. In 1980, *Hibernia* suggested that the regulations announced for the introduction of family planning services under the 1979 Act implied that clinics would be able to continue their activities,

---

[37] *Catholic Standard*, 4 May 1973.   [38] IFPA annual report 1975.
[39] IFPA annual report 1978.
[40] For example, *Women's Choice*, 8 November 1973; 20 March 1975.

provided that they were not involved in abortion referrals. The article claimed that 'it was clear to those in the know' that the other clinics [other than Well Woman] were also referring women for abortion; they concluded that 'There appears to be as much hypocrisy inside family planning clinics as outside'.[41] Well Woman had service agreements with two abortion clinics in London and one in Birmingham, which ensured that their referrals got priority for Saturday appointments. These clinics assigned specific members of staff to care for Irish women. One-tenth of these abortions were carried out free of charge. By the early 1980s, Well Woman was booking up to half of all seats on some Friday-afternoon flights to London. Many women called to the Eccles Street clinic having travelled by bus or train from provincial Ireland, before going to the airport.[42] By 1982, Well Woman was receiving fifty queries a week from women inquiring about abortions, or advice on crisis pregnancies.[43] Dr Áine Sullivan, who worked in the clinic at this time, said that while a majority were single women, there were also a number of married women, who had not informed their husbands about their pregnancy. She was emphatic that the counselling was non-directive; a significant number of women continued with their pregnancy.[44] According to Mary Randles, founder of a family planning clinic in Navan, women borrowed money from the Credit Union to finance their trip to England for an abortion.[45]

The Women's Right to Choose Group – the first Irish feminist organisation calling for abortion on demand – was founded in 1980. Their goal was to secure legal abortion in Ireland; open and accessible to all; free, safe and legal contraception and an end to discrimination against unmarried women and their children in Irish society. They established the Irish Pregnancy Counselling Centre, to provide non-directive counselling for women with crisis pregnancies, and post-abortive counselling. The centre had two trained counsellors and contractual agreements with two private abortion clinics in Birmingham and London. By 1982, 'without any advertising' they were counselling up to 2,000 new clients each year.[46] *Irish Times* journalist David Nowlan noted that other clinics referred women for abortion, but uniquely, the Irish Pregnancy Counselling Centre had no doctor on its staff.[47]

Statistics based on the first 1,000 women referred for abortion by the Irish Pregnancy Counselling Centre showed that 33 per cent were aged 18–21; 26.5 per cent aged 22–25; 13.5 per cent aged 26–29, 10 per cent aged 30–33 per cent; 15 per cent were aged 35 and over and 2 per cent were under 18 years. Almost one-third were in clerical/secretarial jobs; 16 per cent were homemakers, 12 per cent were in professional employment, 11 per cent were students,

---

[41] *Hibernia*, 7 August 1980.   [42] Interview Anne Connolly, 22 August 2013.
[43] *Irish Times*, 8 May 1982.   [44] Interview Monkstown, 19 August 2013.
[45] *II*, 13 May 2021.   [46] *Hibernia*, 11 September 1980; Andrew Rynne, *Abortion*, pp. 38–9.
[47] *IT*, 10 September 1980.

10 per cent were teachers and 10 per cent were unemployed. Just under three-quarters of the women were single, 19 per cent were married, 7 per cent were separated (divorce was illegal and unobtainable) and 2 per cent were widowed; over one-third had never used contraception. Among those using contraception, 28 per cent had used the safe period, a further 8 per cent had used Billings; 28 per cent had used condoms. Almost two-thirds came from Dublin.[48] The profile suggests that women seeking abortions were representative of Irish women of child-bearing years, though a disproportionate number were single.

Irish Times journalist Mary Maher attended a seminar organised by this centre to illustrate its counselling methods. The chief counsellor, who had previously carried out pregnancy counselling in Birmingham, noted the differences between Irish and British women: lack of knowledge about contraception; ignorance of methods other than the pill; the belief that 'nice girls' did not practice contraception unless they were in a steady relationship, guilt, and deep remorse. In her experience, the worst cases were woman who had previously given up babies for adoption. She claimed that there was much less guilt in England; women were much more straightforward about their reasons for seeking abortion.[49] This seminar was followed by a meeting organised by *Status* a new women's magazine, in Liberty Hall which attracted an estimated 1,000 women. They voted by a margin of 283 to 147 in favour of a woman's right to choose; other topics discussed included deserted women and unmarried mothers.[50] Journalist Mary Holland suggested that Irish women should follow the example of French feminists campaigning for abortion by making it known if they had an abortion, but this did not happen. The meeting was chaired by Mary McAleese, a future President of Ireland, who pleaded for 'dialogue and debate rather than confrontation' – to little effect. Speakers included British journalist Jill Tweedie, Dr Mary Lucey of SPUC and Goretti Horgan of Women's Right to Choose Group.[51]

6.1   Protecting the Unborn through a Constitutional Amendment

In 1974, Maurice Dooley, a theologian at St. Patrick's College Thurles, published a paper, 'Contraception and the Irish Constitution', which examined the Irish Supreme Court judgment in the McGee case. He noted the similarities with *Roe* v. *Wade* and concluded that 'We have thus travelled part of the legal road with the American Supreme Court, and a long part of the way to the breakdown in public morality and respect for foetal life'. He alleged

---

[48] *Abortion: A choice for Irish women* (UCD archives, copy in Gemma Hussey, papers. P179/132.
[49] *IT*, 20 February 1981.   [50] *Catholic Standard*, 27 February 1981.
[51] *Catholic Standard*, 20 March 1981.

that Ireland's defence against abortion was dependent on the members of the Supreme Court, 'There seems to be something wrong with a situation where one's rights may be made dependent on the background training of men over whom the citizenry have no control of appointment or dismissal'. He noted that the only Catholic on the US Supreme Court with the 'good Irish name of Brennan' had voted for abortion; 'other traditional Catholic countries have abortion proposals in hand'. In February 1974, less than two months after the McGee judgment, Michael O'Higgins, the Fine Gael leader in the Seanad, tabled an amendment to a Robinson Bill, in a personal capacity, acknowledging 'the ultimate right of the people to decide all questions of national policy according to the requirements of the common good.... it was desirable that the people be consulted as to the enactment or otherwise of legislation which would, or might reasonably be expected to, affect seriously and adversely the quality of life in the State.'[52] A paper published by the Catholic organisation Opus Dei argued that 'if the Government had appointed a different bench... or if they had been educated in different schools, or ....of a different religious persuasion or had sprung from a different class, or happened to be taught a different set of philosophical principles, one might get a different verdict'.[53]

James O'Reilly, an expert on family law, countered that 'there is a radical difference between abortion and contraception in Ireland and suggesting otherwise misrepresents totally what the Supreme Court has achieved'. The Irish Constitution limited the powers of judicial review exercised by the courts.[54] He highlighted differences between the American and the Irish Constitutions – specifically article 41, where the State guarantees to protect the family (marital family) and he drew attention to statements by Mr Justices Walsh and Griffin in the McGee case. Griffin noted that with respect to abortifacients 'entirely different considerations may arise'. O'Reilly concluded that 'In Ireland whatever privacy may mean, it does not mean abortion'.[55] Walsh stated that

To limit family size by endangering or destroying human life must necessarily not only be an offence against the common good but also against the guaranteed personal rights of the human life in question.

Mr Justice Walsh reiterated that position in a 1979 case relating to adoption, where he stated that 'The right to life necessarily implies the right to be born... it lies not in the power of the parent who has the primary natural rights and duties in respect of the child to exercise them in such a way as intentionally or by neglect to endanger the health or life of the child, or to terminate its

---

[52] *SD*, 21 February 1974, col 240.
[53] *Prevailing Winds*, Opus Dei Position Paper. Applications of Church Teaching, Opus Dei Society, Dublin, 1978, NLI.
[54] James O'Reilly, 'Marital privacy and family law', *Studies*, 66, spring 1977, p. 16.
[55] O'Reilly, 'Marital privacy and family law', p. 18.

existence'.[56] William Binchy, another distinguished lawyer, took issue with O'Reilly's interpretation. He argued that the Supreme Court judgment on contraception was probably in advance of public opinion. At a time when opinion on divorce was changing rapidly, the McGee decision 'constitutes live ammunition in the hands of a Court which might again be ahead of public opinion'.[57]

6.2   Abortion and the 1979 Family Planning Act

There is evidence of an increasingly strident campaign against abortion from 1978, which may have been prompted by the impending legislation on contraception. A woman who wrote to the Taoiseach described the Well Woman clinic as an 'abortion warren'; she complained that pirate radio stations – unlicensed, illegal, but with large audiences among young people carried their advertisements and suggested that he should 'tune into Radio Luxembourg (which was off-shore but not a pirate radio station) from 9 pm onwards and you will see what I mean'. This file contains a flyer for a March for Life in Tralee on 16 July 1978, organised by the Christian Life Movement; the march was 'anti-abortion; anti-sterilization, anti-divorce, and anti-contraception'.[58] Anne Connolly, founding director of Well Woman, suggested that the launch of the Women's Right to Choose Group was a factor in the timing of the PLAC.[59]

The government went to considerable efforts to distinguish between contraception and abortion in their Family Planning Bill. A summary of the Minister for Health's consultations noted that views were expressed by a number of bodies including the representatives of the Catholic Hierarchy, that legislation permitting the sale of artificial contraceptives had led in some countries within a short period to legislation permitting abortion, but 'it was indicated, in specific terms, to those who raised this point, that it was the intention to include in the legislation a specific provision indicating that nothing in the legislation was to be construed as permitting abortion'.[60]

The government's efforts to distinguish between their modest relaxation of the laws on contraception and abortion failed to persuade opponents. The national president of the rural organisation Muintir na Tíre, described the Family Planning Bill, as 'abortion in disguise'; others used similar language.[61] The Rape Crisis Centre which opened in 1979 and received a modest grant from the Eastern Health Board was labelled an abortion clinic.[62] The Family

---

[56] As quoted in Mary Maher, 'Five reasons against a referendum' in Mavis Arnold and Peadar Kirby (eds), *'The Abortion Referendum'. The case against* (Dublin, 1982).

[57] William Binchy, 'Marital privacy and family law; a reply to Mr. O'Reilly', *Studies*, 66, winter 1977, pp. 330–5.

[58] NAI DT 2008/148/220.   [59] Interview, 22 August 2015.

[60] NAI DT 2009/16/123 Health Family Planning Bill – memo to government.

[61] *IP*, 11 May 1979.   [62] NAI DT 2010/53/236.

Life Centre at Knock Shrine – which was active in promoting the Billings method, issued a brochure – 'Weep Not for Me. An abortion clinic in your area'; they claimed that it highlighted 'a very real situation in Ireland at the present'.[63] COSC, the Council of Social Concern [in Irish COSC means prevent], a consortium of the Irish Family League; STOP; the Christian political action movement Pro-Fide; Concerned Doctors group; Youth Alert and Veritas Christi, with an address at the headquarters of the Knights of Columbanus, was founded to co-ordinate the anti-abortion campaign. In 1979, Michael Yeats, Fianna Fáil MEP, was forced to refute claims by the Archbishop of Dublin, Dermot Ryan, that the European Parliament would legislate to make abortion available in Ireland.[64] A 1981 report by the European Parliament had recommended that measures should be taken so that women would not have to travel to secure an abortion but could 'obtain the necessary assistance in her own country', but this had no legal standing.[65]

The first resolutions by public bodies demanding a constitutional amendment outlawing abortion were introduced in 1979. In April, Ennis Urban District Council and Kilkee Town Commissioners forwarded copies of an identical resolution to the Taoiseach, calling on the government to arrange for an amendment to Article 40 of the Constitution: The state shall recognise the citizen as a human person from the moment or his or her conception. Similar resolutions followed from Templemore and Athlone UDCs, and this resolution was adopted at the annual conference of municipal authorities.

The debate became more heated in 1980. A programme on abortion, produced by RTÉ Frontline was denounced by COSC as showing 'naked bias'. When the government contacted RTÉ on foot of COSC's complaint, Louis Mc Redmond Head of Information claimed that the programme had highlighted 'a very serious problem'. He argued that the broadcasting service should enable public opinion to discuss contemporary social problems. 'RTÉ does not advocate abortion or promote any opinion of its own. It does however attempt to put forward a balanced and impartial view of matters which are of grave national importance....But public opinion itself cannot be informed unless such discussion takes place'.[66] The documentary team accompanied one woman who was travelling to Liverpool for a termination. The Irish Press suggested that it 'made no judgment but allowed those for and against to have their say', describing it as 'low-keyed in presentation....a major step in bringing facts to the viewer – although that can be manipulated depending on the speaker'.[67] COSC called for a reformed complaints commission for RTÉ, and

---

[63] NAI DT 2010/53/201.   [64] IP, 30 March 1979.

[65] Report on the position of women in the European community, June 1981, quoted in Chrystel Hug, The politics of sexual morality in Ireland (Macmillan, Basingstoke, 1999), p. 144.

[66] NAI DT 2010/53/201.   [67] IP, 16 January 1980.

a constitutional amendment 'protecting human life from the moment of conception or fertilisation'. It also recommended that 'if needs be' abortions carried out outside Ireland should be criminalised to prevent abortion referrals and advertising these services. Although RTÉ stood firm on this occasion, the opposition may have influenced their later coverage of the PLAC.

The Irish Doctors' Guild, founded in 1970, following the collapse of the Guild of St. Luke, SS Cosmas and Damien was another key player. Pat Brennan in *Magill* cited a chat between Galway gynaecologist Eamonn O'Dwyer and a fellow member of the Guild in the summer of 1980, when they discussed whether abortion might be introduced into Ireland. Professor O'Dwyer was the Irish representative on the Council of the Royal College of Obstetricians and Gynaecologists in 1967 when the British Abortion Act was introduced. He claimed that British doctors 'ran away from their responsibility when they chose to leave the decision to Parliament'. In September 1980, Trinity College Dublin hosted an international conference organised by Professor John Bonnar under the auspices of Doctors who Respect Human Life. The non-denominational group, based in the Netherlands, had a large Catholic membership and was committed 'to defending the sanctity of the human person from conception to death'. Brennan suggested that

At this conference Dr Julia Vaughan made her public debut as an anti-abortionist and the pro-life campaign began to develop. It was at this time that the medical core of the Catholic Doctors' Guild joined forces with 'moral issues' groups. The presence of campaigning anti-abortionists from Britain and America added to their sense of urgency.

She claimed that Irish doctors who attended this conference 'were led to believe that there was strong pressure from agencies such as IPPF to influence abortion laws in countries such as Ireland. This allegation of an IPPF pro-abortion international conspiracy is one of the cornerstones of the campaign for a constitutional referendum'.

During this conference, the anti-abortion movement held a separate meeting in Carysfort College (a college of education run by the Sisters of Mercy). This conference, organised by Dr Peggy Norris and Dr Margaret White, was attended by members of The Responsible Society, SPUC; CURA and several doctors who were attending the conference in Trinity College. The speakers included Fr Paul Marx, who attended the conference in Trinity and spoke at an event organised by the Family Life Centre at Knock.[68] When Alan Browne (a former Master of the Rotunda) wrote about the origins of the PLAC in the *Church of Ireland Gazette* in 1983, he mentioned the 1980 Trinity conference. He was invited to co-chair the session on abortion, with Dr Tom Murphy, President of UCD. 'Predictably this was a fairly tough session at which a

[68] *Magill,* July 1982.

number of speakers from the UK and America contributed, often with some vehemence'. He claimed that during the course of the congress, private meetings of Roman Catholic participants took place, 'which can probably be pinpointed as being the origin of the Pro-Life Amendment Campaign'[69] – this may refer to the Carysfort meeting.

In 1980, two UK groups, SPUC and the Responsible Society, formed Irish branches. Brennan described the Responsible Society as a 'British based group known to members of the Catholic Doctors Guild long before the Irish branch was established'. They had co-operated with the Irish Knights of Columbanus on a meeting to discuss 'The Permissive Society'.[70] SPUC had been holding meetings in Ireland since 1973. In the summer of 1980, John Smeaton, secretary general of SPUC and director Phyllis Bowman, toured Ireland. Their main target was Irish women travelling to Britain for abortion. Smeaton claimed that the Hierarchy 'should be much more forthright in their condemnation of abortion'… 'If they came out with the same courage as they showed when Catholic teaching training colleges [in Britain] were threatened with closure they might have had the muscle to overthrow the British Abortion Act of 1967'. SPUC urged the Minister for Health to halt the 'abortion trail' to Britain. By July, they claimed to have five branches in Dublin, and branches in Bray and Greystones. Smeaton addressed a meeting at Dublin's Mater Hospital. Mrs Bowman claimed that there was a witch hunt underway in Britain against foetuses with Down syndrome or spina bifida.[71] In September, the *Catholic Standard* carried an advertisement for public meetings organised by SPUC – 'The case against abortion'; five in Dublin and others in Limerick, Cahir (Tipperary), Cork and the greater Dublin area.[72] The primary purpose behind the advertisement was obviously to publicise the movement, because several meeting had already taken place. Loretto Browne, who became the Irish face of SPUC, claimed that they had twenty Irish branches. She urged all members to write to their TDs demanding an end to the 'abortion racketeers'.[73] Most SPUC meetings took place in Catholic parish halls.

The Irish campaign was linked with developments in Britain, where the Corrie Bill – a private members' bill designed to roll back the 1967 Act – appeared to have some prospects of success. There was a heated debate on abortion at the annual conference of Irish medical students in January 1980, where most of the focus was on doctors who referred women for abortions. An editorial in the *Catholic Standard* in March made a direct appeal to the medical profession on that topic: 'now is the time for doctors and social workers to bestir their conscience'.[74] Journalists attached to fifteen provincial papers

---

[69] *Church of Ireland Gazette*, 30 September 1983.   [70] *Magill*, July 1982.
[71] *Catholic Standard*, 18 July 1980.   [72] *Catholic Standard*, 5 September 1980.
[73] *Catholic Standard*, 19 September 1980.   [74] *Catholic Standard*, 15 March 1980.

issued a statement against abortion which would appear to have been in reaction to a resolution passed by the National Union of Journalists. In June, the *Catholic Standard*, carried a story headed, 'Pro-life man defies union and risks job'; a journalist in Wexford had resigned from the NUJ in protest against their support for the 1967 Abortion Act, and was in danger of losing his job because of the requirement that all journalists be NUJ members.[75] The INO held a seminar on abortion in September 1980, where midwives were warned that although Ireland was unlikely to move to wholesale acceptance of abortion, they should expect strong pressure for the introduction of scanning during pregnancy with a view to aborting severely handicapped infants. Theologian Denis O'Callaghan told the audience that 'morally speaking there was very little difference between abortion and infanticide'. Irish Catholics should learn from what had happened in Britain.[76] Bernadette Bonar (a pharmacist and active member of the IPU), chairwoman of the Responsible Society's Irish Branch, described a recent seminar held by the Council for the Status of Women as a 'field day for radical feminists and the ultra-left'. She criticised the fact that the organisers had permitted a group campaigning for abortion to have a stand, whereas a similar request by SPUC was refused.[77]

On 28 December 1980, the Feast of the Holy Innocents, SPUC organised an anti-abortion march through Dublin, which attracted a crowd of 5,000. The march was addressed by the Lord Mayor of Dublin, Fine Gael TD, Fergus O'Brien. The *Catholic Standard* claimed that virtually all 181 parishes in the Dublin archdiocese had been contacted about the march, as had clergy of other denominations, schools and caring organisations. The organisers placed a wreath outside Leinster House in memory of Irish babies aborted in Britain and demanded the closure of Dublin's abortion referral clinics.[78] The archbishop of Dublin Dermot Ryan spoke about the dangers to Irish society from pro-abortion pressure groups when he addressed the Dublin Rotary Club some weeks later; he referred specifically to the media and suggested that the growing acceptance of abortion would soon be followed by the killing of grandmothers.[79]

In the United States, 'the cultural roots' of the pro-life campaign have been described as 'complex and tangled'. The most significant factors were church attendance and opposition to euthanasia.[80] Many Irish campaigners viewed their activism as part of a wider campaign against sexual permissiveness, divorce and feminism. They drew on rhetoric about Ireland's history and

---

[75] *Catholic Standard*, 28 March 1980; 20 June 1980.
[76] *Catholic Standard*, 26 September 1980.   [77] *Catholic Standard*, 12 December 1980.
[78] *Catholic Standard*, 26 December 1980, 2 January 1981.
[79] *Catholic Standard*, 30 January 1981.
[80] Keith Cassidy, 'The right to life movement', in Critchlow,(ed.) *The politics of abortion and birth control*, p. 130.

identity – an amalgam of faith and fatherland that indicates confusion about the respective spheres of church and state. Changing sexual behaviour, including the use of contraception was often represented as a modern invasion of Ireland. In 1982, an editorial in *Magill* described the proposed pro-life referendum as having 'little to do with the actual issue of abortion but a great deal to do with re-asserting the Catholic nature of this state and reversing recent trends towards a pluralist society'.[81]

A letter sent to Liam Cosgrave asked; 'Do you want to split the Catholic Family. Where was she (Mary R) or Dr O'Brien when people were fighting for Freedom from 1916 to 1921? Such men as your Father and [Michael] Collins'; Mná na hÉireann asked 'WHY SHOULD WE NOT HAVE GOOD CATHOLIC JUDGES IN OUR OWN CATHOLIC COUNTRY?' An anonymous correspondent wrote 'I can't believe your Catholic government is going to give the go ahead to the sale of contraceptives and destroy the souls of the Irish Youths'. A correspondent from Cavan claimed that: 'it looks as if a native Irish government in its hour of freedom is about to undo officially the work of St Patrick although our ancestors suffered three hundred years to be true to him'. According to a Dublin correspondent, 'There is a dreadful battle going on now to drag down this little country and also everyone who wants us to remain a Christian one. All the great Irish men and women in the past fought so hard to remain loyal to God – even with their blood and in the famine years they still adhered to it and it would be so sad to see such a small minority ruining us'.[82]

An Opus Dei paper warned that 'It is quite on the cards that due to our pleasant easy-going "live and let live" attitude to life (which is our inheritance) we will, without realising it, destroy the very society which has given us these traits. We have a fine capacity to love the sinner and hate the sin, to live in harmony with people who disagree with us theologically, politically and even sociologically....But in recent years some of us – certainly a very vocal minority – have been spreading it abroad that the principles underlying Irish life are defective and oppressive of even God-given human rights....And our natural Irish reaction is to wonder: "Perhaps they are right"'.[83]

Addressing a crowd outside Leinster House in January 1981, Loretta Browne claimed that 'if Ireland passed a law permitting abortion its 700 year struggle for self-determination would have given way after 60 years of independence to self-destruction'.[84] Whitty suggested that the PLAC 'commenced because Ireland, like other western countries witnessed an increased prominence of conservative pressure groups in the late 1970s and 1980s. Reacting to

[81] *Magill*, July 1982.   [82] NAI DT 2012/90/880.
[83] Opus Dei position paper no. 59, Editorial 'Look before you leap', n.d., but appears to be late 1970s; NLI.
[84] *Catholic Standard*, 2 January 1981.

a growing demand for legislative action on issues such as illegitimacy, divorce, contraception, homosexuality, sex education, and property rights for women – policies that would directly repudiate the traditional role of Irish women and thereby alter Irish identity – they determined that abortion was the issue, that would best consolidate their political influence'. To support this argument, he quoted John O'Reilly, described as 'the leading instigator of the campaign for a referendum'.

Ireland's progress down the anti-life road has been relatively rapid. From a nation where there was practically no contraception and absolutely no divorce 15 years ago, we have now come to the point where we have freely available contraceptives even in our Third Level Colleges and we are aborting babies to the extent of at least five per cent of our birth-rate. Another six percent of our birth rate is born outside wedlock, nearly double what it was ten years ago. When we add the abortion rate and the illegitimacy rate, we find that we have 7, 514 unwanted conceptions in 1981 – increased from 1,557 in 1963.[85]

6.3   The PLAC

The campaign for a constitutional amendment was organised by the PLAC. Hesketh's extensive account of the campaign identified the seven key individuals, and the links between PLAC and COSC, NAOMI, SPUC, the Irish Responsible Society and the Irish Catholic Doctors' Guild (ICDG). The main organisers were John O'Reilly (PLAC, SPUC, COSC and the Responsible Society); pharmacist Bernadette Bonar (SPUC and the Responsible Society); Dr Arthur Barry, former Master of Holles St (PLAC, NAOMI and ICDG); Professor John Bonnar (PLAC, NAOMI and the Responsible Society); Professor Eamon de Valera Holles St consultant (PLAC, NAOMI and ICDG); Loretta Browne (PLAC, SPUC, the Responsible Society); and Dr Dominic O'Doherty (PLAC, ICDG and the Responsible Society).[86] The list does not include Dr Julia Vaughan, an assistant master (registrar) at Holles Street, who was appointed chair, Michael Shortall CYMS – Catholic Young Men's Society, the secretary, Denis Barror Responsible Society treasurer, and Cornelius O'Leary, the professor of politics at Queen's University Belfast the vice chair. The choice of Dr Vaughan was not accidental – she was one of very few women gynaecologists. John Bonnar expressed the view that 'it was a bad thing for men to be to the forefront of the emerging campaign 'especially as senior academic gynaecologists [who] looked like a stuffy old bunch'.[87]

[85] Whitty, 'Law and the regulation of reproduction in Ireland', p. 863.
[86] Hesketh, *The second partition of Ireland*, App 1, p. 384; Emily O'Reilly, *Masterminds of the right* (Attic Press, Dublin, 1988), pp. 39–62 gives additional information.
[87] *Magill*, July 1982.

The initial strategy was to collect up to a million signatures demanding a referendum. In 1979, journalist Brian Trench suggested that the anti-contraception groups that wrote letters to the newspapers and politicians 'have been losing credibility among public representatives.... Much of the gorier literature circulated to Oireachtas members goes by a fairly short route to the waste-paper basket'. He claimed that these strident campaigns were giving way to a more targeted opposition organised by the Knights of Columbanus, who had close connections with public representatives.[88] PLAC abandoned the signature campaign in favour of securing the support of the main political parties for an amendment.[89] Collecting mass signatures had been central to SPUC's unsuccessful campaign against the British 1967 Act,[90] which may have been a factor, likewise the advice of Professor Cornelius O'Leary, who indicated that a general election was imminent, and candidates should be canvassed to secure their support for a constitutional amendment.[91]

The PLAC was formally launched at a press conference on 27 April 1981 where they unveiled their draft amendment; 'The State recognises the absolute right to life of every unborn child from conception and accordingly guarantees to respect and protect such right by law'. Julia Vaughan expressed the hopes that a successful referendum could have implications for the pro-life movement 'far beyond Ireland....If Ireland manages, against all earlier expectations to stem the abortionist tide, it may yet prove an example to the rest of Western Europe. It we do, it won't be the first time in history that the Irish have been responsible for preserving – and then re-propagating Christian values'.[92] PLAC requested meetings with the Taoiseach Charles Haughey and the Fine Gael leader, Garret FitzGerald. Mr Haughey referred this request to the Cabinet, and they agreed that 'the general line should be that if as a result of a court decision it was necessary to promote legislative changes then these changes would be undertaken'. The Minister for Health and Social Welfare, Michael Woods, would outline the Government's position on television.[93]

PLAC leaders held separate meetings with the Taoiseach and the leader of Fine Gael three days later. Government files contain a formal record of the meeting with the Taoiseach. PLAC alleged that a campaign was underway to legalise abortion through a legal challenge to the constitutionality of the 1861

---

[88] *Magill*, Jan 1979.
[89] Hesketh, *The second partition of Ireland*, pp. 9–13.
[90] Hindell and Simms, *Abortion law reformed*, p. 97.
[91] Hesketh, *The second partition of Ireland*, p. 10.   [92] *Catholic Standard*, 1 May 1981.
[93] NAI DT 2011/127/817 Pro-Life Amendment Campaign mainstream action.

Act. (No evidence of this has come to light.) Mr Haughey was cautious: he indicated that he was not against an amendment, in principle, but he described it as 'delicate issue', and suggested that the law reform commission might be asked to advise on the matter. Professor de Valera, a member of the delegation, suggested that the matter was urgent, while a referendum 'would be emphatically endorsed' at the present time, they could not rely on such support in coming years, 'especially in face of the abortionists' campaign'. Mr Haughey questioned whether there was widespread support for abortion among young people 'outside of the university campus'. He promised to ensure that the law reform commission would respond within months.[94]

Mr Haughey also received a letter claiming to represent the views of thirty-four lawyers, twelve of them senior counsels. They were unanimous that the constitutions in Ireland and the USA included similar provisions on the right to life; neither contained a specific declaration as to the rights of the unborn, which meant that the US courts could concede the right to abortion. While 'nobody doubted the unequivocal statements that the present Government was totally opposed to abortion', that could not prevent the courts from finding that sections of the 1861 Act were unconstitutional 'in a specially selected "hard" case'. They acknowledged that the government would not introduce legislation decriminalising abortion, but if the courts were to declare sections of the 1861 Act unconstitutional the only way to retrieve the situation would be through a referendum.[95]

Mr Haughey also received a personal note from Professor Eamonn O'Dwyer, a member of PLAC, informing him 'that the weight of legal advice to the Pro-Life Group will be that the law as it now stands may not be adequate.... And from the medical point of view, I could see the 1861 Act being challenged as unconstitutional and perhaps being overturned'. He added 'for your own private ear. The feed-back today is that Garret FitzGerald is reported (for what it is worth) to have indicated his interest in and sympathy for such an amendment which he would be prepared to sponsor. This of course may be only so much talk, but I have told you. I am concerned about abortion in the long run'.[96]

Professor O'Dwyer was correct that FitzGerald had committed Fine Gael's support for a pro-life amendment. His report that FitzGerald was willing to sponsor a private-members' bill, if the expected general election did not take place, is consistent with a later statement by Loretta Browne.[97] In his memoirs, FitzGerald claimed that his decision was 'influenced in part by my personal antipathy to abortion and conscious of the opposition of the vast majority of people in Ireland, North and South, Catholic and Protestant, to abortion – one

---

[94] NAI DT 2012/90/671; 30/4/81.   [95] NAI DT 2011/127/817.
[96] NAI DT 2011/127/817.   [97] Hesketh, *The second partition of Ireland*, p. 16.

of the issues on which there was a united view'. He conceded that he had
'failed to appreciate...the extraordinary difficulty of drafting a constitutional
amendment that would have the desired effect ....and secondly, the need to
make continued provision for the termination of pregnancies in cases where
the life of a mother was at risk'.[98]

The interventions by the lawyers and Professor O'Dwyer persuaded
Mr Haughey to support a referendum. On 14 May, he gave a solemn assurance
on behalf of the government to introduce an appropriate constitutional amendment 'to give effect to their position... as soon as circumstances permit'. A
general election was called on 21 May. A special meeting of the EHB passed a
unanimous resolution supporting PLAC and other health boards followed their
example. On 28 May, a group of lawyers announced the formation of the Irish
Association for the Defence of the Unborn. They contacted Mr Haughey asking for his support and informed him that they had already secured the support
of Garret FitzGerald.[99]

The timing of the PLAC was highly advantageous, because the unstable
political arithmetic gave this lobby group considerable leverage. An election in
June 1981 returned a minority Fine Gael Labour government that was dependent on the votes of independent TDs. This government collapsed in January
1982 having failed to secure a majority for its budget. A general election in
February resulted in a minority Fianna Fáil government that was also dependent on independent TDs. That government collapsed in the autumn, and a
third general election resulted in a Fine Gael/Labour government with a stable
majority.

SPUC sent a questionnaire to all candidates standing in the 1981 general
election asking whether they supported the Pro-Life Amendment; whether,
if elected they would fight for a referendum, and for the closure of family
planning clinics and pregnancy advice clinics that referred 'girls' to Britain or
elsewhere for an abortion. A PLAC information sheet explained that they were
pursuing a vigorous campaign to inform and persuade the political parties; if
that met with 'less than total support' they would circulate a nationwide petition seeking a referendum.[100] Hesketh states that 137 of 404 candidates replied
to the SPUC questionnaire, including 60 who were elected – that is less than
half of incoming TDs; forty-seven answered 'yes' to all three questions – less
than 30 per cent of the membership of the twenty-second Dáil. They included
twenty-two Fianna Fáil, eighteen Fine Gael, seven Labour TDs and eight others. The leaders of Fianna Fáil and Fine Gael had given commitments to introduce an amendment without consulting their parties. Labour did not commit
to a referendum, though seven of the party's fifteen TDs (a higher proportion

---

[98] FitzGerald, *All in a life*, p. 416.   [99] NAI DT 2011/127/243.
[100] NAI DT 2011/127/243.

than the other parties) had indicated their support; several later changed their position.[101]

Although FitzGerald had committed Fine Gael to introducing a constitutional amendment, this commitment did not feature in the legislative programme of the Fine Gael/Labour government. A woman who was a member of SPUC wrote to him: 'I know that you have had pressing problems to deal with since your government came into power, but I want to point out that if this most basic of all Human Rights....is given the priority it should receive in a Christian Society then all our other problems most pressing though they seem can be tackled with hope of success'. Several women wrote to Joan FitzGerald, Garret's wife, who was known to exercise considerable influence. An Irishwoman, living in Birkenhead, who sent FitzGerald a picture of Padre Pio with a copy of a prayer, told him, 'Better the guns of Ian Paisley, God help him, than immorality and the loose living of the pagans who call themselves Christians....Ian Paisley, Margaret Thatcher and Garret FitzGerald are in my prayers; the first two know no better, but you, Mr FitzGerald should'.[102] In July 1981, Julia Vaughan wrote to FitzGerald, noting that the government had not committed to introducing a referendum, and 'in consequence some apprehensions have been voiced throughout our constituent and supporting organisations'. She requested 'a brief note with which we could reassure our members'. He reassured her that the government was 'unalterably opposed' to abortion; the Attorney General was examining the matter.[103] Hesketh claimed that there were divisions within the PLAC between the low-key approach favoured by the doctors, which concentrated on lobbying political leaders, and the more strident grass-roots activists, who preferred graphic images of aborted foetuses and letter-writing campaigns.

These divisions were evident in the summer of 1981. Dr Mary Lucey (SPUC) asked all members to lobby the government and their TDs 'requesting that the Pro-Life Amendment be brought in forthwith'. Signs of an expanding grass-roots movement are evident in the volume of correspondence and motions submitted to government in the autumn/winter of 1981, including a letter signed by over 100 members of the Castlecomer branch of SPUC; letters from Praesidia of the Legion of Mary and the Kerry Down Syndrome Association.

SPUC demanded the closure of the Well Woman Clinic. The government responded that the clinic had neither sought nor secured a licence under the 1979 Act; enforcing the law was a matter for gardaí. A draft response to a telegram from Mary Lucey noted that any constitutional amendment would only apply to abortions carried out within the state; abortion referrals were a

---

[101] Hesketh, *The second partition of Ireland*, pp. 113–5; 129–34.
[102] NAI DT 2012/90/879, 17 July 1981.   [103] NAI DT 2011/127/243.

separate matter. It was decided not to send this telegram, which would presumably have prompted demands for an even stronger amendment. In November the Taoiseach was informed (the memo was labelled confidential information) that in the opinion of the Director of Public Prosecution (DPP) referring pregnant women to foreign clinics, or giving them assistance or advice with a view to their seeking or obtaining abortions abroad would not under Irish law amount to an offence capable of being prosecuted in Irish courts.[104] A note from the DPP's office to the Garda Commissioner confirmed that position. 'There is no precedent for the assumption of jurisdiction by our courts in cases such as this, and the judicial authorities on this topic make it clear that any extension of the criminal law would be a matter for the legislature and not for the Courts'.[105]

SPUC sent FitzGerald a telegram, demanding a statement of government policy. Mayo TD and future Taoiseach Enda Kenny submitted several queries on behalf of constituents, including a number from Westport secondary schoolgirls, and letters with many signatures from west Mayo. The impact of the Family Life Centre at Knock is apparent in his repeated requests for guidance. Letters continued to arrive to government ministers, demanding action, and they were more direct than in earlier anti-contraception campaigns: fewer prayers, medals and holy pictures. This was a more focused campaign. Correspondents received a pro forma response stating that the government was 'unalterably opposed' to any legislation permitting abortion; the Attorney General was examining the matter.[106]

6.4   Legal Advice

Although the Haughey government had given a commitment to support a pro-life amendment, there is no evidence that they discussed the matter before the 1981 general election. In August 1981, Peter Sutherland, Attorney General in the Fine Gael/Labour government, submitted the first of many memoranda outlining the legal issues. He sent this to FitzGerald, apparently in a personal capacity, not to the government. Sutherland emphasised that there were rights implicit in the Constitution that were not specifically enumerated. He claimed that these implicit rights included the right to life. It was his opinion 'that the right to life has been clearly enunciated by the Courts and that in the circumstances, the constitutional amendment is unnecessary'. It would be 'positively undesirable to amend the Constitution in this regard'. If this amendment was introduced, he wondered what would be the position of other unspecified rights? He opined that an amendment declaring a fundamental right to life

---

[104] NAI DT 2011/127/244.   [105] NAI DT 2012/90/667, 25 November 1981.
[106] NAI DT 2011/127/243.

from the moment of conception 'is also of little avail without an implementing penal code....In summary it is the criminal law that matters and the criminal law has no place in the Constitution. Treason is the only offence described in the Constitution and that only in a restricted form'. He concluded by noting that 'the view which I have expressed may cause some embarrassment. I would be quite willing to so express it publicly as my advice should this be desirable'.[107]

To suggest that this memorandum might 'cause some embarrassment' was an under-statement. Officials struggled to draft a response to representations from PLAC supporters in light of the Sutherland opinion. One version reiterated that the government was unalterably opposed to abortion; 'complex constitutional and legal issues' were involved; the question of a specific amendment was being considered by the Attorney General 'in the context of the overall review' of the Constitution. They noted that this statement was 'somewhat of a step back from the absolute guarantee given previously' and suggested that the Attorney's considered opinion should be submitted to the government.

Seán Ó Riordáin, a principal officer, suggested that Sutherland's opinion was 'more of a personal letter' to the Taoiseach. He queried whether, if this opinion was accepted the Government can satisfy the pro-life people 'in view of the strong commitment given'. The only acceptable alternative that would make it possible for the Government not to hold the referendum '**but at the same time satisfy the pro-life people …. would be a decision by the Supreme Court'.** [my bold]. He suggested that the government could introduce a Bill and ask the President to refer it to the Supreme Court, such as – 'a case for dealing more harshly with abortion referrals of Irish girls to England'. There was no guarantee that the President would refer the bill, and in the context of a constitution for the whole of Ireland, such a bill would probably be seen as divisive. Another possibility was to initiate a Declaratory Action in the High Court that the 1861 Act was consistent with the constitution.[108]

Government initiatives on Northern Ireland had ground to a halt because of the IRA hunger strikes, which resulted in ten deaths. In August 1981, FitzGerald convened a two-day conference with a small number of ministers and civil servants, where a decision was taken to carry out a review of the 1937 Constitution to make it more acceptable to Ulster unionism. FitzGerald and Sutherland floated the idea through press interviews, and the Taoiseach gave an RTÉ radio interview on the topic. Initial soundings of the views of Northern Unionists, carried out by DFA's Michael Lillis suggested that their objections extended beyond articles 2 and 3.[109] It was envisaged that the review

---

[107] NAI DT 2011/127/817, 28 August 1981, Sutherland to Taoiseach.
[108] NAI DT 2011/127/817 S O'Riordan, 8 October 1981 to Richard Stokes and Secretary to the Government.
[109] FitzGerald, *All in a life*, pp. 375–81.

of the constitution would consider the ban on divorce. There appeared to be a contradiction between introducing a pro-life amendment and drafting a new constitution that would take the views of Ulster unionists into consideration. One Dublin man, who described himself as a 'life-long' member of Fine Gael expressed horror at FitzGerald's proposal 'to tinker with the Constitution' and warned, 'If you think by opening the door to divorce you will influence the Orangemen in the North you can think again'. SPUC suggested that article 41.3 (relating to marriage and divorce) should be amended– to bring civil and ecclesiastical law into conformity![110]

PLAC was concerned that a decision on a pro-life amendment would be subsumed into a wider review of the constitution. The more militant wing demanded that FitzGerald be given an ultimatum to set a date for the referendum.[111] In November, Julia Vaughan informed him that the implied delay was unacceptable to the PLAC Council, 'amounting in its view to a weakening of that governmental resolve which we had so heartily welcomed'. She asked to meet him, ahead of a special meeting of the Council, and she informed him that she was in regular communication with two Fine Gael backbenchers – Godfrey Timmons and Kieran Crotty.[112] The Taoiseach met a delegation on 10 December. PLAC was determined that an amendment should proceed independent of a wider constitutional review; they expressed concern that there might not be sufficient support for a revised constitution and consequently their amendment could fail. They again raised the spectre of an imminent constitutional challenge to the 1861 Act, and they expressed the opinion that a pro-life amendment would restrict the capacity of the European Court to force abortion on Ireland. The Taoiseach dismissed the prospect that the Supreme Court would permit abortion but promised action if that happened. He hoped that a review of the constitution would be concluded by February 1982, with a referendum in 1983. Dr Vaughan dismissed 1983 as 'too late' and threatened to issue a public statement expressing PLAC's dissatisfaction.[113]

Following this meeting, FitzGerald apparently tried to find some means of placating the pro-life lobby. A letter in his name was drafted to the Minister for Justice inquiring about possible legislation to curb abortion referrals by Irish clinics, asking for this to be dealt with 'expeditiously'. This letter was not sent, apparently on the advice of his private secretary Declan Kelly who had controversially been transferred from DFA.[114] However a reply to a Limerick priest who had written to Michael Noonan TD stated that the Department of Justice was examining abortion referrals. On 8 March 1982, the last day in office of the FitzGerald government, the office of the Minister for Justice indicated

---

[110] NAI 2012/90/879.   [111] Hesketh, *The second partition of Ireland*, pp. 24–6.
[112] NAI DT 2012/90/667, 23 November 1981.   [113] NAI DT 2012/90/667, 10 December 1981.
[114] FitzGerald, *All in a life*, pp. 365–6.

that legislation on abortion referrals could be enacted, 'that would have a fair degree of effectiveness', though it might be difficult to bring all 'code words' within the scope of the law.[115]

Hesketh suggests that PLAC was in disarray by December 1981, but their position was transformed when a general election was called for February 1982.[116] The Family Life Centre at Knock sent a cyclostyled sheet to outgoing TDs titled 'Promises to Keep' reminding them of their promise before the last general election that a Bill would be introduced providing for a referendum. TDs were asked to indicate their position on a referendum before 15 February; failure to reply would be regarded as a 'no'. SPUC sought similar assurances from TDs who were seeking re-election. FitzGerald gave an unequivocal commitment to take 'such steps as are necessary' to provide constitutional protection for the unborn child during the course of the next Dáil, though he failed to indicate the timing. PLAC demanded that it should be addressed during the next session. Mr Haughey gave a commitment to do so during 1982 'without reference to any other aspect of constitutional change'.[117] SPUC issued a press release five days before the General Election, 'while noting the commitment of both leaders to the amendment, the PLAC now urges the Taoiseach to agree to bring forward this important amendment as a separate issue from his general constitutional review.'[118]

On the coalition's last day in office, Peter Sutherland submitted an opinion on a proposed wording for the amendment. Given that a change of government was probable, it would appear that he wished to leave this on record for his successor. The wording considered was that

The state acknowledges the right to life of the unborn, and with due regard to the equal right to life of the mother, guarantees in its laws to respect, and, as far as practicable by its laws to defend and vindicate that right.

He described the wording as 'ambiguous and unsatisfactory... Far from providing the protection and certainty which is sought by many of those who have advocated its adoption, it will have a contrary effect'. It was unclear what life was being protected, and whether that protection applied from the moment of fertilisation. On the question of 'equal rights', he concluded that 'a doctor faced with the dilemma will be compelled by the wording to conclude that he can do nothing'. He concluded that the logical interpretation of the proposed amendment was that 'the right to life of the unborn is absolute'. He highlighted the differences in principle between ordinary legislation and a statement in the constitution. A statement in the constitution should stand the test of time. 'Uncertainty as to its meaning and effect could have the most serious

[115] NAI DT 2012/90/667.   [116] Hesketh, *The second partition of Ireland*, pp. 27–28.
[117] Hesketh, *The second partition of Ireland*, pp. 118–9.   [118] NAI DT 2012/90/667.

consequences'.[119] This prophetic statement anticipates the legal issues that arose in the aftermath of the 1983 Amendment.

When a minority Fianna Fáil government took office, the Department of the Taoiseach alerted the new Attorney General, Patrick Connolly to the fact that 'your predecessor had reservations' and gave him a copy of Sutherland's statement. On 23 March, Mr. Haughey announced the government's intention to introduce legislation to enable the holding of a referendum during 1982. He received congratulatory messages from pro-life organisations. Julia Vaughan described it as 'an act of political leadership of a high order, and [that] it will be recognised as such in Ireland and internationally'. She committed PLAC to ensuring 'a massive turn-out' for the referendum.[120]

The commitment was foolhardy, given the difficulties of drafting suitable wording. The anti-abortion movement in the United States had reacted to *Roe* v. *Wade* by organising a campaign to introduce a constitutional amendment affirming the right to life, but there was widespread disagreement over the wording and scope of an amendment. Cassidy notes that 'it is hardly surprising that in the decade following the Roe decision the movement was racked by end-less controversy over an amendment strategy'. In 1980, an Amendment stating that: 'A right to abortion is not secured by this Constitution' was defeated in the US Senate by fifty votes to forty-nine (with one abstention).[121]

In June 1982, the Attorney General sent a memo to the Taoiseach, which began by asking what precisely was being sought in the referendum. There were 'certain worrying ambiguities', in the PLAC attitude. He noted that Article 40 of the Constitution is a guarantee of the right to life of living per-sons. 'It is important that any amendment... should not be so framed as to reduce the guarantee of the right to life of the living or elevate the guarantee of the right to life of the unborn above the right to life of the living'.

A commentary by Richard Stokes of the Taoiseach's Department focussed on contraceptives that prevented implantation; abortion following rape, and cases of anencephalic deformity. He suggested that once the 'moment of fertil-ization' was not mentioned, it should be possible to perform a D and C [dila-tion and curettage] in the immediate aftermath of rape. On anencephaly, he could 'see no logic from a humanitarian point of view in seeking to have an exemption for a deformed fetus which will not survive and not for a deformed foetus which will live. Quite the reverse in fact because the need for an abor-tion is less warranted for anencephaly where nature's course will quickly end a harrowing situation'.

When Mr. Haughey approved the circulation of draft memos for Government to the Departments of Justice, Health and the Attorney General, Frank Murray,

[119] NAI DT 2012/90/667, 8 March 1982.   [120] NAI DT 2012/90/667, March 1982.
[121] Casssidy, 'The right to life movement' in Critchlow, pp. 144–5.

a senior official in the Department of the Taoiseach, suggested that DFA should also be circulated because of the potential implications for north–south relations. Before the matter was submitted to Government, there was a need to have 'precise details on existing medical practice by Catholic and non-Catholic doctors in relation to interference with pregnancies...... and how any of the formulae proposed, or other formulae envisaged would relate to existing procedures'. It would be necessary to consider the proposed amendment 'from the standpoint of the different churches'. This was consistent with the consultations carried out before drafting the 1979 Family Planning Act.

The Attorney General offered three possible wordings:

The State acknowledges the right to life of the unborn. The State therefore condemns abortion and, subject to the right to life of other persons, guarantees in its laws to respect and as far as practicable by its laws to defend the right to life of the unborn.

First Alternative: The State acknowledges the right to life of the unborn and, guarantees in its laws to respect, and as far as practicable by its laws to defend that right.

Second Alternative: The State acknowledges the right to life of the unborn. The State therefore condemns abortion and, subject to the right to life of other persons, guarantees in its laws to respect and as far as practicable by its laws to defend that right.

The response of the Department of Justice was in conformity with Catholic teaching; they claimed that nobody had suggested making it a criminal offence to carry out an abortion by removing the womb. Justice was emphatic that the existing law on abortion was 'understood to be applicable from the time of fertilisation'. 'If one accepts ....that the life of the unborn is human life, it is doubtful if respect for it can without violation of principle be declared to be subject to the right to life of others'; this phrase 'even on the narrowest interpretation' would 'represent an important change in principle in the existing position'. They noted that the German abortion laws had been challenged as too restrictive under the European Convention of Human Rights; any constitutional amendment giving effect to the wishes of the pro-life supporters would seem likely 'sooner or later to come into conflict with the Convention'.[122]

The chief medical officer in the Department of Health submitted a confidential memorandum, expressing support for the first alternative wording. He agreed that the proposed amendment might present difficulties for contraceptive pills and the IUD. He also submitted a statement on current medical practice. Dublin obstetrical opinion was 'adamant that the only areas where a living fetus might be destroyed is in the areas of ectopic pregnancy or cancer'. However obstetrics textbooks noted that severe vomiting in pregnancy might develop into a toxic state, and they recommended inducing labour in such circumstances (regardless of gestation); termination was also recommended in cases of severe kidney failure – though he claimed that this should no longer

[122] NAI DT 2012/90/667, 29 July 1982 D J.

arise because of dialysis and the outlook for pregnant women with severe cardiac disease had changed in recent years, though in 1980, a woman who was twenty weeks' pregnant had died due to a heart condition. He noted that termination was sometimes recommended in cases of diabetes or TB. On foetal abnormalities, 'in general there is a feeling that the congenitally abnormal may not justify the same care as the normal child and this is projected to the situation where recognised cases of mental or physical handicap during pregnancy become a justification for termination'. There was no recognised practice in cases of rape, though some doctors would administer large doses of oestrogens (morning after pill) and other had been known to do a D and C to prevent possible conception; introducing an IUD would have a similar effect.

In August 1982, the Taoiseach received a letter from journalist Mary Kenny, who was writing a book about abortion. She advised him that it was 'important to avoid, in the wording of any referendum, any implication of controlling or punitive attitudes to women....The wording....should thus emphasise the positive with a phrase such as "that we honour and respect human life from its commencement until its natural end".... It might also be a valuable and positive affirmation to the world that Irish people are not, as a general rule, in favour of taking human life as is sometimes imagined....emphasise the positive...and not the negative'.[123]

The timetable for agreeing a wording for the amendment was thrown into disarray, when Malcolm MacArthur, a suspect in two murders, was found to be staying in the apartment of the Attorney General Patrick Connolly, who was on holidays. Connolly resigned and was succeeded by John Murray. The Cabinet agreed to hold an all-day meeting on 22 September devoted to the parliamentary programme for the coming session – including the PLAC legislation.

The documents submitted to Cabinet included three new wordings. O'Riordan commented that 'I am not sure that the waters are any clearer.... The amendment is about balancing those rights and I have seen no formula nor can advance any myself, which in my view would do that successfully... An ironic factor in all this may be that the Pro-Life people, in advocating a Constitutional amendment may well replace the absolute right of the unborn recognised in McGee with a qualified right which in time could be tested and found wanting. The Pro-Life movement may have hastened abortion in Ireland. Existing medical practice cannot be ignored but to recognise it may be to recognise abortion'.[124]

The approach of Attorney General John Murray suggests a greater commitment to a constitutional amendment than Sutherland or Connolly displayed. The objective was to protect – 'from the time of conception'. He quoted from an unpublished paper by two Holles St consultants which examined the case

---

[123] NAI DT 2012/90/881.   [124] NAI DT 2012/90/668, 21 September 1982.

histories of all expectant women who died within forty-two days of confinement in the years 1970–79 in that hospital's care. He claimed that abortion would not have saved any lives. However, there were cases other than ectopic pregnancy and cancer of the uterus, where potential difficulties might arise – anti-cancer drugs and radiation had the potential to damage, or kill the unborn baby; likewise, some medical procedures following a motor accident – but he claimed that the medical profession believed that these would be immune from litigation because of the absence of intent to commit abortion. Medical practitioners appeared to regard the existing law as permitting 'indirect abortion' where the life of the mother is threatened, but 'There is a degree of uncertainty ...as to the exact meaning of the existing law and further what medical procedures are considered to be in accordance with the present law'. He suggested that the proposed amendment was 'designed not to make the present law more restrictive or more liberal'. Murray set out four possible wordings for the amendment, but none of these were adopted by Cabinet. A wording was finally agreed on 29 October:

The State acknowledges the right to life of the unborn, and with regard to the equal right to life of the mother, guarantees in its laws to respect, and, as far as practicable, by its laws to defend and vindicate that right.

Hesketh, citing 'a source who wished to remain anonymous' claimed that this wording was drafted by supreme court judge Anthony Hederman – a former Fianna Fáil Attorney General though Martin Mansergh, an adviser to the Taoiseach, suggested that the wording was not the work of any individual.[125] This is credible, given the variations, sometimes minor, found in government papers. An erratum, added to Hesketh's book after publication, stated that Mr Justice Hederman did not formulate the wording; the Attorney General 'was responsible for and formulated that amendment'.

Responsibility for drafting legislation was given to the Department of Health. A text was circulated on 2 November. The government was under pressure from multiple fronts; leadership challenges within Fianna Fáil, possible defeat in Dáil Éireann, and pressure from the Pro-Life lobby. Hesketh claims that the publication of the draft Bill was not primarily prompted by electoral considerations[126] – but that is questionable.

6.5   The All-Ireland, Protestant Dimensions

Opposition to the 1967 British Abortion Act was not confined to Catholics. SPUC loaded its committee with non-Catholic members.[127] The anti-abortion movement in the United States included 'Roman Catholics and fundamentalists,

---

[125] Hesketh, *The second partition of Ireland*, pp. 157–8.
[126] Hesketh, *The second partition of Ireland*, pp. 159–62.
[127] Hindell and Simms, *Abortion law reformed*, p. 182.

moderate evangelicals, members of mainstream Protestant denominations, Mormons, Orthodox Jews and some...who profess no religious beliefs at all'.[128] In 1982, a group of English Anglican clergy wrote to the London *Times*, expressing their support for the principles laid down by the Catholic bishops and the Chief Rabbi about the sanctity of life.[129] When delegations of the Irish Protestant churches met Mr Haughey in relation to the family planning legislation, they all expressed clear hostility to abortion. So, it was not unrealistic to expect that the proposed constitutional amendment might attract some support from the Protestant churches. Those hopes were dashed in May 1982 when the Board of Community Affairs of the Irish Council of Churches (ICC) – whose membership included the main Protestant churches and organisations, such as the Salvation Army – approved a resolution affirming their opposition to 'indiscriminate abortion' but expressing the opinion that 'the State's regulation of this and other matters affecting morals should be a matter for legislation by the Oireachtas, and not for definition by the Constitution'.[130] Most member organisations sent copies of similar resolutions to the government. In June, the Executive Committee of the ICC issued a statement to the effect that the proposed amendment would divide the community. Catholic moral teaching allowed abortion in some exceptional cases; if these were incorporated into the constitution 'then the teaching of one religious denomination is to be enshrined into the Constitution'; it asked why 'the exceptional situations' that many Protestant churches would view as justifying abortion should not also be 'considered for inclusion'.[131] An editorial in the *Church of Ireland Gazette* dismissed the proposed referendum as 'extraneous to all genuine argument on the subject'; it would 'perpetuate this hypocritical state of affairs', where although divorce, abortion and contraception were illegal 'in general little notice is taken of individuals who find ways around the ban'. It accused Mr Haughey of 'shameless political opportunism'[132] but failed to note that the same might be said of Garret FitzGerald.

Despite these unpromising signals, the government went to considerable efforts to secure Protestant support. Hesketh suggests that the PLAC made efforts to distance itself from the Catholic church; the leadership was entirely lay, and there was no formal organisational link between PLAC and the Catholic hierarchy.[133] But there was no Protestant among the PLAC leadership, and the fact that the only medical/surgical interventions that they viewed as acceptable – ectopic pregnancy and cancer of the uterus – conformed to Catholic teaching, gave the referendum a strong Catholic flavour. A Galway

---

[128] Cassidy, 'The right to life movement', p. 136.
[129] *Church of Ireland Gazette*, 15 January 1982.   [130] *IT*, 19 May 1982.
[131] NAI DT 2012/90/881 statement, 21 June 1982.
[132] *Church of Ireland Gazette*, 25 June 1982.
[133] Hesketh, *The second partition of Ireland*, pp. 50–2.

woman, a Fine Gael supporter, alerted FitzGerald to what had happened that morning at Mass: 'The priest read out about a meeting of the Pro-Life group tomorrow night. He said they were writing to you and all the TDs about their attitude to the Pro-Life issue. He said that your government were to have introduced it at the last sitting of the Dáil but you failed to do so. He said he would let everyone in the Cathedral know the politicians' views on it before the election and that we should only vote for candidates who were Pro-Life. It now appears that the election in the West will be won or lost for your Government on that issue and not on the Budget. [I myself could not in conscience vote for a Government who would not bring in Pro-Life legislation]'.[134]

Mr. Haughey emphasised that 'particularly from the Anglo-Irish side, it will be necessary to consider the proposed amendment from the standpoint of the different churches'.[135] In June 1982, his advisor, Martin Mansergh, had breakfast in Belfast with Rev Sidney Garland, an evangelical Presbyterian minister, who was chairman of the Northern Ireland branch of LIFE – an international pro-life movement. Garland claimed that LIFE had approximately 1,000 members in Northern Ireland, the majority Presbyterians and was expanding into the Republic. He had contacted Mansergh, offering his support for the amendment, because he believed that a successful outcome might prove to be a turning point in the LIFE campaign worldwide. He claimed that 'the pro-family ethos' in the Republic was one of the most attractive features for northern Protestants.

In a memorandum to the Taoiseach, Mansergh expressed the view that the government was 'honour-bound' to introduce a referendum; it was also right that a matter on which people had strong feelings should be decided directly by the people, as opposed to being left to the Oireachtas or the courts – as would be the position if the constitutional prohibition on divorce was to end. He cautioned that the issue was 'turning into a major political struggle', and he was uncertain whether those campaigning for the referendum 'were serving their own best interests, since they would make abortion for the first time a major subject of debate'. He then set out some wider philosophical issues:

A Whether Ireland is to become a secular Western state like any other (sharing with many continental countries a mainly Catholic background) or whether it will remain a State with its own individuality which upholds certain distinctive Christian values. The progress of secularization has been extremely rapid in Ireland over the last twenty years, and the PLAC can be seen as an attempt to posit a *ne plus ultra* (it being clear that the divorce ban may not last indefinitely and with the abolition of illegitimacy would become increasingly irrelevant anyway).

B On a political level an attempt to make even the possibility of achieving a united Ireland dependent on the State divesting itself completely of any specifically Catholic

[134] NAI TD 2012/90/879, 7 February 1982.   [135] NAI TD 2012/90/668, 14 July 1982.

ethos. Some churchmen see a heaven–sent opportunity for consolidating partition, by branding this part of the country a Catholic or better still a Sectarian state, or alternatively of leveraging itself into an equal society, which their numbers scarcely justify. This is not to decry the genuine uneasiness of members of minority churches…

He suggested that the PLAC 'cruelly exposes the contradictions and inconsistencies at the heart of Dr FitzGerald's constitutional crusade launched without due care or reflection'. He warned that the PLAC

may have a considerable influence on the perception of the Northern Ireland problem for some years to come. The Protestant Churches have moved with almost indecent haste to "sectarianize" the issue without even waiting for the wording…It is already clear that the secularists/feminists will shelter behind and thereby magnify the impact of the sectarian argument. They appear to be using this as their "trump" card.

PLAC would be used by 'our opponents in the North' to suggest that there was no prospect of a pluralist Ireland, 'and that a united Ireland is therefore a pipedream'. In Britain, where 'most of our well-wishers in Labour actually believe that Abortion should be legalised in the North, doubts would be reinforced'. 'Every care should be taken to avoid potential damage' in the wording and how the referendum was presented. He noted that abortion was available in Belfast in cases of anencephaly. [A 2019 court case suggests that this was either inaccurate or obstetrical practice became more restrictive in later years.][136]

Mansergh recommended that any public presentation should emphasise that the State 'was giving positive recognition to values common to Irish people North and South. We have a distinctive way of life here, are proud of it, and wish to protect and develop it. The State is taking a positive stand against what is perceived to be one of the evils of our time'. It should emphasise that all Churches were opposed to abortion, which was not available in Northern Ireland. LIFE was not a Catholic organisation, so abortion cannot be represented as a sectarian issue. This argument would be 'greatly strengthened… if the wording….is such that it does not reflect exclusively Catholic teaching'. He warned that there were indications of 'growing intransigence in the hitherto-supine Protestant community'. Proposals that the government introduce legislation recognising annulments granted by the Catholic church – as an alternative to removing the constitutional ban on divorce, and the recent family planning act were both seen as enshrining Catholic teaching in law.[137] His reference to annulment and family planning legislation was based on a sermon by Victor Griffin Dean of St Patrick's Cathedral.[138]

David Neligan, an assistant secretary in DFA reported that 'the proposed amendment has serious implications for Anglo-Irish policy…… Given the

---

[136] My conversation with the late Dr Jim Dornan, FRCOG, who practised for many years in Belfast, would suggest the latter.
[137] NAI DT 2012/90/667.   [138] *Church of Ireland Gazette*, 1 May 1981.

Government's commitment to fostering reconciliation between the two major traditions in Ireland, it is necessary to examine carefully any proposal which attracts the unanimous condemnation of Unionist politicians who will see in it the introduction of a sectarian provision into the Constitution and confirmation thereby of their view that the State is a Roman Catholic State which aspires to Irish unity, so as to impose domination on the Protestant people of Northern Ireland'. Some Northern Catholics expressed reservations – they included the SDLP's deputy leader, Seamus Mallon. Wally Kirwan of the Taoiseach's Department issued a warning that the memorandum for government should deal with the matter from the all-Ireland standpoint'.[139] Although the main Protestant churches opposed indiscriminate abortion, they tolerated a wider range of exceptions than the Catholic church, and they had stated their opposition to any constitutional amendment; 'it seems reasonable to assume that any of the formulae set out in the draft memorandum would be opposed by the Protestant Churches'. This would setback North–South relations and progress towards Irish unity. Neligan recommended that 'Having regard to Northern sensitivities the proposed amendment should be as pluralist and non-sectarian as possible'. The Taoiseach had given an undertaking to consult the Protestant churches on the wording – if their agreement could be secured this would mark 'a very positive advance' in the Government's objectives on Northern Ireland'.

The Department of Justice had concluded that 'a pluralist text' was 'unattainable', but Frank Murray reiterated that 'the objective should be to produce an amendment which from the point of view of any religious denomination, would be as neutral as possible'. He referred to an *Irish Times* article by Kevin Boyle, Professor of Law at UCG and an early member of the Northern Ireland Civil Rights Association, which was highly critical of the proposed amendment but suggested that 'Pluralism is the concept that we should use to get ourselves out of this mess … It is a measure of how far we in the South have to travel towards the United Ireland that we wish to see that no one has thought other than that the amendment is an internal 26-county debate'. The Protestant churches opposed the proposed amendment, 'while resisting the English abortion law'. Murray suggested that the Government should appoint a Commission that was representative of all interests to advise on laws, 'which reflect the absolute abhorrence, North and South, to liberal abortion laws'.[140]

According to Dr Mansergh, David Bleakley (ICC Chairman) expressed the opinion that 'all Churches could accept a pro-life statement that did not alter the legal status quo'; Ireland North and South operated under the same legislation with respect to abortion. He suggested that Mansergh should contact leaders of the Presbyterian and Methodist churches and try to secure agreement

---

[139] NAI DT 2012/90/668 20, September 1982.   [140] *IT*, 5 August 1982.

on a wording.[141] But Una Bhean Uí Mhathúna of the Irish Housewives' Union wrote 'that we fail to see why they should be consulted at all in the matter'. Her organisation wanted to see the draft.[142]

The files do not contain any record of Mansergh's meetings with Dr Henry McAdoo, Church of Ireland Archbishop of Dublin, though Hesketh suggests that they were critical, and 'the draft ultimately formulated was heavily influenced by McAdoo's concerns' – that it should be 'positively pro-life; that the mother's rights should be clearly stated; that the beginnings of life should remain undefined; that the status quo in relation to legal and medical matters should be safeguarded; and that the formula should be worded in such a manner that it would be capable of "evolution"'. Hesketh claims that Monsignor Gerard Sheehy (Chancellor of the Dublin Archdiocese) and Dr McAdoo were shown advance copies of the wording and approved it.[143] Garret FitzGerald also stated that Dr McAdoo had seen and approved the proposed wording.[144] Some members of the PLAC were concerned that it failed to define the beginning of life. However, it attracted the support of Capuchin priest Fr Brendan O'Mahony, who had previously opposed the referendum, and positive statements from Dr McAdoo, Methodist Minister, Rev Desmond Gilliland, the Chief Rabbi, David Rosen and others. Garland was the only protestant clergyman to give his unequivocal support. Mansergh thanked him: 'While we will be seeking the support of all the Christian Churches as well as other groups for the Amendment, we are particularly glad of your support as a Northern Ireland Protestant and as one active in the LIFE organization'.[145] On 24 November, Garland addressed a press conference called by the Northern Ireland branch of LIFE outlining their services for unmarried mothers and their children and expressing support for the amendment.[146]

6.6   The Doctors

The PLAC had secured the support of many of the country's leading obstetricians, and some played a prominent role in the campaign. In June 1982, the Institute of Obstetricians, which was chaired by Stanley Hewitt (a member of PLAC) debated whether to issue a statement. Opinion was divided; Conor Carr, who opposed the referendum, was in favour of formulating a policy that took account of members' views; John Bonnar wanted a canvass of the membership and a public statement on the Institute's position. Dr John Murphy described the amendment as 'unnecessary and divisive'; he believed that the Institute would only 'add to the confusion of this unnecessary debate

---

[141] NAI DT 2012/90/669 Report on visit 12–13 October.   [142] NAI DT 2012/90/881.
[143] Hesketh, *The second partition of Ireland*, pp. 157–8.   [144] FitzGerald, *All in a life*, p. 417.
[145] NAI DT 2012/90/881.   [146] *IT*, 25 November 1982.

by coming out in favour or against'. George Henry reported that consultant staff at the Rotunda believed that the Institute should make a statement. The Executive Council could not reach agreement and the topic disappeared from the agenda for almost a year.[147] In January 1983, the IMA issued a statement that 'the Amendment contained nothing which was contrary to the policy of the Association, which was opposed to abortion', and there was no need to discuss whether it was necessary. This can be read as an attempt to distance themselves from the controversy.

In May 1983, Fergus Meehan, consultant obstetrician in Galway and a member of the Institute, expressed concern about the potential impact on medical practice, in the treatment of pregnant women, the use of IUCDs and post-coital contraception. He was supported by a group called Concerned Doctors against the Amendment, who presented themselves as pro-life but opposed to the amendment. They included Conor Carr, who had written to the *Irish Times* in January, expressing his opposition because the amendment entailed the majority imposing its views on the minority – 'the antithesis of democracy'. He suggested that 'if the Catholic Church cannot persuade its members to accept its teachings then this is a failure of the Church and the State should not be required to bolster this failure'.[148] In June, Hewitt sent a letter to members stating that the treatment given to pregnant women would not be altered 'in any respect whatsoever' by a referendum; there was 'not the slightest risk' that they would face legal proceedings if the amendment was passed. He circulated this letter without the executive's approval or prior knowledge. At the next meeting of the executive, he claimed that the letter was a discussion document that should only have been circulated to the executive, but it had 'inadvertently' been sent to all members and leaked to the press. The outcome was a decision to call an extraordinary general meeting. Meanwhile, the leading gynaecologists, who were patrons of PLAC, published a statement to the effect that the proposed amendment was 'designed not to interfere with established medical practice'. Hesketh described this as 'a pre-emptive strike'. The EGM of the Institute on 22 July 1983 was marked by confusion: uncertainty as to the procedures/standing rules for this first EGM; whether to issue a statement, take a vote, permit proxy votes. Many members expressed fears that the Institute might split. Dermot MacDonald, a PLAC patron, opposed a vote 'as the Institute may be too immature to handle this national issue'. The attendees were divided as to whether the amendment would have an impact on medical practice. An initial vote was in favour of issuing a statement, but that was challenged on procedural grounds, and some members left the meeting. A statement was finally issued reaffirming the Institute's opposition to abortion and acknowledging that the meeting 'could not reach a consensus with regard

---

[147] Minutes, 19 June 1982.   [148] Carr, *The lucky twin*, pp. 216–21.

to the implication for medical practice'.[149] Feelings were running high; several of those present later alleged that one member who opposed the referendum was assaulted outside the meeting room.

6.7   The Opposition

The 1981 European Values Survey showed strong disapproval of abortion in the Republic 'stronger than in the North and stronger than in most other European countries'. However,

Protestants and especially the non-religious disapprove of abortion less, if indeed the view expressed by "convinced atheists" can be called disapproval at all. Otherwise, it is only in the youngest age group, in the intermediate occupational groups (skilled manual workers and "non-manuals"), and among the unemployed that disapproval of abortion diminishes (and barely so), to the margin between "strong" and "moderate".[150]

When asked about justification for abortion (presumably of those who believed it could be justified in some circumstances), 43 per cent of Irish respondents cited risks to a mother's health; the corresponding figure in Northern Ireland was 76 per cent and 90 per cent in Britain.[151]

Once the main political parties had expressed support for a Pro-Life Amendment there was little prospect that it would be defeated. The opposition had to tread an almost-impossible path – explaining why this referendum was unnecessary and potentially dangerous to women's lives and health but avoiding the label of being pro-abortion. The nuanced nature of their argument did not lend itself to snappy slogans or a mass campaign, whereas the PLAC could call on an extensive and often simplistic repertoire of emotional images and phrases.

The official Anti-Amendment Campaign (AAC) was launched in June 1982; Hesketh describes it as 'a mixture of theological and political, liberal and secular – all welded together by a common antipathy to a pro-life constitutional amendment'. The membership included Protestant clerics, liberal politicians and secular interest groups.[152] Several women's groups joined the campaign, including the Well Woman Clinic, the Women's Right to Choose Group, the Council for the Status of Women and the Irish Housewives Association, though the Ireland's largest women's organisation – the ICA supported the amendment. Family planning groups were predictably, in the opposition camp. The involvement of Protestant churchmen was significant, though Hesketh notes that 'Though Protestant spokesmen proclaimed their staunch

---

[149] RCPI, Minutes of the Institute of Obstetricians and Gynaecologists, EGM 22 July 1983.
[150] Michael Fogarty, Liam Ryan, Joseph Lee, *Irish values & attitudes. The Irish report of the European value systems study* (Dominican publications, Dublin, 1984), pp. 46–47.
[151] Fogarty et al, *Irish values*, p. 200.   [152] Hesketh, *The second partition of Ireland*, p. 57.

opposition to abortion, the doctrinal chasm which separated them from the
Catholic Church – and therefore from P.L. A. C – was far from hidden'.[153]
The trade union movement was divided, as were the major political parties,
except Fianna Fáil. The AAC highlighted five key points: (1) the amendment
would do nothing to solve the problem of unwanted pregnancies; (2) it allowed
no exceptions, even in cases of rape or incest; (3) it was sectarian, seeking to
enshrine the teaching of one church in the constitution; and (4) it would impede
discussion and possible legislation on abortion, and it was a waste of public
funds.[154] Only one TD Jimmy Kemmy, and three senators, Robinson, West
and Shane Ross were listed among the initial supporters; supporting doctors
included George Henry and pathologist Dermot Hourihane, founding members
of the Fertility Guidance Centre.

In the AAC's pamphlet, *The Abortion Referendum: The Case Against*, journalist Mary Holland emphasised that the referendum, if passed, would enshrine
Catholic teaching in the constitution. This would seriously impede the development of a pluralist society, and improvements in north-south relations; 'It
is ….impossible to envisage how the current campaign for the introduction
of civil divorce…could make any progress' and the 'political climate' would
become 'more antagonistic' to those wishing to decriminalise homosexuality,
or broaden the laws on contraception. She suggested that 'the rigid viewpoint
which this amendment seeks to enshrine' would affect attitudes to unmarried
mothers, illegitimacy, rape and other matters. 'Its effect will be to create a
more punitive, *less* caring society'. Almost half of her contribution focused
on the implications for relations with Ulster Protestants, and their fears about
the influence of the Catholic church in Irish society. The remainder of this
pamphlet included short pieces (some reprinted from newspapers) by lawyers
Kevin Boyle and Adrian Hardiman, a range of religious/ethical contributions
and sections on the medical issues by Drs Andrew Rynne and Moira Woods.[155]

The broad church that constituted the AAC was problematic. The Women's
Right to Choose affirmed abortion as a right. Moderates emphasised the difficulties associated with a constitutional amendment, as opposed to the question of abortion. Hesketh noted 'the almost complete disappearance of the
Women's Right to Choose Campaign', as an indication that the AAC was
dominated by moderates. He claimed to have only discovered one statement
issued by the AAC that could be described as pro-abortion.[156] The campaign
gradually attracted support from members of the legal profession, doctors, academics, and a growing number of politicians, including the then leader of the

[153] Hesketh, *The second partition of Ireland*, p. 63.
[154] Hesketh, *The second partition of Ireland*, p. 75.
[155] Mary Holland 'Introduction' in Mavis Arnold and Peadar Kirby, *The Abortion Referendum:
the case against.*
[156] Hesketh, *The second partition of Ireland*, pp. 87–8.

Labour Party Michael O'Leary and senior trade unionists. Lawyers against the amendment was formed in October 1982 with over eighty members, including several future members of the Supreme Court and UCG Professor Kevin Boyle. Academics against the amendment was launched on 6 December 1982, by Dr P.J. McGrath, a former priest and professor at Maynooth; doctors against the amendment, which claimed to represent over 120 doctors announced its campaign on 26 January 1983 and barristers against the amendment, which claimed to represented 98 barristers, including 18 senior council was formed in February 1983.[157] Hug comments that more lawyers supported the AAC than the PLAC; the reverse was true of doctors.[158] Hesketh suggests that opinion was moving against the PLAC in the autumn of 1982; an opinion poll carried out by Irish Marketing Surveys showed 43 per cent in favour but 41 per cent against the amendment. But when those surveyed were presented with a draft wording 'No Irish Government may introduce laws to permit abortion' the figures were 47 per cent in favour and 36 per cent against. *Irish Independent* journalist Tom Rowley read these results as indicating that many Irish voters were 'caught in a dilemma' – opposed to a referendum, but if one was held, they would vote in favour.[159]

6.8   Politics

Fianna Fáil published the proposed wording for the referendum on 2 November. The *Irish Independent* described it as 'vague', but there were indications that it would be acceptable to most Catholic and Protestant churchmen. Maynooth theologian Dr Denis O'Callaghan criticised the omission of the phrase 'from conception'.[160] The vague wording; the 'equal rights' accorded to the 'unborn' (undefined) and the mother; and the further qualification 'as far as practicable' highlighted the potential legal challenges. Mary Robinson stated that it 'would throw the entire matter into the lap of the courts'.[161] Una Bhean Uí Mhathúna described the wording as 'a limited abortion bill' that weakened the 1861 Act. She claimed that '"Unborn" could mean anything animal, or vegetable'. As successive Attorneys General were incapable of drawing up a suitable amendment she suggested that the Taoiseach should do it himself 'similar to the excellent Article on divorce' in the 1937 Constitution. She rejected suggestions that the views of Protestants and unionists should be considered: 'Given the total denial of human and civil rights to the nationalist people of the Six-Counties and considering the brazen sectarianism of the Protestant rulers there

---

[157] Hesketh, *The second partition of Ireland*, pp. 202–3.
[158] Hug, *The politics of sexual morality in Ireland*, p. 149.
[159] Hesketh, *The second partition of Ireland*, pp. 103–4.   [160] *II*, 3 November 1982.
[161] Hesketh, *The second partition of Ireland*, pp. 156–69.

we fail to see why there should be any question of pleasing the tiny number of Protestants in the 26 Counties.'[162]

Two days after the publication of the proposed wording, the government was defeated on a motion of censure, and a general election was called for 24 November. Garret FitzGerald indicated that the Fine Gael parliamentary party had unanimously decided to commit 'to having it put to the people by 31st March next'. The referendum would 'not be delayed by any other consideration'.[163] In his memoirs, he expressed relief 'that the draft .... was one in conscience that I could accept'.[164] No member of Fine Gael questioned the wording during the course of the election campaign; politicians such as Maurice Manning TD who had reservations feared that 'the election would be side-tracked'.[165] Labour leader Dick Spring reiterated his party's unequivocal opposition to abortion and announced that he would discuss his reservations about the proposed wording with other party leaders after the election – effectively leaving his position and that of his party open.[166] Democratic Socialist TD Jimmy Kemmy – an unequivocal opponent of the referendum lost his seat following a campaign where opponents alleged that he supported abortion. Michael D. Higgins, probably the first Labour politician to express his support for the AAC, was also defeated. Pro-life supporters followed him throughout the campaign, disrupting canvassing and making allegations against him. Kemmy and Higgins were both vulnerable, irrespective of the PLAC, though it was undoubtedly a factor.[167]

The election resulted in a Fine Gael/Labour coalition which took office in mid-December. The joint programme for government reiterated FitzGerald's commitment that legislation providing for an amendment would be adopted by 31 March 1983. Mr Haughey had assigned responsibility for the amendment to the Minister for Health, Michael Woods. Because Labour TD Barry Desmond, who was Minister for Health was opposed to the amendment, the Minister for Justice, Michael Noonan was given responsibility. On 27 January, the Taoiseach confirmed that the bill enabling a referendum (which had lapsed when the Dáil fell) would be reintroduced, and a referendum held before 31 March. Rumours began to fly that Fine Gael was divided. In late January, Attorney General Peter Sutherland presented FitzGerald with his formal legal opinion on the wording.[168] Some members of the parliamentary party, notably Maurice Manning, Monica Barnes, and John Kelly, a distinguished constitutional lawyer, expressed concerns, and the Dublin South constituency party

---

[162] NAI 2012/90/991, 12 November 1982.
[163] Hesketh, *The second partition of Ireland*, pp. 172–3.   [164] FitzGerald, *All in a life*, p. 471.
[165] Hesketh, *The second partition of Ireland*, pp. 194–5.   [166] *IT*, 10 November 1982.
[167] Hesketh, *The second partition of Ireland*, pp. 183–6; Brian Girvin, 'Social change and moral politics: the Irish constitutional referendum 1983', *Political Studies*, 34, 1986, p. 72.
[168] FitzGerald, *All in a life,* p. 440.

passed a motion unanimously condemning the proposed amendment. Barnes threatened to vote against the amendment.[169] The government received a lengthy report from doctors who opposed the amendment setting out the consequences for clinicians and women.

Peter Sutherland's Opinion opened by stating that: 'The requirements of the Pro-Life lobby relating to the legislature and the Courts cannot be complied with by any formula of words. If the Supreme Court is to be precluded from permitting abortion, in any circumstances, through the implication of a right vesting in the mother then where can the authority be found, for example for operations relating to carcinoma of the uterus other than from the legislature'. PLAC would not permit any legislation providing for intent to abort. If the wording permitted the Court to balance the conflicting rights of mother and foetus, 'the Supreme Court ultimately have an interpretative power, which would permit the balancing in favour of the mother' and might well favour the mother. 'Either the Court or the legislature had to be given power to interpret, or the legislature retains it'.

Sutherland favoured a confirmative amendment: 'Nothing in this Constitution shall be invoked to invalidate any law on the ground that it prohibits abortion'. This would prevent a *Roe* v. *Wade* outcome, while leaving the Oireachtas free to legislate and 'to respond to social changes or developments in medical practice'. He suggested that this approach would address the concerns expressed by the Protestant churches. The only objection was that it left it open to the Oireachtas to legislate to permit abortion.[170] The Department of Justice disputed the Attorney General's opinion and his proposal for a revised wording. They argued that a narrow amendment would not be worthwhile and would not meet the wishes of the PLAC. Justice believed that the original proposed wording would not threaten existing practice with regard to carcinoma of the uterus, or ectopic pregnancy; in other words, that Catholic-approved practices would not be challenged. The Attorney expressed concerns that neither draft dealt with post-coital contraception and IUDs. He suggested that they were probably illegal on the basis of current statute law and might be proven to be unconstitutional. Any amendment would probably make it unconstitutional to terminate anencephalic pregnancies. He noted that 'The text was avoidably (his underlining) vague on a central issue – what is meant by "the unborn"'. The 'deliberate and unavoidable ambiguity' in the wording 'is calculated only to make it inevitable that there will be expensive litigation, with, at the end of the day the right of decision being handed over unnecessarily to the Supreme Court'. He concluded:

[169] Hesketh, *The second partition of Ireland*, pp. 209–14.
[170] UCD Archives Gemma Hussey Papers, P179/132.

In summary: the wording is ambiguous and unsatisfactory. It will lead inevitably to confusion and uncertainty, not merely amongst the medical profession to whom it has of course particular relevance, but also amongst lawyers and more specifically the judges who will have to interpret it. Far from providing the protection and certainty which is sought by many of those who have advocated its adoption it will have a contrary effect. ....doctor's dilemma saving the life of the mother....will be compelled by the wording to conclude that he can do nothing.[171]

The court challenges and later referendums, and the death in 2017 of Savita Hallappanavar confirm the validity of this assessment.

The DPP also had reservations that became known to the media.[172] Caught between the reservations expressed by its two senior legal officers, and pressure from PLAC, the government determined to introduce the second reading of the bill and postpone the committee stage 'to permit the Minister to reflect on the matter'. The Minister for Justice proposed contacting PLAC to explain that the present text 'gave rise to problems and could have repercussions in a direction very different to what they would wish'. He hoped to communicate with representatives of the Jewish community and the Protestant churches, because of the 'serious risk at the moment of sectarian divisions – arising in part from the harshly worded statements being made by some opponents of the amendment'. The memo noted that 'there may be a risk of a backlash'. Agreement might be impossible (presumably among the various religious denominations), but an attempt should nevertheless be made to secure one.[173]

When FitzGerald and Noonan met the leaders of the PLAC, they indicated that the proposed wording must be re-examined, and the referendum delayed, but FitzGerald expressed the hope that an amended wording 'commanding widespread support' would be produced quickly. He reminded the PLAC that their initial request was to ensure that the Supreme Court could not strike down, as constitutional, legislation prohibiting abortion. PLAC emphasised their determination that the legislature should be incapable of legislating for abortion in the future, so removing the capacity of the court would not satisfy their demands.[174] [Some have contended that this marked a shift in their position, but Hesketh suggests that it didn't].[175] Andy Ward, Secretary of the Department of Justice, who had assumed the key role, with an official from the EU division, held an informal 'off the record' discussion with Brendan Shortall, the PRO for PLAC on 21 February 'with the concurrence of the Taoiseach'. Ward reported that PLAC did not share the reservations expressed by the Attorney General; they would oppose any amendment that left open

---

[171] NAI DT 2013/98/27.

[172] *IT*, 3 May 1983. For a detailed account, see Hekseth, *The second partition of Ireland*, pp. 216–8.

[173] NAI DT 2013/98/23.   [174] NAI DT 2013/98/23.

[175] Hesketh, *The second partition of Ireland*, pp. 218–9.

the possibility that the Oireachtas could legislate at some future date to permit abortion. They rejected claims that the amendment would not prevent a single abortion; that it would worsen relations with Northern Protestants; they did not accept that it would enshrine Catholic teaching in the constitution or constitute an improper invasion of personal and sexual privacy. Incorporating the PLAC as a human right would enable the State under article 60 of the European Convention to resist any judgment of the European Court.[176]

In March, following lengthy deliberation, the Minister for Justice introduced an alternative wording in Dáil Eireann – 'Nothing in the Constitution shall be invoked to invalidate any provision of a law on the grounds that it prohibits abortion'. This addressed PLAC's original argument that abortion could be introduced into Ireland by a judgment of the Supreme Court. By this stage, PLAC had become much more demanding, and neither PLAC nor the Catholic church were prepared to accept this alternative formula. The Dáil rejected it by eighty-seven votes to sixty-five. Fianna Fáil voted *en bloc* against this wording, as did thirteen Fine Gael and Labour backbenchers.

The Fianna Fáil wording was put to voters in a referendum on 7 September 1983 and approved by 66.9 per cent of those who voted; turnout was only 54.6 per cent. Over 80 per cent of voters in Cavan, Monaghan, Roscommon, Mayo, Donegal and Cork North-West approved the amendment; all five constituencies that voted to reject it were in Dublin.[177] Girvin claims that 80 per cent of Fianna Fáil voters and 61 per cent of Fine Gael voters supported the amendment; a majority of Labour voters were opposed.[178] Taoiseach Garret FitzGerald and the Labour party urged voters to oppose the referendum as did the Methodist Church and the Church of Ireland. The conference of Irish bishops urged people to be guided by their conscience.[179] However statements by individual bishops supporting the amendment were read at Sunday masses.[180]

The campaign, which was often unpleasant, pitted a determined PLAC, against a coalition of individuals and interest groups who were trying to articulate complex arguments. The relentless single-minded determination of the PLAC was evident in the limited coverage of the campaign on RTÉ; when they failed to secure a veto on the presence of two politicians on the main current affairs programme *Today Tonight*, they boycotted the event.[181] The emotional impact was wholly on the side of the PLAC. It invoked Irish exceptionalism, Catholicism and anti-Britishness, which had been aggravated by the deaths of IRA prisoners on hunger strike. In my hometown of Carrickmacross

---

[176] NAI DT 2013/98/23.   [177] Hesketh, *The second partition of Ireland*, appendix 5.

[178] Brian Girvin, 'Church, state and society in Ireland since 1960', *Eire/Ireland* 43, no 1 and 2, 2008, p. 87.

[179] Vicky Randall, 'Irish abortion politics: a comparative perspective', *Canadian Journal of Irish Studies*, 18, no 2, December 1992, p. 108.

[180] Hesketh, *The second partition of Ireland*, p. 304.   [181] *IT*, 24 and 25 August 1983.

(close to the border with Northern Ireland), meetings of the PLAC ended with prayers for those who had died on hunger strike. Abortion was presented as a barbarous practice tolerated in Britain, but not in Ireland.[182] Earner-Byrne and Urquhart have published a photograph of a pro-life march where a woman carries a banner: 'Let Ireland lead the world in the protection of the unborn'.[183]

Randall suggests that the key elements of the campaign were the active involvement of elite doctors in leadership roles; the weakness of left-wing parties; divisions among Irish feminists on the question of abortion, and the strong position of the Catholic Church. The Catholic Church did not take a formal leadership role; they relied on lay groups.[184] By 1983, tens of thousands of Irish women had travelled to Britain for abortions,[185] but most women travelled in secret and often their families or close friends did not know of their abortion. Their stories were not told in public, and neither were the stories of the mothers who gave birth to foetuses with fatal abnormalities, such as anencephaly. Public discussion of rape and its impact on women was only beginning; the Rape Crisis Centre had only recently been founded, and some PLAC activists were keen to associate it with abortion. All the sympathy and emotional engagement was with the PLAC. They could draw on networks such as NAOMI, the groups that had opposed contraception and on international expertise. The AAC found it difficult to craft an argument that was simple and emotionally compelling. The opposition case was not helped by confusion – not least the fact FitzGerald, who ultimately opposed the referendum, had signed up to the Pro-Life Amendment, not once but twice.

6.9   Aftermath

Despite this pre-emptive attempt to preserve what was seen as a distinct Irish way of life, to present an alternative model for the world, the number of Irish women travelling to Britain for abortions continued to rise. There is no evidence of efforts before 1983 to prevent women from accessing information about abortion in Britain, or travelling to Britain for an abortion, and travel was not prohibited under Irish law. In October 1986, however, SPUC took a case in the High Court against the Well Woman Clinic and Open-Door Counselling to prevent them from referring women to clinics outside the state for abortion.[186]

---

[182] Ruth Fletcher, 'Post-colonial fragments: representations of abortion in Irish law and politics', *Journal of Law and Society*, 28, no 4, December 2001, pp. 568–89; see also Cara Delay, 'Wrong for womankind and the nation: anti-abortion discourses in 20th century Ireland', *Journal of Modern European History*, 17, no 3, 2019, pp. 312–25.

[183] Earner-Byrne and Urquhart, *The Irish abortion journey*, p. 76.

[184] Randall, 'Irish abortion politics', pp. 107–116.

[185] By 1989, the number was estimated at 50,000. Diane Munday, Colin Francome, Wendy Savage, 'Twenty-one years of legal abortion', *BMJ*, pp. 1231–34.

[186] *IT*, 8 October 1986.

The High Court determined that it was illegal to refer women for abortion outside the state – a decision based on the 1983 amendment. The clinics were ordered to cease doing so by 12 January 1987.[187] On 3 January 1987, the *Irish Times* reported that the Well Woman Clinic was completely booked out until 12 January, with women seeking information and advice.[188] Ruth Riddick of Open Line Counselling announced that she would continue to give advice to women on her private phone line.[189] Well Woman ceased doing so, though they continued to offer post-abortion counselling. The Chairman of the Irish College of General Practitioners, and the vice chairman of the IMO – both speaking in a personal capacity – expressed fears that legal action might be taken against GPs who provided advice and abortion referrals, and they specifically referred to 'entrapment'.[190] Although no doctor faced a legal challenge, a GP known to me claimed that he had experienced attempted entrapment. In 1988, the Supreme Court confirmed the High Court ruling by Mr Justice Hamilton (a future Chief Justice).[191] SPUC subsequently obtained an injunction against the students' unions in TCD and UCD, preventing them from publishing phone numbers and addresses for British abortion clinics in student union handbooks. Some British periodicals began to redact such information from copies sold in Ireland, but *Cosmopolitan* and a number of other publications continued to carry advertisements.[192]

The prohibition on providing information about abortion was appealed to the EU Court in Luxembourg and the European Court of Human Rights in Strasbourg. The latter found against the ban on information; however, the EU court made a contrary decision and SPUC was granted a permanent injunction against the student unions.[193] In 1991, the Irish government secured the addition of a special protocol to the Maastricht Treaty, the treaty that established the Single European Market, stating that it did not affect the application of the 1983 constitutional amendment. That same year when the High Court granted an injunction against a fourteen-year-old pregnant girl, who had been raped – the X Case – travelling to England for an abortion, the decision was overturned by the Supreme Court, who determined she had a right to abortion in order to protect her life. She had threatened to commit suicide. This case gave rise to public outrage; two-thirds of those polled wanted some easing of the constitutional position.[194] This Supreme Court judgment was followed by three referendums in 1992. Two were passed – affirming the right to information about abortion and the right to travel for an abortion, a third, reversing the

---

[187] *IT*, 20 December 1986.   [188] *IT*, 3 January 1987.   [189] *IT*, 30 December 1986.
[190] *IT*, 23 January 1987.
[191] Ursula Barry, 'Abortion in Ireland', *Feminist Review*, 29, Summer 1988, p. 62.
[192] Barry, 'Abortion in Ireland', p. 62.   [193] Hug, *The politics of sexual morality*, pp. 158–60.
[194] Randall, 'Irish abortion politics', pp. 107–116.

Supreme Court judgment on the X Case was rejected. This referendum was again rejected in 2002.[195]

One interesting feature is the absence of any legal challenge, under the Eighth Amendment to post-coital contraception. In 1984, Adrian Hardiman SC, a future member of the Supreme Court, drafted an opinion on this topic for the Well Woman Clinic, which they shared with the network of family planning clinics. He believed that the prospect of a prosecution being taken by the 'ordinary prosecuting authorities', that is, the state was remote, but he could not predict what 'fringe groups' might do. He considered the prospect of defending an action against an injunction (to dispense the post-coital pill) to be 'good considering the near impossibility of proving that fertilisation had taken place and the modus operandi of the post-coital doses of the oral contraception involved. The risk on the criminal side (prosecution for administering a drug with intent to procure a miscarriage) would be higher because all that would be required to be shown in such a case would be the administration with intent....not necessary to show that fertilisation or implantation had taken place'. Such a case would raise questions about definitions of 'the unborn', and he determined that it would be 'eminently fightable'. He reiterated 'that the service should be provided as widely as it is needed but without unnecessary ostentation or publicity. I believe that the longer it is provided without legal challenge the stronger will its position be in the event of such a challenge'.[196] No prosecutions were taken against the importation or use of early-stage abortion pills which became available by the end of the 1980s.

Abortion was banned in Ireland until the second decade of the twenty-first century. This was possible because women could travel to Britain; the prohibition did not result in illegal/back-street abortions with inevitable risks to women's lives and health. The impact on clinical practice has not been researched. Improvements in scanning resulted in more and earlier diagnoses of foetuses that would not survive birth; some women had no option but to continue their pregnancy to term – willingly or unwillingly – others bore the significant emotional and financial costs of a late-stage abortion in Britain. In 1992, when there appeared a prospect that the government might legislate to implement the Supreme Court judgment, the Institute of Obstetricians and Gynaecologists canvassed its membership on the subject. They received replies from 54 members, just under half of the 120 members (from Ireland north and south). Twenty-six favoured a complete ban on abortion, including twenty of the thirty-five in active practice in the Republic; others wished the current practice to continue. There was general agreement that any legislation should allow present practice to continue in the following areas:

[195] Earner Byrne and Urquhart, *The Irish abortion journey*, pp. 85–6.
[196] UCDA Derek Freedman Papers, P276/5.

1. Treatment of malignant diseases in the mother should be carried out as necessary, regardless of risk to the baby.
2. Conditions requiring treatment by delivery of the infant before the present legal viability date of twenty-eight weeks – for example, severe toxaemia at pregnancy 23-28 weeks should continue to be valid indications of delivery (many of these babies will survive).
3. ectopic pregnancies – remove
4. Legislation should not affect a medical decision to terminate after viability has been achieved.[197]

The correspondence and minutes indicate serious divisions among the Institute's members. One stated: 'I have actually heard obstetricians say that to deliver somebody with fulminating pre-eclampsia at 26 weeks is a termination and nothing more!' A member based in Belfast recommended adopting practices similar to those in Northern Ireland where the number of terminations was small; most were for significant congenital malformations detected early in pregnancy. A member based in the Republic claimed that in his thirty-six years working in obstetrics he knew of no case where the lives of the mother and the foetus were in conflict, 'nor, in which the mother's life due to illness could not be satisfactorily treated awaiting the normal outcome of pregnancy'. However, a farmer's wife who wrote to the Institute claimed that 'Every farmer worthy of the name values the life of the mare above that of the foal, the cow above that of the calf ... until the young are born'. A member who was based in the Republic stated that 'As regards proper counselling of woman seeking abortion in my experience it is practically impossible to dissuade a woman from having an abortion once she has made her mind up to have one. A scan showing the foetus moving around is always helpful, but I would imagine most would refuse to have one'.[198]

In October 1992, thirteen practising obstetricians who were subsequently described by some colleagues as the 'dirty dozen' published a letter in the *Irish Times*, highlighting the potential risks to women's lives, from continuing pregnancies. They cited cases of maternal mortality in the UK in the years 1985–87 where a maternal death might have been averted if the pregnancy had been terminated: women with severe cardiac conditions; women with severe hypertensive disease in early pregnancy; and women who were diagnosed with cancer, especially cancer of the cervix in early pregnancy, where treatment was postponed. They emphasised such cases were rare, but they posed a real risk to women's lives. Only three of the thirteen signatories worked in Dublin, three were based in Cork, and the remaining seven worked in Galway, Letterkenny,

[197] Carr, *The lucky twin*, pp. 222–6.
[198] Institute of Obstetricians and Gynaecologists – abortion files 19 June 1992 chairman's report.

Limerick, Portlaoise, Tralee, Wexford and Waterford.[199] In the same year, Emily O'Reilly highlighted the case of Sheila Hodgers, a young mother whose cancer treatment was suspended when she was pregnant because of the potential damage that the drugs would inflict on her child. She died two days after the birth.[200]

The Medical Council issued a statement in March 1993 noting that 'Situations arise in medical practice where the life and or health of the mother or of the unborn, or both are endangered. In these situations it is imperative ethically that doctors shall endeavour to preserve life and health....While the necessity for abortion to preserve the life or health of the sick mother remains to be proved, it is unethical always to withhold treatment beneficial to a pregnant woman, by reason of her pregnancy. Departure from these principles in practice may leave the doctor open to a charge of professional misconduct'.[201]

The death of Savita Hallapanavar in 2012 prompted national and international outrage. She was seventeen weeks pregnant and public opinion blamed her death on the pro-life amendment. The cause was severe sepsis, following prolonged rupture of the membranes. The report on her death highlighted

a lack of recognition of the gravity of the situation and of the increasing risk to the mother which led to passive approaches and delays in aggressive treatment.

This appears to have been due either the way that the law was interpreted in dealing with the case or the lack of appreciation of the increasing risk to the mother and early need for delivery of the fetus.[202]

Savita Hallapanavar was not the only Irish woman to suffer a life-threatening medical condition during pregnancy – yet no similar death has been highlighted to date, which would suggest that doctors intervened when pregnant women's lives were threatened in similar circumstances. Maternal mortality, which was low by 1983, continued to decline. In 1983, at 12 per 100,000 births, it was equal to Scotland, lower than that in Northern Ireland but higher than that in England and Wales. By the year 2000, it was significantly lower than in England and Wales or Scotland, and among the lowest in the world, though Murphy and O'Herlihy have suggested maternal mortality in Ireland has been underreported.[203] In 2010, three women took a case to the European Court, claiming that their rights had been violated because of the absence of safe legal

---

[199] *IT*, 24 October 1992. Signatories, Patricia Crowley, Andrew Curtain, Brian Davidson, Anthony Dempsey, John Doyle, Vincent Fenton, George Henry, Rosemary Jordan, Harry Murphy, Michael Mylotte, Timothy O'Connor, Walter Prendeville and Edgar Ritchie.

[200] O'Reilly, *Masterminds of the right* (Attic Press, Cork, 1992), pp. 7–9.

[201] RCPI, Institute of Obstetricians and Gynaecologists – abortion files.

[202] HSE, Investigation of incident 50278 from the time of patient's self-referral to hospital on the 21st October 2012 to the patient's death on 28th October 2012. June 2013, p. 4.

[203] Cliona Murphy and Colm O'Herlihy, 'Maternal mortality statistics in Ireland. Should they carry a health warning', *IMJ*, 100, no 8, September 2007, 574.

abortion in Ireland; the Court rejected two of the cases, but found in favour of C, who became pregnant while undergoing treatment for cancer, and had travelled to Britain for an abortion. The European Court closed its case in 2014, following the enactment of the 2013 Protection of Life During Pregnancy Act, permitting abortions in cases where a woman's life was endangered, including the danger of suicide. In 2018, the Irish electorate voted by a margin of two to one, to repeal the Eighth Amendment.

This chapter might appear to intrude into a narrative that is focussed on contraception; however, it is central to a recurring theme in this work: the belief in Irish exceptionalism, and Ireland's capacity to withstand trends that were evident in other western countries. The 1983 constitutional amendment can be seen as the last throw of the dice for those who were determined to stem social and moral change. It captured the emotional sympathies of many people who were undoubtedly opposed to abortion and may have known little of the circumstances that drove Irish women to seek abortion. Their mobilisation was also invaluable in the defeat of the 1986 referendum to overthrow the constitutional ban on divorce. Yet the success of the PLAC was primarily symbolic, a reinforcement of the mythology of Irish exceptionalism following the 1979 Family Planning Act. The numbers travelling to Britain for abortions continued to rise, as did pre-marital/extra-marital sexual relations and pregnancies; the amendment probably had adverse consequences for the health and lives of pregnant women and may have delayed the rollout of foetal screening and the development of foetal medicine. The fact that the Amendment did not have greater consequences in terms of maternal mortality, and human tragedies is a reflection of the strong element of hypocrisy within Irish society; the successful efforts by many gynaecologists to finesse the regulations and continue to save women's lives despite the potential danger of a legal challenge, and above all, the fact that many women continued to travel to Britain for abortions, a journey that imposed emotional and financial costs.

7 'Bona Fide Family Planning'
The 1980s and 1990s

The number of births peaked in 1980, the year when contraception became legal for 'bona fide family planning' purposes. At 21.78 per 1,000, Irish fertility was significantly above the average for the EU 15,[1] of 13 per 1,000. Irish fertility was higher in 1980 than in the years 1956–61 (21.2 per 1,000), and only marginally below the figure for 1961–66, of 29 per 1,000. Superficially, it might seem that nothing had changed. But during the 1960s and 1970s, a much higher proportion of young adults had married than in the past, and they had married at an earlier age, yet family size had fallen significantly. In 1960, almost one baby in five was born to a mother who had previously given birth to 5–9 infants, and 2.5 per cent were born to mothers of ten or more previous births. By 1980, only 7.6 per cent of births were to mothers of 5–9 infants, and 0.5. per cent were to mothers of ten or more infants. By 1979, the number of actual births was 24 per cent lower than would be expected if the fertility patterns of 1971 had continued, and the decline was greatest among older women. The fertility of married women aged 40–44 had declined by almost 40 per cent; for married women aged 35–39, the figure was 33 per cent. The fertility of married women aged less than thirty-five had fallen by 20 per cent. The transformation in one decade was significant. Although there were regional variations in fertility decline, the figures showed 'a surprising consistency'; the decline in Dublin was less than half the national average – but in 1971, marital fertility was lower than elsewhere, and in 1980, Dublin city and Dun Laoghaire had the lowest fertility rates; the greatest decline was in Limerick and Cork cities, and in Cavan, a predominantly rural county.[2] By 1980, therefore, despite the lack of legal access to contraception, the fertility of Irish couples had fallen substantially.

The decline in marital fertility, already pronounced by 1980, continued over the following decades. Smaller families coincided with a significant rise in the

---

[1] The fifteen western European countries that constituted the European Union in the late 1990s: Austria, Belgium, Denmark, Finland, France, Greece, Ireland, Italy, Luxembourg, Netherlands, Portugal, Spain, Sweden, West Germany and United Kingdom. Not all were members of the then EEC in 1980.

[2] Brendan Herlihy, 'Changing pattern of reproduction', *Journal Irish Medical Association*, 74, no. 4, April 1981.

number of married women of childbearing years in paid employment. During the 1980s, the number of marriages fell sharply, and a growing number of single women appear to have focused on their careers,[3] and the birth rate fell to 15.1 per 1,000, still the highest in the EU but much closer to the EU15 rate of 12 per 1,000. In 1990, the Irish total fertility rate, the number of births necessary to sustain a stable population, was only marginally above the replacement figure.[4]

In 1980, 5 per cent of registered births were non-marital; by 1990, this had almost trebled to 14.6 per cent. In 1983, the 'Kerry babies', a complex and troubling story of Joanna Hayes, a single mother who was falsely charged with murdering two newborn infants, captured public attention. Earner-Byrne and Urquhart describe the public inquiry into that event as 'a display of mysogny writ large'.[5] The death the following January of fifteen-year-old Ann Lovett and her new-born infant beside a Marian grotto, prompted an even greater wave of emotion, which is captured in the many letters written to the mass-audience radio show, *The Gay Byrne Programme*.[6]

Irish fertility and family patterns were coming into line with other countries in western Europe (fertility in the United States remained significantly higher), and that process was well underway before contraception was legally available.

The 1979 Family Planning Act was both restrictive and enabling. It made contraceptives legal for the first time but sought to limit access by requiring a prescription (even for condoms), and only for 'bona fide family planning purposes'. Commentators often claim that this meant that only married couples could obtain contraceptives, but the wording was deliberately ambiguous, and it was never subjected to legal challenge. Girvin asserts that the Act 'reflected the continuing influence of the Catholic church on moral issues',[7] but I would support those who see it as marking a formal break with Catholic church control over moral legislation,[8] and the fact that the Catholic church apparently acquiesced, however reluctantly, in this legislation is significant. The ambiguity at the core of the Act reflected a similar evasiveness in Irish society.

---

[3] Brendan Walsh, 'Labour force participation and the growth of women's employment, Ireland 1971–1991', *Economic and Social Review*, 24, no. 4, 1993, pp. 369–400.

[4] D. A. Coleman, 'The demographic transition in Ireland in international context', in J.H. Goldthorpe and C.T. Whelan (eds), *The development of industrial society in Ireland* (Oxford University Press/The British Academy, Oxford, 1992), p. 67.

[5] Earner Byrne and Urquhart, *The Irish abortion journey*, p. 63. On the 'Kerry babies' story, see Tom Inglis, *Truth, power and lies, Irish Society and the case of the Kerry babies* (UCD Press, Dublin, 2005).

[6] For a summary of the contents of these letters, see *Report of the Commission on Mother and Baby Homes and related matters* (Dublin, 2021), chapter 12, pp. 150–153.

[7] Brian Girvin, 'An Irish solution to an Irish problem', p. 2.

[8] Hug, *The politics of sexual mortality*, p. 115; Aiden Beatty, 'Irish modernity and the politics of contraception, 1979–1993', *New Hibernia Review*, 17, no 3, 2013, pp. 100–18.

By making contraception legal, in however limited a fashion, and highlighting the need for training, information and education on family planning, the environment had changed. The lengthy consultations surrounding the Act, and the extensive debate in the Oireachtas meant that the topic was discussed more widely than before and becoming aware that it is possible to control fertility is the first step towards using contraception.

Máire Nic Ghiolla Phadraig noted that the legislation brought about 'the medicalisation of all types of contraception' and 'those who are legalistically inclined may, rather than conforming or working out a principled judgement on the issue look instead to an alternative source of authority, which would justify their use of Church prohibited methods' – they could seek medical advice.[9] The Catholic church did not concede defeat: they hoped that evidence showing the effectiveness of church-approved methods, especially Billings, would limit the spread of contraception, particularly in provincial Ireland. Otherwise, they concentrated their efforts on abortion, and preventing female sterilisation. The limitations of the 1979 act and the widespread understanding that it was a compromise meant that successive governments remained under pressure both to extend and to restrict access to contraception.

Studies carried out in the late 1970s and early 1980s highlighted serious shortcomings in terms of information and access to family planning. A survey of 120 post-natal mothers in Wexford in 1978 (interviewed within five days of giving birth) revealed that 64 per cent of the pregnancies were unplanned; 32 pregnancies had resulted from family planning failures. Socio-economic status was a key determinant of contraceptive use: only four of the twenty professional or upper-middle-class women interviewed had not used family planning, compared with half from a working-class background. Most women had received no advice from a doctor; one in ten had attended a family planning clinic – the numbers were equally divided between those using natural and other methods; 70 per cent wanted more advice and almost half were unable to get the type of family planning that they wanted. The main sources of information were friends and relatives, forty; books, magazines and other media, twenty-seven; family doctors, twenty-five; family planning clinics, twelve and maternity hospitals, three. One woman in four was undecided as to her future family planning; few mothers wanted more than four children.

A survey by Dr Conor Carr carried out in 1979/80 among 379 patients attending ante-natal clinics in Portiuncula Hospital in Ballinasloe showed that the calendar method, used by 27 per cent remained the most popular; Billings at 11.8 per cent was slightly below the 12.6 per cent who used the Pill; 36 per cent had used no method. He suggested that 'some at least of those who claimed not

[9] Maire Nic Ghiolla Padraig, 'Social and cultural factors in family planning', in *The changing family* (Family Studies Unit UCD, 1984), p. 93.

to have used any family planning method were probably either using some form of calendar method or coitus interruptus, since a number of women stated that pregnancy was either accidental or due to "taking a chance"'. Approximately 30 per cent described their pregnancy as unintended. Seventy-eight of the 140 couples who were using natural methods had an unplanned pregnancy, as did just under a quarter of those using other methods. Although it was generally believed that the contraceptive pill was widely used, only 12.7 per cent listed it as their most recent form of contraception, though one-third had used the Pill at some time in the past. He concluded that 'at present a large number of couples attempting to plan their families were not succeeding, whilst over one-third are not planning at all'.[10]

Another survey carried out in Dublin's Rotunda Hospital, among post-partum mothers and their partners, focused on working-class attitudes towards 'artificial' contraception: 98 per cent of those surveyed were Catholic; 31 per cent had one child; 55 per cent had 2–4 children; and 12 per cent had five or more children. All 100 women completed the survey but only 50 of the 80 husbands/partners. One man declined because he believed that such surveys 'would ruin the moral standards of this country and encourage women to be loose'. About 53 per cent of women had used artificial contraception and 75 per cent would do so in future, but 19 per cent were undecided. Most of the latter were uncertain what they would do to prevent a future unwanted pregnancy; 5.5 per cent indicated that they would use natural methods. Only 8 per cent had never used 'artificial' contraception and did not plan to in future – they all believed that it was wrong, citing religious belief, side effects, or opposition from their husbands. This survey indicated a growing use of contraception among women in their twenties and early thirties: 60 per cent of women aged thirty-six or over had never used contraception, nor had 80 per cent of mothers who were under twenty years of age. By the 1980s, contraception was commonly used in other countries by women who had not yet given birth, but 61 per cent of first-time Rotunda mothers had never used 'artificial' contraception.

Dublin women had better access to family planning services than their Wexford counterparts: 54 per cent of the Rotunda women using 'artificial' contraception had obtained it from a family planning clinic, hospital or GP; 38 per cent said that their main source of information was medical, though 48 per cent cited magazines, TV, books or friends. Almost two-thirds of the Rotunda women felt that their knowledge was adequate, but the authors of the report claimed that 'more objective findings... indicated their knowledge to be quite poor'. About 14 per cent believed that artificial contraception was

---

[10] Angela Moore and Patricia Murphy, 'Attitudes, knowledge and extent of use of artificial contraception in social classes IV and V in Ireland', *JIMA*, 73, no 9, September 1980, pp. 342–6.

wrong, yet only 3 per cent cited religious beliefs as the sole objection; 12 per cent believed that their husband/partner was opposed to 'artificial' contraception – a majority of these couples had discussed family planning. Half of all pregnancies were unplanned; 70 per cent of these women had done nothing to prevent conception; most of the remainder were due to failures of natural methods. Asked about future child-bearing wishes, almost half of the women did not want any more children; a similar proportion wanted at least one more child, but none wanted a baby within one year; 74 per cent believed that 2–4 children were the ideal family size. Over one-quarter of these recent mothers did not know how they would prevent another pregnancy.

Two-thirds of the men surveyed had used some form of 'artificial' contraception in the past, and the same proportion would welcome more information on this subject. One-quarter had used medical sources – GPs or clinics; 90 per cent believed that their partners' knowledge of family planning was adequate – but only 67 per cent of the women agreed and the survey team believed that this figure was inflated. A surprising 18 per cent of men (compared with 12 per cent of women) believed that 'artificial' contraception was wrong, but only 2 per cent gave religion as the sole objection. Although 92 per cent believed that family planning should be a joint decision, 20 per cent had never discussed contraception with their partner. A higher proportion of men than women would rely on 'natural' methods to prevent an immediate pregnancy. The authors concluded that the men believed that it was the woman's duty to be better informed; male criteria for 'adequate knowledge' were 'considerably lower than the women's'. On the revelations that 20 per cent of men had never discussed contraception with their wife, that 100 per cent of women but only 80 per cent of men did not want another child within a year, they commented that 'This lack of communication in Irish marriages seems to us to be truly astounding'. If couples were contemplating a vasectomy or using an IUD, there was evidence of a close correlation between the views of both partners, indicating that they had discussed the matter, but with regard to 'less radical methods', there was often a marked discrepancy.[11]

These surveys indicate widespread demand for family planning services – which begs the question whether the 1979 Act would meet this demand. One obvious limitation was that the Act only extended to 'bona-fide family planning' purposes. This restriction *might* have been respected (one feature of the Irish story is the absence of a significant black market for contraceptives until the 1970s) if the legislation had been introduced a decade earlier. During the 1970s however, traditional patterns of family, marriage and fertility began to change. Fertility of married couples was falling, and the proportion of babies

---

[11] Moore and Murphy, 'Attitudes, knowledge and the extent of use of artificial contraception among social classes IV and V in Ireland'.

born to single mothers was increasing. By the end of the decade, a majority of single women were keeping their babies and the number of cohabiting couples was rising. An increasing proportion of clients attending family planning clinics were single. Students Unions were providing unrestricted access to contraceptives; non-medical contraceptives were available in some pubs and night clubs, and some Dublin pharmacies were selling them without prescription, so there was little prospect that the law would be observed (whatever it meant). Comments on government files suggest that this was tacitly acknowledged. For many politicians and public servants, the 1979 Act was regarded as a formal statement that the Irish state did not condone premarital/extra-marital sexuality. A review carried out in 1984 concluded that 'Put shortly, it is the doctor and nobody else who decides what is bona fide family planning ... If he considers that an unmarried couple are seeking contraception for the stated purpose, his opinion on the matter is final'.[12]

Hug claimed that the new law 'seems to have closed more doors than it opened, on paper at least',[13] but the critical phrase is 'on paper'. Implementation reflected a complex mixture of conservative Catholic conviction, cowardice – avoiding the key issues – and cupidity, with certain interest groups determined to reap the financial benefits accruing from the legal contraception, at the expense of other providers. The Galway Contraception Action Programme interviewed 110 households before the legislation came into effect; the majority were living in local authority housing. As the interviews were carried out during working hours, 90 per cent of interviewees were women. Eighty-three per cent were aware of the Family Planning Act; 20 per cent believed that it would make contraception easier to obtain; 38 per cent believed that it would become more difficult, and 40 per cent answered 'don't know', which was probably the appropriate reply. Only 12 per cent believed that access would become easier for medical card holders; 15 per cent believed it would be more difficult, a significant majority plumped for no change or don't know; 52 per cent of respondents believed that single people would face greater difficulties accessing contraception than before.[14] Hug claims that condoms doubled in price, even before VAT was levied, at the luxury goods rate of 35 per cent. She quotes a representative of the IFPA who claimed that UK suppliers had previously been supplying condoms at low prices in order to create a market for their products.[15] In 1982, a report on the Cork Family Planning Clinic highlighted the impact of rising prices for condoms (almost £3 for a pack of twelve), on clients

---

[12] NAI DT 2017/2/1189 Fennelly to Matt Russell.
[13] Hug, *The politics of sexual morality*, p. 114.
[14] UCDA Barry Desmond Papers unlisted Box 352.
[15] Hug, *The politics of sexual morality,* p. 114 Information about VAT on contraceptive products, *IT*, 9 January 1984.

who lived in 'appalling economic conditions'.[16] The 1979 Act did not prevent an individual (married or single) from importing contraceptives for personal use. Customs officers could determine whether the quantity imported was for personal use, or resale (which was prohibited).[17]

7.1   The Providers: Health Boards, GPs, Hospitals and Pharmacists

In theory, the 1979 Act gave primary responsibility for family planning to the health boards. Section 3 (i) of the Statutory Instrument setting out the implementation of the Act stated that 'A health board shall make available a family planning service' – either directly or by devolving that responsibility to 'a body or person' under the 1970 Health Act. Others wishing to provide a family planning service had to apply to the Minister for Health for a license. The service must comply with the regulations and must be provided by a registered medical practitioner. But Mr Haughey's meeting with the health boards had indicated that they were unwilling to provide a comprehensive service, even one restricted to married couples, and it became evident that they preferred to leave the task to GPs.

The EHB, which covered the Dublin region held a special meeting in January 1981 to consider the operation of the Act. Labour Councillor Mary Freehill proposed a motion demanding that the EHB insist that medical and para-medical personnel should have access to courses on family planning, 'at least of the standard already being provided by the Irish Family Planning Association, which is already recognised by the Department of Health'. She asked the Board to draw up a list of doctors who were willing to provide 'an objective service with expertise and recognition in all methods of contraception', and a list of pharmacies that were willing to fill prescriptions within the terms of the act. Professor J.S. Doyle (a paediatrician) proposed a motion that the EHB would not support the use of IUDs because they were abortifacients. The EHB programme manager reported that the Board had decided not to establish any clinics until the position with respect to costings, staff and related matters had been clarified and the role that GPs and voluntary organisations (which presumably included family planning clinics) would play. Although the EHB had held discussions with GPs and pharmacists it was unclear how many would provide a service within the Act. The programme manager gave a commitment to endeavour to ensure 'a reasonable spread of services throughout its area', and to ensure that GPs had access to training programmes, and information enabling them to refer patients for specialist services. The EHB had been

---

[16] UCDA P276/11 Derek Freedman papers.   [17] *IT*, 28 June 1979.

in contact with the CMAC, medical organisations, maternity hospitals and the IFPA.[18] *Irish Times* medical correspondent Dr David Nowlan described this debate as 'one of the most muddled and ragged in the Board's history'.[19] Although the EHB approved a modified version of Freehill's motion,[20] the IPU and the medical organisations refused to provide the information necessary to compile a directory of providers. Medical organisations claimed that this would constitute advertising.[21] There is evidence that the EHB maintained a restrictive stance on contraception. One social worker, based in Inchicore (a working-class area), told FPS that the Board would only permit her to display notices about natural family planning services on the noticeboard outside her office; she proposed to have leaflets about other forms of family planning available in her office.[22] The EHB passed a resolution against the use of IUDs.[23]

A survey of 41 of the 413 doctors on the EHB General Medical Services panel carried out in 1982 or 1983 reported that two-thirds gave instruction in natural methods and referred patients seeking this; 90 per cent prescribed the Pill, 43 per cent prescribed condoms and 51 per cent prescribed spermicides. Almost three in four agreed that there was a need for additional family planning services. In 1983, Eithne FitzGerald, a Labour councillor (and future minister), proposed that the EHB should develop a comprehensive family planning service and officials should devise a feasibility plan.[24] They outlined three options – continuing the existing services, which were heavily dependent on GPs, with the possibility that a group of GPs might provide a dedicated family planning clinic at a Health Board clinic; designating a number of public health doctors and nurses to provide a family planning service to supplement the current GP service, or making arrangements with bodies such as NAOMI, CMAC and IFPA to provide additional services in areas where that was considered necessary. They agreed to investigate the third option.[25] At the next meeting, officials reported that the IFPA was unable to establish additional clinics but would assist by training personnel, providing literature and on-going support, and they would provide staff with a new clinic during the initial training period. CMAC were considering their response; NAOMI indicated that they were unlikely to become involved. A group of doctors was considering establishing a family planning clinic in a health board clinic. In light of these responses, the EHB decided to consider the possibility of providing some family planning services, perhaps in conjunction with the women's health screening clinics that were being established in a number of suburban areas.[26] A family planning

---

[18] EHB Minutes, 15 January 1981, accessed on Lenus website, 15 August 2017.
[19] *IT*, 16 January 1981.   [20] EHB Minutes, 15 January 1981.
[21] *IPU Review*; EHB Minutes, 3 November 1983, p. 131.
[22] UCDA P276/4 Derek Freedman Papers, 1983.   [23] EHB Minutes, 3 November 1983, p. 131.
[24] EHB Minutes, 3 November 1983, p. 130.   [25] EHB Minutes, 3 November 1983, p. 138.
[26] EHB Minutes, 15 November 1983, p. 149.

clinic, staffed by GPs, was opened in the health board clinic in Finglas in the mid-1980s.[27]

The health boards failed to assume a major role in providing family planning services, though they gave financial support to groups who provided instruction in 'natural methods'. In 1986, the EHB stated that 'Policy in relation to Family Planning Services remains to be finally settled by our Board'.[28] A study of maternity and infant schemes reported that 48 per cent of mothers had received no family planning advice. Health Boards were only legally obligated to provide family planning services in 1993.[29] The failure of the health boards to promote family planning clinics was of greatest significance in provincial Ireland. Women and men who lived at a distance from a major city had to rely on GPs and local pharmacies. In some communities, the sole GP was unwilling to prescribe the Pill or non-medical contraceptives. This problem was most acute for those holding medical cards because they would have had to pay to consult another doctor. Even if the doctor was willing to prescribe contraceptives, the local pharmacist might refuse to dispense them.

The 1979 Act enabled maternity hospitals to give more publicity and information to their family planning activities, though the hospitals appear to have been cautious. The 1982 clinical report from the Rotunda stated crisply that 'During the year a Family Planning Service was established in the Hospital'. One clinic directed by a midwife, provided natural methods exclusively; another, led by a doctor and a midwife, provided 'cap fittings and general advice'. They reported an increasing demand for IUDs and expressed the hope that they would fit these in future; however, 'it was felt that until such time as the Family Planning legislation is updated, the Hospital should not insert these devices'.[30] In 1986, Winifred O'Neill reported that most Irish maternity hospitals provided advice on 'natural' methods, only one (unnamed) offered a comprehensive family planning service.[31]

A motion that 'The IUD is not a contraceptive' was tabled at the IMA annual conference in April 1979. The outcome of the debate was a proposal by Michael Solomons that a committee should examine the workings of the IUD. Consultant gynaecologists Brendan Murphy, John Bonnar, George Henry, Eamonn O'Dwyer and Michael Solomons plus GP Ray Hawkins consulted the literature and met on six occasions, but they were unable to give an unequivocal answer.[32] Their report, published in the *JIMA*, concluded that

[27] Winifred O'Neill, 'A profile of family planning need', UCD, M. Soc. Sc. Thesis, 1986, pp. 1–71.

[28] EHB Minutes, 22 January 1986, p. 56.

[29] Earner-Byrne and Urquhart, *The Irish abortion journey*, p. 63–4.

[30] Rotunda Hospital clinical report, 1982, p. 56.

[31] As O'Neill regarded sterilisation as part of a comprehensive service it is possible that this hospital was the Victoria in Cork.

[32] Solomons, *Pro-life*, pp. 47–8.

'The consensus of opinion at the present time is that the currently available IUDS do not inhibit ovulation. While some effect on sperm transport may occur, especially with the medicated devices, the changes induced in the uterine milieu by the IUD which prevent or interfere with the process of implantation of the blastocyst are considered to be the principal mode of action of the IUD'.[33] David Nowlan claimed that this report contained nothing new, though he expressed the hope that it would provide the basis for further balanced debate.[34] The same issue of the *JIMA* published a signed editorial by one member of the group, Eamonn O'Dwyer outlining his dissenting argument. He exaggerated the adverse side-effects of an IUD and concluded by stating that 'While the Committee has not stated that an IUD is an abortifacient whatever prevents the implementation of a fertilised ovum is in effect an abortifacient'.[35] The next issue of the *Journal* carried a letter signed by two members of the IMA, expressing surprise that the report had been published before first being seen by the Council, and stating that 'The opinion at the end, ambiguously entitled "Conclusion" does not state any new information and appears to be designed to avoid an attempt to answer the controversy about whether or not the devises are abortifacient'.[36] The Institute of Obstetricians and Gynaecologists rejected demands from the Knights of Columbanus that they endorse the finding that IUDs were abortifacients.[37] Family planning clinics continued to fit IUDs, as did a number of doctors, but it would appear that the devices had to be imported surreptitiously, as was the case before the 1979 Act came into effect.

7.2   Education and Training: The Medical Profession

Although doctors were involved in family planning during the 1970s, the profession was divided. The Institute of Obstetricians and Gynaecologists sat on the fence. In 1973, it was suggested that they should determine a policy on family planning, but the executive decided that they should first discuss the question of abortion – which Michael Solomons (a member of the Institute) described as 'putting the cart before the horse'.[38] In the following year, they endorsed two statements on family planning: the first, a statement approved by the National Health Council in 1972, which was identical to the resolution passed by the 1968 UN Conference on Human Rights in Tehran: 'That

---

[33] Brendan Murphy; John Bonnar; Ray Hawkins, George Henry, Eamonn O' Dwyer Michael Solomons and J.A. Byrne (secretary to the committee), 'Report on IUCDS', *JIMA*, 73, no 5, May 1980.

[34] *IT*, 2 June 1980.   [35] *JIMA*, May 1980, report by Murphy et al.

[36] *JIMA*, July 1980.   [37] *JIMA*, February 1980; Solomons, *Pro-life*, p. 48.

[38] RCPI, Minutes Executive Committee of the Institute of Obstetricians and Gynaecologists, 1 June 1973 and 7 September 1973.

the Conference considers that couples have a basic right to decide freely and responsibly on the number and spacing of their children and the right to adequate education and information in this respect'. The second was the statement of the *Commission on the Status of Women* (quoted in Chapter 4). But there is no evidence that the Institute took any steps to make these resolutions a reality, and the Institute was not invited to participate in the Department of Health consultations prior to drafting the 1979 Act, and they did not seek a meeting or make a written submission. When the Institute discussed the proposed legislation in January 1979, Kieran O'Driscoll urged that they should be seen to take a lead in the provision of family planning services. At his suggestion, a resolution was passed 'That the Institute enthusiastically supports the concept of family planning'. They agreed to contact the Irish section of the Royal College of GPs with a view to working with them to devise a training programme in family planning for GPs.[39] The committee drafting this programme consulted widely: INO, IMA, Medical Union, Department of Health, Royal College of Psychiatrists Irish Division, FPA Dublin, FPA Cork, CMAC, NAOMI and Family Life Centre Cork.[40] Some members of the executive objected to any programme that would give instruction on how to insert an IUD. The compromise agreed was that 'the Institute had a responsibility to educate, but not to train family doctors in the various methods of Family Planning', which presumably ruled out 'training' in how to insert IUDs or diaphragms. Professor Bonnar, who was involved in devising the programme, emphasised that the 1979 Act had placed family planning in the hands of the profession and 'the Institute must provide a programme to polarised views and furthermore since the Institute represented all Ireland it must look at family planning as objectively as possible'.[41] When some members urged that the Institute should not advocate any method 'which may interfere with the continuing development of the human fertilised egg', Drs O'Driscoll and Bonnar sought to distinguish between education and advocacy. The Institute decided to hold a scientific meeting to discuss IUDs, but there is no indication that they did so.

A 1981 survey of 100 GPs conducted by the CAP, which only attracted a 49 per cent response rate, showed that almost two-thirds of respondents had no training in family planning; 10 per cent had a diploma, and 28 per cent claimed to have some other unspecified qualification.[42] Many GPs and obstetricians, who were in favour of contraception, were genuinely conflicted over the 1979 Act – especially the requirement to write prescriptions for condoms. I know of several doctors who wrote prescriptions, with great reluctance because refusal would present significant difficulties for their clients. In March 1981, a total

[39] RCPI, Minutes Executive Committee, Institute of Obstetricians and Gynaecologists, 13 January 1979; 5 September 1981.
[40] Minutes, 17 February 1979.   [41] Minutes, 8 December 1979; 2 February 1980.
[42] *II*, 17 July 1981.

of 240 doctors signed letters that were presented to the Minister for Health, declaring that they reserved the right to break the law and provide condoms to patients if their professional judgement indicated that this was advisable.[43]

In September 1983 – the fact that this coincided with the referendum on the right to life of the unborn was probably not coincidental – the ethical and executive committees of the IMA approved what *Irish Times* medical correspondent David Nowlan described as 'an extremely positive statement on the subject of family planning' – judged by the 'traditional standards of establishment medicine in Ireland'. This was a draft statement to be approved at a forthcoming meeting of the World Medical Association expressing approval of family planning, urging member organisations to become actively involved in family planning education and encouraging all medical schools to include it in the curriculum.[44]

The first training programme run by the Institute of Obstetricians and Gynaecologists and the Irish College of GPs took place in May 1981. In response to a query from Michael Solomons, the Institute confirmed that IUDs were included. Approximately 100 doctors attended the two-day course, which was sponsored by the EHB. The Institute had decided not to accept sponsorship from pharmaceutical companies or firms that provided contraceptives. This initial course provided no clinical training, and it was decided to explore how this could be added. Some members expressed concern at the possibility that doctors would be sent to family planning clinics for practical training.[45] Plans to introduce clinical training sessions progressed slowly. In 1982, the membership of the Institute's training committee was expanded to include regional representation; one of the new members was Edgar Ritchie, a founding member of the Cork family planning clinic. The expanded committee recommended a number of practical sessions (included counselling) and arranged that these would be delivered in hospitals, family planning clinics, GP surgeries, in-service training and natural family planning centres. In 1985, George Henry suggested that the existing programme requiring three sessions in natural family planning centres, and three in 'artificial' [the word minuted] family planning should be modified to provide for more sessions in 'artificial' family planning. It was later agreed that there should be flexibility with respect to the number of sessions dedicated to particular methods.[46] By 1986, this programme was providing GPs with a comprehensive training in family planning. However, the Institute declined to make it a required component of

---

[43] *IT*, 27 June 1983.   [44] *IT*, 14 September 1983.

[45] RCPI Minutes Executive Committee Institute of Obstetricians and Gynaeologists, 21 March 1981; 5 September 1981; 3 October 1981.

[46] RCPI, Institute of Obstetricians and Gynaeologists, AGM Minutes, 29 March 1985; Minutes Executive Committee, 6 January 1986.

the Diploma in Obstetrics, a post-graduate qualification that was held by most Irish GPs, on the grounds that the diploma was taken by some doctors who were not working in Ireland.[47] This decision was confirmed in 1992;[48] it meant that not all future Irish-based GPs were trained in family planning.

The slow evolution of this post-graduate diploma meant that the IFPA retained a key training role. In 1981, the Association of Irish Family Planning Clinics reported that the RCOG in London had decided that they would no longer grant certificates in family planning to doctors who had received their training in Ireland. They were unclear as to the basis for this decision but suggested that Professor Bonnar had convinced the Joint Committee that the IFPA course was not appropriate; this may have been an attempt to divert trainees to the Institute of Obstetricians and Gynaecologist's programme. In 1982, the AGM of family planning clinics was told that counselling was now a required component in UK training courses, and should be included, if they wished to secure reciprocal recognition.[49] Rivalries between the IFPA and the medical organisations eased following the decision to involve the IFPA clinics in providing practical training for doctors taking the Postgraduate Diploma in Family Planning. A key figure in this development was Edgar Ritchie, who was a member of the Association of Irish Family Planning Clinics and a member, and later chair of the joint committee of the Institute and the RCGPI.

7.3   'Natural' Family Planning

'Natural' family planning was a major beneficiary of the 1979 Act. State funding enabled NAOMI and CMAC to recruit and pay administrative staff. The services evolved – with more training sessions and new models, such as Couple to Couple training – where a male/female couple who were experienced in 'natural' methods instructed another couple. It would appear that the 'natural' family planning organisations continued to operate independently of the medical services. A draft report on family planning and GPs produced by the IMA in 1984 emphasised that family doctors should have an input into local services.

Family doctors should be in a position to refer and consult with the medical and lay personnel who organise and staff these centres and their local natural family planning centre in particular. Family doctors should have the ability to communicate with the same ease and regularity with these centres as they do with any of their consultant colleagues or any other agency to which they refer their patients. Such liaison and communication between family doctors and the staff of the natural Family Planning centres would be of immense value to both the instructors and the patients and

---

[47] Minutes, 9 June 1984.   [48] Minutes, 14 February 1992.
[49] AGM Minutes, 22 June 1982.

promote mutual confidence in each other and in the methods which they are using and their success.[50]

It is unclear when the use of natural methods began to decline in Ireland. David Geiringer claims that in England, it began to 'significantly wane in popularity' in the 1980s.[51] A midwife who was involved with 'natural' family planning in the National Maternity Hospital and through the CMAC suggested that use of 'natural' family planning declined in Ireland during the 1990s.

7.4   The Pharmacists

The Irish Pharmaceutical Union – the representative body for retail pharmacists – was one of the most aggressive players in the unfolding of the 1979 Act. The IPU was a relatively new organisation, founded in the early 1970s, and contraception featured prominently in their deliberations almost from the outset. Many members objected to pharmacists supplying the Pill; some proposed resolutions supporting 'natural' methods (which would have provided pharmacists with no significant income). Members protested that the Pharmaceutical Society – the professional regulatory body – required licensed pharmacists to dispense the contraceptive pill (though I suspect not all pharmacies complied).[52]

In 1978, a pharmacist with an address in Kilkee (Clare) wrote to *the IPU Journal*, stating that a prescription for any recognised contraceptive was 'perfectly legal'. He drew members' attention to a Department of Health memorandum circulated to each Health Board, stating that '"the services which a Health Board is empowered to provide under the Health Act 1970, must relate to the prevention or treatment of a defective condition of health". If, for the prevention or treatment of such a condition it is necessary that a person undergo a vasectomy operation or have an intra-uterine device fitted or be required to make use of contraceptive pills or appliances, there is power for these services to be provided under Chapters 2 and 3 of part 4 of the 1970 Act'. [I have failed to find a copy of this circular.] He suggested that this indicated that health boards had a legal right to supply contraceptives. The Mid-Western Health Board had reimbursed him for Ortho diaphragms and contraceptive creams dispensed on GMS prescriptions; he had submitted these for payment under the 'special items' heading.[53] This letter prompted a strongly worded attack from a Limerick pharmacist, who alleged that these contraceptives had a high failure rate and resulted in venereal disease and cervical cancer. He could not 'see how a Catholic pharmacist could possibly supply contraceptives

[50] UCDA Derek Freedman Papers, P276/6 Draft report 22/4/85.
[51] Geiringer, *The Pope and the Pill.*   [52] See *IPU Review*, May 1977, report of AGM.
[53] *IPU Review*, August 1978 – contraceptives on GMS.

to anyone without himself becoming guilty of participating in his neighbour's moral wrong doing'.[54] A Dublin pharmacist called on members, 'with a cry from the heart – I implore you, my fellow pharmacists, to heed well and take to heart the solemn teaching of the supreme pastor which condemns not only the practice of contraception as being always morally evil but warns the rulers of nations not to legalise the sale and distribution of contraceptives in their respective countries'.[55]

The prospect of legislation legalising contraception precipitated the formation of an Irish branch of the Catholic Guild of Pharmacy. The Irish founders claimed that 'The fabric of Irish Catholic family life is threatened'; the guild aimed to encourage members to preserve and promote the Catholic ethos in the practice of their profession; to defend and sustain the traditional values of Irish family life, and liaise with other guilds of Catholic pharmacists and association of Catholic doctors and nurses.[56] They circulated all retail pharmacists before the 1979 act came into effect urging them not to co-operate.[57] The *IPU Review* gave regular coverage to meetings organised by the Catholic Guild of Pharmacy.

The IPU determined that it would not give members directions about whether to dispense contraceptives. They modified their stance when the PSI – the regulatory body for pharmacists – approved an amendment to the bill permitting family planning clinics to dispense contraceptives, without consulting the IPU.[58] The Minister for Health and a senior official met IPU representatives on 20 June 1979, to smooth relations. The IPU was 'disturbed' at not being consulted about this amendment. They opposed the emergence of 'a new type of pharmacy', that is in a family planning clinic and announced that this amendment had made their poll of members null and void. Mr Haughey tried to diffuse tensions, suggesting that family planning clinics would only be licensed where a service was not being provided (through GPs and pharmacies). The licensing power was a reserve position to be determined by the Minister. The IPU was free to direct members not to operate a pharmacy in a family planning clinic; they indicated that they would do this. He undertook to give a written guarantee that no clinic would be licensed without prior consultation with the Union.[59] [I have found no evidence that they were consulted, but that does not mean that it didn't happen.]

Despite these assurances, in August 1979, the IPU announced that they would not operate the Act because the family planning clinics proposed to establish pharmacies to dispense contraceptives. They claimed that the clinics would circumvent the Act by employing a pharmacist in some capacity,

---

[54] *IPU Review*, October 1978 and January 1979.   [55] *IPU Review*, February 1979.
[56] *IPU Review*, April 1979.   [57] *IP*, 15 December 1980.
[58] *IPU Review,* June 1979.
[59] UCDA Barry Desmond papers, unlisted Box 210, 21 June Leinster House.

while leaving the dispensing to an assistant. Dr John McManus, a GP and member of the Workers' Party, denounced this as an attempt by the IPU to secure a monopoly on supplying condoms; he claimed that many pharmacies had supplied condoms for some years without prescription.[60] FPS records confirm that four of the five chemists in Tallaght had been supplying condoms without prescription for some years.[61] The IPU directed its members not to take employment in pharmacies established by family planning clinics or in pharmacies that were owned by non-pharmacists. The Federation of Family Planning Clinics responded by accusing the IPU of using the clinics as scapegoats in their campaign to secure a closed shop of pharmacy ownership. Others accused the IPU of attempting to prevent wholesalers supplying the clinics.[62]

When the Act came into effect on 1 November 1980, the IPU claimed that a majority of members were refusing to dispense contraceptives (presumably other than the Pill). They asked members not to reply to Health Boards who were attempting to compile lists of pharmacies that would operate the Act. A survey by the *Irish Press* in December 1980 reported that none of the Dublin pharmacies that they entered was willing to give a firm reply, when asked whether they stocked condoms. The article described 'a middle-aged woman chemist [who] rushed crimson faced into the back of the shop' in Talbot Street in central Dublin. Some pharmacists claimed that there was little point in stocking condoms as they were readily available in pubs and discos. No pharmacist supplying condoms could be found in Cork city. In Wexford town, four of eight pharmacists said that they would not stock them; the others declined to reply. The Limerick family planning clinic reported that only three of the fourteen local pharmacists would supply non-medical contraceptives.[63] The *Sligo Champion* claimed that local doctors and pharmacists had 'adopt[ed] a wait and see approach'.[64] Two Dublin pharmacists wrote to the *IPU Review* early in 1981 about 'the appalling situation which exists with regard to the availability of non-oral contraception'. They alleged that a majority of pharmacists 'seem to be using the so-called "conscience clause" as a means of **not** (in original) providing this very important part of the Health Service'. They noted that very few pharmacists had expressed conscientious objections to dispensing oral contraception. They asked the IPU 'to comply with this important service', but a note by the editor stated that the national executive had agreed that the operation of the family planning act should not involve compulsion.[65] In May 1981, the IPU President complained that 'no opportunity was lost by a myriad or (sic) pressure groups, and professional people who should know better, to level the finger of vilification at the community pharmacist, coupled with allegations that the Act was unworkable simply because pharmacists didn't want to work

[60] *IT*, 10 August 1979.   [61] UCDA Derek Freedman Papers, 276/11.
[62] *IPU Review*, August/September 1979.   [63] *IP*, 15 December 1980.
[64] *Sligo Champion*, 28 November 1980.   [65] *IPU Review*, February 1981.

it'. He criticised the fact that family planning clinics continued to operate 'in breach of the act and apparently a blind eye is being turned'. He alleged that there was little demand for non-medical contraceptives; three pharmacists in Bray were considering returning stock to the wholesaler because of lack of demand; a local family planning clinic and a newsagent sold condoms.[66]

Pharmacists were accused of having it both ways – failing to supply contraceptives and attempting to prevent others from doing so.[67] In 1981, the London Rubber Company, a major provider of condoms claimed that only 150 of approximately 1,200 chemists, were prepared to stock them. It was claimed that under the 1979 Act, pharmacies that were limited companies – that is part of a retail network, were not permitted to stock condoms. If that interpretation was correct, it would exclude roughly one-third of retail chemists.[68] A survey carried out by the IFPA (not an organisation that was viewed favourably by the pharmacists) in the summer of 1981 reported that 46 per cent of pharmacists would not supply contraceptives (presumably other than the Pill), a further 39 per cent declined to co-operate with the survey, only 15 per cent indicated that they supplied contraceptives.[69] Evidence suggests that sales of non-medical contraceptives through chemist shops developed slowly. By the end of 1980, ten import licenses for contraceptives had been issued – eight to wholesalers and two to chemists, but no licences had been issued for the importation of IUDs.[70]

7.5   Family Planning Clinics

Family planning clinics and mail order providers had operated in a legally grey zone in the aftermath of the McGee case. The 1979 Act ended that ambiguity. One critical issue was whether clinics could continue to supply non-medical contraceptives. 'Donations' in return for condoms constituted their major source of income, subsidising the running costs and the individual consultations and training sessions. In 1979/80, they accounted for 46 per cent of the IFPA's income.[71] In March 1979, the *Irish Times* reported that when the Ballymun Branch of the Socialist Party asked the IFPA to establish a clinic in that area, which had a large working-class population, many of child-bearing years, they replied that they were not in a position to provide further services in light of the proposed legislation, though they would be willing to instruct local doctors in family planning.[72] When the Association of Irish Family Planning Clinics met shortly after the publication of the Family Planning Bill, they concluded that the provision that those providing family planning (GPs or clinics) could not sell, supply or stock any type of contraceptive would jeopardise their

[66] *IPU Review*, May 1981.   [67] *Evening Herald*, 3 May 1982.
[68] UCDA Derek Freedman Papers, P276/10.   [69] *II*, 17 July 1981.
[70] *SI*, 16 January 1981.   [71] *IT*, 26 August 1980.   [72] *IT*, 9 March 1979.

existence. It would also create difficulties for clinics fitting diaphragms; how could they do so, if they were unable to stock them? They doubted that the health boards could provide a replacement service, because few doctors were qualified in family planning. They suggested that 'a peculiar double standard [is] to operate, that only those methods approved by the Roman Catholic church are available throughout the country without any restriction whatsoever. No minimum training is required of those teaching natural methods, and this, despite the very rigorous and lengthy training required by the O M A S'.[73]

A government amendment introduced at the committee stage enabled family planning clinics to sell contraceptives, provided that this was done through a pharmacy, and the clinic had secured a license from the Minister for Health.[74] Michael Solomons, a founding member of the IFPA, claimed that this amendment was the outcome of lobbying by clinics and their clients. '"Phone your TD Today" posters were plastered around cities and towns in an attempt to encourage our supporters to put pressure on their public representatives to amend the bill and prevent the closure of the clinics'.[75]

During the long delay (approximately one year) between the passing of the Act and the issuing of the Statutory Instrument setting out detailed requirements, the clinics debated whether to apply for a licence, or challenge the constitutionality of the Act. The advice given by James O'Reilly, UCD academic and family law expert, to the Association of Family Planning Clinics was based on the assumption that clinics would apply to the Minister for Health for a licence and would employ a dispensing chemist as required under the Act. He suggested that any client purchasing condoms by mail order should sign a form stating that they were required for bona fide family planning purposes. The staff would draw up a list of persons who had signed this statement, which would be counter-signed by a medical practitioner 'in purported compliance with the Act'. He cautioned that he had not yet had sight of the regulations, and there were indications that 'a strict regime will be applied when the regulations are made and come into effect'. Based on existing regulations governing pharmacies, a pharmacist could not divide his (sic) time between several clinics, and it was not possible under the Pharmacy Acts to purchase prescriptions through the post. A decision about a constitutional challenge should be deferred until the regulations were published. One possible ground for a challenge was the different requirements applying to those who provided a range of contraceptive services, compared with those providing 'natural' family planning.

Hugh O'Flaherty SC (a future Chief Justice) focussed on the term, 'bona fide family planning' – which the Minister had studiously avoided defining during the course of the debate –and the failure to define family. He referred

---

[73] Derek Freedman Papers, P276/1.   [74] Barry Desmond Papers unlisted Box 21,
[75] Solomons, *Pro-life*, pp. 43–4.

to the McGee case, and the Nicalaou judgment (re adoption) both based on the family founded on marriage. He suggested that 'if the phrase is given the meaning that permitted unmarried persons to have recourse to contraception – although the right was not absolute but required some element of continuity in the relationship, no matter how difficult that might prove for those who have to implement the provisions of the Act – nevertheless it might well be sufficient to preserve its constitutionality'. He also advised against taking a constitutional challenge until regulations had been drafted, 'since the Courts do not like having to try cases unless there are a discernible set of facts on which they can base their judgements'. He did not believe that the Act infringed religious freedom as set out in the Constitution, and unlike O'Reilly, he was not concerned about having a chemist present at all times, but he was concerned about the implications for mail order sales.

Paul McNally SC gave some comfort to the clinics by citing a Supreme Court Judgment, Donegal Marts 1967, which argued that 'the Minister must exercise his licensing powers in accordance with the principles of constitutional justice'. Family planning clinics would have a right to a hearing if refused a licence; the fact that they existed gave a further defence relating to their property rights. He commented that it was 'significant' that the Minister had discussed the drafting of the Bill, 'with almost every relevant body except the family planning clinics' despite their expertise in this field. The failure to consult them before drafting the legislation (though the Minister and Department of Health officials had met representatives of the IFPA) amounted to a breach of the constitutionally guaranteed right of constitutional justice as established in the case of In re Haughey 1971:

Throughout the whole history of the pre-drafting consultations, the drafting and the passing of the Bill through the two Houses of the Oireachtas, the Minister appears to have regarded the existing family planning clinics as renegades or outlaws whose only raison d'être arises from a defect in the legislative network arising from the Supreme Court decision in McGee.

He suggested that these prejudices 'may result in his Family Planning Bill being declared unconstitutional in the courts'. The fact that a married couple might be unable to purchase condoms without travelling long distances might be deemed to infringe on their constitutional rights. A doctor who refused contraception to a married couple would be obliged to indicate the reasons for refusal and listen to their point of view, otherwise, he would be guilty of infringing the constitutional right of natural justice. Requiring a couple to approach a doctor to seek a prescription for condoms could breach their constitutional right to marital privacy.[76]

---

[76] UCDA Derek Freedman Papers, Box 1, 6 November 1979 – Counsel's opinion.

FPS, which was incorporated in 1972 to supply contraceptives by mail order and to clients who visited their premises, faced particular difficulties, and perhaps for that reason, they would appear initially to have adopted a more militant attitude. A meeting in September 1979 examined the possibility of FPS mounting a constitutional challenge. Eamonn Walsh SC suggested that 'it would weaken both the case and position of FPS if a case were to be run on the lines of making contraceptives available to unmarried people'. He agreed that the new legislation prohibited giving away contraceptives or sending them through the post. While Section 2 imposed an obligation on the Minister to provide a comprehensive natural family planning service, it imposed no obligation to provide any form of service that involved the use of contraceptives. Health Boards were required to provide natural family planning, but clinics providing access to contraception would only be licensed if the Minister was satisfied that is in the public interest and meets a particular need. On that basis, he suggested that the bill was discriminatory – supporting natural family planning and discouraging alternatives. As to whether it was unconstitutional, he suggested 'the critical test appears to be the reasonable availability of contraceptives and advice and information'. If pharmacies and GPs implemented the Bill, it would be difficult to have it declared unconstitutional. He believed that the bill was constitutional. If a constitutional challenge was mounted, it would be unwise for FPS to be the sole plaintiff. Eamonn Walsh and Hugh O'Flaherty both expressed the opinion that a legal challenge would be stronger if a clinic had attempted to operate the Act unsuccessfully. FPS would be in a much stronger position to mount a legal challenge if they were refused a licence. Whether to operate within the Act or outside, with a consequent risk of prosecution was a matter for the FPS Board.

At a further briefing in May 1980, Aidan Browne indicated that FPD – the trading company wing of FPS, which supplied contraceptives to family planning clinics and individual clients, would be in a different place to the clinics, because of the commercial nature of the business. He felt that they had no real choice other than to proceed with a declaratory action as soon as the regulations were published, on the basis of reasonable access to contraception. He suggested that they identify three married couples who were willing to take a legal challenge – two from outside Dublin, one having been deprived of mail order contraception, the second denied contraceptives by their local chemist; the third should be from Dublin. He advised that 'we should [not] allow ourselves to be carried away on extreme examples, such as that of a person living on an island whose Doctor is a conscientious objector'; the State was not bound to make contraception available in the same way as it is bound to provide free primary education. There was some discussion about taking a case to the European Court.[77]

---

[77] UCDA Derek Freedman Papers, P276/1. Summary of briefing with Aidan Browne on 15 May 1980: present Frank Crummey, Anne Connolly (solr) and Brigid Barry JC.

When the regulations were eventually published in August 1980, many key issues remained unresolved. Clinics could operate only with the minister's consent, however in a statement, the Minister noted that a pharmaceutical chemist 'may sell contraceptives in connection with the service he provides in keeping open shop at a place where family planning services are made available'. The IPU gave a less dogmatic response to the opening of pharmacies in family planning clinics, and it would appear that they had dropped their threat not to co-operate with the Act if the clinics were licensed.[78]

The message from legal experts was that clinics should apply for a licence. But the 1979 Act conflicted with the core values of those who ran family planning clinics.[79] The CAP – a left-wing feminist group that advocated free access to contraception for all and a liberal approach to abortion – urged clinics not to apply for licenses.[80] But CAP did not operate a clinic, so their stance presented no difficulties. When the Association of Family Planning Clinics met shortly after the regulations were published, they expressed the opinion that the regulations contained 'a clear hint that health boards could sublet a family planning service for medical card holders' and suggested that they should discuss this possibility with the health boards. The section on advertising was ambiguous – they believed that clinics could continue to advertise, and it should be possible to frustrate government interference if they applied for and received consent to operate a clinic. The outcome of a 'lengthy discussion' is perhaps best summarised by Robert Cochran of FPS, who had previously favoured mounting a constitutional challenge. His position had changed from one of outright opposition to viewing the legislation as a purely tactical question.[81] The IFPA announced that it would apply for consent to operate, but this would not preclude them from expressing opposition to the legislation and supporting clinics that opted not to seek the minister's consent. IFPA information officer Christine Donaghy claimed that the legislation was so complicated that Senior Counsel 'were already unable to offer interpretations of it'.[82]

When the Act came into effect in November 1980, the IFPA and clinics in Cork, Galway and Bray had applied for licences. Well Woman decided to defy the law, likewise the Family Planning Centre in Merrion Square,[83] the Limerick clinic was undecided, though they later secured a licence. In the final days of October, the *Irish Times* reported panic buying of condoms. One Dublin clinic claimed that sales had increased four-fold in recent weeks with

[78]   *IT*, 2 August 1980 also the regulations.
[79]   UCDA Derek Freedman Papers, P276/1 Minutes meeting 21 June 1980.
[80]   *IT*, 19 August 1980.
[81]   Derek Freedman Papers, P276/1. Minutes 19 August 1980.   [82]   *IT*, 26 August 1980.
[83]   This would appear to be the clinic operated by Dr James Loughran, who had parted company with the IFPA, and continued to operate a clinic in Merrion Square, the location of Ireland's first stand-alone family planning clinic.

people buying Durex by the gross.[84] There were queues outside the IFPA clinic in central Dublin.[85] Minister for Health Michael Woods issued a licence to the IFPA, but he refused them permission to sell contraceptives in their clinics. The IFPA announced that they would seek to open a pharmacy, but they feared that the Minister might prevent this, and even if they were permitted to do so, the cost of the pharmacist and pharmacy would reduce their income.[86] Supplemental advice issued by James O'Reilly shortly after the regulations came into effect, suggested that the key issues for the clinics related to the Pharmacy Acts. 'By applying and incorporating the Pharmacy Acts into the sale and supply of contraceptives, the 1979 Statute in effect places contraceptives in a similar position to poisons and medicines'. The Act could not be interpreted as giving a doctor the power to dispense contraceptives, and there was no provision for mail order sales.

The legalisation of sales of non-medical contraceptives created new commercial opportunities. Family planning clinics were precluded from holding a licence to import contraceptives. FPD, which had supplied condoms to the clinics, ceased trading in the summer of 1980 and was planning to go into liquidation. When this was discussed at a meeting of the clinics, 'a number of people expressed the view that the mutual trust among Clinics had gone'.[87] FPS set up a new company, Dearsley, which secured a licence to import contraceptives. Although Dearsley sales doubled between October and December 1981 – indicating that the 1979 Act had almost certainly increased access to non-medical contraceptives – it was only marginally solvent by the end of 1981.[88] The London Rubber Company, a leading manufacturer of condoms, recommended that Dearsley concentrate on supplying family planning clinics and not attempt to supply chemists, which would require three to six sales representatives.[89] The LRC was intent on securing a significant share of the Irish market and appeared to be seeking a more commercial importer/distributor. When Dearsley decided to increase its prices, this led to tensions with the family planning clinics. Well Woman threatened to change its supplier. A sales report by Dearsley noted that from October to December 1981, clinics accounted for 81.5 per cent, 87 per cent and 90 per cent of total sales, respectively, which suggests that many couples continued to secure contraceptives from clinics, rather than seek a doctor's prescription or face the possibility that their local chemist might not supply them. Pharmacies accounted for approximately 10 per cent of sales. The balance came from sales to doctors.

When Dearsley approached wholesalers who supplied retail pharmacies, one said that they were reluctant to get involved on a national level 'because they

---

[84] *IT*, 29 October 1980.   [85] *EH*, 30 October 1980.
[86] *EH*, 30 October 1980.   [87] Derek Freedman Papers, P276/3, 21 June 1980.
[88] UCDA Derek Freedman Papers P276/3, FPS supplies 1980–81 meeting, 10 December 1981.
[89] UCDA P276/3, 28 October 1981; 5 November 1981.

felt this is a sensitive area which could damage the reputation of their other products'. A second distributor gave an almost identical response; a third was only interested, if they secured exclusive rights to distribute Durex throughout Ireland.[90] Well Woman apparently attempted to secure the Durex franchise. Commercial companies were also interested; there is evidence of a transition to a more commercial environment. A growing number of pharmacies were supplying non-medical contraceptives without prescription, and FPS feared that this would affect sales.[91]

Data in the Dearsley records, which appear to date from 1982, lists 127 pharmacies that they supplied: 38 in Dublin city and county; elsewhere in Leinster – Carlow 1, Kildare 4, Louth 1, Kildare 4; Kilkenny 3, Meath 4, Longford 2, Louth 1; Offaly 1, Westmeath 2, Wexford 8, and Wicklow 3. They supplied eight pharmacies in Cork, city and county, two in Kerry, five in Limerick, five in Tipperary and five in Waterford, four in Monaghan, four in Donegal but only one in Cavan, one in Clare, one in Leitrim, two in Roscommon, five in Galway and a surprising ten in Mayo. Dearsley was one of several suppliers; nevertheless, the pattern is interesting. The large number of outlets in Mayo may reflect the fact that Dearsley supplied Ballina-based, United Drug, who distributed condoms in that region. The absence of stockists in Louth suggests that people were sourcing supplies across the border and perhaps selling them locally without a prescription; the same might apply in Cavan. But Kerry, a large county, distant from Northern Ireland, had only two supplying pharmacies.[92] In 1983, journalist Nell McCaffrey, writing about the 'Kerry babies' – a complex story where an unmarried mother was charged with murder of her baby/babies, noted that no pharmacy in the nearby town [Listowel] sold condoms.[93] Dearsley's figure of 127 pharmacies is broadly in line with evidence assembled by Minister for Health Barry Desmond that there were pharmacies supplying condoms in 118 towns.[94] The patchy supply meant that some doctors defied the Act by supplying patients directly. Dearsley supplied thirty-eight doctors – many were GPs, but the list includes gynaecologists and eight doctors had addresses in Dublin or surrounding suburbs.

No clinic closed because of the 1979 Act, and their compliance with the legislation was partial, at best. FPS and the IFPA introduced training/advice on Billings as required under the law. Each clinic designated a medical director, which presented no difficulty, because all had medical personnel attached. Some continued to supply condoms without prescription, and they became a

[90] UCDA, P276/10, Dearsley, progress report, 1 December 1981.
[91] UCDA P 276/11 Directors' meeting, 16 June 1983.   [92] UCDA, P276/11.
[93] Cited in Earner Byrne and Urquhart, *The Irish abortion journey*, p. 63. On the 'Kerry babies' story, see Inglis, *Truth, power and lies, Irish Society and the case of the Kerry babies*.
[94] NAI DT 2015/88/611 Health Family Planning Amendment Bill 1984.

major source of contraception for single people. FPS continued to offer a mail order service. In April 1981, one-quarter of sales by family planning clinics was through illegal mail orders. The IFPA, who accounted for 40 per cent of Dearsley's sales, employed a pharmacist for 7–8 hours a week, but they were warned that 'this front to the law is wafer thin'.

In April 1981, the directors of FPS concluded that the risks of prosecution were extremely slim. That assumption was challenged some months later when an inspector from the local garda station visited their offices and asked to speak to 'someone in charge'. His inquiries concerned a long-running advertisement by FPS in the *Sunday World*, offering discounts on sales of condoms. Advertisements targeting the public infringed Section 3 of the 1979 Act. The inspector reported that he was acting on a request sent to several garda districts. He was not taking a statement, merely reporting on the situation. FPS explained that they had applied for a license in November 1980, but the application was still pending, over a year later. When the inspector asked whether FPS was selling contraceptives, they 'fudged' the issue by talking about the need to have diaphragms for fitting and emphasising that they provided a high-quality medical service.[95] FPS discontinued the advertisements for a brief period. In March 1982, the directors were asked to appear at Donnybrook garda station, but this summons was dropped following a letter from their solicitor.

In September 1982, FPS held a seminar marking their tenth anniversary, where they reflected on the current state of family planning services. The absence of government recognition for a comprehensive family planning service provided through health boards and private clinics 'has both curtailed and stifled the activities of private clinics who have had to tread carefully and delicately in a number of areas, and, in particularly on matters of advertising'. Family planning clinics remained confined to the cities, and while attendance was rising, the clients were mainly middle class. FPS suggested that the clinics should lobby the government demanding a national service. The constraints of the 1979 Act were most evident, with respect to advertising. Unlicensed 'pirate' radio stations had been willing to carry advertisements in the past, but with indications that the government was considering licensing private radio stations, Radio Nova and Sunshine Radio were refusing to carry advertisements, though Nova had carried an interview about the work of FPS.[96] FPS continued to publish small advertisements in any publication that would accept them. They were shifting from upmarket/specialist publications to free sheets, and publications that reached a rural audience. By the early 1980s, the *Irish Farmers' Journal* was carrying advertisements for family planning services,

---

[95] UCDA Derek Freedman Papers, P 276/3 R Cochran memo to FPS directors, 22 December 1981.
[96] UCDA Derek Freedman Papers, P 276/3, FPS, 11 February 1982.

and not simply 'natural' family planning as was the case in the 1970s; one advertisement in 1983 was placed close to a 'Lonely Hearts' advertisement, which claimed that many farmers wished to meet 'girls'.[97] FPS would continue to advertise in *Image* (a glossy woman's magazine) 'since it leads to a quality image and reaches more women aged 15–34 than any other quality magazine'. Having failed to place advertisements in the ICA magazine, they were targeting *The Woman's Club*, which had a rural circulation of 13,300 'and whatever newspapers needed to reach women in rural areas'.[98] In February 1983, FPS was contacted by Sunday Newspapers Ltd, who reported that the advertising standards authority had stated that their advertisements did not now contravene the advertising code, which enabled them to advertise in mass media.

In December 1982, Dr Andrew Rynne, a prominent advocate of family planning, appeared in Naas District Court on charges of having supplied condoms to a patient; this was the first court case under the 1979 Act. Gardaí raided his surgery and seized condoms, which had been supplied by Dearsley. The case was adjourned for six months. A local pharmacist claimed that 'three packets of 12 [condoms] will last me at least a month', because Dr Rynne was supplying at least 200 packets to clients. FPS lawyers recommended that Dearsley set up a shelf company and obtain an import licence as a precaution in case they were pursued by the Director of Public Prosecution.[99] Dr Rynne was fined £500; an *Irish Times* article by Mary Maher suggests that he may have been targeted because of his prominence in the campaign against the Pro-Life Amendment.[100] Twenty-eight women members of the socialist group in the European Parliament offered to pay his fine, but his sentence was cancelled on appeal and he was given the Probation Act. He told the court that he would continue to defy the Act.[101]

Despite the difficulties presented by the 1979 Act, the evidence suggests that family planning clinics extended their services. Well Woman, which did not apply for a licence, opened new premises in the north inner city, which became their base for handling abortion referrals and travel arrangement to Britain.[102] The clinics introduced new services in fields such as sexual health, psycho-sexual counselling, holistic programmes relating to women's health, including the menopause, male sterilisation and adolescent sexuality.[103] They co-operated with the Health Education Bureau in providing information on these topics and expert speakers for sessions in community centres. FPS was working with the Rutland Centre – an addiction treatment centre. They noted

---

[97] *Irish Farmers Journal*, 26 March 1983.
[98] UCDA Derek Freedman Papers, P276/3 FPS tenth anniversary seminar, 16 September 1982.
[99] UCDA P 276/3 FPS, 10 December 1982.   [100] *IT*, 27 June 1983.
[101] *IT*, 13 July 1983, 8 December 1983; 9 December 1983;   [102] Anne Connolly interview.
[103] See List of IFPA files held in RCPI.

that a nurse from Holles St had visited their clinic and asked about the services provided; she had taken a supply of leaflets and a practice diaphragm.[104]

FPS failed to secure a licence, presumably because it was involved in distributing contraceptives. In 1983, they claimed that their application was 'in limbo'; it was neither rejected nor granted.[105] The goal was to reach a more working-class clientele, and they explored various options, including a mobile clinic. They opened a clinic one morning a week, in Bawnogue Shopping Centre in Clondalkin in the offices of a local GP, and they contacted the EHB with a proposal to run family planning sessions in EHB clinics in communities with a large working-class and younger population. One doctor with a practice in Tallaght suggested that they should hold a clinic in his surgery fitting IUDs and diaphragms, but he was not keen that they would 'take his pill practice away'. When FPS suggested that they would probably need 'some pill practice' plus sales of condoms to make the clinic viable, he reported that condoms were available without prescription in Tallaght chemist shops – yet another example of how changing circumstances disrupted the business model that had underpinned the family planning clinics.[106] The Bawnogue clinic opened in June 1982; a clinic in Tallaght opened some months later. But Bawnogue was described as developing 'slowly', Tallaght 'even more slowly'.

In 1984, the medical director attached to FPS presented a report to the board setting out current developments and ways of improving their service. Many clients were seeking advice on gynaecological problems, infertility and sexuality.

Subjects which were previously taboo were being responded to. Because there was no precedent to follow clinic staff were often unprepared, in terms of training and experience, to deal with these needs. Naturally our responses were sometimes inadequate and clumsy. However, we learned as we went along and we can now see that what the public expects from the staff of a family planning clinics is a comprehensive family planning, well-woman and sexual health service.... Because all these areas are sexually-related and because most people who visit the clinic will have grown up and lived in an atmosphere of sexual repression, ignorance and prejudice, they will generally have feelings of anxiety and/or guilt and/or fear when they arrive. They may well feel intimidated by the articulate, seemingly confident and sexually healthy staff. They will probably feel sexually inadequate. In such circumstances they may not be able to articular their needs or anxieties and will often leave the clinic not having got what they really wanted. They may use a request for contraception or a pregnancy test or complaint of vaginal discharge, etc. as a 'visiting card' in the hope that what is really troubling them will come out one way or another. All members of staff must be aware of these issues and know how to respond.[107]

[104] UCDA Derek Freedman Papers, P276/4.
[105] UCDA Derek Freedman Papers, P276/4, 2 November 1983.
[106] UCDA Derek Freedman Papers, P276/4 FPS, 23 June 1982.
[107] UCDA Derek Freedman papers, P276/5, 16 February 1984 meeting of directors.

The number of callers to IFPA clinics rose steadily, and the number who were described as working class almost doubled between 1979 and 1982 – from 15,683 to 30,631. There was only a marginal increase in the number of middle-class clients – from 11,243 to 11,997.[108] By 1982, 59 per cent of working-class and 53 per cent of middle-class clients were single.[109] In 1984, Mary Maher described Saturday morning visitors to the Cathal Brugha Street clinic in central Dublin, as mostly young and male. IFPA staff told her that clients were less concerned about remaining anonymous, and they no longer had to keep a list of sympathetic priests who would speak to clients; 60 per cent of IFPA income came from sales of condoms.[110] A flyer for the IFPA clinics dating from the mid-1980s listed the services offered: the Pill, cap/diaphragm fitting, IUCD insertion, Billings and rhythm instruction, smear tests, cytology, breast examination, sterilization, menopause sexual problems counselling, pregnancy testing and counselling. Non-medical contraceptives were sold by a pharmacist in the clinics and by post.[111]

In 1982, Well Woman organised a seminar, which was open to the other clinics, to examine the medical and legal aspects of post-coital contraception, with contributions from Dr Moira Woods and Adrian Hardiman, SC.[112] While Well Woman had no inhibitions about supplying post-coital contraception, there appears to have been a strong consensus among FPS staff against doing so. They described the treatment as 'controversial'; if it proved ineffective, they would be faced with requests for abortion referrals, which they were unwilling to supply. FPS decided to make it known that they did not supply post-coital contraception, but they would compile a report on the usage of the drug in other countries including the failure rate, together with a list of medical practitioners 'who are particularly experienced in this field and who could refer for abortion in cases of rape'.[113] In 1983, 3–4 per cent of callers to the IFPA's Synge Street clinic sought post-coital contraception, and it would appear that they were facilitated.[114] The provision of contraception to young people under eighteen years was another issue for discussion. FPS determined that nobody would be turned away on the basis of age.[115]

7.5.1   Amending the 1979 Act

Despite the undoubted limitations of the 1979 Act, access to contraception improved in the early 1980s. A survey carried out by the EHB in December

---

[108] Máire Nic Ghiolla Phadraig, 'Social and cultural factors in family planning', pp. 69–72.
[109] Nic Ghiolla Phadraig, p. 72.   [110] *IT*, 9 January 1984.   [111] RCPI, IFPA archives, box 10.
[112] UCDA Derek Freedman Papers, P 276/3 FPS medical report, June 1982.
[113] UCDA Derek Freedman Papers, P 276/3 FPS, 15 April 1982, medical report for March Director's meeting, 22 April 1982.
[114] *IT*, 9 May 1984.
[115] UCDA Derek Freedman Papers, P 276/3FPS October 1982 medical report.

1985 showed that 85 per cent of GPs who were participating in the GMS scheme wished to be included in a list of family planning providers that the Board was planning to compile; 81 per cent indicated that they provided instruction on the calendar method; 76 per cent on the temperature method and 66 per cent provided instruction on Billings. About 93 per cent prescribed the Pill; 71 per cent prescribed spermicides but only 32 per cent wrote prescriptions for condoms; 42 per cent fitted diaphragms and 30 per cent fitted IUDs. A majority (57 per cent) claimed to have specific training in family planning, and one-third held a qualification in family planning. This suggests that the range of services and expertise provided by GPs had increased significantly. Pharmacists in the EHB area appear to have modified their attitude; 75 per cent were willing to be listed as providing services under the Act; 89 per cent dispensed the Pill; 56 per cent dispensed contraceptive jelly and creams; 71 per cent dispensed condoms and 26 per cent dispensed diaphragms. A majority of those who were not currently dispensing contraceptives did not intend to do so in future.

The main limitation of this survey is the poor response rate: 40 per cent of GPs and 34 per cent of pharmacists. It is probable that the non-respondents included a disproportionate number of conservative doctors and pharmacists. The directors of Community Care reported that family planning services were adequately spread and readily available throughout the EHB area.[116] Nevertheless, a study 190 post-natal mothers interviewed in the Rotunda in October 1985 concluded that there had been no increase in the use of birth control since 1980 by working-class women and their knowledge of their personal fertility remained poor. Women who used family planning were more likely to belong to higher socio-economic groups hold private health insurance and have completed second level schooling. However, it also concluded that family planning services provided by GPs in the EHB region appeared adequate. Women who had used these services reported a high level of satisfaction, though many working-class women were not aware of their existence.[117]

There was no prospect that the 1979 Act would end the debate over contraception. A general election in 1982 resulted in a stable Fine Gael/Labour Coalition that lasted until 1987. Labour TD Barry Desmond became Minister for Health. The programme for government included a commitment to review the legislation relating to contraception. By February 1983, the Department of Health had determined that contraceptives could be purchased on prescription in 118 towns, but they were not available in large areas of provincial Ireland. When the Minister met FPS, they reported that he appeared to have data showing that 360 chemists sold contraceptives. In 1985, Barry Desmond informed the Dáil that the Department's review showed that only one-quarter of pharmacies sold contraceptives.

---

[116] EHB Minutes, 9/1/1986, pp. 9–10.
[117] O'Neill, 'A profile of family planning need', p. vi.

The 1983 conviction of Dr Andrew Rynne for selling condoms prompted the Council of the IMA to write to the Minister for Health, Barry Desmond, urging him to honour his commitment to reform the 1979 Family Planning Act, as a matter of urgency.[118] The Minister was keen to remove the requirement for a prescription to buy condoms, which had prompted many complaints from the medical profession. In 1984, he performed the official opening of an FPS clinic in Dun Laoghaire, knowing that it was not licensed and would sell condoms without a prescription. The *Evening Herald* carried the story under the headline 'Minister opens law-breaking clinic', reporting that 'That "Irish solution to an Irish problem" took on a ludicrous dimension today as the Minister for Health opened a clinic which will operate in breach of the current Family Planning Act'. It noted that as Barry Desmond opened the clinic the Well Woman Centre faced prosecution for selling condoms 'on a non-prescription basis'.[119]

There were risks associated with any amending legislation because a number of Fine Gael and Labour TDs were opposed to even minor reform, and in November 1984, seventeen medical consultants (many of them veterans of the PLAC) warned that more liberal access to contraceptives would result in increased promiscuity, rampant venereal disease and an increasing incidence of cervical cancer. These assertions were countered by a smaller group of doctors.[120] The government gave approval for revised legislation, though a note from the parliamentary draftsman would appear to suggest that the reference to 'bona fide family planning purposes' should remain; the Minister was determined to remove it.[121]

The draft legislation removed the requirement for a prescription for non-medical contraceptives; it expanded the outlets permitted to supply and sell contraceptives to include doctors' surgeries, health board hospitals and recognised family planning clinics. Non-medical contraceptives were not to be supplied to those under eighteen years – the submission to Cabinet noted that this restriction 'has regard to currently accepted views about the age at which young people may be regarded as having reached maturity'. State funding for family planning remained confined to methods that met the approval of the Catholic church.[122]

Garret FitzGerald does not mention the 1985 Act in his extensive memoirs.[123] The Bill was debated against the background of the divisive 1983 Pro-Life Amendment, a sharp fall in the birth rate among married couples and a substantial rise in births to single mothers, including many teenage mothers. The 1983 death in childbirth of fifteen-year-old Anne Lovett beside a religious

---

[118] *IT*, 13 July 1983.   [119] *EH*, 16 April 1984.
[120] Barry Desmond, *Finally and in conclusion. A political memoir*, (New Island Books, Dublin, 2000), pp. 238–40.
[121] NAI DT 2017/2/1189 Health family planning amendment bill.
[122] NAI DT 2015/88/611 Health Family Planning Amendment Bill 1984; 6 November 1984.
[123] Beatty, 'Irish modernity and the politics of contraception 1979–1993', p. 108.

grotto in Granard had prompted emotional outrage and a debate over teenage sexuality. The bill should also be seen in the context of the government's New Ireland Forum,[124] which had debated the question of legislation that reflected the views of a particular religious community. Senator John Robb, a Northern Ireland surgeon from a liberal Protestant tradition, claimed that rejecting the bill would boost partition.[125] The measure was opposed by Fianna Fáil, a number of Labour and Fine Gael deputies and senators, and by individual bishops, but not by the Catholic hierarchy acting collectively.[126] It formed the theme of Lenten pastorals from the Archbishop of Armagh, Cardinal Cahal Daly, Archbishop of Dublin, Kevin McNamara, Bishop of Limerick Dr Newman and Dr Conway of Elphin. Cardinal Daly denounced contraception as morally wrong; his warning of the grave social consequences that would follow any liberalisation of the current law was supported by sixty priests in the Armagh diocese. Barry Desmond responded by asking who ran the country – the church or the state? The intense pressure reflected the government's slim majority, and the fact that several back-bench government deputies were known to oppose the measure. A number of government deputies were subjected to considerable personal abuse. This was not new – what was new was the fact that they made it publicly known; two Galway deputies were given garda protection. A summary of local newspapers in the *Irish Times* suggests that traditional moral outrage still flourished – the *Donegal Democratic* denounced the legislation as 'A licence for immorality', but the *Kilkenny People* had absorbed the message of the New Ireland Forum; it referred to the old Northern Ireland government legislating to enforce the majority Unionist point of view and ignoring the views and needs of the Catholic minority. When the bill passed the second reading, by a narrow majority of 83 to 80, Minister for Foreign Affairs, Peter Barry, claimed that it had met the Forum challenge.[127]

Barry Desmond described the debate as 'intensive, frequently emotional and invariably party partisan'. His most intemperate opponents included Fine Gael deputies Oliver J. Flanagan and Alice Glenn. Fianna Fáil leader, Charles Haughey, determined without consultation that his party should oppose the measure, a decision that prompted some opposition among TDs. In the end, only Des O'Malley failed to oppose the bill, and he was expelled from the party for his action.[128] The Fianna Fáil deputies voting against the Bill included John O'Connell, who had co-sponsored legislation on family planning in the early 1970s. In 1992, as Minister for Health, he removed all restrictions on sales of non-medical contraception.

---

[124] The Forum for a New Ireland 1983–84 was established by Taoiseach Garret FitzGerald to debate the issues that needed to be resolved in order to improve north/south relations.
[125] *IT*, 14 February 1985.   [126] Hug, *The politics of sexual morality*, p. 119.
[127] NAI DT 2017/77/171, Press cuttings mainly February 1985.
[128] Desmond, *Finally and in conclusion*, pp. 241–4.

Having failed to prevent the Bill being passed by the Oireachtas, opponents tried to persuade the President not to sign it into law. This campaign appears to have been initiated by Family Solidarity. A handwritten note from the Secretary to the President noted that the bill had 'generated a lot of heat inside and outside the Dáil', mainly in relation to 'free votes', 'matters of conscience', etc., and the President had received many letters asking him not to sign the bill, but to refer it to the courts. The official concluded that 'Much of the writing has been organised, with advertisements from one group appearing in last Sunday's paper urging people to write to the President'. He claimed that none of the letters presented 'any case of substance'. Many came from inveterate protesters against earlier contraceptive bills, and representatives of organisations such as Parent Concern and the Family Rights Council. Letters writers included Fr James McDyer a priest who was active in rural development in the west of Ireland and a parish priest, writing 'on behalf of the people of Clonmacnoise'.[129] The Secretary to the President had spoken to 'a few influential Churchmen' and had pointed out the implications of referring a Bill to the Supreme Court; he noted that these churchmen 'will, of course, unfortunately remain silent'.[130] [If the President refers a Bill to the Supreme Court and they determine that it is constitutional, it cannot be challenged in future.] There is a decided irony in the efforts of these conservative interest groups to have the legislation referred to the Supreme Court, given that the PLAC campaign had centred on fears that the Supreme Court might legalise abortion, following a legal challenge.

The reformed legislation made life much easier for family planning clinics and GPs who were willing to supply contraceptives, but a motion at a meeting of the EHB demanding a substantial commitment to providing family planning was not carried.[131] The 1985 budget reduced the rate of VAT on contraceptives from 35 per cent to 23 per cent. The market for non-medical contraceptives had grown at an annual rate of 9 per cent over the previous three years. The growing availability of non-medical contraception removed the major source of income for family planning clinics. The emergence of AIDS as a then-fatal disease meant that the market expanded even more rapidly in later years. Community pharmacists had overcome their reservations and were now the main source of non-medical contraception.

7.6   Availability of Contraception by Health Board Area: Figures Dating from 1987

Western 136 GPs and 113 Pharmacies
Mid-Western 121 GPs and 101 Pharmacies

---

[129] Letters are on NAI DT 2015/77/94.   [130] NAI DT 2015/77/93.
[131] EHB Minutes, 22 January 1986.

Southern 202 GPs and 191 Pharmacies
North-Western 88 GPs and 89 Pharmacies
Midlands 84 GPs and 78 Pharmacies
South-Eastern 221 GPs and 109 Pharmacies
North-Eastern 104 GPs and 96 Pharmacies
Eastern 379 GPs and 396 Pharmacies

In December 1987, FPS held an extraordinary AGM to amend the memo-randum of association which set out the objects for which the company was established, following the example of the IFPA by focussing its efforts on education, training and problems relating to fertility and sexual relations.[132]

By the mid-1980s, family planning had become an integral part of the lives of most young married couples. A survey with 100 first-time pregnant married women and 100 first-time pregnant single women who attended the National Maternity Hospital in 1986 showed that 81 per cent of married women had used contraception, compared with 36 per cent of single women.[133] Only 20 per cent of single Irish women who had abortions in England in 1984 had used contraception.[134] Seventy-five per cent of the single women included in the National Maternity Hospital study who had not intended to become pregnant, had not used contraception, and this was not a reflection of religious scruples, education or any factor other than their single status. Greene et al concluded that

lack of sex education, lack of information on contraception, poor access to contraceptive methods and social embarrassment and difficulties about the use of contraception may be important determinants of the single women's failure to use contraception – despite its wide acceptability to married women.[135]

Conservative groups continued to achieve intermittent successes. Plans for a clinic in Cavan were foiled on three occasions when selected premises proved to be no longer available. In 1991, the IFPA was fined £500 for unlaw-fully selling condoms in Dublin's Virgin Megastore.[136] IPU members were instructed not to stock the brand sold by Virgin because the IPU believed that it would shortly be on sale in supermarkets. By the early 1990s, improving access to condoms was increasingly linked with efforts to prevent the spread of AIDS. The first cases in Ireland were diagnosed in 1982, but the number diagnosed annually remained in single figures until 1987. It peaked at seventy-five cases in 1994 and again in 1995. In contrast to other western countries, the

---

[132] UCDA Derek Freedman Papers, P276/8.
[133] Sheila Greene, Marie-Therese Joy, J.K. Nugent and P. O'Mahony, 'Contraceptive practice of Irish married and single first-time mothers', *Journal of Biosocial Science*, 21, 1989, p. 380.
[134] Geoffrey Dean, A Walsh, D. O'Hare & H. Mc Louglin, (Medico-Social Research Board, Dublin, 1985), *Termination of pregnancy England 1984: women from the Republic of Ireland.*
[135] Greene et al, 'Contraceptive practice of Irish married and single first-time mothers', p. 384.
[136] Hug, *The politics of sexual morality*, p. 122.

largest number occurred among intravenous drug users, 40 per cent of diagnoses between 1983 and 1999 were in intravenous drug users, compared with 30 per cent in homosexual males. Because homosexual acts remained illegal in Ireland until 1993, the health authorities were unwilling to play a major role in providing health advice on AIDs; that gap was filled by Gay Health Action and other voluntary groups, who urged the importance of condoms and communicated their message to intravenous drug users.[137] The IFPA cited the growing risk of AIDS in its defence against prosecution for selling condoms in the Virgin Megastore, which had longer opening hours than pharmacies and was welcoming and accessible to young people. Condom Sense, a group who installed condom vending machines in pubs, night clubs and other locations identified as AIDS activists, not as promoters of family planning.[138] In 1992, Minister for Health John O'Connell introduced legislation lowering the age for purchasing contraceptives to seventeen – the age of consent for heterosexual sex; younger users would have to be married or secure a prescription, but there is no evidence that these requirements were enforced. Sales outlets expanded, but the ban on vending machines continued. The minister conceded that these residual restrictions were maintained to respect 'the concerns of many groups, and individuals, not least parents'.[139] In 1993, Minister for Health Brendan Howlin removed condoms from the definition of contraceptives which meant that no minimum age applied and they could be sold through vending machines. Restrictions on advertising were also lifted. The legislation was uncontroversial; only three TDs opposed the legislation.

7.6.1   Male and Female Sterilisation

When we look at the long-drawn out and often heated debates on contraception, sterilisation is the dog that didn't bark. Although male and female sterilisation for contraceptive purposes was contrary to the teaching of the Catholic church, vasectomy and tubal legation were never illegal in Ireland, and there is no evidence that any government minister or civil servant attempted to restrict these clinical practices. The topic was avoided, not discussed. Access was restricted by members of the medical and nursing professions, hospital ethics committees and others, who were determined to implement Catholic Church

---

[137] Kate O'Donnell, Mary Cronin, Derval Igoe, *Review of the Epidemiology of AIDS in Ireland, 1983–1999* (National Disease Surveillance Centre, Dublin, n.d.), downloaded from Lenus website 22 March 2022; David Kilgannon, 'Responsible, collective and caring': Gay Health Action, AIDS activism and sexual health in the Republic of Ireland, 1985–1898', *IESH*, 2021, pp. 1–18; Fiona Smith, 'Cultural constraints on the delivery of HIV/AIDS prevention in Ireland, *Social Science and Medicine*, 46, no 6, March 1997, pp. 661–72.

[138] Mairead Enright and Emilie Cloatre, 'Transformative illegality': how condoms became legal in Ireland', *Feminist Legal Studies*, 2018, 26, pp. 261–84.

[139] As quoted by Whitty, 'Law and the regulation of reproduction in Ireland', p. 756.

teaching in their professional roles. Sterilisation is a heavily gendered story. Vasectomy, or male sterilisation, was widely available by the 1980s, but tubal ligation was not. Although Dublin led the way with respect to family planning, women living outside Dublin who relied on public medical services had greater access to tubal ligation until the 1990s.

Some of the modern history of sterilisation is extremely troubling. Eugenicists favoured sterilising women, and to a lesser extent, men with intellectual or physical disabilities, and sterilization was also deployed against ethnic minorities. In the early twentieth century, it was widely believed that women who gave birth outside marriage were often mentally ill, and in some countries, they were at risk of forced sterilisation. In the 1920s, thirty-five US states introduced eugenic sterilization programmes, which resulted in the forcible sterilisation of 64,000 people, who were described as 'feebleminded' or 'genetically defective'. These programmes were most widespread in the southern states. Afro-Americans and Native Americans were disproportionately targeted.[140] There were close links between eugenicists and birth control advocates, and the American Birth Control League was in favour of sterilising those deemed to be insane or feebleminded.[141] Several states in the southern USA attempted to introduce laws in the late 1950s and early 1960s, providing for sterilisation that targeted poor black families, in the hope of reducing welfare spending; only the threat that they would lose federal funding deterred them from doing so.[142]

In Europe, as is widely known, compulsory sterilisation was deployed by the Nazis against Jews and gypsies, and those with disabilities and chronic health conditions, including alcoholism. It was also deployed against poor single women, especially women who had given birth to more than one child by more than one father.[143] Between 1933 and 1945, an estimated 1 per cent of the German population, the majority were women, underwent forced sterilisation.[144] Compulsory sterilisation of those with physical or mental disabilities was not unique to the United States or the Nazi regime. In the 1950s, forced sterilisations took place in Mexico, Puerto Rico, Panama and Japan. In Puerto Rico, one-third of women of child-bearing age were sterilised between 1930 and 1970, and coercive sterilisation appears to have been common. Sweden, Finland Denmark and Norway all had eugenically determined sterilisation programmes that were in marked contrast with their social democratic traditions.

---

[140] Linda Gordon, *The moral property of women. A history of birth control politics in the United States* (University of Illinois Press, Urbana and Chicago, 2007), p. 342.

[141] Gordon, *The moral property of women*, p. 229.

[142] Gordon, *The moral property of women*, p. 290.

[143] Michelle Mouton, *From nurturing the nation to purifying the Volk: Weimar and Nazi family policy, 1918–1945* (Cambridge University Press, Cambridge, 2007), Chapters 3 and 5.

[144] Patrick Zylberman, 'Les damnés de la démocratie puritaine: stérilisations en Scandinavie, 1929–1977, *Le Movement Social*, 187, 1999, p. 99.

Sterilisation was sometimes mandatory if a woman with a physical or intellectual disability wished to leave an institution to live in the community.[145] Sweden was later forced to pay compensation to women who were compulsorily sterilised. Switzerland's programme of sterilisation to control the country's gypsy population, first introduced at the end of World War I, only ended in 1972.[146] Stories of men in India being offered portable radios, blankets and other gifts if they agreed to be sterilised featured in Irish and British newspapers in the late 1960s. These incentives were introduced when the government was forced to abandon plans for compulsory sterilisation following public protests. By 1973, more than seven million men had received payments for undergoing a vasectomy.[147]

In 1972, the UK National Health Service (Family Planning) Amendment Act authorised vasectomies for contraceptive purposes; this measure was introduced because the law in the UK and especially in Scotland was unclear whether the operation was legal, if done for contraceptive purposes and NHS surgeons were reluctant to perform vasectomies for this reason. In Ireland, it was widely believed that sterilisation, male or female was illegal, but no legal challenge was ever mounted to the procedures.

Second-wave feminism in the United States did not advocate female sterilisation (presumably because of the embarrassing involvement of earlier American feminists with eugenics). The medical profession was also cautious about this permanent form of fertility control. Nevertheless, by the late 1970s, sterilisation was the most common form of birth control for American women over twenty-five years of age. Poor women and those with less education were more likely to have been sterilised; vasectomy was more common among well-educated, middle-class men, and twenty-nine times more common among white men than among blacks.[148]

The links between sterilisation and eugenics and evidence of forced sterilisations provided Catholic periodicals with a strong argument that could be deployed to influence public opinion on the topic of voluntary sterilisation. During the 1970s, the *Catholic Standard* carried regular articles about the compulsory sterilisation of young black women in the USA, and other instances of forced sterilisation; these stories carried veiled warnings against the introduction of female sterilisation in Ireland. In 1973, for example, they reported on a disputed sterilisation of two young black 'girls' in Alabama, which was

---

[145] Zylberman, 'Les damnés de la démocratie puritaine', pp. 99–125. On Denmark, see Birgit Kirkabæk, 'Sexuality as disability: the women on Sprogø and Danish society', *Scandinavian Journal of Disability Research*, vii, 3–4, 2005, pp. 194–2005.
[146] M.J. Drake, I.W. Mills, D. Cranston, 'On the chequered history of vasectomy', *BJU International*, 84, 1999, p. 478.
[147] *Evening Echo*, 12 March 1968; Drake et al, p. 480.
[148] Gordon, *The moral property of women*, pp. 342–4.

discussed in the US Senate; the following year they reported claims by a bishop in Puerto Rica, that sterilisation was compulsory in that US protectorate.[149]

The Papal Encyclical *Casti Connubii* condemned compulsory sterilisation. When Pius XI was asked a year later, whether 'direct sterilization is lawful', his response was 'no'. Pius XII (1939–58) issued several unequivocal statements condemning sterilisation. The first, in 1940, stated that 'any direct sterilisation, whether of man or of woman, whether perpetual or temporary, is forbidden by the Law of Nature'. He condemned sterilisation in the course of his speech to the Italian Catholic Society of Midwives giving papal endorsement to the safe period, and again, shortly before his death in 1958.[150] Noonan, having examined Catholic teaching on 'mutilation' a term that also encompasses plastic surgery and organ transplants, concluded that 'it becomes even more difficult to see why sterilisation was not, in some cases lawful'.[151] Papal condemnation of voluntary sterilisation was 'not of the solemn authority of *Casti Connubii* on interference with the procreative function in the exercise of coitus'[152]; it did not carry the same level of papal prohibition. In 1968 however, Paul VI made an unequivocal statement on the topic in *Humanae Vitae*: 'Equally to be condemned, as the magisterium of the church has affirmed on many occasions, is direct sterilization, whether of the man or of the woman whether permanent or temporary'.[153]

7.7   Hysterectomy: 'The Irish Tubal Ligation'?

While Catholic teaching condemned male or female sterilisation, it did not condemn hysterectomy – a radical form of female sterilisation, which could be justified by the 'double effect' – removing a womb because it was diseased, or a woman suffered from heavy menstrual bleeding. The proportion of births to women who were over thirty-five years, and high parity was much greater in Ireland than in other developed countries, and these two factors gave rise to substantially increased risks of maternal morbidity and death. In 1979, during the debate on the Family Planning Bill, Noel Browne noted that in 1973, maternal mortality for women under the age of 35 was 8 per 100,000, rising to 30 per 100,000 for women aged 35–40, and 120 per 100,000 for women aged 40–45.[154] Some older married women underwent hysterectomies in order to prevent future conceptions. One doctor described hysterectomy as 'the Irish tubal ligatation'.[155]

The annual reports of the Dublin maternity hospitals provide extensive details about obstetrical procedures, including anonymised maternal and infant

---

[149] *Catholic Standard*, 27 July 1973; 6 December 1974.
[150] Noonan, *Contraception*, pp. 451–2.   [151] Noonan, *Contraception*, p. 456.
[152] Noonan, *Contraception* p. 452.   [153] *Humanae Vitae*, para. 15.
[154] DD, 10 May 1979.   [155] *IT*, 7 February 1986 quotation from Dr Andrew Rynne.

deaths, but they are markedly less informative about gynaecological procedures. Hysterectomies were also carried out in general hospitals and private
nursing homes. In the late 1970s, a US Ph.D. student interviewed a forty-four-
year-old Dublin woman, who had never used contraception. She underwent
twenty pregnancies including six sets of twins; the family was extremely poor
as the husband was long-term unemployed. Rhesus incompatibility resulted in
the death of nine children. Following the birth of her eighth surviving child, the
couple attempted total abstinence, but when she mentioned that in confession
her parish priest criticised her for 'shirking her "wifely duties" and denied her
absolution'. Her ninth suriviving child was born less than nine months later. At
this delivery – which may have been by caesarean section, though this is not
stated – 'a sympathetic physician performed a hysterectomy'.[156]

In his memoirs, Dr Michael Flynn, programme manager in the Midlands
Health Board in the 1970s, described the case of a woman who had a caesarean hysterectomy on her tenth pregnancy, because she did not wish to have
additional children, and another case of a Traveller woman, mother of thirteen children, who had a hysterectomy. He described the use of hysterectomy
to prevent future conception, as 'bad medicine and undesirable'.[157] Journalist
Ronit Lentin quoted a general practitioner who claimed that doctors who had
ethical objections to sterilisation 'would whip a womb out without a second
thought'; she also suggested that women who were private patients found it
easier to secure a hysterectomy for contraceptive purposes. However, a female
doctor claimed that the incidence of hysterectomy was lower than in England
because Irish doctors preferred to sustain a woman's capacity to bear children:
in cases of prolapse of the uterus, Irish doctors were more likely to carry out
surgery to repair the uterus, rather than a hysterectomy.[158]

The mother of Mary McAleese (President of Ireland), who grew up in
Belfast, had a hysterectomy following the birth of her ninth child. Her family
doctor, referred her to a Protestant gynaecologist who performed a hysterectomy. A priest who was a friend of the family, learned of this, 'possibly from
the hospital's Catholic chaplain [and] in front of us children he berated my
parents demanding to know why his permission had not been sought, since my
mother was still of "child-bearing" age'.[159]

There is no evidence that therapeutic female or male sterilisations were performed in Ireland before the 1970s (except via hysterectomy). The first reference
that I have found to vasectomy was in 1970 when Janet Martin, editor of the
women's page in the *Irish Independent* reported that two Dublin hospitals had
performed vasectomies, and the IFPA had referred four men for vasectomies in

---

[156] Reilly, 'Population dynamics and family planning in Ireland', pp. 115–6.
[157] Michael P. Flynn, *Medical doctor of many parts* (Kelmed, Ireland, 2002), pp. 162–5.
[158] *II*, 12 March 1981.
[159] Mary McAleese, *Here's the story. A memoir* (Penguin Ireland, Dublin, 2020), p. 59.

the past year. When she attempted to get statistics on the number performed in Ireland, she discovered that 'a great many men had never even heard of the operation'. These vasectomies were carried out under general anaesthetic, whereas in Britain, most vasectomies were out-patient procedures performed under local anaesthetic. Martin stated that vasectomies were 'legally permissible here'; they were done 'because of the loose definition of the contraceptive ban'. She claimed that the Voluntary Health Insurance would pay for the procedure: 'two brave souls' had been reimbursed. The cost to a private patient was £20–£25.[160]

This story together with a report in an unnamed Irish medical journal appears to have prompted Fine Gael TD and medical doctor Hugh Byrne to table a series of parliamentary questions to the Minister for Health: 'whether the operations carried out were of a purely optional nature', and whether this procedure was covered by VHI. His tone indicated disapproval; he asked whether the Minister condoned surgical beds being used for vasectomies, given a shortage of beds. The Minister, Erskine Childers, replied that hospitals were not required to inform him about the details of medical procedures; this was a matter for medical practitioners. He did not propose to investigate the reports.[161]

In 1972, when a committee of Protestant gynaecologists wrote a report on contraception for the Church of Ireland's role of the church committee, they included a paragraph on sterilisation. This stated that any decision should be made 'by the individual family unit. Gynaecologists should neither perform nor advise such a procedure without full discussion with the persons concerned including some psychological evaluation of the possible consequences'. They expressed the opinion that sterilisation should be available 'when it is considered that it is in the best interests of the patient and her husband that it should be done'.[162] As sterilisation was irreversible it should only be used when a couple has determined, for medical or social reasons to have no further children. The procedure should be generally available. Doctors had the right in conscience to refuse to carry out sterilisations, but in such cases, the patient should be referred to another medical practitioner.[163]

The 1973 annual report of the IFPA noted that Dr Caroline Deys had demonstrated how to perform vasectomies to the medical staff, and she had performed vasectomies on nine clients on the clinic's waiting list. Two members of the medical staff were undergoing training, to enable the IFPA to start regular sessions.[164] In the following year, Drs Deys and Altman performed twenty-five vasectomies and Dr Andrew Rynne began to hold regular sessions in the Synge Street clinic, where he carried out thirty-four vasectomies under local anaesthetic. The IFPA was also referring clients to a private medical practitioner.[165]

[160] *II*, 30 March 1972.   [161] DD, vol 260, 12 April 1D972, col. 20.

[162] *Church of Ireland Gazette*, 8 February 1974 – memo submitted re Family Planning Bill.

[163] *Church of Ireland Gazette*, 8 February 1974.   [164] IFPA Annual Report 1973.

[165] IFPA Annual Report 1974.

There is evidence that Health Boards funded the cost of sterilisation in some circumstances. A memorandum circulated by the Department of Health, apparently in the 1970s, stated that 'the services which a Health Board is empowered to provide under the Health Act 1970, must relate to the prevention or treatment of a defective condition of health. If, for the prevention or treatment of such a condition it is necessary that a person undergo a vasectomy operation or have an intra-uterine device fitted or be required to make use of contraceptive pills or appliances, there is power for these services to be provided...'[166] In 1976, the IFPA carried out 148 vasectomies; the number had almost trebled to 414 by 1978, and in later years, they performed approximately 400 each year.

Dr Rynne and two IFPA colleagues, Maeve Keelan and Katherine Acheson published a report on vasectomies carried out by the IFPA between June 1974 and December 1977. Of 631 clients assessed during this period, 552 or 87.4 per cent had a vasectomy. They refused to perform a vasectomy on the male partner in a childless couple, both in their early twenties. One in four clients was referred by a family doctor. Few of the remainder had discussed vasectomy with their GP and did not wish her/him to be informed. In England, by contrast, a majority of referrals came from GPs. Half of those, who were not referred by a GP, did not indicate how they became aware that the IFPA performed vasectomies, the remainder got that information through magazines, the media, social workers or a friend. Most clients were in their thirties, married 6–10 years, parents of 2–4 children; 79 per cent lived in cities or towns. The mean age and mean family size were marginally higher than for clients seeking vasectomies in England. A rather surprising 42 per cent had used no form of contraception other than natural methods or coitus interruptus. About 82 per cent opted for a vasectomy because they regarded their families to be complete, two-thirds expressed a dislike of using long-term contraception.[167]

Male sterilisation expanded with little publicity throughout the 1970s and 1980s. FPS commenced vasectomies in 1979; in 1981, they carried out 238. A review carried out post 1985 reported that in 1 per cent of cases, there was recanalization, which meant that the vasectomy had failed.[168] Well Woman began a vasectomy clinic in 1978, carrying out approximately 10 each week, but ceased in 1981 allegedly for financial reasons.[169] A PhD thesis completed in 1981 noted that the IFPA adopted a very careful protocol with respect to vasectomies – potential clients were screened and some were rejected, whereas they claimed that another [unnamed] clinic, which would appear to be Well

---

[166] *IPU Review*, August 1978, quoted in a letter from John Williams MPSI Kilkee.
[167] *JIMA*, 72, no 2, 16 February 1979, 'Vasectomy in Ireland: a preliminary report' by Maeve Keelan, Andrew Rynne and Katherine Acheson.
[168] UCDA P276, Derek Freedman Report on Vasectomy Service in FPS – n.d.
[169] *IT*, 28 August 1981.

Woman 'was far more relaxed in attitude'; any man who requested a vasectomy 'would be given the operation on the following weekend'.[170]

By 1984, vasectomies were being carried out in family planning clinics in Limerick, Cork and Galway. The Adelaide Hospital – a voluntary hospital with a stated Protestant ethos – was the only hospital providing in-patient vasectomies, under full anaesthetic which required an overnight stay. Some provincial hospitals performed them as an out-patient procedure; others were done in GP surgeries outside normal surgery hours. Family planning clinics played a critical role in expanding access, by training local doctors. In Limerick, vasectomies were originally carried out once a month by a visiting doctor from Dublin, but the service expanded when local doctors gained expertise. Journalist Helen Shaw claimed that 2,000 Irish men had vasectomies in 1983. She noted that two doctors, who counselled couples before surgery, regarded the rise in vasectomies as an indication that men were taking greater responsibility for fertility control. The procedure cost £90, which was considerably cheaper than female sterilisation.[171] An article describing the FPS vasectomy clinic noted that many clients lived in areas where they were unable to secure regular supplies of contraceptives, and this was a factor in their decision.[172] In 1983, FPS noted that a growing number of social workers were referring clients for vasectomies, noting that 'they tend to be exceedingly hard cases with multiple problems – (not always just large families)'. One social worker had persuaded 'the medical office' – presumably the regional health authority to pay for the procedure; FPS hoped that this would prove to be a precedent.[173] In 1986, the *Irish Independent* reported that Seamus McGee, husband of Mary McGee, the plaintiff in the 1973 Supreme Court case, had a vasectomy under the GMS scheme. Mrs McGee had given birth to two additional children in the early 1980s.[174] The fact that vasectomies could be carried out in a GP surgery without a nurse or additional staff meant that the procedure was immune from scrutiny. That was not the case with female sterilisation.

7.8   State and Church Responses

In 1975, *Human Life is Sacred*, a lengthy pastoral letter issued by the Irish Hierarchy noted that sterilization was being carried out 'in some places in this country' and reiterated that it was contrary to papal teaching. The reference was brief, and it appeared at a late stage in this lengthy document.[175] In the same year, the Council of Europe passed a resolution demanding that

---

[170] O'Reilly, 'Population dynamics and family planning in Dublin Ireland', p. 95.
[171] *IT*, 24 February 1984, Helen Shaw, 'The operation that improves your love life'.
[172] *EH*, February 1985.   [173] UCDA P276, Derek Freedman Papers, Box 2, April 1983.
[174] *II*, 4 December 1986.
[175] *Human Life is Sacred*. Pastoral letter of the Archbishops and Bishops of Ireland, Para 118.

sterilisation for family planning purposes should be available in member countries under the health service.[176] Vasectomy does not appear to have prompted action or explicit statements by the Catholic church. By contrast, female sterilisations were obstructed by ensuring the non-cooperation of hospital staff and the formation of ethical committees. The exercise of ethical opt out was widely understood within Irish hospital medicine; many doctors, nurses and other health professionals had worked in Britain, where some had exercised their right not to be involved, directly or indirectly in abortions. Female sterilisation may have been the first occasion when ethical opt-out was applied in Irish hospitals.

When the Minister for Health Charles Haughey met the IFPA in 1978 to discuss his proposed family planning bill, Dr George Henry raised the question of sterilisation. He informed the Minister that the IFPA was carrying out several hundred vasectomies annually, but tubal ligation could only be carried out in hospitals, and some doctors and nurses were reluctant to carry out the procedure. The IFPA had sought legal advice as to whether sterilisation was legal. Mr Haughey informed the delegation that there was no law prohibiting sterilisation, and he did not intend to include sterilisation in the legislation.[177] He reiterated this when he met a delegation of the Irish Episcopal Conference. When the National Health Council met the Minister in relation to the family planning bill, they tabled a memorandum by Dr de Courcey Wheeler, who was not present, urging that male sterilisation should be more widely available, and female sterilisation should be an acceptable practice. Dr de Courcey Wheeler claimed that the objections were 'mainly moral'. He urged that sterilisation should be available free of charge to all medical card holders. Several members of the National Health Council who were present disagreed.[178] One member stated that sterilisation was carried out 'in a limited number of medically approved cases and he would prefer if it were not commented on at all either by the Council or in legislation'.[179] This encapsulates the attitude of the government, Department of Health officials and many doctors at this time.

A summary of the meeting between the IMA and the Department reiterated the IMA's opposition to sterilisation. Dr Boyle (Coombe) explained that sterilisations were performed in two hospitals (unnamed); in each case, they had to be approved by an ethics committee.[180] When the Family Planning Bill was going through the Oireachtas, Noel Browne tabled an amendment at the Committee Stage providing for the inclusion of vasectomy and tubal ligation.

---

[176] The Council of Europe on Fertility and Family Planning. Resolution 75, 29, 14 November 1975. *Population and Development Review*, 2, no 2, June 1975, pp. 313–5.

[177] UCDA Barry Desmond Papers box 210 IFPA, 24 April 1978.

[178] UCDA Barry Desmond Papers box 210 National Health Council.

[179] Box 210 National Health Council, 2 March 1978.

[180] Box 210 IMA, 26 January 1978.

Mr Haughey rejected this amendment, claiming that whether 'voluntary tubal ligation or voluntary vasectomy, are suitable or legitimate forms of family planning is not relevant to this legislation'. At a later point, he emphasised that 'Nobody is being denied access to these types of operations as a result of this Bill'.[181]

7.9   Female Sterilisation

1973 appears to be the year when references to sterilisation begin to appear in women's magazines. *Woman's Choice* February 1973 quotes a letter from a twenty-four-year-old mother of four, asking about sterilisation. She was told that this could be done in Ireland but only for medical reasons; they referred her to the IFPA clinic. The magazine received a similar query some weeks later, and a thirty-seven-year-old mother of eight, who was on the pill wrote that she was considering sterilisation.[182] When another woman asked for the name and address of a doctor who would perform female sterilisation, she was told that this was 'not yet common' and could only be done on medical grounds following a referral. As she had mentioned that her husband was not keen on her having this operation, the columnist suggested that he should consider a vasectomy, which was a much easier procedure to arrange.[183] Another correspondent was a mother of two in her late twenties, who suffered 'bad nerves' lived in difficult home circumstances and had tried several methods of contraception without finding a satisfactory one. Her husband had decided to be sterilised, but 'as we live in a small town, he does not know how to go about it'. He also 'wonders if it is possible for him to have it done without any bother concerning his religion'.[184]

The first recorded female sterilisations appear to have been carried out in the Adelaide Hospital. In 1975, the Irish Family League claimed that six women had been sterilised in the Adelaide hospital 'because of results of the pill; 4 with deep venous thrombosis; 1 cerebrovascular incident and 1 chest pain' – all cited as evidence of the dangers of the contraceptive pill. Given the League's hostility to all forms of contraception that statement should not be taken as authoritative. They suggested that the Adelaide should be asked to supply evidence about sterilizations carried out in the hospital.[185] Michael Solomons states that George Henry was carrying out tubal ligations 'at his own hospital' (the Adelaide) but soon found that his waiting list was 'out of control'.[186] Demand

---

[181] DD, 9 May 1979.
[182] *Woman's Choice*, 22 February 1973; 5 April 1973; 24 May 1973.
[183] *Woman's Choice*, 6 September 1973.
[184] *Woman's Choice*, 6 no 12 – appears to be in late 1973.
[185] NAI DT 2003/133/215 Family Planning Resolutions 1975.
[186] Solomons, *Pro-life*, p. 38.

increased as the health risks of the contraceptive pill for older women became known, and a growing number of women sought a reliable means of preventing future pregnancies. In 1978, the social work department of the Rotunda noted that a number of women, most of whom had severe social or psychological problems, wanted a guarantee of no future pregnancies, but although their husbands agreed with their wish, few were willing to undergo a vasectomy. They noted that existing provision took no account of these women's needs, 'sometimes the "best" they could hope for was vasectomy'.[187] A survey of contraceptive intentions in the Rotunda in 1980 among post-partum mothers showed that 4 per cent of husbands had either undergone a vasectomy or intended to do so.

The main impediment to providing tubal ligation was access to hospital facilities. The procedure had to be permitted by the hospital board, and it required the co-operation of nursing and other para-medical staff. Michael Solomons, a pioneer in Irish family planning, carried out very few tubal ligations:

as I was conscious that many of my nursing staff had ethical objections to the procedure. I had too much regard for their profession to ignore their beliefs. Whether or not a doctor was able to perform this operation was a lottery. The matron and theatre sisters in Baggot Street [a voluntary, general hospital], came up with a solution. 'Ask the parish priest they said'. If he approves, we'll have no objections we will get two nurses who are willing to assist you'. It was a different story in Mercer's [another voluntary general hospital] where the otherwise co-operative theatre sister stated, 'You are not going to do that in my theatre'.[188]

The closure of several Dublin voluntary hospitals during the 1970s and 1980s – including Baggot Street and Mercer's – probably reduced access to tubal ligation in the city. In the Midland Health Board area, Dr Michael Flynn stated that 'occasional ligations of fallopian tubes were performed, not without difficulty, as not many nurses were willing to assist'. In the mid-1970s, the bishop of Meath, Dr McCormack asked the CEO of the MHB to come to see him. The CEO reported that the bishop had expressed his displeasure at the fitting of IUDs and sterilisation in a MHB hospital, and he requested that these practices be discontinued. The CEO 'stood his ground' saying that what was being done was not illegal; if women asked for a tubal ligation and the doctors were willing to carry it out, they would be permitted. 'No one would be obliged to participate, and nurses were free to opt out if they had a conscientious objection'. Dr Flynn reported that the consultant obstetrician appointed to the county hospital in Portlaoise 'performed the occasional tubal ligation.... The matron in Portlaoise Hospital, a nun, told me that the local parish priests had questioned the sterilisation operations being performed in the hospital. Her response was that what went on in the operating theatre was a matter for

[187] Rotunda Hospital Clinical Report 1978, p. 70, signed by Holmes and Burns.
[188] Solomons, *Pro-life*, p. 39.

the doctors and nurses and she would not interfere'. This theatre sister, a nun raised no objections to sterilisations, but when she retired, she was due to be replaced by a married woman, who was opposed to sterilisation. In this case, a compromise was reached. When a doctor gave advance notice that a sterilisation would be carried out, another nurse would take her place. Dr Flynn reported the number of tubal ligations performed in his annual returns of hospital and out-patient procedures. But the procedure was dependent on willing staff, and a resignation or retirement could bring tubal ligations to a halt. He suggested that 'it might be said that our approach in the midlands was 10 to 15 years in advance of other public hospitals'.[189] While this might sound like self-congratulations, his claim is valid.

Dublin maternity and gynaecological services were concentrated in voluntary hospitals, which meant that access to tubal ligation was almost non-existent for many years. In 1979, the Archbishop of Dublin Dr Dermot Ryan issued an ethical code for hospitals in the archdiocese. This emphasised the right not to take part in any procedure if the person had a conscientious objection. This code explicitly ruled out direct abortion and artificial insemination. He recommended that all hospitals should establish ethics committees. It stated that 'no person can, in any circumstances demand the use of hospital facilities for any operation, procedure, treatments or research which the hospital authority judges to be inconsistent with the ethical policy and accepted practices of the hospital....Those who accept appointments or employment in any hospital should do so on the understanding that they will not violate the ethical policy and accepted practices of the hospital'.[190] The Archbishop may have issued this code in anticipation of the imminent enactment of a Family Planning Act, and the renegotiation of contracts for hospital consultants.

Medical consultants employed in Catholic voluntary hospitals had a different contract to those who were employed in public hospitals. An editorial in the *JIMA* in 1981 commented on the apparent contradiction between acknowledging the consultant's right to exercise independent judgement on ethical matters, and the right of the hospital authority to safeguard the ethical principles on which the character and constitution of the hospital is based. It noted that sterilisations were not

in themselves contrary to the norms of medical practice, although the vast majority of doctors in practice in Ireland find it repugnant to sterilise healthy individuals. The position of the Catholic Church on this matter is well known and widely followed. A hospital Board of Management which is avowedly Catholic would be altogether inconsistent were it to permit such operations within its precincts. The fact that an individual doctor wants to do such an operation does not give this doctor the right to do so in a particular institution.

---

[189] Flynn, *Medical doctor of many parts*, pp. 162–5.   [190] *II*, 1 March 1979.

In the case of the Health Board hospitals the precedence held by the hospital is not so strongly stated and in certain circumstances it would be within the ambit of the contract for the consultant's views to prevail.[191]

In the case of what the Department of Health termed 'Catholic contracts', the views of the hospital carried a greater weight, and hospital staff could not carry out procedures that contravened Catholic teaching. When the Mater Hospital (a large general hospital that provided gynaecological treatment) issued a code of ethics and set up an ethics committee in 1981, it emphasised that the Mater was a Catholic hospital with a responsibility 'to reflect in its policies and practices the moral and ethical teaching of the Catholic church', and it repeated the key principles set out by Archbishop Ryan in 1979.[192]

In 1981, there were reports that the Erinville hospital in Cork – which was under the Southern Health Board – was considering a limited tubal ligation service for women who had strong medical grounds for avoiding future pregnancies. Gynaecologist, Professor David Jenkins, indicated that this was in response to demand from local GPs and patients.[193] The SHB sought legal advice; they noted that each case would be considered individually by an ethics committee representing medical and nursing staff.[194] A consultant radiologist at the Erinville, who was a member of the SHB made repeated efforts to have these operations deemed illegal, without success. The numbers were small – six in 1981, two at the Cork Regional Hospital and four at the Erinville. In the following year, the SHB determined that the matter should be 'thrashed out by the government'.[195] In January 1983, the *JIMA* published an editorial on sterilisation, prompted by the debate at the SHB. It suggested that many important issues had 'hitherto been swept under the carpet'. Tubal ligations were not done on a large scale in any hospital in the state, and no hospital performed them 'when requested for social reasons by the healthy'. It reiterated that sterilisation was contrary to the tenet of the Catholic church; it was not permitted in Catholic hospitals, and many nurses would not assist with the procedure. The editorial suggested that there was a clear distinction between voluntary sterilisation of the healthy and sterilisation of women who would be at risk in a future pregnancy. The SHB had received legal advice that the decision whether to carry out a tubal ligation 'was one properly within the professional judgement and responsibility of the consultant to decide. Of interest is the further legal opinion that it was not permissible to limit the consultant's judgement by an Ethics Committee who would examine individual cases proposed for ligation'. The *JIMA* editorial believed that this decision only related to sterilisations for medical reasons. It noted that 'one of the disturbing facts to emerge from the

[191]   *JIMA*, August 1981, p. 211.   [192]   *IT*, 27 March 1981.
[193]   *Cork Examiner*, 30 January 1981.   [194]   *Cork Examiner*, 14 April 1981.
[195]   *Cork Examiner*, 6 July 1982.

Southern Health Board legal opinion was the legal lack of standing of a hospital Ethics Committee. Such Committees are coming into existence in many hospitals, but it appears that in Health Board Hospitals, in any event, they are toothless. In voluntary hospitals it would seem to be preferable that these bodies be Committees of the Boards of Governors and that decisions based on their advice should emanate from the Board'. The IMA had not formulated a policy on sterilisation.[196] This was consistent with its practice of avoiding decisions that might split the membership.

Statistics on the number of tubal ligations performed reveal dramatic differences between the regional health boards and between voluntary and health board hospitals.

7.10   Female Sterilisation: Health Boards and Voluntary Hospitals, 1982–1984

	1982	1983	1984	Total
Health Boards	68	127	241	436
Dublin Voluntary	11	20	24	55
Victoria Cork	453	638	810	1901

Female Sterilisations Performed in Health Board Hospitals, 1982–1984

Eastern Health Board, 0;

Southern Health Board, 31;

South Eastern Health Board, 0;

North-Western Health Board, 7;

Western Health Board, 104;

Mid-Western Health Board, 190;

Midland Health Board, 36;

North-Eastern Health Board, 0;

Total   369.

[Barry Desmond Papers Box 210. The second total is lower than the figure given in the previous table. This appears to relate to an under-reporting of the number carried out in the Western Health Board; 436 appears to be the correct figure.]

The Rotunda performed a small number of tubal ligations every year from 1977; if they were performed before 1977, they were not recorded in the annual clinical report. But the numbers, 5 in 1978, 3 in 1979, 5 in 1980; none noted for 1981, 5 in 1982, 13 in 1983, 15 in 1984, and 18 in 1985 – suggest that they were only carried out where a woman would be at serious medical risk in the

---

[196] *JIMA*, August 1982.

event of a future pregnancy. It was not until 1989, when the number rose to 141, that it exceeded 100. The first tubal ligation in the National Maternity Hospital was carried out in 1978 by Dr Dermot MacDonald, on a multiparous woman who had had a succession of stillbirths because of rhesus incompatibility. There was no prospect that she would give birth in future to a living child. As a candidate for master of the hospital, Dr MacDonald had indicated that he would carry out tubal ligation where there was an overwhelming clinical argument for doing so. He was assisted in the operating theatre by Declan Meagher – his predecessor as master. The occasion proved very divisive in the hospital. Matron collected the signatures of staff nurses who undertook not to co-operate with the procedure; a number of senior medical and nursing staff contacted the Archbishop of Dublin Dr Dermot Ryan, and board members were canvassed in favour of Dr MacDonald's dismissal. He warned his wife that they might have to emigrate to Canada. He survived, because he told the board that in the event of his dismissal, he would inform the media as to the reasons, and the Board backed down.[197] It may be noteworthy that this happened before Archbishop Ryan had published his ethical code.

Department of Health statistics for the years 1982–4 show that six tubal ligations were carried out in the National Maternity Hospital; three in the Coombe; thirty-three in the Rotunda; eleven in the Adelaide and one each in Sir Patrick Duns and Baggot St Hospitals. By the 1980s, all the Dublin maternity hospitals had appointed ethics committees, who determined whether a woman would be approved for tubal ligation. The six-member committee in the Coombe consisted of representatives of medical and nursing staff and different religious denominations. The nine-person committee at Holles St comprised three doctors, three nurses, a priest, a theologian and the secretary to the Board. The Rotunda committee included a geneticist but no religious representatives.

The INO was overwhelmingly opposed to sterilisation. Andrew Rynne claimed that 'The power that is being wielded by those nurses in hospitals is quite extraordinary. ….Nurses have a right to opt out but they shouldn't have a right to veto the procedure for somebody else'. An unnamed source in Holles St claimed that 'by and large, there isn't very much of a problem, even among conservative doctors, but there's a very strong feeling among nurses…. Because of the hierarchical structure, junior nurses will follow the instructions of senior nursing staff, who are very conservative'.[198]

Barry Desmond, who became Minister for Health in 1982, was the first Minister for Health to express his support for sterilisation. He was criticised

---

[197]   Interview with the late Dr Dermot McDonald; interview with Maeve O'Dwyer 7 August 2013. Peter Boylan, *In the shadow of the eighth. My forty years working for women's health in Ireland* (Penguin Ireland, Dublin, 2019), Chapter 5.
[198]   *IT*, 6 February 1986.

for failing to supply information on their availability in public hospitals, allegedly because he feared that 'ethical committees would spring up all over the
place'. An article in the *Irish Times* in 1986 reported that the Rotunda carried
out 31 tubal ligations in 1985; there were three in Holles St and none in the
Coombe, whereas 100 were carried out in the Regional Hospital in Galway.
For the Dublin figures to be proportionate to the respective populations, the
number should be 350.[199] The small number carried out in the Rotunda reflects
the opposition of nursing staff (many of them Catholic), and perhaps other
non-medical staff. But the refusal of nurses to participate does not explain the
low numbers in the Adelaide, a voluntary hospital with a declared Protestant
ethos and a Protestant nursing staff. A file in Barry Desmond's papers suggests
that Dr John Bonnar carried out an average of six tubal ligations annually in
the Adelaide – all for medical reasons. The number increased in the mid- and
late 1980s following the appointment of new consultants. By the early 1990s,
the Adelaide was carrying out approximately 400 tubal ligations a year; there
was a two-year waiting list.[200]

In December 1983, the EHB rejected a motion proposed by Labour councillor Eithne FitzGerald that female sterilisation should be made available in
an EHB hospital. In 1985, Pronsias de Rossa made a similar demand, again
without success.[201] The dramatic differences in the provision of tubal ligations
between the various health boards reflected the attitudes of medical personnel,
and the presence or absence of voluntary hospitals. An article in the *Sunday
Press* in 1985 noted that tubal ligations had been available in three hospitals
in the MHB region: Mullingar, Tullamore and Portlaoise, but by 1985, they
were only carried out in Port Laoise, where Dr Corristine conducted them,
mainly for medical reasons and when a woman's social circumstances offered
no alternative. The appointment of a new consultant in Mullingar meant that
tubal ligations had resumed, and 'a small number of vasectomies' were being
carried out. But a campaign was underway to stop all sterilisations: when the
consultant was on holidays, a petition was compiled, allegedly signed by every
nurse in Mullingar Hospital urging an end to sterilisations. The closure of the
maternity unit in Tullamore meant an end to sterilisations at that hospital; the
Sunday Press claimed that the consultant – Dr David Mortell, who had transferred to Mullingar, would be unable to carry out sterilisations there, reducing
overall availability.[202]

The large number of tubal ligations carried out in the mid-western and western health boards reflects the commitment of consultant obstetricians Anto

---

[199] *IT*, 6 February 1986.
[200] Boylan, *In the shadow of the eighth*, Chapter 5 Barry Desmond Papers, unlisted box 210.
[201] *IT*, 4 November 1983; 9 December 1983 EHB minutes 1983; *Evening Herald*, 5 November 1985.
[202] *Sunday Press*, 25 August 1985 – cutting in Barry Desmond Papers.

Dempsey in Limerick, and Michael Moylette in Galway, and their determination to overcome opposition within and outside the hospital. They had to deal with incidents such as porters refusing to wheel a woman to theatre, or staff walking out.[203] In the summer of 1985, the *Sunday Press* reported that Michael Moylette was performing approximately 100 tubal ligations a year in the Galway Regional Hospital – for women with clear medical and social problems, and Anto Dempsey was performing 65–70 a year in Limerick using similar criteria: 'it's for people who have finished their families and have compelling medical or psycho-social reasons'. The publicity prompted the bishop of Galway Eamonn Casey to circulate local doctors reminding them that sterilisation is 'repugnant to Christian teaching'. Shortly after Dr Casey's letter, there were calls for the establishment of an ethics committee in the hospital,[204] but sterilisations continued.

Dublin women seeking a tubal ligation had to travel and/or pay for surgery in a private clinic. Health board hospitals would not perform sterilisations on women from outside their region. By the late 1970s, women from all parts of Ireland were travelling to the Victoria Hospital in Cork, a small voluntary hospital with a Protestant ethos. The gynaecologist, Edgar Ritchie, a graduate of Trinity College Dublin, had trained as a junior doctor in Lancashire with Harold Steptoe – a pioneer of laparoscopy, and one of the doctors who successfully achieved the first test-tube baby. He worked as a Methodist medical missionary in Biafra during the years of the Biafran war, where he was involved in setting up the charity Biafra Concern, now Concern. In 1969, he was appointed as a consultant gynaecologist at the Victoria Hospital and the Erinville Hospital. His initial involvement in family planning began when a woman patient, he had attended, who was seriously depressed, committed suicide, because of an unwanted pregnancy. He was a founder of the Cork Family Planning Clinic in Tuckey Street.

The Victoria became the major centre for tubal ligation in Ireland because it was a small hospital, with a close-knit and predominantly Protestant staff. Close co-operation between Edgar Ritchie, anaesthetist Ted Hobart and a theatre sister 'who would take responsibility' was crucial. In the early years, the procedure was performed free of charge for women with a medical card. Dr Ritchie told me that he was earning substantial fees 'which I did not need' from his expertise in laparoscopy (a procedure used in some cases of female infertility), and he used this money to buy equipment needed for tubal ligation. He reflected that it was 'surprising how much freedom at that time a consultant had'. His professional autonomy, together with the co-operation of a few like-minded colleagues, explains the Victoria hospital's major role in tubal ligation. He is doubtful whether he sought the approval of the Hospital Board, but he would have discussed what he was doing with one or two members. As a small, Protestant hospital, the Victoria also took the lead in other initiatives. Cork needed a clinic for sexually transmitted diseases, but it was 'not very welcome at St. Finbarr's' [a health board hospital] so the Victoria offered to run it. They also set up a sexual assault unit 'at a time when sadly the Irish medical profession and the IMA would have been very conservative'.[205] In 1983, Dr Ritchie began to carry out tubal ligations at the Erinville.

Women were warned that the procedure might fail, and there was a risk of a subsequent pregnancy, and an increased risk of tubal pregnancy (which could be fatal). All the women signed a consent form. The Victoria Hospital generally sought the consent of their partner but they waived that in cases where he had a history of schizophrenia or violence towards his partner. Many women had travelled over 100 miles for the procedure which complicated the question of consent; some women only underwent counselling on the eve of surgery, and they might not have secured their husband's written consent. Given the long waiting lists, the Victoria had to give priority to certain cases: the hospital never saw itself as meeting the needs of most Irish women seeking sterilisation. By 1984, demand was so great that there were reports that the Victoria was refusing to take any further appointments.[206]

The long waiting lists for tubal ligations meant that women were travelling to Britain or Northern Ireland. The 1978 annual report of the IFPA expressed regret that the majority of gynaecologists in Ireland were unwilling to perform the procedure. During the past year, they had referred twenty-five patients to Liverpool. By the early 1980s, it would appear that they were referring patients to the Bandon Nursing Home; the annual report for 1981 noted a concern that this home might be forced to close – but that was averted when it secured a loan to remain in business. The Federation of Family Planning Clinics considered buying a private nursing home in the Dublin area where tubal ligations could be carried out; they estimated that they would need a minimum of twenty cases a week to make it viable. It would cost approximately £200,000 to buy and equip a clinic, and there were fears that demand would fall sharply 'when the Dublin Gynaecologists had the courage of their Cork colleagues' and introduced the procedure in city hospitals.[207] In 1983, a counsellor in the Well Woman Centre claimed that the number of women seeking sterilisation had increased five-fold in the past year; Well Woman provided counselling, secured the consent of their partners and referred women to clinics in Liverpool and London.[208]

When Dr Andrew Rynne decided to set up a private hospital in Clane, county Kildare, near Dublin, the IFPA considered investing in the hospital,

[205] Interview with Dr Edgar Ritchie in Killarney, 10 September 2012.
[206] UCDA P276 Derek Freedman, papers box 2, 1984.
[207] Derek Freedman, papers, October 1982 Federation of Family Planning Clinics.
[208] *IT*, 9 December 1983.

which was to be used as a centre for female sterilisation, but decided against doing so.[209] This clinic, which also carried out a range of other procedures, was opened in August 1985 by Monica Barnes TD.[210] This was not the first private clinic to provide tubal ligation in the Dublin area. The eleven-bed Whitethorn Clinic opened roughly one year earlier in a nearby village of Celbridge, and within two months, there were over 200 women on the waiting list. It was owned by a GP who carried out the advance consultations including counselling the women and their partners, but the procedure was performed by a doctor who travelled from Britain. Initially he was carrying out fifty operations a month, but he increased his visits to two sessions a week to meet demand. Statistics of the first 500 sterilisations at Whitethorn showed an average age of thirty-six years; 83 per cent of the women were Roman Catholic, the majority were middle or professional class. This is not surprising given the cost of £290, which was dearer than in a UK clinic, though not, when travelling costs were included. The VHI would pay for tubal ligation if it was carried out for medical not family planning reasons.[211]

The Catholic Bishop's 1985 Lenten pastoral *Love is for Life*, revisited a range of sexual topics, including pre-marital and extra-marital sex, cohabitation, abortion and contraception. The section on sterilisation opened by referring to sterilisations carried out in Nazi Germany, before reiterating that 'Catholic hospitals may not provide facilities for such operations. Catholic medical personnel may not cooperate with them'. It alleged that sterilisation could have adverse psychological consequences for both women and men.[212] In the same year, a group of Galway doctors sought to buy the Calvary Hospital, a small private hospital owned by a religious congregation. A clause in the sale contract precluded its use to carry out tubal ligations. Under the constitution of the religious congregation, the hospital could not be sold without the permission of the diocesan bishop.[213]

The absence of tubal ligations in the North-Eastern Health Board area reflected the fact that the region's largest maternity hospital was Our Lady of Lourdes Hospital Drogheda, a Catholic voluntary hospital with an ultra-conservative attitude towards contraception. The consequences of that culture were revealed in the 2006 *Inquiry into Peripartum Hysterectomy* at that hospital, by Judge Maureen Harding-Clarke, which was established to examine the rate of hysterectomies carried out on women coincidental with a caesarean section.

Section 5 headed 'The ethical position as practised by the MMM [Medical Missionaries of Mary] states:

[209] Freedman, box 2, 1984.   [210] *Evening Herald,* 26 August 1985.
[211] *Evening Herald,* 28 September 1984; *IT*, 25 January 1985.
[212] *Love is for Life*, 12.4, paras 103–8.   [213] *Evening Herald,* 19 September 1985.

5.1 The Catholic ethos prohibited the use of all forms of contraception. The only family planning advocated and permitted was the natural method of the safe period, or the Billings method. Information on other forms of family planning methods was not allowed even in circumstances where another pregnancy was dangerous. Sterilisation for contraceptive purposes was not permitted. The ethos allowed for "indirect sterilisation" where the primary purpose was for medical reasons, although the end result was that the woman could no longer become pregnant. The accepted practice in Catholic hospitals was to "isolate the diseased organ" by removing the uterus. Tubal ligation – i.e. the tying off a woman's fallopian tubes to prevent the passage of ova to the uterus for fertilization – was not acceptable.

5.2 There was an abundance of evidence that indicated the unwritten ethical code was rigidly applied. For many years, Dr. Neary and Dr. Lynch had sought clarification from the Department of Health, the Medical Defence Union and the Health Board of their legal position with regards to patient choice on offer in other hospitals. They never received what they considered adequate answers from any source, and they were obliged to operate in a grey area of "indirect sterilisation". It seemed to us that a tubal ligation for medical reasons was more likely to raise queries than the number of peripartum hysterectomies.[214]

The introduction to this report noted that 'The obstetricians there, in common with obstetricians in other Catholic hospitals with a Catholic ethos, may have carried out hysterectomies to protect the woman's health from a further pregnancy'.[215] In the report of a 1998 inquiry into obstetrical/gynaecological practices at the hospital by three Irish-based consultant obstetricians, two obstetricians concluded that 'Having reviewed the case notes, we are of the opinion that all of the nine cases reviewed can be justified in the prevailing situation. We note that if female sterilisations were available in the Lourdes Hospital the incidence of caesarean hysterectomy would be reduced by 50% immediately.' Hysterectomies were carried out as a form of 'indirect sterilisation'.[216] The review group appointed by the Institute of Obstetrics noted that 'In previous years, in Ireland, some patients may have had a peripartum hysterectomy as a method of sterilisation and although some of Dr Neary's patients may have fitted the criteria for indirect sterilisation, in the opinion of the Review Group, the choice of peripartum hysterectomy for the purposes of sterilisation is not now acceptable'.[217] The Harding-Clark inquiry determined that

---

[214] Department of Health and Children. *The Lourdes Hospital Inquiry.* An inquiry into peripartum hysterectomy at Our Lady of Lourdes Hospital Drogheda by Judge Maureen Harding-Clark, SC, 2006.
[215] *The Lourdes Hospital Inquiry*, 2.7.   [216] *The Lourdes Hospital Inquiry*, p. 4.
[217] *The Lourdes Hospital Inquiry*, 1.16.

'Dr. Neary's fears that any observed deviation from the ethos of the MMMs [Medical Missionaries of Mary] would result in dismissal were well founded'. He had referred a number of private and public patients to hospitals in Newry (Northern Ireland) for tubal ligation but would not use the Lourdes Hospital headed notepaper when writing referral letters.[218]

By the 1990s, tubal ligation was becoming more widely available. Peter Boylan, who was Master of Holles St at this time, noted that the Adelaide hospital was carrying out approximately 400 every year, but there was a two-year waiting list. The Coombe was reviewing its policy of restricting sterilisation to women with strong medical indications. When he secured the approval of the hospital's executive committee to extend the number carried out in Holles St in 1992, the Archbishop of Dublin, Desmond Connell, asked him and the matron to meet him, 'It wasn't so much an invitation as a command'. He described the atmosphere of the meeting with Dr Connell and auxiliary bishop Dr Moriarity as 'arctic... an ocean of mutual incomprehension between us across the table', but the meeting had no discernible outcome. Holles St carried out 321 tubal ligations in 1994 and 445 in 1997.

7.11   Conclusions

The 1980s is generally represented as a bleak decade, when Irish people voted in favour of the Pro-Life Amendment and continuing the constitutional prohibition on divorce, and the stories of Ann Lovett and Joanne Hayes shone an uncomfortable light on Irish attitudes towards extra-marital pregnancy. It was also the decade when contraception became more generally available to both married couples and single people. By the mid-1980s, it would appear that a majority of married couples were using contraception, before the birth of their first child. Contraception among single women was significantly lower; this is at least partly a reflection of the limitations of the 1979 Family Planning Act. Although a growing number of single people were accessing contraceptives from family planning clinics and other outlets, it would have been difficult for single women and men, living in rural and small-town Ireland to secure contraception. From 1985, the laws were gradually relaxed to reflect the reality of an Ireland with a high rate of pre-marital and extra-marital sexual activity.

During the 1980s, family doctors and community pharmacies emerged as the main providers of contraception. With a much wider choice of contraceptive methods available from GPs who were trained in family planning, and more widespread outlets in pharmacies, the battle increasingly shifted to female sterilisation. This battle was fought through ethical committees and hostile staff in

---

[218] *The Lourdes Hospital Inquiry*, 15.30; 15.18.

various hospitals; it did not impact on Dáil Éireann, and it featured to only a minor extent in the media. Successive Ministers for Health, senior departmental officials and officials and members of the regional health boards, failed to confront the reality that many women were unable to secure a tubal ligation because they lived in a particular health board area and could not afford the cost of travel or paying for private treatment, or the fact that some doctors were precluded from carrying out tubal ligations by the ethical code that prevailed in particular hospitals. The 1990s saw a major extension of tubal ligation, especially in the Dublin maternity hospitals; this was achieved because a growing number of hospital staff were prepared to defy Catholic church teaching. The battle against contraception had effectively concluded by the mid/late 1990s. Statistics on extra-marital pregnancies, teenage pregnancies and cohabitation indicated that any hopes that Ireland would remain an outlier in sexual practices and contraception had disappeared.

Conclusion

> Each discussion began with a specific theme – abortion, divorce, contracep-
> tion – but the underlying agenda related to something more profound and
> fundamental; what kind of people we were, what we wanted to become, and
> who was standing in the way of progress and change. At some time, not long
> before, an invisible line had been drawn across the path between The Past
> and Modern Ireland. It was though a count of heads was being undertaken to
> establish how many people were on either side of the line. Mobility between
> the two appeared almost unthinkable. The two Irelands had value systems
> that had little or no common ground.
>
> John Waters, *Jiving at the Crossroads* (Belfast, Blackstaff, 1991)

Central to the history of family planning in Ireland is the interaction between
religious observance and expressions of Irishness, and how that changed in
response to domestic political and socio-economic developments, and to international forces. The history of twentieth-century Ireland's engagement with
contraception is a story of unfolding divisions across decades of social change.
An Irish identity imagined around rural living, Catholicism, large families,
traditional gender roles and sexual puritanism was promoted and pursued,
before coming under immense pressure. And yet the decline of this imagined
Irishness was not unopposed; indeed, many lamented its passing.

The Irish Free State which came into existence in 1922 consisted of
twenty-six of Ireland's thirty-two counties. Catholics accounted for over 93
per cent of the population. The industrial revolution was mainly confined to
north-east Ulster. By the beginning of the twentieth century, rural Ireland
was dominated by small and middling-sized family farms. The proportion of
the population in urban areas was low; and small and medium-sized towns
reflected the values of the countryside. The family was central, and a family's interests generally took precedence over those of the individual members – marriage partners were commonly chosen on the basis of the social
standing of their family and arranged marriages were common; marriage,
dowries and inheritance were closely linked. Emigration provided a safety
valve removing the rebellious and the non-heirs. It enabled generations of

Irish couples to produce large numbers of children in the knowledge that they would not have to provide for all their children within Ireland. Religious life was another outlet for children who did not marry or inherit the farm, and many farming or business families had several daughters or sons in religious life. Such a society demanded strict social controls, especially over sexual morality – because early or improvident sexual encounters would jeopardise the social order.

In the late nineteenth century, Irish Catholic families were not noticeably larger than Protestant families, though that was beginning to change. By 1911, there is evidence of declining fertility among Protestant couples and an emerging differential Catholic/Protestant fertility. The 1930 Lambeth Conference when the Anglican community gave a qualified approval to family planning, and the hastily drafted papal encyclical *Casti Connubii* meant that by the 1930s, the Catholic church was the only major religious denomination to oppose contraception. Although there is no evidence that the members of the Church of Ireland welcomed the 1930 ruling, the distinction appears to have strengthened the denominational divide with respect to family size and family limitation in Ireland, north and south. The fertility gap between Catholic and Protestant couples widened, as did the fertility gap between Ireland and Northern Ireland. Many Irish people regarded church teaching on marriage, sexuality and the family (together with popular religious devotions) as core aspects of their Catholicism and their identity. This teaching was enforced through the confessional. The political and economic aspects of Catholic teaching that were synonymous with Catholicism in other parts of Europe, such as vocationalism, solidarism and the primacy of the family over the state, were only known and understood by an educated minority, and anti-communism, though frequently expressed, was tantamount to tilting at windmills. The Irish state reflected the values of its politicians and citizens, introducing stringent censorship of films and publications, a constitutional ban on divorce and legislation banning access to contraceptives or information about contraception. There is no evidence of any serious challenge to this moral code, except from a small cohort of intellectuals, and that remained so until the 1960s.

In 1961, Ireland was poor, agrarian and almost universally churchgoing, with the highest marital fertility (number of children born to married couples) in the developed world, by a considerable margin. The post-war wave of economic growth throughout western Europe had passed Ireland by. The most common employment for women was in domestic and institutional service, or within the family economy. Married women did not work outside the family home, family farm or business. At that time, 'Irish women had among the "least modernised" fertility patterns in the western world.... For Irish women, therefore the dominant choice was still between either having no children (through non-marriage) or having a lot (if they did marry)'.[1] Contraception was not discussed; and many adults were quite ignorant about the possibilities of controlling fertility; others feared the wrath of priests in the confessional if they attempted to do so. For many – perhaps a majority – of the couples, limiting the number of children was not within 'the calculus of choice'. With the security of a population that was overwhelmingly Catholic, and almost universally churchgoing, and the legal ban on contraception and providing information about contraception, the Irish Catholic church denied couples access to information and training in church-approved methods of family planning that was readily available to Catholics elsewhere. This decision to hold the line and to continue to teach that the purpose of marriage was to beget children – a message that had been largely abandoned by Catholic clergy in the United States and western Europe – was reactionary and dogmatic. But from the church's perspective, it may not have been unwise, given the evidence that couples who tried 'natural' family planning and experienced failure or sexual frustration tended to seek more reliable methods that were not approved by the Catholic church.

During the 1960s, the social structures that emerged in the decades following the great famine and were reinforced in the 1920s, following independence, began to crack. In 1961, over 23 per cent of births were fifth or higher-parity births. By 1981, less than 8 per cent of births were fifth or higher parity; by 1991, the figure was under 5 per cent. The arrival of the contraceptive pill, the first legally permitted reliable contraceptive available in Ireland, and the delay in the Vatican's decision as to whether the Pill was compatible with Catholic teaching, was liberating for Ireland, because it became possible for the first time to speak openly about contraception.

The 1968 papal encyclical *Humanae Vitae*, reaffirming traditional Catholic church teaching on contraception ranks as a major turning point for Catholicism. Its impact on Ireland was slower to become evident. Church attendance remained extremely high until the 1990s, but a growing proportion of those formally participating in religious services were not complying with Catholic teaching on contraception, and there is little evidence that Irish clergy tried to craft a moral and theological compromise that would enable Catholic couples to square that circle. However, the Pandora's Box of contraception had been opened and could not be closed. The Northern Ireland civil rights campaign, focussing on the grievances of the Catholic minority, and the ensuing violence, prompted questions about the rights of the Protestant minority in Ireland, launching a fraught debate about Irish identity/ies and the relationship

---

[1] Tony Fahey, Helen Russell and Emer Smyth, 'Gender equality, fertility decline and labour market patterns among women in Ireland', in Brian Nolan, Philip O' Connell and Christopher Whelan, *Bust to boom? The Irish experience of growth and inequality* (Institute of Public Administration, Dublin, 2000), p. 247.

between Catholicism, Irishness and minority rights. In the face of this emerging debate, in 1971, the Catholic Hierarchy effectively abandoned their traditional argument against contraception – that it was contrary to church teaching. They now claimed that any relaxation of the laws on contraception would usher in 'the permissive society' and undermine core values of Irish society.

There was a moment in the early 1970s when it appeared possible that Ireland might relax its stringent legislation against contraception and repeal the constitutional ban on divorce, and likewise, there was a prospect that the political relationship between Ireland and Northern Ireland would be transformed. Neither happened. In December 1973 however, coincidentally within days of the Sunningdale Agreement,[2] the Supreme Court decision in the McGee case, affirmed the right of a married couple to use contraception to plan their family. This judgment imposed a responsibility on government to introduce legislation permitting married couples to gain access to family planning, but this was not enacted until 1979. The 1979 Family Planning Act restricted access to contraceptives to 'bona fide family planning purposes', though this phrase was not defined in the act, or the accompanying statutory instrument. The legal vacuum during the 1970s made it possible for family planning services to expand – though only in cities and some larger towns. It also facilitated the emergence of a black market and mail order market in contraceptives. By 1979, despite restrictive legislation, it was no longer possible to control their spread, or to confine contraception to married couples. The number of births peaked in 1980, seven years after the peak in the marriage rate, and the year when access to contraceptives became legal. Yet by 1980, the fall in Irish fertility was well entrenched despite the absence of legal access to contraception. The decline was greatest among women aged over thirty-five years, and it happened throughout Ireland, not just in the cities. This suggests that the diffusion of 'natural' family planning (and perhaps greater use of withdrawal) was primarily responsible for falling fertility among older women. Nevertheless, Irish families remained the largest in Europe, and surveys of post-partum mothers in the early 1980s show that a high proportion of pregnancies were unplanned; evidence shows that many couples were using less-reliable means of contraception.

Diarmaid Ferriter claims that 'in rising in the 1970s, Irish feminists were facing a 1980s that would, in many respects seek to push them back'.[3] But despite the restrictive nature of the 1979 Family Planning Act, and the 1983 Pro-Life Amendment Campaign, the 1980s was the decade when it became evident that

[2] The December 1973 Sunningdale Agreement negotiated between the British and Irish governments and Northern Ireland politicians provided for a power-sharing executive in Northern Ireland and measures to accommodate 'an Irish-dimension'. It collapsed within six months.
[3] Diarmaid Ferriter, *Ambiguous Republic: Ireland in the 1970s* (Profile Books, London, 2012), p. 679.

the tide had turned. Against the backdrop of a depressed economy, falling male employment and high rates of unemployment, the number of married women in the workforce rose significantly, and fertility fell sharply. In 1977, only 14.4 per cent of married women were in paid employment; by 1989, this had risen to 23.7 per cent and this trend accelerated in the following decade.[4] By the early 1990s, Irish fertility was still the highest in Europe, but only by a small margin, and it was lower than in the United States. Fahey et al describe Irish fertility in the mid-1990s as 'mid-Atlantic rather than wholly European'; in other words, it was no longer exceptional. In 1986, 75 per cent of first-time married mothers in the National Maternity Hospital had used contraception. There was a much greater prospect that a married woman could secure informed advice on contraception and access to a variety of methods (other than sterilisation) from a trained GP; male sterilisation was readily available, and single adults could obtain condoms, though not without difficulty. The 1979 Family Planning Act, restricting contraception to 'bona fide family planning purposes', failed to take account of changing sexual practices, among single people, particularly among teenagers, who would have found it almost impossible (outside Students' Unions) to secure reliable contraception. In the mid-1980s, the overwhelming majority of single women having abortions in England or giving birth in the National Maternity Hospital had not used contraception. From 1980 to 1996, the proportion of births to single mothers rose five-fold, from 14 per cent to 48 per cent of total births,[5] and although divorce was still prohibited by the constitution, the number of separated and co-habiting couples had risen significantly. But while many of these children were born to cohabiting couples, in 1990, teenagers accounted for 30 per cent of births to single mothers.

The changes in Irish society from the 1960s to the 1990s were not all in the direction of liberalism. Conservative interest groups emerged as countervailing forces, and although they have often been viewed as evidence of a continuation of traditional Irish Catholicism, these movements were different both in terms of leadership and their *modus operandi*. The groups who campaigned against contraception were led by laity, often by women, and they owed much to US and British anti-abortion activists and their methods. In addition to fighting against the legalisation of contraception, they promoted the Billings method of family planning, as a church-approved reliable alternative to 'artificial' contraception. The failure to prevent the enactment of the 1979 Family Planning Act and the rising number of Irish women seeking abortions in Britain were key factors in their determination to mount the campaign that led to the approval of a constitutional amendment in 1983 affirming the rights of the unborn.

---

[4] Margret Fine-Davis, *Changing gender roles and attitudes to family formation in Ireland* (Manchester University Press, Manchester, 2016), p. 7.
[5] Fahey et al, 'Gender equality', pp. 246–58; quotation on p. 249.

The passing of the 1983 Pro-Life Amendment was a formal statement that Ireland *was* different: that the society with which John Waters' bus passengers identified,[6] had spoken. But many supporters of the amendment were conscious that this was a last attempt to shore up the ethos of a conservative Catholic society. In 1981, the obstetrician, Professor Eamon de Valera, who was heavily involved in the amendment campaign told the Taoiseach Charles Haughey that, while a referendum 'would be emphatically endorsed' at the present time, they could not rely on such support in coming years.[7] The evidence of continuing falling marital fertility, rising extra-marital births, cohabitation and a steadily rising abortion trail to Britain suggests that this was a hollow victory, though the constraints on women's lives and obstetrical practice, following the 1983 referendum should not be under-estimated. The tensions between a traditional and a changing Ireland had not disappeared by the 1990s. In 1997, the referendum removing the constitutional prohibition on divorce was passed by a wafer-thin margin, and legislation to bring Irish law on abortion into line with the 1992 Supreme Court verdict in the X case was not enacted until the second decade of this century.

One intriguing feature of Irish efforts to preserve traditional sexual morality is the failure to enlist any significant support from the Protestant community. This is in marked contrast with the United States. The women and men who bombarded Irish media and politicians with anti-abortion, anti-contraception messages deployed the rhetoric of faith – Catholic – and fatherland – nationalist. The letters that they sent to politicians and their speeches often cite Ireland's battle to preserve Catholicism despite the penal laws, and the struggle for independence from 'England' and these references are blended with an insistence on traditional gender roles and traditional sexual morality. Many correspondents were opposed to any concessions to Ulster unionism or Irish Protestantism. They failed to recognise that there was considerable common ground between Ireland north and south, and Irish Catholics and Irish Protestants, on social and sexual mores. Deep-seated divisions with respect to religion and identity, meant that this common moral ground was not acknowledged or deployed. Ultimately religious and national identities proved stronger than common moral values.

Most writing to date about family planning in Ireland highlights the role played by second-wave feminism, but the picture is arguably more complex than commonly suggested. There was no systematic mainstream feminist campaign to reform the laws on contraception, and the Council for the Status of Women, the umbrella group for women's organisations, was not consulted about the 1979 Family Planning Act, and did not seek to be involved. Their

---

[6] John Waters, *Jiving at the crossroads* (Blackstaff Press, Belfast, 1991).
[7] NAI DT 2012/90/671; 30/4/81.

cautious attitude towards contraception is further evidence that this was a sensitive and divisive issue. But second-wave feminism played an important, albeit indirect role. The 1973 report of the *Commission on the Status of Women*, together with Irish membership of the EEC, resulted in the removal of many barriers affecting women's rights with respect to employment, property, and welfare. The emergence of women journalists with strong feminist credentials who focused on social issues was vital in raising women's awareness of birth control. But the expanding female voice and female presence in public life was not all on the side of liberal change. There has been a failure to acknowledge that Ireland had not one but two polarised women's movements, and while a majority of well-educated, articulate women, including most women journalists favoured contraception, divorce and a more liberal society, a significant number of women were engaged in counter-movements. The latter have been largely excluded from history – they deserve serious consideration. The role played by the expansion in higher education has also been under-appreciated. The establishment of family planning clinics in Galway and Limerick and the radical approach taken by the Well Woman Clinic were driven by current and former student activists.

There is likewise need for more investigation of gender relationships in Irish society with a focus on men. Before the arrival of the contraceptive pill, the primary responsibility for controlling fertility rested with men. Hera Cook suggests that in Britain until the 1960s, most of the initiative with respect to family limitation was taken by men. The history of fertility decline, before 1960, suggests that abstinence and coitus interruptus were the main methods deployed. But they required male co-operation, and while the evidence is scant, it suggests that Irish men were not to the fore in efforts to limit family size. The fact that Ireland, unlike some other European countries, did not display major gender difference with respect to religious practice; that most Irish men not only attended Sunday mass but went regularly to confession, served to reinforce Catholic teaching on fertility control. In 1958, one priest claimed that many Irish Catholics had 'a confession complex'.[8] Many Irishmen apparently failed to consider the impact of multiple births, and pregnancies past the age of forty, on the health and well-being of their wives, and many couples failed to discuss these topics.[9] Irish Catholicism, well into the 1960s, continued to teach that the purpose of marriage was the begetting of children, whereas by then, clergy in most other western countries were emphasising the 'companionate marriage'.

---

[8] Louise Fuller, *Irish Catholicism since 1950: The undoing of a culture* (Gill & Macmillan, Dublin, 2002), p. 119.

[9] For a harrowing account of male callousness, see John McGahern, *Memoir* (Faber & Faber, London, 2005). McGahern's father continued to have sexual relations with his wife following her treatment for breast cancer, and her pregnancy – she was in her early forties – probably shortened her life.

Many Irish men subscribed fully to traditional Church teaching on marriage, while providing little financial or personal support to their wives and families. Raymond Cross, a gynaecologist attached to the Rotunda Hospital, commented that 'ignorance, drunkenness, selfishness and non-co-operation unfortunately seemed to go hand in hand with ill-health and grand multiparity' in 1960s Ireland. Foley, writing about Irish couples and the safe period in the 1960s, states that, 'The non-cooperation of men emerges as a theme in the many discussions of the rhythm method'.[10] It is also evident from the letters to women's magazines that family planning could be a fraught issue for many couples, especially where one partner wished to continue to attend confession and the sacraments. A 1980 survey of post-partum mothers in the Rotunda, and their partners (cited in Chapter 7) revealed some disquieting divergences between men and women on whether to have another child and decisions about contraception, with the men adopting more conservative attitudes towards contraception, and apparently not for religious reasons. Until the 1980s, most condoms sold in Irish family planning clinics were purchased by women. The gendered aspect is also important in relation to sterilisation. By the 1980s, vasectomy was readily available in Ireland, and it was cheap. The acute medical risks that some women faced in pregnancy, for example older women suffering from haemolytic disease, could have been resolved if their husband had a vasectomy, yet many men were apparently unwilling to undergo this procedure. Improvements in education among women, and men; increasing employment in industry and services, as opposed to farming and family businesses, and an end to arranged marriages and dowries resulted in greater equality between couples, and this was most important in rural Ireland.[11] Opinion polls carried out in the 1970s show that farming households were consistently the most conservative with respect to contraception, but that did not result in a long-term difference in family size between rural and urban Ireland.

The role of the medical profession is mixed. The first family planning services in Ireland were introduced by doctors, who were concerned to address the medical and social consequences for women of frequent pregnancies. This was also the case in Spain, another conservative Catholic country, where contraception was illegal until 1978.[12] Some doctors were pioneers in setting up family planning clinics and sterilisation services; others played a prominent role in the PLAC. The majority opted for a quiet life, avoiding controversy; this was a characteristic of Irish Catholic professionals, reflecting the failure

---

[10] Foley, '"Too many children"', p. 148.

[11] Damien Hannan and Louise Katsaiouni, *Traditional families? From culturally prescribed to negotiated roles in farm families* (ESRI, Dublin, 1977).

[12] Teresa Ortiz-Gómez and Agata Ignaciuk, 'The fight for family planning in Spain during late Francoism and the transition to democracy, 1965–1979', *Journal of Women's History*, 30, no 2, 2018, pp. 41–5.

of educated Irish Catholic laity to develop a distinct voice. The many letters in women's magazines from women who were afraid to ask their doctor for contraception, raise wider issues about communication, authority and social hierarchy in doctor–patient relationships, though these are not unique to Ireland. The role of nurses and pharmacists in Irish family planning has hitherto been ignored. From the 1920s onwards, both professions were dominated by men and women who subscribed to the values of Catholic Action. Catholic training hospitals and lay and religious matrons appear to have exercised considerable influence on staff nurses and trainee nurses, and the hierarchical nature of the nursing profession promoted conformity, despite a growing number of married nurses, though family planning clinics had no problem recruiting nurses. In the case of pharmacists, and the medical profession, it is probable that the Knights of Columbanus were influential, though arguably the stance taken by pharmacists and by many doctors, was primarily motivated by professional interests. The story of female sterilisation highlights the difference between hospitals under the control of the health boards, and voluntary hospitals, and it refutes simplistic impressions that Dublin was more progressive; in the 1980s, women who wished to have a tubal ligation had a much greater prospect of securing one without having to pay if they were resident outside Dublin, or the North-Eastern Health Board area.

The primary responsibility for bringing Irish laws on contraception into line with the needs of the population and Supreme Court judgments rested with politicians, and, with a few exceptions they led from behind. For many years, they failed to introduce legislation that was required to take account of the 1973 Supreme Court judgment on the McGee case, and in later decades, they likewise failed to legislate to reflect the 1992 judgment in the X case, which permitted abortion to save a woman's life. The conservatism of the regional health boards, where local authority representatives tended to be older men, because membership was highly prized (primarily for the travelling expenses),[13] ensured that the public health system failed to play a significant role in family planning. In more recent years, and beyond the scope of this book, there has likewise been a failure to legislate on the questions of sperm donation and surrogacy; both operate within a legally grey zone, that is reminiscent of the family planning clinics in the 1970s.[14]

The success of the 1983 Pro-Life Amendment Campaign reflects the pusillanimity of Irish political leaders, and the capacity of a relatively small, albeit noisy interest group to exploit a volatile political environment. The complicated and nuanced arguments of the Anti-Amendment Campaign were drowned by

---

[13] I am indebted to Eithne FitzGerald, a former member of the Eastern Health Board, for this insight.
[14] In 2022, the Oireachtas began the process of legislating on surrogacy.

the PLAC's emotive messages communicated in circular letters to politicians and at public meetings. The bulky files of letters and lurid pamphlets in the National Archives, expressing opposition to contraception and abortion considerably dwarf the number of submissions about events in Northern Ireland. By contrast, there is very little material relating to the Sexual Offences Act, prohibiting homosexual acts between consenting adults, which was repealed in 1993. That is not to suggest that gay men and women did not experience discrimination within Irish society; they did. But the Irish theology journal *The Furrow* published fifty articles on contraception, and fifteen on homosexuality. There is no evidence that the Catholic church or conservative lobby groups denounced male sterilisation, whereas female sterilisation faced strong opposition. This suggests that the Catholic church and Irish society accorded a heightened significance to *female* sexuality and reproduction.

This is both a national and an international story. There were strong external influences at play: such as the comparisons between the McGee case and *Roe* v. *Wade*. Many Irish doctors and nurses had worked in England, and their experiences of the 1967 Abortion Act had a strong bearing on Irish attitudes to abortion in both professions. On a more positive note, doctors and nurses who had worked outside Ireland were to the fore in establishing family planning services; most of the founders of the Fertility Guidance Clinic had worked outside Ireland.

The history of family planning also offers a lens on the changing influence of the Catholic church. In the early years after independence, very little by way of church–state division came into the public sphere. The church exercised its influence on senior politicians, public servants and the judiciary quietly, behind closed doors often without controversy because they shared a common culture, family ties, church schools and shared socialisation. The dispute over the 1951 Mother and Child Scheme (which is as much a dispute between the state and the medical profession, as it is a church–state dispute) only became public because the Minister for Health Noel Browne released correspondence with politicians and the Catholic Hierarchy after he resigned. The delicate political brokerage between the 1951–54 Fianna Fáil government and the Hierarchy that resulted in a modified version of the Mother and Child scheme being introduced in 1953 (Health Act) only became known thirty years later when the files in the National Archives were opened.

By contrast, most of the debate on contraception took place in public, which, I would suggest, can be seen as evidence of declining church authority. From the 1970s onwards, the campaigns to maintain the conservative line were fronted by lay men and women, and it would be foolhardy to suggest that they were merely the puppets of clerical masters. Many Irish men and women were extremely uncomfortable with the social consequences of making contraceptives readily available, or the idea of abortion. In twenty-first century Ireland, the decline in influence of the Catholic church is generally explained by reference to the involvement of Catholic clergy in child sexual abuse, and the treatment of children and unmarried mothers in church-run institutions, but there is a strong case for suggesting that its uncompromising stance on contraception – post 1968 – was also crucial, as couples who dissented from church teaching on contraception ceased to attend church regularly or follow the leadership of the clergy. In the aftermath of Vatican Two, regular confession also assumed a less prominent place in religious practice.

One interesting feature of Ireland's long-drawn out debate over fertility control and abortion is that it did not trigger the formation of a right-wing political party. All the main political parties (with the possible exception of Fianna Fáil) had members with both conservative and liberal views on these matters. In recent years, two new parties, Renua and Aontas, have been formed by politicians who left their original parties in protest against those parties supporting the repeal of the Eight Amendment to the Constitution (the 1983 Pro-Life Amendment) and the introduction of legislation permitting abortion, but neither has shown the capacity to establish more than a minor presence in Irish politics. Indeed, one paradox is that these long-drawn out and often heated debates over fertility control had only a marginal impact on electoral politics.

The gradual pace of change with respect to contraception and the battles that ensued is an index of wider social change in late twentieth-century Ireland. A majority of Irish people continued to attend church regularly, and religious rites of passage remained near universal until the late 1990s; the constitutional ban on divorce ended in 1997 with a wafer-thin majority in the referendum, the legal prohibition on adult homosexual practice was removed without much controversy in 1993. It was only in the late 1990s, with increasing immigration, an accelerating decline in religious practice that the rhetoric of Ireland's distinctiveness with respect to sexuality, began to crumble, and only in the second decade of the twenty-first century, that a new Irish identity – that of a modern, multi-cultural, diverse society began to be constructed.

Ultimately, at the core of this story, there is an idealised image of Ireland, as a country with a tradition of large families, sexual purity and a strong belief in Catholicism and nationalism, and while this stereotype was questioned and there was growing evidence to refute it, it retained widespread popular support until the closing decades of the twentieth century, especially in rural Ireland and among older generations. This image combined with a belief in Irish exceptionalism – that Ireland could withstand the changes that were underway in twentieth-century western society in relation to sexual behaviour, the role of women and the merits of large families, while simultaneously securing the benefits of a prosperous modern society. These images/stereotypes were reinforced by the dominant place of Irish Catholicism in people's lives. Many Irish people had no close friends or relatives who were not practising Catholics, and their understanding of religious or cultural diversity was minimal. The Catholic church played a prominent role in Irish society, as a major provider of educational, health and welfare services, so perhaps it is not altogether surprising that many people who wrote to government ministers expressing their opposition to reforming the laws relating to contraception failed to distinguish between the respective spheres of church and state. By the 1970s, the disruptive forces of economic growth, a rising population of young adults and university graduates, and growing evidence of a demand for contraception, and Irish women travelling to England for abortions, challenged this image. The onset of violence in Northern Ireland added a further ingredient to this volatile mixture because it prompted a debate over civil rights, and the need to take account of minority opinion. In the face of these powerful forces pressing for change, it is significant that the moral legislation enacted in the first decades after independence survived until the closing decades of the twentieth century, which might suggest that Ireland was exceptional.

Bibliography

Unpublished Primary Sources

National Archives of Ireland (NAI)

Department of the Taoiseach files
Hilda Tweedy Papers

Newberry Library Chicago

Solon Toothaker Kimball Papers

Dublin Diocesan Archives

John Charles McQuaid Papers

Galway Diocesan Archives

Browne Papers

National Library of Ireland Manuscripts Room

Irish Countrywomen's Association Papers

Royal College of Physicians of Ireland

Minutes of the Executive Committee of the Institute of Obstetricians and Gynaecologists
Minutes of Annual General Meetings of the Institute of Obstetricians and Gynaecologists
Irish Family Planning Association Papers

UCD Archives

Barry Desmond Papers unlisted
Gemma Hussey Papers P 179

Derek Freedman Papers P 276

Brendan Walsh Papers: privately held

Dáil and Seanad Debates

Irish Government Publications

Report of the Committee on Evil Literature (Dublin, 1926)
Iris Oifigiúil, Register of Prohibited Publications
Commission on Emigration and Other Population Problems, 1948–1954 (Dublin, 1955)
Commission on the Status of Women (Dublin, 1972)
Department of Health and Children. *The Lourdes Hospital Inquiry.* An inquiry into peripartum hysterectomy at Our Lady of Lourdes Hospital Drogheda by Judge Maureen Harding-Clark, SC, 2006
Report of the Commission of investigation into Mother and Baby Homes and related matters (Dublin 2022)

Other Official Publications

Royal Commission on Population, 1948–1949 (London Cmnd. 7695)
Disturbances in Northern Ireland. Report of the Commission appointed by the Governor of Northern Ireland (Belfast 1 September 1971)
Minutes of the Eastern Health Board – available on Lenus website

Newspapers, Magazines and Serial Reports

Clergy Review
The Catholic Standard
Church of Ireland Gazette
Cork Examiner
Family Planning News
Hibernia
Irish Ecclesiastical Record
Irish Farmers' Journal
Irish Independent
Irish Medical Times
Irish Pharmaceutical Union Review
Irish Press
Irish Times
Journal of the Irish Medical Association, later Irish Medical Journal
Magill
Sunday Independent
Sunday Press
This Week
Woman's Choice

Woman's Way
World Medicine
The Coombe Hospital Lying-in Hospital, Clinical Reports
The National Maternity Hospital, Holles Street, Clinical Reports
The Rotunda Hospital Clinical Reports
Irish Family Planning Association Annual Reports

Books and Journal Articles

Adams, Michael, *Censorship. The Irish experience* (Dublin: Sceptre, 1968).
Anderson, Stuart and Virginia Berridge, 'The role of the community pharmacist in health and welfare, 1911–1986', in Joanna Bornat, Paul Thompson, Robert Perks, Jan Walmsley (eds), *Oral history health and welfare* (London: Routledge, 2000), pp 47–74.
Arbarbanel, A. R., *Journal of the American Medical Association*, May 1961 letter re efficacy of the fertility testor.
Arnold, Mavis and Peadar Kirby (eds), *'The abortion referendum', The case against* (Dublin, 1982).
Bailey Martha T., '"Momma's got the pill": How Anthony Comstock and Griswold v. Connecticut shaped US child-bearing', *American Economic Review*, 100, no 1, 2010, pp 98–129.
Bargy Castle Meeting, *'Humanae vitae'*, *The Furrow*, 19, no 11, 1968, pp 565–8.
Barry, Ursula, 'Abortion in Ireland', *Feminist Review*, 29, 1988, pp 57–66.
Becker, Gary, *A treatise on the family* (Cambridge: Harvard University Press, 1991 edition).
Betts, Katharine, 'The Billings method of family planning: an assessment', *Studies in Family Planning*, 15, no 6, 1984, pp 253–66.
Biever, Bruce, *Religion, culture and values. A cross-cultural analysis of motivational factors in native Irish and American Irish Catholicism* (New York: Arno Press, 1976).
Billings, J. J., *The ovulation method* (Melbourne: Advocate Press, 1964).
The ovulation method of natural family planning. Based on a lecture by Dr Billings – no date, NLI accession stamp is 22 October 1974.
Binchy, William, 'Marital privacy and family law; a reply to Mr. O'Reilly', *Studies*, 66, 1977, pp 330–5.
Blanshard, Paul, *The Irish and Catholic power* (London: Derek Verschoyle, 1954).
Bongiorno, Frank, *The sex lives of Australians* (Victoria: Collingwood, 2015 edition).
Bowman, Emer Philbin, 'Sexual and contraceptive attitudes and behaviour of single attenders at a Dublin family planning clinic', *Journal of Biosocial Science*, 9, 1977, pp 427–45.
Boylan, Peter, *In the shadow of the eighth. My forty years working for women's health in Ireland* (Dublin: Penguin Ireland, 2019).
Brooke, Stephen, *Sexual politics. Sexuality, family planning, and the British left from the 1880s to the present day* (Oxford: Oxford University Press, 2011).
Campbell, Flann, 'Birth control and the Christian Churches', *Population Studies*, 14, no 2, 1960, pp 131–47.
Carr, Conor, *The lucky twin, an obstetrician's tale* (no publication details given).
The Teachings of Pope Pius XII. Compiled and edited with the assistance of the Vatican Archives by Michael Chinigo (London: Methuen, 1958).

Chesser, Eustace, Joan Maizels, Leonard Jones and Brian Emmet, *The sexual, marital and family relationships of the English woman* (London: Hutchinson's Medical Publications, 1956).

Christiano, Kevin J., 'The trajectory of Catholicism in twentieth century Quebec', in Leslie Woodcock Tentler (ed), *The Church confronts modernity. Catholicism since 1950 in the United States, Ireland & Quebec* (Washington, DC: Catholic University of America, 2007).

Clear, Caitriona, *Women of the house. Women's household work in Ireland 1922–1961* (Dublin: Irish Academic Press, 2000).

Clear, Caitriona, *Women's voices in Ireland: Women's magazines in the 1950s and 1960s* (London: Bloomsbury, 2016).

Cloatre Emilie and Máiréad Enright, '"On the perimeter of the lawful": enduring illegality in the Irish family planning movement, 1972–1985', *Journal of Law and Society*, 44, 2017, pp 471–500.

Coleman, D. A., 'The demographic transition in Ireland in international context', in J. H. Goldthorpe and C. T. Whelan (eds), *The development of industrial society in Ireland* (Oxford: Oxford University Press/The British Academy, 1992), pp 53–79.

Conway, William, 'The recent papal allocution: the ends of marriage', *Irish Theological Quarterly*, 19, no 1, 1952, pp 75–9.

Cook, Hera, *The long sexual revolution, sex and contraception, 1800–1975* (Oxford: Oxford University Press, 2004).

Corsa, Leslie, 'The United States: public policy and programs in family planning', *Studies in Family Planning*, 3, 1968, pp 259–76.

Critchlow, Donald T. (ed), *The politics of abortion and birth control in historical perspective* (University Park, PA: Pennsylvania State University, 1996).

Crummey, Frank, *Crummey v Ireland. Thorn in the side of the establishment* (Dublin: Londubh Books, 2009).

Cunningham, John, '"Spreading VD all over Connacht" Reproductive rights and wrongs in 1970s Galway', *History Ireland*, 19, no 2, 2011, pp 44–7.

Curtin, Chris, Pauline Jackson and B. Connor (eds), *Gender in Irish society* (Galway: Galway University Press, 1987).

Curtis, Maurice, *The splendid cause. The Catholic Action movement in Ireland in the twentieth century* (Dublin: Original Writing, 2008).

Dalla-Zuanna, Gianpiero, 'Tacit consent. The Church and birth control in Northern Italy', *Population and Development Review*, 17, no 2, 2011, pp 361–74.

Daly, Ann, '"Veiled obscenity"; contraception and the Dublin Medical Press, 1850–1900', in Elaine Farrell (ed), *'She said she was in the family way'. Pregnancy and infancy in modern Ireland* (London: Institute of Historical Research, 2012), pp 15–34.

Daly, Mary E., *The slow failure: population decline and independent Ireland, 1920–1973* (Madison: University of Wisconsin Press, 2006).

Daly, Mary E., 'The primary and natural educators? The role of parents in the education of their children in independent Ireland', in Maria Luddy and James Smith (eds), *Children, childhood and Irish Society 1500 to the present* (Dublin: Four Courts, 2014), pp 65–81.

Daly, Mary E., *Sixties Ireland. Reshaping the economy, state and society, 1957–1973* (Cambridge: Cambridge University Press, 2016).

Dean, Geoffrey, A. Walsh, D. O'Hare and H. McLouglin, *Termination of pregnancy England 1984: women from the Republic of Ireland* (Dublin: Medico-social Research Board, 1985).

Delay, Cara, 'Pills, potions and purgatives: woman and abortion methods in Ireland, 1900–1950', *Women's History Review*, 28, no 3, 2019, pp 479–99.

Delay, Cara, 'Wrong for womankind and the nation: anti-abortion discourses in 20th century Ireland', *Journal of Modern European History*, 17, no 3, 2019, pp 312–25.

de Lestapis, S. SJ. *Family planning and modern problems* (London: Herder and Herder, 1961), translation of *La Limitation des Naissances* (Paris, second edition 1959).

Derosas, Renzo letters, and Frans van Poppel, *Religion and the decline of fertility in the western world* (Dordrecht: Springer, 2006).

Desmond, Barry, *Finally and in conclusion. A political memoir* (Dublin: New Island Books, 2000).

Dols, Chris and Marten van den Bos, '*Humanae Vitae*: Catholic attitudes to birth control in the Netherlands and transnational church politics, 1945–1975', in Alana Harris (ed), *The schism of 1968. Catholicism, contraception and Humanae Vitae in Europe, 1945–1975* (London: Palgrave Macmillan, 2018).

Dorr, Noel, *Sunningdale: The search for peace in Northern Ireland Sunningdale* (Dublin: Royal Irish Academy, 2017).

Doyle, J. B. and Frank Ewers, 'The fertility testor', *Journal of the American Medical Association (JAMA)*, 170, no 1, 1959, pp 45–6. Accessed 14 March 2022.

Doyle, J. B., letters, *JAMA* 176, no 6, May 1961, pp 174–5. Accessed 14 March 2022.

Drake, M. J., I. W. Mills and D. Cranston, 'On the chequered history of vasectomy', *British Journal of Urology International*, 84, 1999, pp 475–81.

Dupont, Wannes, 'Of human love: Catholics campaigning for sexual aggiornamento in post-war Belgium', in Harris (ed), *The Schism of '68*.

Earner-Byrne, Lindsey, *Mother and child. Maternity and child welfare in Dublin, 1922–60* (Manchester: Manchester University Press, 2007).

Earner-Byrne, Lindsey and Diane Urquhart, *The Irish abortion journey, 1920–2018* (London: Palgrave Macmillan, 2019).

Enright, Mairead and Emilie Cloatre, '"Transformative illegality": how condoms became legal in Ireland', *Feminist Legal Studies*, 26, 2018, pp 261–84.

Fahey, Tony, Helen Russell and Emer Smyth, 'Gender equality, fertility decline and labour market patterns among women in Ireland', in Brian Nolan, Philip O'Connell and Christopher Whelan (eds), *Bust to boom? The Irish experience of growth and inequality* (Dublin: Institute of Public Administration, 2000), pp 244–67.

Family Regulation, 'The Catholic View, address to the Dublin branch of the Guild of St Luke, SS Cosmas and Damien', *Irish Theological Quarterly*, 30, 1963, pp 163–8.

Farmar, Tony, *Holles St, 1894–1994. The National Maternity Hospital. A centenary history* (Dublin: A&A Farmar, 1994).

Farrell, Elaine (ed), *'She said she was in the family way'. Pregnancy and infancy in modern Ireland* (London: Institute of Historical Research, 2012).

Fennell, Nuala, *Political woman: a memoir* (Dublin: Currach Press, 2009), p. 61.

Ferriter, Diarmaid, *Occasion of sin: sex and society in modern Ireland* (London: Profile, 2012).

Fine-Davis, Margret, *Changing gender roles and attitudes to family formation in Ireland* (Manchester: Manchester University Press, 2016).

Fisher, Kate, *Birth control, sex & marriage in Britain 1918–1960* (Oxford: Oxford University Press, 2006).

Fitzpatrick, David, *The two Irelands, 1912–1939* (Oxford: Oxford University Press, 1998).

FitzGerald, Garret, *Towards a new Ireland* (Dublin: Torc, 1973).

FitzGerald, Garret, *All in a life. An autobiography* (Dublin: Gill &Macmillan, 1992).

FitzGerald, Garret, *Ireland in the world. Further reflections* (Dublin: Liberties Press, 2005).

Flynn, Michael P., *Medical doctor of many parts* (Ireland: Kelmed, 2002).

Fogarty, Michael, Liam Ryan and Joseph Lee, *Irish values & attitudes. The Irish report of the European value systems study* (Dublin: Dominican Publications, 1984).

Foley, Deirdre, '"Too many children?" Family planning and *Humanae vitae* in Dublin, 1960–72,' *Irish Economic and Social History*, 46, no 1, 2019, pp 142–60.

Freedman, Ronald, Paschal Whelpton and Arthur Campbell, *Family planning, sterility and population growth* (New York: McGraw-Hill, 1959).

Fuchs, Joseph, 'The Pill', *Studies*, 53, 1964, pp 352–71.

Fuller, Louise, *Irish Catholicism since 1950. The undoing of a culture* (Dublin: Gill & Macmillan, 2002).

Gauvreau, Michael, '"They are not of our generation." Youth, gender, Catholicism and Quebec's dechristianizaton, 1950–1979', in Leslie Woodcock Tentler (ed), *The Church confronts modernity. Catholicism since 1950 in the United States, Ireland & Quebec* (Washington, DC: Catholic University of America Press, 2007).

Gavreau, Danielle and Peter Gossage, 'Empechez la famille. Fecondité et Contraception au Quebec, 1920–1960', *Canadian Historical Review*, 78, no 3, 1997, pp 478–510.

Geiringer, David, *The Pope and the pill* (Manchester: Manchester University Press, 2020).

Gervais, Diane, 'Morale catholique et détresse conjugale à Quebec. La réponse du service de régulation des naissances, Seréna 1955–1970', *Revue de l'histoire de l'amerique francaise'*, 5, no 2, 2001, pp 188–95.

Gervais, D. and D. Gauvreau, 'Women priests and physicians: family limitation in Quebec, 1949–1970', *Journal of Interdisciplinary History*, 34, no 2, 2003, pp 293–314.

Gillis, John, Louise Tilly and David Levine (eds), *The European experience of declining fertility* (Oxford: Oxford University Press, 1992).

Girvin, Brian, 'Contraception, moral panic, and social change in Ireland, 1969–79', *Irish Political Studies*, 23, no 4, 2002, pp 555–76.

Girvin, Brian, Church, state and society in Ireland since 1960', *Eire/Ireland*, 43 no 1 and 2, 2008, pp 74–98.

Girvin, Brian, 'An Irish solution to an Irish problem. Contraception, Catholicism and change', *Contemporary European History*, 27, no 1, 2018, pp 1–22.

Glass, D. V., 'National programs', in *Family planning and population programs. A review of world development* (Chicago: University of Chicago Press, 1966: Proceedings of the International Conference on Family Planning Programs, Geneva, 1965, pp 188–92

Glass, D. V., 'Western Europe', in *Family planning and population programs. A review of world development* (Chicago: University of Chicago Press, 1966: Proceedings of the international conference on family planning programs Geneva, August 1965), pp 183–8.

Goldscheider, Calvin, 'Religion, family and fertility: what do we know historically and comparatively?', in Derosas and van Poppel, *Religion and the decline of fertility*, pp 41–58.

Goldthorpe, J. H. and C. T. Whelan (eds), *The development of industrial society in Ireland* (Oxford: Oxford University Press/The British Academy, 1992).

Gordon, Linda, *The moral property of women. A history of birth control politics in the United States* (Urbana and Chicago: University of Illinois Press, 2007).

Greene, Sheila, Marie-Therese Joy, J. K. Nugent and P. O'Mahony, 'Contraceptive practice of Irish married and single first-time mothers', *Journal of Biosocial Science*, 21, 1989, pp 379–86.

Grzymala-Busse, Anna, *Nations under God. How Churches use moral authority to influence policy* (Princeton: Princeton University Press, 2015).

Guinnane, Tim, *The vanishing Irish. Households, migration, and the rural economy in Ireland, 1850–1914* (Princeton: Princeton University Press, 1997).

Hannan, Damien and Louise Katsaiouni, *Traditional families? From culturally prescribed to negotiated roles in farm families* (Dublin: ESRI, 1977).

Haring, Bernhard, *Sociology of the family* (Cork: Mercier, 1959, translation of *De Ehe in dieser Zeit*, first published 1954).

Harris, Alana, *Faith in the family. A lived religious history of English Catholicism, 1945–82* (Manchester: Manchester University Press, 2013).

Harris, Alana, 'Love divine and love sublime: The Catholic Marriage Advisory Council, the Marriage Guidance Movement and the State', in Alana Harris and Timothy Willem Jones (eds), *Love and romance in Britain, 1918–1970* (London: Palgrave Macmillan, 2015), pp 211–12.

Harris, Alana, '"The writings of querulous women": contraception, conscience and clerical authority in 1960s Britain', *British Catholic History*, 32, no 4, 2015, pp 557–85.

Harris, Alana, 'A Gallileo moment....', in Harris. (ed), *The Schism of 68*.

Harris, Alana (ed), *The Schism of 68. Catholicism, contraception and Humanae Vitae in Europe, 1945–1975* (London: Palgrave Macmillan, 2018).

Harrison, R. F., J. Bonnar and W. Thompson, *Fertility and sterility. The Proceedings of the XIth World Congress on Fertility and Sterility, Dublin, June 1983* (Lancaster and Boston: MTP Press, 1984).

Hesketh, Tom, *The second partitioning of Ireland. The abortion referendum of 1983* (Dun Laoghaire: Brandsma Books, 1990).

Hindell, Keith and Madeleine Simms, *Abortion law reformed* (London: Owen, 1971).

Hug, Chrystel, *The politics of sexual morality in Ireland* (Basingstoke: Macmillan, 1999).

Humphreys, Alexander, *New Dubliners. Urbanization and the Irish family* (London: Routledge and Kegan Paul, 1966).

Inglis, Tom, *Truth, power and lies, Irish society and the case of the Kerry babies* (Dublin: UCD Press, 2005).

Irish Pregnancy Counselling Services, *Abortion: A choice for Irish women.*

Irish Women's Liberation Movement, *Chains or change* (Dublin: Irish Women's Liberation Movement, 1971).

Jackson, Julian, *A certain idea of France. The life of Charles de Gaulle* (London: Penguin, 2018).

Jackson, Pauline, 'Outside the jurisdiction: Irishwomen seeking abortion', in Curtin, Jackson and O' Connor (eds), *Gender in Irish society* (Galway: Galway University Press, 1987), pp 203–23.

Jackson, Pauline, 'Abortion trials and tribulations', *Canadian Journal of Irish Studies*, 18, no 1, 1992, pp 112–20.

Jain, Anrudh K. and Irving Sivin, 'Life table analysis of IUDS: problems and recommendations', *Studies in Family Panning*, 8, no 2, 1977, pp 25–47.

Jones, Greta, 'Marie Stopes in Ireland: the mothers' clinic in Belfast, 1936–1947', *Social History of Medicine*, 5, 1992, pp 255–77.

Kaiser, Robert Blair, *The encyclical that never was. The story of the pontifical Commission on Population, Family and Birth 1964–66* (London: Sheed and Ward, 1985).

Keenan-Thomson, Tara, *Irish women and street politics, 1956–1973* (Dublin: Irish Academic Press, 2010).

Kelly, Brendan and Muiris Houston, *Psychiatrist in the chair: the official biography of Dr Anthony Clare* (Dublin: Irish Academic Press, 2020).

Kelly, Gerald SJ. *Medical-moral problems* (Dublin: Clonmore and Reynolds, 1957).

Kelly, Laura, 'Irishwomen United, the Contraception Action Programme, and the campaign for free, safe and legal contraception, c. 1975–81', *Irish Historical Studies*, 43, no 164, 2019, pp 269–97.

Kelly, Laura, 'The contraceptive pill in Ireland, c. 1964–1979: activism, women, and doctor-patient relationships', *Medical History*, 64, no 2, 2020, pp 195–218.

Kelly, Laura, 'Debates on family planning and the contraceptive pill in the Irish magazine, Woman's Way, 1963–1973', *Women's History Review*, 3, 2021, pp 971–89.

Kennedy, Robert, *The Irish. Emigration, marriage and fertility* (Berkeley, Los Angeles, London: University of California Press, 1973).

Kertzer, David I., 'Religion and the decline of fertility: conclusions', in R. Derosas and Frans van Poppel (eds), *Religion and the decline of fertility in the western world*, pp 259–70.

Klaus, Hanna, Miriam Labbok and Diane Barker, 'Characteristics of ovulation method acceptors: a cross-cultural assessment', *Family Planning*, 19, no 5, 1988, pp 299–304.

Knödel, John, 'From natural fertility to family limitation: the onset of fertility transition in a sample of Germany villages', *Demography*, 16, no 4, 1979, pp 493–521.

Latz, Leo, *The rhythm of sterility and fertility in women* (Dublin: Veritas, 1939).

Lawman, Geoffrey (ed), *Hamish Fraser. A memorial volume. Fatal Star* (Long Prairie, Minnesota: The Neumann Press, 1987).

Loughrey, Mark, *A century of service. A history of the Irish Nurses and Midwives Organisation, 1919–2019* (Newbridge: Irish Academic Press, 2019).

Luddy, Maria and Mary O'Dowd, *Marriage in Ireland, 1660–1925* (Cambridge: Cambridge University Press, 2020).

MacCormaic, Ruadhán, *The Supreme Court* (Dublin: Penguin Ireland, 2016)

MacNamara, Trent, *Birth control and American modernity. A history of popular ideas* (Cambridge: Cambridge University Press, 2018).

Marks, Lara, *Sexual chemistry. A history of the contraceptive pill* (Yale: Yale University Press, 2001), p. 187.

Marques, Tiago Pires, 'The politics of Catholic medicine: "The Pill" and *Humanae Vitae* in Portugal', in Alana Harris (ed), *The Schism of' 68*.

Marshall, John, 'The prevalence of mucous discharge as a symptom of ovulation', *Journal of Biosocial Science*, 7, 1974, p. 50.

Marshall, John, *Love one another. Psychological aspects of natural family planning* (London: Sheed & Ward, 1995).

Marshall, John, *Fifty years of marriage care* (London: Catholic Care, 1996).

Martin, Peter, *Censorship in the two Irelands, 1922–1939* (Dublin: Irish Academic Press, 2006).

May, Elaine Tyler, *America and the pill. A history of promise, peril and liberation* (New York: Basic Books, 2010).

McAleese, Mary, *Here's the story. A memoir* (Dublin: Penguin Ireland, 2020).

McAvoy, Sandra, '"Its effect on public morality is vicious in the extreme": defining birth control as obscene and unethical, 1926–32', in Elaine Farrell (ed), *'She said she was in the family way'* (London: Institute of Historical Research, 2012), pp 35–54.

McAvoy, Sandra, '"A perpetual nightmare": women, fertility control, the Irish state, and the 1935 ban on contraceptives', in Margaret Preston and Margaret Ó hÓgartaigh (eds), *Gender and medicine in Ireland, 1700–1950* (New York: Syracuse University Press, 2012), pp 189–202.

McCarthy, Canon John, *Problems in theology, vol 2. The Commandments* (Dublin: Browne & Nolan, 1959).

McCormick, Leanne, '"The Scarlet Woman in Person": the establishment of a family planning service in Northern Ireland, 1950–74', *Social History of Medicine*, 21, no 2, 2008, pp 345–60.

McCormick, Leanne, *Regulating sexuality. Women in twentieth-century Northern Ireland* (Manchester: Manchester University Press, 2009).

McDonagh, Enda, 'Moral theology to-day. Marriage and family planning', *Irish Theological Quarterly*, 29, no 1, 1962, pp 70–5.

McDonagh, Enda, 'Christian marriage in an ecumenical context', *The Furrow*, Jan 1968, pp 3–11.

McGahern, John, *Memoir* (London: Faber & Faber, 2005).

Mc Laughlin, Loretta, *The Pill, John Rock and the Church: the biography of a revolution* (Boston: Little, Brown and Company, 1982).

McQuillan, K., 'When does religion influence fertility?' *Population and Development Review*, 30, no 1, 2004, pp 25–56.

Meehan, Ciara, *A just society for Ireland? 1964–1987* (Basingstoke: Palgrave Macmillan, 2013).

Moore, Angela and Patricia Murphy, 'Attitudes, knowledge and extent of use of artificial contraception in social classes IV and V in Ireland', *JIMA*, 73, no 9, 1980, pp 342–6.

Morrison, Desmond, 'Natural methods of family planning', *The Furrow*, 25, no 10, 1974, pp 322–3.

Mouton, Michelle, *From nurturing the nation to purifying the Volk: Weimar and Nazi family policy, 1918–1945* (Cambridge: Cambridge University Press, 2007).

Munday, Diane, Colin Francome and Wendy Savage, 'Twenty-one years of legal abortion', *British Medical Journal,* 5, 1989, pp 1231–4.

Murphy, Brendan, John Bonnar, Ray Hawkins, George Henry, Eamonn O' Dwyer Michael Solomons and J. A. Byrne (secretary to the committee), 'Report on IUCDS', *JIMA*, 73, no 5, 1980, pp 188–9.

Murphy, Cliona and Colm O'Herlihy, 'Maternal mortality statistics in Ireland. Should they carry a health warning', *IMJ*, 100, no 8, 2007, p. 574.

Murphy, Gary, *Charles Haughey* (Dublin: Gill, 2021).

Murphy, Harry, Diarmaid O'Driscoll, Michael Brogan, Lorraine Hickey and Kevin O'Gorman, 'Opinions of post-natal mothers regarding family planning', *JIMA* 72, no 2, 1979.

Nolan, Brian, Philip O' Connell and Christopher Whelan, *Bust to boom? The Irish experience of growth and inequality* (Dublin: Institute of Public Administration, 2000).

Noonan, John, *Contraception. A history of its treatment by the Catholic theologians and canonists* (Cambridge: Belknap Press, 1965).

O'Brien, John A. (ed), *The vanishing Irish. The enigma of the modern world* (New York: McGraw-Hill, 1953).

O'Brien, Conor Cruise, *States of Ireland* (London: Hutchinson, 1972).

O'Callaghan, Denis, 'Fertility control by hormonal medication', *Irish Theological Quarterly*, 27, 1960, pp 1–15.

O'Callaghan, Denis, 'After the encyclical', *The Furrow*, 19, no 11, 1968, pp 633–41.

O'Callaghan, Margaret, 'Language, nationality and cultural identity in the Irish Free State, 1922–7', *Irish Historical Studies*, xxiv, no 94, 1984, pp 226–45.

Ó Gráda, Cormac and Niall Duffy, 'The fertility transition in Ireland and Scotland c.1880–1930', in *Conflict identity and economic development, Ireland and Scotland 1600 –1939* (Carnegie: Preston, 1995).

O'Leary, Olivia and Helen Burke, *Mary Robinson. The authorised biography* (Dublin and London: Sceptre/Lir, 1999).

Olszynko-Gryn, Jesse, 'The feminist appropriation of pregnancy testing in 1970s Britain', *Women's History Review*, 28, no 6, 2019, pp 869–94.

Opus Dei position paper no. 59, Editorial 'Look before you leap', No date, but appears to be late 1970s.

O'Reilly, James, 'Marital privacy and family law', *Studies*, 66, 1977, pp 8–24.

Ortiz-Gómez, Teresa and Agata Ignaciuk, 'The fight for family planning in Spain during late Francoism and the transition to democracy, 1965–1979', *Journal of Women's History*, 30, no 2, 2018, pp 41–5.

Park, A., 'An analysis of human fertility in Northern Ireland', *JSSISI*, 11, 1962, pp 1–13.

Phadraig, Máire Nic Ghiolla, 'Social and cultural factors in family planning', *The changing family* (Dublin: Family Studies Unit, UCD, 1984), pp 58–97.

Pope Pius XII, *Marriage and the Moral Law. What the Pope really said* (London: Pontifical Court Club, 1957) 57 a foreword by Dr Godfrey President of the Pontifical Court Club, p. 13.

Praz, Anne-Françoise, 'State institutions as mediators between religion and fertility: a comparison of two Swiss regions, 1860–1930', in Derosas and Van Poppel (eds), *Religion and the decline of fertility*, pp 147–76.

Quinlan, Jane, *The Billings method.* Information, books charts and stamps (Cork: Ovulation Method Advisory Service, (OMAS), 1976).

Quinlan, Jane, *The Billings method*, Revised edition 1979 Compiled by Ovulation Method Advisory Service (OMAS) Cork).

Rafferty, Oliver, *Catholicism in Ulster 1603–1983. An interpretative history* (London: Hurst, 1994).

Randall, Vicky, 'Irish abortion politics: a comparative perspective', *Canadian Journal of Irish Studies*, 18, no 2, 1992, pp 121–8.

Reed, James, *From public vice to private virtue. The birth control movement and American society since 1830* (New York: Basic Books, 1978).

Reed, James, 'The birth control movement before Roe v. Wade', in Donald T. Critchlow (ed), *The politics of abortion and birth control in historical perspective* (University Park, PA: Pennsylvania State University 1996).

Rev. A Regan, CSSR, 'The Catholic approach to marriage', *Irish Theological Quarterly*, 21, 1954, pp 252–64.

Riordan, Susannah, '"A reasonable cause": the age of consent and the debate on gender and justice in the Irish Free State, 1922–35', *Irish Historical Studies*, 34, no 147, 2011, pp 427–46.

Rock, John, *The time has come. A Catholic doctor's battle to end the battle over birth control* (London: Longmans, 1963).

Rohan, Dorine, *Marriage Irish style* (Cork: Mercier, 1969).

Rowntree, Griselda and Rachel M. Pierce, '"Birth control in Britain" Part I', *Population Studies*, 15, no 1, 1961, pp 3–31.

Rowntree, Griselda and Rachel M. Pierce, '"Birth control in Britain" Part II', *Population Studies*, 5, no 2, 1961, pp 121–60.

Ryan, Paul, *Asking Angela McNamara, An intimate history of Irish lives* (Dublin: Irish Academic Press, 2012).

Ryder, Norman and Charles Westoff, *Reproduction in the United States, 1965* (Princeton: Princeton University Press, 1971).

Ryder, Norman and Charles Westoff, *The contraceptive revolution* (Princeton: Princeton University Press, 1977).

Rynne, Andrew, *Abortion. The Irish question* (Dublin: Ward River Press, 1982).

Santow, Gigi, 'Coitus interruptus in the twentieth century', *Population and Development Review*, 19, no 4, 1993, pp 767–92.

Schoonbeim, Marloes, *Mixing ovaries and rosaries. Catholic religion and reproduction in the Netherlands, 1870–1970* (Amsterdam: Aksant, 2005).

Segalen, Martine, 'Exploring a case of late French fertility decline: two contrasted Breton examples', in John Gillis, Louise Tilly and David Levine (eds), *The European experience of declining fertility* (Oxford: Oxford University Press, 1992), pp 227–50.

Sharpless, John, 'World population growth, family planning, and American foreign policy', in Critchlow (ed), *The politics of abortion and birth control*, pp 72–102.

Smith, James, 'The politics of sexual knowledge: the origins of Ireland's containment culture and the 1931 Carrigan report', *Journal of the History of Sexuality*, 13, no 2, 2004, pp 208–33.

Solomons, Michael, *Pro-life. The Irish question* (Dublin: Lilliput Press, 1992).

Sprull, Marjorie J., *Divided we stand. The battle over women's rights and family values that polarized American politics* (London: Bloomsbury, 2017).

Statement from the Irish bishops' conference on proposed legislation dealing with family planning and contraception, *The Furrow*, 29, no. 8, August 1978, pp 525–7.

Stopper, Anne, *Mondays at Gajs. The story of the Irish Women's Liberation Movement* (Dublin: The Liffey Press, 2006).

Suenens, Leon, *Love and control* (London: Burns & Oates, 1961), translation of *Un Problème crucial: amour et matrice de soi*, Bruges 1960).

Sutherland, Halliday, *Laws of life* (London: Sheed & Ward, cheap edition 1946).

Szreter, Simon, 'The idea of demographic transition and the study of fertility change: a critical intellectual history', *Population and Development Review*, 19, no 4, 1993, pp 659–701.

Szreter, Simon, *Fertility class and gender in Britain, 1860–1940* (Cambridge: Cambridge University Press, 1996).

Tentler, Leslie, *Catholics and contraception. An American history* (Ithaca: Cornell University, 2004).

Tentler, Leslie (ed), *The Church confronts modernity. Catholicism since 1950 in the United States, Ireland and Quebec* (Washington, DC: Catholic University of America Press, 2007).

Thornton, Patricia and Sherry Olson, 'The religious claim on babies in nineteenth century Montreal', in R. De Rosas and F. W. A. Van Poppel, *Religion and the decline of fertility*, pp 207–34.

Tichenor, Kimba Allie, *Religious crisis and civic transformation. How conflicts over gender and sexuality changed the West German Catholic church* (Waltham: Brandeis University Press, 2016).

Tietze, Christopher, and Robert G. Potter Jr., 'Statistical evaluation of the rhythm method', *American Journal of Obstetrics and Gynecology*, 84, no 5, 1962, pp 692–98.

Trussell, James and Laurence Grummer-Strawn, 'Contraceptive failure of the ovulation method of periodic abstention', *International Family Planning Perspectives*, 16, no 1, 1990, pp 5–15.

Urquhart, Diane, *Irish divorce. A history* (Cambridge: Cambridge University Press, 2020).

Van der Kaa, Dirk, '"Ready, willing, and able": Ansley J. Coale, 1917–2002', *Journal of Interdisciplinary History*, 34, no 3, 2004, p. 509.

van Heek, F., Roman Catholicism and fertility in the Netherlands: demographic aspects of minority status, *Population Studies*, 10, no 2, 1956, pp 125–38.

Vassalle, Francesca and Massimo Faggioli, 'A kind of reformation in miniature: the paradoxical impact of Humanae Vitae in Italy', in Harris (ed), *The Schism of 68*.

Walsh, Brendan, Some Irish population problems reconsidered *ESRI paper 42* (Nov 1968).

Walsh, Brendan, 'Religion and demographic behaviour in Ireland', *ESRI paper 55* (May 1970).

Walsh, Brendan, 'Labour force participation and the growth of women's employment, Ireland 1971–1991', *Economic and Social Review*, 24, no 4, 1993, pp 369–400.

Waters, John, *Jiving at the crossroads* (Belfast: Blackstaff Press, 1991).

Weissman, M. C., L. Foliaki, E. L. Billings and J. J. Billings, 'A trial of the ovulation method of family planning in Tonga', *Lancet*, ii, 1972, p 813.

Whitty, Noel, 'The law and the regulation of reproduction in Ireland, 1922–1992', *The University of Toronto Law Journal*, 43, no 4, 1993, pp 851–88.

Whyte, John, *Church and state in modern Ireland, 1923–79* (Dublin: Gill & Macmillan, 1982).

Wilson-Davis, Keith, 'The contraceptive situation in the Irish Republic', *Journal of Biosocial Science*, 6, no 4, 1974, pp 483–92.

Wilson-Davis, Keith, 'Irish attitudes to family planning', *Social Studies: Irish Journal of Sociology*, 3, no 3, 1974, pp 264–76.

Wilson-Davis, Keith, 'Some results of an Irish family planning survey', *Journal of Biosocial Science*, 7, no 4, 1975, pp 435–44

Zylberman, Patrick, 'Les damnés de la démocratie puritaine: stérilisations en Scandinavie, 1929–1977', *Le Movement Social*, 187, 1999, pp 99–127.

Theses

O'Neill, Winifred, 'A profile of family planning need'. M.Soc.Sc, UCD, 1986.

O'Reilly, Richard Kevin, 'Population dynamics and family planning in Dublin', PhD University of Connecticut, 1981.

Rose, R. S., An outline of fertility control, focusing on the element of abortion in the Republic of Ireland to 1976 (Stockholm PhD thesis); copy in. Barry Desmond Papers, box 352.

Index

abortifacients, 26, 171, 182, 184–86, 209,
 See also intra-uterine devices (IUDs);
 post-coital contraception
 contraceptives alleged to be, 167
abortion, 29, 302, *See also* anti-abortion
 movement
 British Abortion Act (1967), 5, 95, 148,
 197, 199, 212, 213, 228
 Catholic church and, 25, 104, 183, 203, 214
 counselling, 141, 206, 243, 245
 doctors' deliberations on, 200, 212, 244, 257
 indirect or therapeutic, 201, 228
 information on, 22
 Irish criminal law and, 198
 and Irish medical professionals in Britain,
 197, 288, 311
 letters to politicians on, 166, 201
 medical grounds for, 178
 medical students debate, 213
 Northern Ireland and, 5, 199
 nurses and midwives and, 152, 214
 practised illegally, 199
 Protestant and unionist views, 5, 171, 185,
 229, 231, 237
 public opinion and, 235, 237
 women's right to advocated, 142, 207,
 208, 236
abortion referrals and travel, 3, 220, 222
 abortions kept secret by women, 141, 242
 C case, 247
 contraception not used by most women
 seeking, 279, 306
 court ruling prohibiting referrals, 242
 criminalisation of referrals advocated, 212,
 214, 223
 family planning clinics and, 134, 183,
 205, 206
 Family Planning Services (FPS) and, 274
 information on, 205, 242
 Irish doctors and, 206, 243
 Irish Family Planning Association (IFPA)
 and, 206

option of travel facilitates legal prohibition
 of abortion, 244
 profile of women referred, 207
 right to travel affirmed by referendum, 243
 student union referrals, 132, 206
 travel to Britain, 7, 198, 200–204, 206, 207,
 211, 213, 242, 247, 313
 Well Woman Clinic and, 140, 206, 272
Adelaide Hospital, 159, 287, 289, 294,
 295, 300
AIDS, 278, 279
Alfrink, Cardinal Bernard, 69
Ally (crisis pregnancy organisation), 206
American Birth Control League, 36,
 281, 310
amniocentesis, 95, 141
anti-abortion movement. *See also* Pro-Life
 Amendment Campaign (PLAC); Society
 for the Protection of the Unborn Child
 (SPUC)
 in America, 151
 'anticipative' character in Ireland, 197
 absence of Protestants, 8
 British and American influences, 7, 147,
 201, 204
 contraception and abortion linked by, 92,
 124, 147, 165, 197, 201, 204, 210
 graphic nature of campaigns, 124, 201
 international forces believed to be
 promoting abortion, 212
 Irish expatriates and, 198
 US Supreme Court precedent feared, 208
 women as leaders of, 148
Anti-Amendment Campaign (AAC), 235, 238,
 242, 310
artificial insemination, 141, 199, 291
Association for Deserted and Single Parents
 (Adapt), 139
Association of Irish Family Planning Clinics,
 260, 264
Association of Irish Priests, 114
Australia, 11, 29, 62, 153, 158, 201

Printed by Printforce, the Netherlands